The Archaeology of Clwyd

BRITISH COAL
OPENCAST

gwasanaeth archaeoleg
clwyd
archaeology service

edited by
John Manley, Stephen Grenter
and Fiona Gale

In the 13th and 14th centuries the church at Llanynys in the Vale of Clwyd was one of the richest in North Wales. The medieval wall painting of St. Christopher is attributed to the period 1400 - 1430 and the painting was executed by an artist of the first rank. Originally the halo around the head of Christ was covered in gold foil.

In Memory of

Canon Ellis Davies
Vicar of Whitford 1913-1951

and author of

Prehistoric and Roman Remains of Denbighshire	**1929**
Prehistoric and Roman Remains of Flintshire	**1949**
Flintshire Placenames	**1959**

Conventions

cms	=	centimetres
m	=	metres
km	=	kilometres
ha	=	hectares
OD	=	Ordnance Datum
C^{14}	=	Carbon Fourteen

CONTENTS

Dedication	3
Preface	7
Radiocarbon dating/Clwyd Archaeology Record	8
List of Contributors	9
Chronological coverage of each chapter	11
The Environment: Past & Present by David A. Jenkins	13
The Palaeolithic and its Quaternary Context by Stephen Green	26
Mesolithic by Kenneth Brassil	47
The Neolithic by William J.Britnell	55
The Bronze Age by Frances Lynch	65
The Iron Age by Fiona Gale	82
Small Settlements by John Manley	97
The Romano-British period by Kevin Blockley	117
The Dark Ages by Nancy Edwards	129
Offa and Wat's Dykes by David Hill	142
Mottes and Moated Sites by Jack Spurgeon	157
The Stone Castles by David Cathcart King	173
Medieval Settlement by Glanville Jones	186
Vernacular Architecture by A.J.Parkinson	203
Clwyd in the Industrial Revolution by Stephen Grenter and Ann Lloyd Williams	219
Bibliography	231
Index	247

PREFACE

Clwyd was born as a county in 1974, as a result of Local Government re-organisation. With this publication I think I can say that Clwyd has now come of age. On the following pages you will see that Clwyd lays claim to its history, and what a long history that is.

It is certainly the longest in Wales, as the discovery of the remains of Neanderthal people and their tools, at Pontnewydd Cave indicate. The first family groups of hunters and gatherers reached Clwyd nearly a quarter of a million years ago. And it is certainly one of the most varied, with magnificent hillforts crowning the hill-tops, superb castles controlling the valleys and extensive industrial remains which still underline the part the people of Clwyd played in the Industrial Revolution.

We are also lucky in Clwyd to have had such a variety of historians and archaeologists working in our county. The fruits of their painstaking researches are evident on every page of this book. We thank them both for undertaking this project and for contributing such excellent articles to this publication.

It is fitting that this book is dedicated to Canon Ellis Davies who wrote those two pioneering volumes on the prehistoric and Roman remains of Denbighshire and Flintshire. His works have stood the test of time and are still consulted today. Without his contributions our knowledge of the archaeology of Clwyd would have been greatly impoverished.

W. R. Thomas
Chairman, Clwyd County Council

RADIOCARBON DATING

Radiocarbon dating is a technique of dating ancient organic material by measuring the amount of a radioactive isotope remaining in a sample. There is still some dispute about the relationship between radiocarbon years and true or calendar years. Until the relationship is resolved it is customary when quoting 'radiocarbon years' to suffix them bc or prefix them ad rather than BC and AD which are reserved for calendar years. Broadly speaking, the older the material, the more radiocarbon dating underestimates true dates.

CAR - CLWYD ARCHAEOLOGICAL RECORD

There are more than 6,000 archaeological sites in the county of Clwyd, ranging in age from the remote palaeolithic period to sites from the much more recent industrial era. A minority, about 400, are legally protected as scheduled ancient monuments. They vary in size from large masonry castles and hillforts to a handful of pottery sherds or a scatter of flints. Each 'site' has its own discrete number; or CAR number, this number is then used to refer to the site on maps and record cards held by the Clwyd Archaeology Service. Each year new sites and finds are discovered and these records, complete with new CAR numbers, are added to the Clwyd Archaeological Record. This record contains details of all known archaeological sites in the county of Clwyd.

A bronze age ceremonial monument above Llandrillo. CAR 795 (Photo Clwyd Archaeology Service).

List of Contributors

Kevin Blockley	Formerly of Clwyd-Powys Archaeological Trust
Kenneth Brassil	Clwyd-Powys Archaeological Trust
William Britnell	Director, Clwyd-Powys Archaeological Trust
Nancy Edwards	Department of History University of Bangor
Fiona Gale	Archaeological Assistant Clwyd County Council
Stephen Green	Keeper of Archaeology and Numismatics, National Museum of Wales
Stephen Grenter	Archaeologist, Clwyd County Council
David Hill	Department of Extra Mural Studies, University of Manchester
David Jenkins	Department of Soil Science, School of Agricultural Forest Sciences, University of Bangor
Glanville Jones	Department of Historical Geography, University of Leeds
David Cathcart King	Formerly a school master in Clevedon, Avon. Author of numerous scholarly publications on Castles in Wales and England.
Frances Lynch	Department of History University of Bangor
John Manley	Principal Archaeologist Clwyd County Council
Anthony Parkinson	Royal Commission, Ancient and Historic Monuments (Wales)
Jack Spurgeon	Royal Commission, Ancient and Historic Monuments (Wales)
Ann Lloyd Williams	Curator, Bersham Industrial Heritage Centre

CHRONOLOGICAL COVERAGE OF EACH CHAPTER

Palaeolithic *	250,000 — 8,000BC
Mesolithic *	8,000 — 4,300BC
Neolithic *	4,300 — 2,300BC
Bronze Age	2,300 — 600BC
Iron Age	600BC — AD43
Small Settlements	600BC — AD410
Roman	AD43 — 410
Dark Ages	AD410 — 1066
Offa's & Wat's Dyke	AD750 — 800
Mottes & Moats	AD1066 — 1400
Stone Castles	AD1200 — 1400
Medieval Settlement	AD1066 — 1450
Vernacular Architecture	AD1450 — 1800
Industrial Archaeology	AD1700 — 1950

* The palaeolithic, mesolithic and neolithic mean respectively, the old, middle, and new stone ages. Throughout these three periods of time human beings used stone tools and metals were unknown. During the old and middle stone ages daily food was obtained by a mixture of hunting, gathering and fishing. During the new stone age the advent of farming as a way of life gradually replaced hunting and gathering.

THE ENVIRONMENT: PAST AND PRESENT
by David A. Jenkins

The present environment is something which can be experienced directly. Having experienced it, we can then understand it in terms of its various components. The physical nature of the land surface reflects the underlying solid geology, that is, the particular rock types and their disposition. The surface detail has been determined by a succession of processes which have produced characteristic landforms and associated superficial deposits. Upon this surface has developed a diversity of soils which have established, in combination with the climate, the varying fertility of the area and thus the vegetation, and ultimately the land-use and history of human occupation. All these components combine to produce the distinctive and diverse character of Clwyd, from the bleak Hiraethog moorland to the wooded limestone valleys and the rich agricultural lowlands of the Vale of Clwyd. But it was not exactly this environment that our predecessors experienced; certain aspects have changed, and indeed man has been partly instrumental in this change, whereas other factors such as climate and sea level have varied inexorably with time, and indeed are still doing so.

In describing the environment of Clwyd in an archaeological context, it is therefore necessary to extrapolate back in time to landscapes that would be relatively unfamiliar. Unfortunately, such reconstructions often rest on meagre and controversial evidence, but perhaps that is their challenge and attraction. This paper will present a brief outline of the various components of the environment in Clwyd attempting, where possible, to trace the course of their evolution through the period of human occupation. It will deal successively with the solid geology, the geomorphology, the soils and the climate, and conclude with one of the few examples where it has been possible to integrate the history of the environment with that of man.

Solid Geology

The solid geology constitutes the framework for the environment and has remained effectively unchanged during man's occupation. The rocks which now outcrop in Clwyd range in age from the Ordovician (c.$450 x 10^6$ years ago) to the Triassic (c.200×10^6 yrs. ago) and are a major determinant of the landscape. Thus each of the major rock types sets the character of the derived landsurface and so the geological map provides a convenient basis for the subdivision of Clwyd (Fig.1). In broad terms this resolves into: a large area of lower palaeozoic rocks which comprise the Silurian of the Hiraethog Moors to the west and extend down into the Ordovician of the Berwyn Range to the south; two strips of Carboniferous limestone from Colwyn and Prestatyn in the north to Ruthin and Llangollen, respectively, in the south; a flanking strip to the east of Millstone Grit and Coal Measures from Flint in the north to Oswestry in the south; and finally the softer New Red Sandstones which are glimpsed in the Vale of Clwyd and underlie the County's extension into the Cheshire basin. It is a pattern that has been known in outline since the pioneering mapping by William Smith in 1815; it is summarised in the Regional Geological Memoir by Smith & George and detailed in a number of more specific recent publications.

The Lower Palaeozoic rocks are dominated by mudstones and sandstones of Silurian age with a general easterly dip of around 10-30°. The relative homogeneity tends to give a subdued relief of smooth, rounded slopes, with harder beds of sandstone forming small scarps. This is in contrast to the more dramatic scenery of Snowdonia to the west where harder igneous

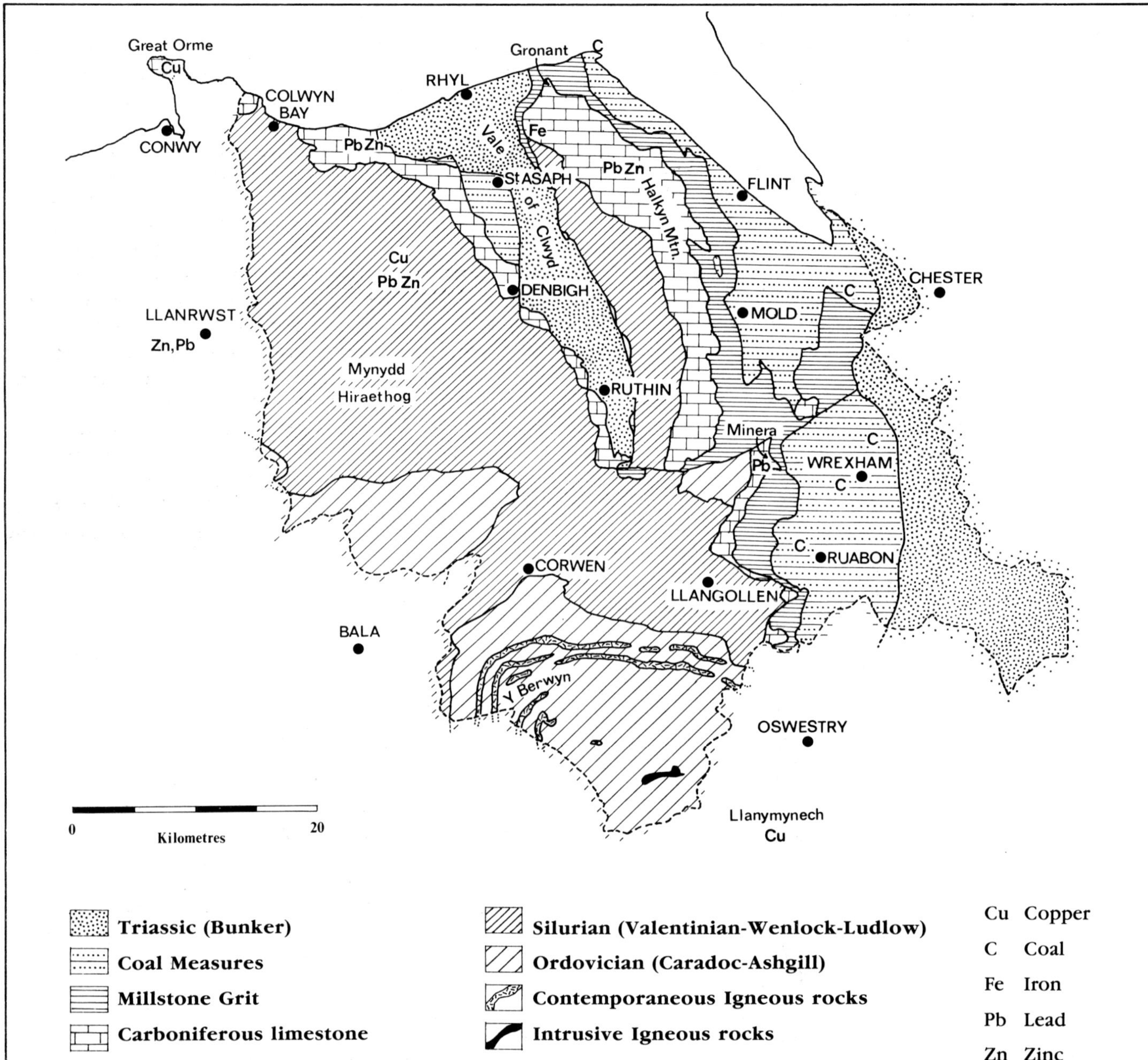

Fig.1 The solid geology of Clwyd showing location of rock types, coal and metal deposits.

rocks are interspersed among the softer sedimentary rocks: only in the Ordovician rocks of the Berwyn Mountains in the south of Clwyd are there occasional rhyolitic igneous rocks and comparable scenery. The Silurian rocks were discussed extensively by Boswell and more recently their outcrop in the Hiraethog Moor has been mapped and described in detail by Warren *et al.*. From an environmental viewpoint, these rocks are slow weathering, being in the main non-calcareous and having undergone a low grade metamorphism. The latter has both hardened them to some degree and also imparted a variable fracture cleavage, dipping to the south at angles ranging from 40-90°; this determines the way in which these rocks break up physically. The rocks have also been intensely faulted and (to the south) folded and these structures, together with the associated joints, are also reflected in the details of the present scenery.

These lower Palaeozoic rocks are overlain unconformably by rocks of Lower Carboniferous age which dip eastward at low angles. In places this sequence commences with basal sandstones and conglomerates, but it is dominated by hard, massive, pale grey, crystalline limestones which are variously bioclastic and fossiliferous, or porcellanous, or thin-bedded and dark. Occasionally the limestone has been dolomitised whilst to the east thick beds of chert occur locally (e.g. the "Gronant Chert"). The limestones are hard, and slow to weather physically, although chemical weathering enlarges joints by dissolution and diverts surface drainage underground to form cave systems, such as Hesp Alyn and Ogof Llyn Parc, Minera, leaving the ground above dry. The limestone therefore forms prominent flat-topped ridges or plateaux and can give rise to an impressive scenery of gorges or cliffs, such as the Eglwyseg at Llangollen.

Overlying these rocks to the east is a tract of "Millstone Grit" extending south from Prestatyn, where dark shales occur, to Ruabon, where the rocks comprise mainly decalcified sandstones. Still farther east are the overlying "Coal Measures" whose outcrop extends from the Point of Ayr to Oswestry and comprises coal seams and interbedded blue-grey shales passing up into unproductive sandstones, fireclays and marls. Because of their obvious economic importance, the underground succession and structure of these rocks is known in some detail. The youngest rocks exposed in Clwyd date from the Triassic. They are of a very different nature, comprising red-stained sandstones and marls that were deposited under arid continental conditions. They are relatively soft and weather fairly readily to give fertile soils so that rock exposures are not very common: they underly the protrusion of Clwyd into the Cheshire plain, and also the isolated down-faulted trough of the Vale of Clwyd.

Environmental Significance

The rocks that comprise the solid geology of Clwyd vary in their structure, hardness, chemical composition and susceptibility to weathering. Their influence upon the environment therefore also varies in terms of both the landforms which they engender and also their derived soils and vegetation. This factor has remained relatively unchanged during the course of man's existence in Clwyd and, as discussed below, indirectly influenced the pattern of settlement through the topography and soils. However, it did have a direct effect upon his activities in that it would have contributed to his source of raw materials for tools and building. It is worth noting that rock types such as the limestones were well suited to building, whilst others such as the mudstones were poor in this respect. Clwyd also lacks outcrops of dolerites and other igneous rocks that were apparently favoured elsewhere for axes, ceramic filler and boiling stones, and there are no suitable equivalents of the chilled igneous or adjacent baked rocks that were exploited farther west at Graig Lwyd or Mynydd Rhiw during the neolithic. However, the "Gronant" and "Trelogan" cherts provided substitutes for flint, albeit of inferior quality, in the manufacture of implements during the mesolithic.

Another of Clwyd's resources that has been exploited intensively is its deposits of metal ore. These are dominated by the lead (and associated zinc) deposits in the Carboniferous limestones of the Halkyn Mountain and Minera areas, but there is also mineralisation of the Silurian mudstones of Hiraethog by lead as well as by a little copper, and the latter has been worked in the Carboniferous limestones at Llanymynech and, just to the west of Clwyd, the Great Orme. It is possible that these deposits may have attracted early man to Clwyd and there is now positive evidence of prehistoric exploitation 3,700 - 3,000 years ago at The Great Orme and actual evidence of Roman extraction at Llanymynech. However, most of this evidence would have been obliterated during the major phase of 18th and 19th century extraction whose relics still dominate areas such as parts of Halkyn Mountain.

GEOMORPHOLOGY

Pre-glacial Landscapes

Following the deposition of the Triassic rocks there is little direct evidence of the subsequent history of Clwyd over the next 150 million years. However, the essential features of what is now the landscape of North Wales must have begun to be discernible some 50 million years ago. It has been suggested that a cover of chalk once extended over a planated surface in North Wales, its removal exhuming this platform upon whose gently domed surface our present drainage pattern was initiated. Fragments of an original radial drainage pattern are recognised, for example, in the easterly-flowing upper reaches of the Conwy linking through to stretches of the Dee. An analysis of the distribution of landsurface with altitude reveals a concentration at particular levels which Brown has interpreted as "sub-aerial peneplains" eroded across the flanks of an uplifted landmass, for example around 400m and 300m OD - the "middle" and "lower peneplain" respectively. Most of upland Clwyd relates to these ancient landsurfaces, only the Berwyn Range (825m OD) protruding above it as possible fossil "Monadnocks", linking with the Snowdonian peaks to the west.

Subsequently it is suggested that there was intermittent uplift of the landmass. "Coastal platforms" were then eroded into the marine margins during periods of standstill: such may be the origin of the areas at 185m OD on the northern flanks of Halkyn mountain and elsewhere along the coast of Clwyd, and also of less obvious areas at 135m and 75m OD. There has been surprisingly little development of these models in recent years, although Battiau-Queney has suggested that relict weathering dating from the early part of this (Tertiary) period is still to be seen in a few places in North Wales. However, the major elements in the landscape of Clwyd would have been recognisable by this time.

Glacial Processes and Landforms

The more obvious details of our landscape are of a relatively recent origin. They result from the climatic fluctuations of the last 1.6 million years (the "Pleistocene") during the colder phases of which northern Britain suffered repeated glaciations. Since the pattern of successive

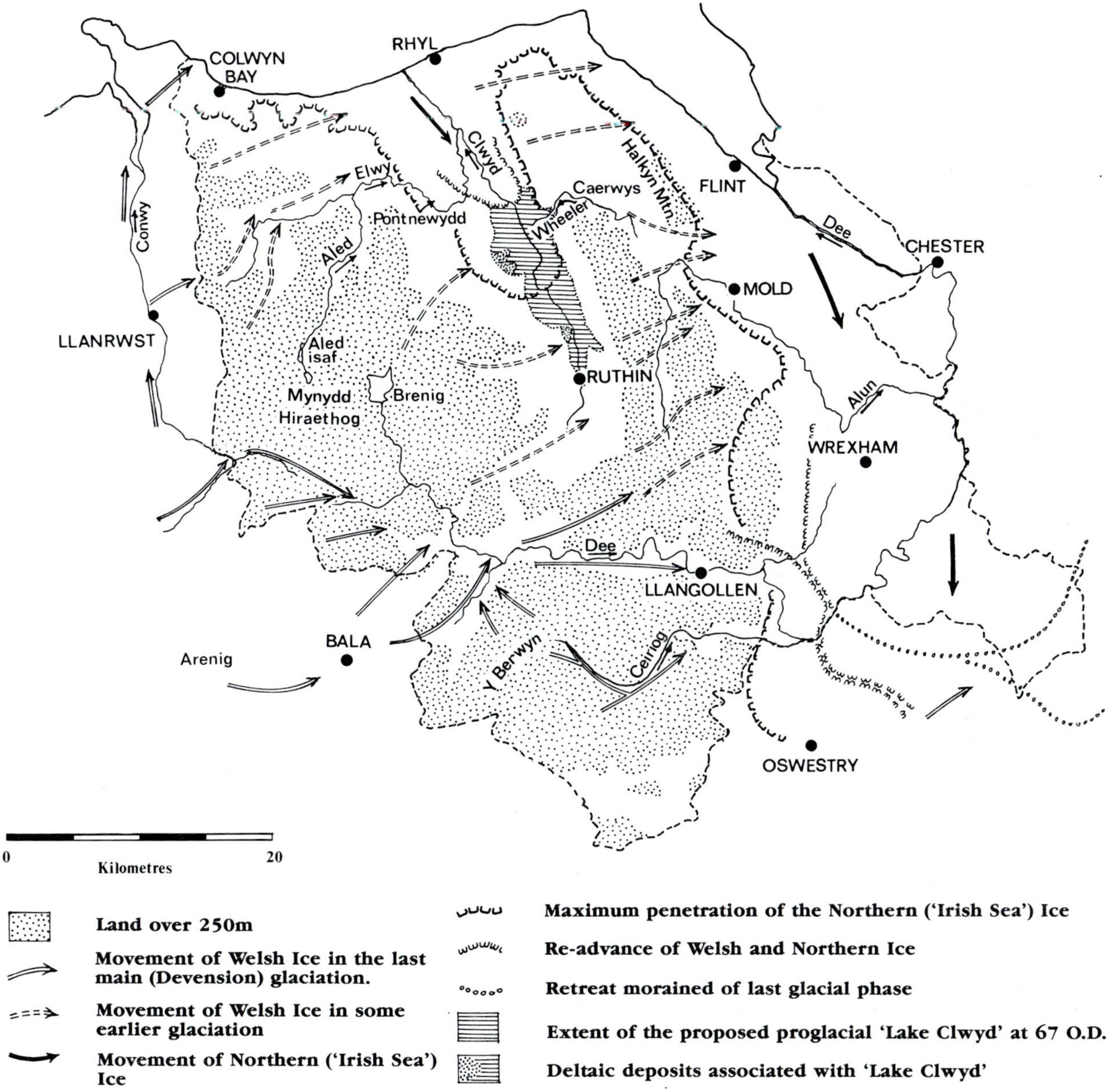

Fig.2 Selected features of the Quaternary in Clwyd.

glaciations would have been generally similar, the effects of earlier glaciations are likely to have been either removed by erosion, or buried under further deposits, during the latest ("Devensian") glaciation. As a result, the detailed history of this period is very difficult to unravel, and it is only in the last few decades that analysis of the continuous sedimentary record preserved in deep sea cores has revealed that the number of such glacial episodes is nearer to 20 than to the 4 previously accepted. Such glaciations extended to varying extents over Britain north of a line from the Severn to the Thames. The Pleistocene is also of particular relevance in that it saw the establishment of man during the warmer "Interglacial" periods.

Clwyd shows abundant evidence of this phase in both its landforms and deposits (Fig.2). As temperatures dropped, snow would have accumulated locally, possibly to form ice on high ground such as Mynydd Hiraethog, Y Berwyn and the Clwydian Range. But Clwyd was also subject to invasion not only by the more powerful ice generated by the higher ground of Snowdonia and the Arenigs to the west, but also by that from the Western Highlands and Southern Uplands of Scotland which coalesced with ice from the Lake District and extended southward down the Irish Sea. The latter brought with it a distinctive suite of erratics and diagnostic "northern" minerals alien to Wales which may be detected microscopically in the sand fraction. Its deposits are a characteristic reddish-brown colour due to contributions from the Triassic sediments eroded from the floor of the Irish Sea: this contrasts with the typical blueish-grey colours of the fresh sediments deposited by local Welsh ice. On meeting ice from North Wales, the "Northern" or "Irish Sea" ice divided at the Great Orme, part deflected to the west across Anglesey and part to the east into the Cheshire Plain, whilst the Welsh ice was in turn also deflected south-west and south-east as it emerged from the high ground.

In Clwyd, little is known about early ("pre-Devensian") glaciations. However, a valuable glimpse into glacial history is afforded by the chance preservations of deposits from an earlier glacial and interglacial period which slumped into the entrance of the cave of Pontnewydd in the Elwy valley some 150,000 years ago and which also carry the earliest record of man in Wales. Devensian deposits left by the northern ice are restricted to a coastal fringe with protrusions into the Vale of Clwyd and the Cheshire Plain. The exact margin between the local and northern ice varied in a complex manner according to the relative strengths of the two ice sheets, as illustrated by its oscillations in eastern Clwyd. In reviewing the evidence of glacial events in Clwyd, the following sequence of events has been suggested by Embleton:

an early glaciation involving powerful Welsh ice extending north-east from Snowdonia to Colwyn Bay and from the Arenigs over the Hiraethog moors, across the Vale of Clwyd (where ice must have been some 600m thick), and up onto the Clwydian range at levels of 560m: Northern ice was excluded.

a later glaciation dominated by Northern ice which left its distinctive deposits up to 295m on Halkyn Mountain and up to 590m on the northern flanks of Snowdonia: Welsh ice was confined to the interior.

a final period of more restricted ice activity with Northern ice, relatively unopposed by Welsh ice, penetrating some 20km up the Vale of Clwyd, and with the Hiraethog moors probably free of significant ice. In the last phase of this episode Northern ice re-advanced up the Vale of Clwyd as far as Trefnant; only this latter phase has been positively dated as later than 18,000 years ago by radiocarbon dating.

However, as Embleton pointed out in his detailed review of glaciation in north-east Wales, such reconstructions of Pleistocene events can only be tentative in view of the limited evidence available.

Glaciation leaves its imprint on the landscape both in the form of erosive features, especially in the uplands where the ice had more energy, and also in the form of deposits of unsorted "till" (or "boulder clay") which tends to blanket large tracts of the lowlands where much of the ice lost energy and finally melted. In Clwyd erosional features are not so dramatically developed as in the classic area of Snowdonia, due to a less favourable pre-glacial landscape and geology and to less vigorous ice movement. Nevertheless weakly developed "cwms" and glaciated valleys may be present margining the eastern side of the Vale of Clwyd (Moel Famau) and the middle Dee valley. Deposition in a variety of forms is more widespread and over 30m thick in places, sometimes with composite sections — Red Northern till usually overlying grey Welsh till. Elsewhere the till has been moulded into distinctive "drumlins" or elongated mounds oriented parallel to the direction of ice flow, the best examples up to 30m high and 320m long occurring south of Llanelidan. The only probable example of a "terminal moraine" is the line of low hills traversing the Vale of Clwyd at Trefnant.

Glaciofluvial Features

Some of the most distinctive features of glacial activity arise from the action of the powerful meltwater associated with retreating ice. This re-sorted glacial till to give localised deposits of glaciofluvial gravels, sands and clays. These take a variety of forms such as pro-glacial terraces (as in the Conwy and Elwy valleys) or deltas (as at Bellan north-west of Mold, and at Wrexham), or as sub-glacial mounds ('kames": as at Colwyn Bay) or ridges up to 1km long and 18m high ("eskers": as at Wrexham). The surfaces of these various deposits may be further pockmarked by depressions ("kettle holes") caused by the melting of masses of entrapped ice: those at Nannerch in the Wheeler valley, for example, are up to 20m deep. The meltwater carved itself deep drainage channels, sometimes sub-glacial but elsewhere draining lakes temporarily impounded by the ice. These features are usually striking anomalies in the pattern of today's drainage: Embleton for example, notes several "overflow channels" margining the Conwy valley to the west and also suggests that sub-glacial drainage initially escaped eastwards from the Vale of Clwyd (Fig.3) uphill through the Wheeler valley.

Much of the local topographic detail in the landscape of Clwyd, experienced by both early and contemporary man, therefore owes its origin to these complex events. However, their reconstruction demands careful and detailed fieldwork, and unfortunately little has yet been carried out in Clwyd. Examples are the studies reported by Brown and Cooke on the impressive deposits of glaciofluvial sands in the Wheeler valley, and by Thomas on the "fan delta" at Rhosesmor.

The Post-glacial: Climate, Soils and Vegetation

Upon retreat of the last glaciers in north Wales some 14,000 years ago, our present environment evolved with the improving climate. But the generally post-glacial or "Holocene" was not a period of simple steady climatic amelioration and our knowledge of its history has had to be built up from scraps of evidence from scattered sites, regrettably few of which are in Clwyd. Such reconstructions have relied heavily on the analysis of fossil pollen from which the past

Fig.3 The rich, fertile Vale of Clwyd framed by the Clwydian Hills rising to the east.

vegetation can be surmised and, from this, the climate inferred: the sequence of pollen preserved in peat and lake deposits is particularly valuable in this respect and large sections of the post-glacial can often be represented at a single site. In some cases the interpretation has been reinforced from other sources, such as analysis of beetle or mollusc remains, or has been placed on an absolute time-scale by radiocarbon dating. The general picture which has emerged for Britain is of a minor climatic set-back around 11,000-10,000 years ago (the "Loch Lomond stadial"), followed by the warming and drying of the climate up to around 5-7,000 years ago (the controversial "post-glacial climatic optimum") after which the climate cooled and became wetter, leading to our present conditions. During this period of changing climate and vegetation, our soils evolved and the landscape suffered further modification by erosion and deposition. From the mesolithic on, early man experienced and responded to successive stages in this changing environment.

Peri-glacial and Post-glacial Landforms

Modification of the landsurface did not cease in the post-glacial and some important localised features developed in this period. In particular, as the ice retreated the area went through a "peri-glacial" phase similar to that experienced today in tundra regions. The effects of freeze-thaw processes are accentuated under such conditions and can often be seen in the churning ("cryoturbation") of stones that is still preserved at depth in many of our soils today. In the summer season, the thaw saturated and de-stabilised the surface layers of soil which migrated downslope and accumulated on lower valley slopes, especially those facing south, to give the extensive "solifluction deposits" or "head" that occur in upland areas of Clwyd, but which are often difficult to distinguish from glacial till. It is also likely that scree deposits developed at the base of cliffs mainly at this time, some still being an obvious feature of our landscape, as at the Eglwyseg (Fig. 4), others having grassed over to give a smooth planar slope; the entrances to limestone caves may well have been sealed by such events. These processes were operative not only as the last Devensian ice disappeared but also during the subsequent climatic deterioration that occurred some 10,000 years ago: in a few protected sites, peri-glacial features may have also survived from previous glacial phases.

Fig.4 Castell Dinas Brân and the impressive limestone scarp of Eglwyseg.

Fig.5 Hanmer Mere and adjacent parkland in the south-east of the county.

The melting of the great ice sheets of the glacial maximum released such volumes of water as to raise sea level some 100m. This ("eustatic") effect was complicated by the simultaneous, but slower, ("isostatic") readjustment of the land surface as the weight of ice was removed, so that the movement of sea-level and thus of the coastline varied from place to place as the Irish Sea and Liverpool Bay were progressively drowned. In Clwyd, Heyworth and Kidson have suggested that the sea level rose rapidly some 100m up to 7,000 years ago and then more slowly the last 5m over the last 5000 years. The geography of "Clwyd" would thus have been very different to neolithic and mesolithic man, with an extensive tract of lowland in what is now Liverpool Bay to the north. At an earlier stage, following the height of the glaciation, palaeolithic man in Wales would only have been separated from Ireland by an extended creek. On land, the climatic amelioration re-established water erosion as the major process. Post-glacial drainage adapted to the rising sea-level and modified the inherited glacial landscape. Gullies developed in the valley sides and rivers cut into the soft unconsolidated glacial deposits on the valley floors, sometimes leaving a sequence of terraces. In limestone areas, seepage from the valley sides has deposited considerable volumes of soft calcareous "tufa", as at Caerwys where a valuable late-glacial and post-glacial succession containing a land snail fauna has been recorded.

Soils and Vegetation

Over the post-glacial period, the soils of Clwyd have developed on this mosaic of varied topography and deposits, in conjunction with a vegetation which also reflected the changing climate. Regrettably few palynological studies have been carried out from which post-glacial history can be reconstructed. Some information has been obtained for the upland site of Brenig and the Cheshire basin to the east (Fig.5) has provided classic sites for the Late Devensian at Chelford and some valuable sections for the post-glacial have come from Snowdonia. The general sequence is one which started with the establishment of pine forest followed by the development of an oak dominated forest with elm, lime and hazel in lowland areas, and birch/alder in the uplands, such forests reaching their climax some 5-7,000 years ago. There then appear indications of localised clearance and cultivation in the form of "weeds", such as plantain and dock. These mark the first major impact of man on his environment — neolithic settlement and de-forestation, especially on the lighter sandy or gravelly soils of alluvial, glaciofluvial, or Triassic parentage. This is a process which gathered momentum and ultimately led to the transformation of the landscape from the woodlands of earlier times to the artificial mosaic of cultivation of today, and one which would have been accompanied by side effects such as soil erosion and changes in drainage. However, this development was punctuated by fluctuations in climatic conditions that saw intermittent colonisation and retreat from upland areas. In particular, Hibbert has suggested that a grass/sedge moorland gave way to heather dominated uplands in the bronze age of Clwyd around 4,000 years ago, with deterioration to colder, wetter conditions at the change to romano-british times around 2,000 years ago.

As might be anticipated from today's climate and topography, the soil map at 1:50,000 produced by the Soil Survey of England and Wales shows a transition from fertile brown earths in the lowland to podzolised soils on the steeper slopes and peaty gleys and stagnopodzols in the colder, wetter uplands. Detailed maps and memoirs have been produced for the areas around Rhyl and Denbigh, Wrexham and Holywell, and a generalized account is given by Rudeforth *et al.* . In lowland areas a distinction

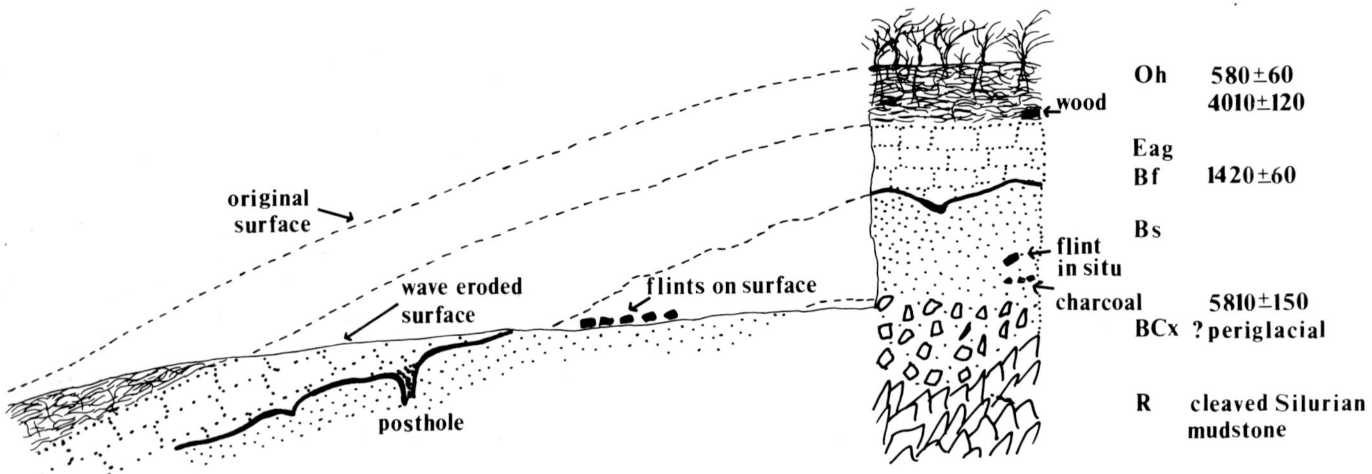

Fig.6 Sketch section which shows the mesolithic flints at Llyn Aled Isaf, as revealed during the dry summer of 1974.

can be made between richer, but often heavy, soils on the reddish brown deposits left by "northern" ice and those on the alluvial deposits derived from local lower palaeozoic shales. Podzols are particularly favoured by the Carboniferous quartz sandstones, whilst the stagnopodzols and gleys of the wetter uplands, whose complex history is discussed below, also reflect the heavier texture and poorer drainage of the Lower Palaeozoic shales. The potential of the present landscape in Clwyd, reflecting soils, climate, and topography, etc., is summarised in "Land Use Classification" maps which show only small pockets of the best ("Grade 1") land in the sheltered Vale of Clwyd, passing up to the poorest ("Grade 5") land in the exposed uplands of Hiraethog and similar areas.

Conclusion: Aled Isaf — A Case History

As part of a detailed study of soil profiles in the Hiraethog uplands, a stagnopodzol profile monolith was collected in 1974 from the shore of Aled Isaf, a reservoir constructed in the 1930s. As a result of a dry summer, the level of the reservoir was unusually low such that a broad platform was laid bare exposing a surface cut through the successive soil horizons. On this surface were found by chance fragments of flint, some of which were later seen to be worked: further detailed collection produced some 4,000 fragments including microliths, scrapers, burins, cores, etc., as well as a few flakes of Gronant chert, and covering in typology the mesolithic and the bronze age. A careful search also located one flint *in situ* at depth in the soil profile at the lake edge; the chances of finding the flints under the peat surface would have been minimal without the winnowing action of waves as the level of the reservoir oscillated. An archaeological survey subsequently revealed evidence of temporary habitation in the form of a hearth and of stakeholes interpreted as belonging to a "palisade trench". Unfortunately, no pollen analyses are yet available for this site but radiocarbon dates have been provided by Prof. Scharpensier for charcoal, wood fragments and the thin cemented "iron pan" in the soil profile, as indicated schematically in Fig.6.

Several interesting points emerge from this study. It would seem that early man hunted in this area over a long period of time. The deep river trench, now flooded, was presumably suitable for the trapping of game, and perhaps a woodland less dense compared to that of the lowlands, together with the gentler climate of those times, made what are now the bleak uplands of today a more attractive environment for mesolithic man. The change from migrating hunter/gatherer to settled pastoralist in the neolithic presumably saw the uplands deserted for the more fertile soils of lowland river valleys (Fig. 7), although under the pressure of an expanding population, and with favourable climatic conditions, man subsequently re-occupied the uplands during the early bronze age; this is evident at Brenig just to the east. An insight can also be gained into the history of the soil profile since it is clear that human occupation coincided with a phase of hillslope erosion, 6,000 to 4,000 years ago, during which half a metre of soil accumulated over fossil peri-glacial material at the foot of the slope. It is also clear that the peaty surface and the thin iron-pan and other "stagnopodzol" features all developed after the human occupation and possibly as a result of climatic deterioration around 2,000 years ago.

The fortunate conjunction of archaeological finds and soil analyses at Llyn Aled Isaf has therefore provided an all too rare glimpse of the past history of a fragment of Clwyd. This example illustrates both the value and the fascination of such palaeoenvironmental studies and the complexity of the interactions between man and his environment. A proper understanding of man's history in Clwyd can only come with the continued accumulation of information from detailed, multidisciplinary, studies.

Fig.7 An impressive aerial view of Moel Famau and lowlands beyond.

THE PALAEOLITHIC AND ITS QUATERNARY CONTEXT

by Stephen Green
with a contribution on Geomorphology by Helen Livingston

Introduction

The palaeolithic of Clwyd — which extends over 250,000 years — can be understood only in the context of the long succession of climatic changes which characterized the Pleistocene. This period saw a long succession of cool, but only occasionally glacial, phases which alternated with more temperate periods, sometimes of fully 'interglacial' status with the development of woodland and with temperatures broadly comparable to those of the present day. These climatic differences affect our understanding in certain directions: for example, periods of cold climate generally had very much lower sea-levels with the result that, for much of the Pleistocene, Britain was joined to the Continent. Dry land would have stretched also from what is now the north coast of Wales to the Isle of Man and beyond. The natural environment, too, would have changed drastically with forest at one extreme yielding to arctic tundra at the other. Again, wildlife would have changed with climate and, accordingly, the potential food supply too would have varied. Perhaps our biggest mental leap is required in recognizing the massive changes which have taken place in the land of Clwyd itself. Here I turn to a contribution by my colleague Dr Helen Livingston, who has for some years been studying the geomorphology of the area between the Vales of Clwyd and Conwy.

Geomorphology

The landforms and stratigraphy of the area between the fault scarp of the Clwydian Hills and the glacial trough of the Vale of Conwy record the later stages in the Quaternary history of the region, which has been glaciated on several occasions during the Pleistocene (Figs.8,9). Ice from two sources entered the area. First, Irish Sea Ice from the Lake District and southern Scotland, the deposits of which are confined to the coast and the lower reaches of the Vales of Clwyd and Conwy. Second, Welsh ice from Snowdonia, Arenig and Berwyn; and possibly from the Hiraethog region of the Denbigh Moors. The evidence for the three phases of glaciation recognized in Clwyd (Fig.9) may be summarized as follows:

I Evidence for "early" glaciation of the region, possibly on more than one occasion, comes, in part, from the erratic lithology and heavy mineral suites of deposits dated to before 225,000 years in Pontnewydd Cave. These suggest an advance of Irish Sea ice into the region, of which the youngest may be correlated tentatively with Oxygen Isotype stage 8 (300-250,000 BP) or even earlier. Some "northern" igneous erratics recorded from tills in the Vale of Clwyd are very weathered and this may likewise reflect their original transport in an early glaciation and subsequent inclusion in later deposits. Evidence comes, in part also, from the putative glacial diversion of the River Elwy. Here, Boswell [1] and Embleton [2] have suggested that the Elwy Valley between Ddol and Cefn Rocks was cut by meltwater marginal to an early Irish Sea ice sheet which diverted the river from a "pre-glacial course" across the Cefn Meiriadog limestone ridge. Pontnewydd Cave opens onto this stretch of valley which clearly must have been cut before northern material could enter the cave. In the absence of any supporting evidence it is only possible to

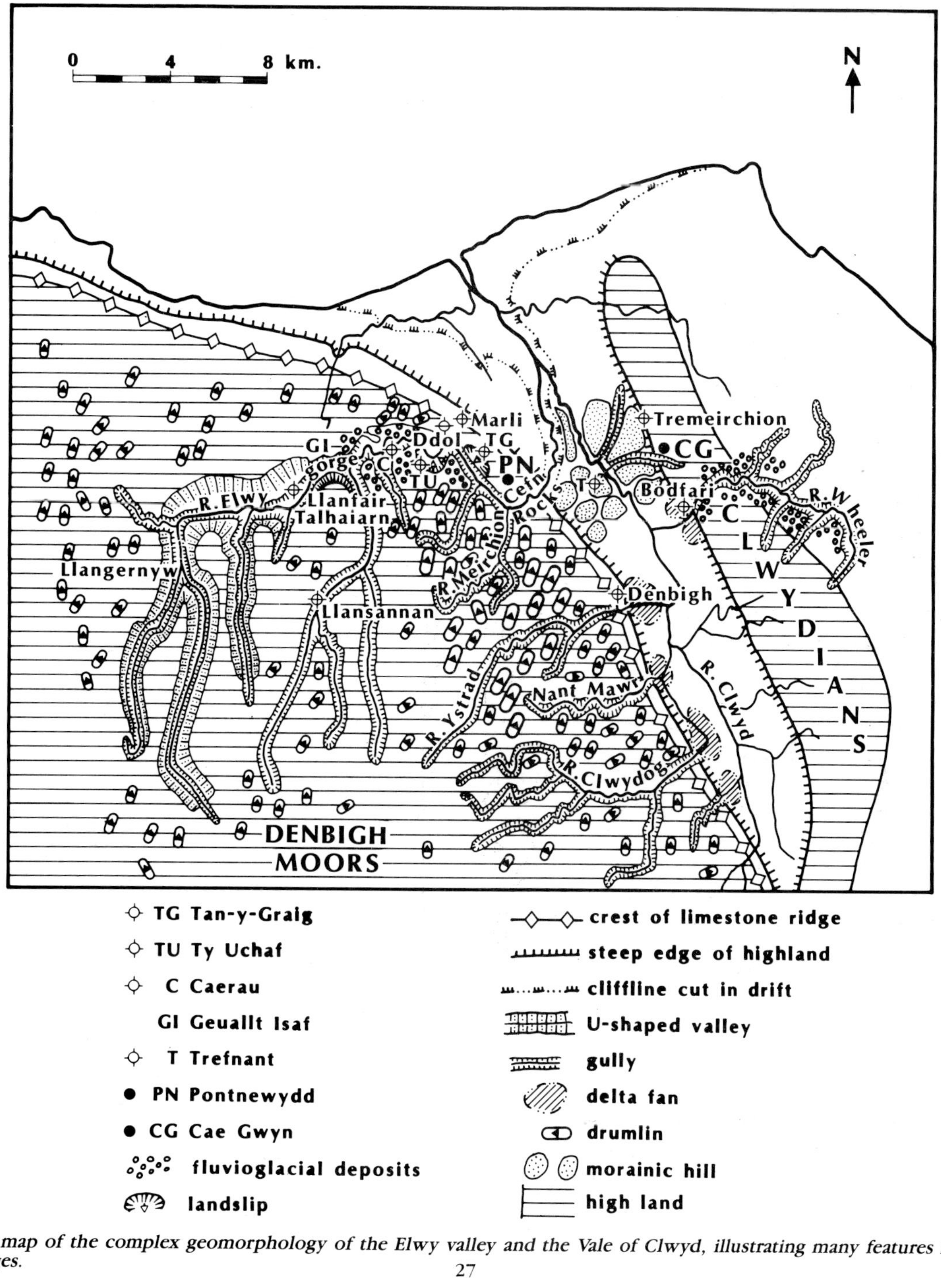

Fig.8 A simplified map of the complex geomorphology of the Elwy valley and the Vale of Clwyd, illustrating many features formed during or after the Ice Ages.

Stage	Geomorphological Event	Pontnewydd Cave Event
Post-glacial	landslipping; lower river terraces	cave mouth exposed by landslips
Zone III	solifluction	Upper Breccia emplacement
Late Devensian Irish Sea Re-advance (post 18ka)	moraine in Vale of Clwyd; till plain in Vale of Clwyd; Irish Sea ice penetrates Elwy Valley;	
	localised ponding in front of Irish Sea ice;	
	glaciofluvial activity from wasting Welsh ice;	
Late Devensian Welsh Ice Re-advance	Welsh ice in Elwy Valley; drumlins are formed in the Upland Zone of the	cave mouth probably blocked by
	Denbigh Moors by ice from the Hiraethog ice cap;	plug of Lower Breccia
Main Devensian Glaciation (post 30ka)	Irish Sea ice ("shelly tills" of Moel Tryfan, Moel Wnion and Halkyn Mountain). Welsh ice ("Arenig till" of the Clwydian Hills).	
Ipswichian Interglacial	accumulation of "Hippopotamus fauna" at Cefn Cave	
Wolstonian Glacial	(Older Irish Sea ice/2nd Welsh ice advances: Midlands)	
Hoxnian or later Interglacial		Lower Breccia (pre-225ka) • Intermediate (pre-225ka)
Anglian Glaciation	(northern drifts of Coventry/1st Welsh ice advance: Midlands)	Lower Sands and Gravels (pre-250ka)
Cromerian Interglacial	?	
Beestonian Glaciation or earlier	Possible Elwy diversion ("Northern drift glaciation")	cave system opened up

• ka = 1000s of years before present.

Fig.9 Chronology of events in the Elwy Valley and Pontnewydd Cave

speculate that the diversion relates either to the Beestonian Northern Drift Glaciation recognised in Oxfordshire [3] or to the even earlier Baventian cold stage.[4]

II In Clwyd two glacial advances can be recognised involving both Welsh and Northern Ice. Evidence for the first event is patchy, and most of the present landforms and deposits date from the most recent glacial phase; but "Higher Level" Irish Sea tills occur to the east of the study area at a height of about 300m OD near Moel y Crio [5] and to the west at 580 and 400m OD on Moel Wnion and Moel Tryfan.[6] It is not known if these deposits all relate to the same early ice advance but as they all occur at high elevations near the coast it is reasonable to assume that they do, and that they relate to a time during which an extensive Welsh Ice sheet prevented northern ice from penetrating inland, causing it to pile up against the coastal hills. The significance of the radiocarbon date of 33,740 + 2100/-1800 BP obtained on shells from Moel Tryfan [7] is unclear, but it is probably safest to accept this as giving no more than a minimum age.

III The latest event has been dated to younger than 18,000 BP, a date derived from the radiocarbon age of 18000 + 1400/-1200 BP (Birm-146) obtained from a mammoth bone probably found in Ffynnon Beuno Cave [8] discussed further below. During this phase the Irish Sea and Welsh ice sheets followed roughly the same flow patterns as before but ice generated on the Hiraethog Moors may have been less influenced by the Merioneth Ice Cap, thus enabling a Denbigh Moors Ice Cap to form.

It is possible that this glacial event was no more than a Late Devensian re-advance of the ice equivalent to the Welsh and Ellesmere readvances of the northern Welsh Marches.[9]

Laminated clays in the Vale of Clwyd "trench" and the low level deltas (below 40m OD) of the Ystrad, Nant Mawr, Clywedog and Wheeler rivers where they enter the Vale provide evidence for a moraine-dammed Lake Clwyd. (Fig.10). When the morainic ice core finally melted, the moraine was breached by the impounded meltwaters, thus initiating the present drainage of the Vale floor.

As regards the late glacial and post glacial periods, evidence from Glanllynnau in north-west Wales [10] suggests that the area was ice-free by 14,468 $\pm$ 300 BP, although it is probable that the morainic ice core persisted for some time after this.

The Flandrian transgression is marked by the 5m "Bryn Carrog" coastline.[11] This inland cliff is cut into the Irish Sea till from Gronant (SJ 092 832) to Penmaen (SH 881 788) where it enters the sea and thence to the Little Orme (SH 817 828). The rivers Elwy and Clwyd both flow in "entrenched" valleys north of the Vale of Clwyd moraine, their steep-sided river-cut bluffs being associated with the coastline and continuing into it. When sea level fell downcutting and excavation extended up the Elwy valley resulting in large-scale landslipping of the valley fill. Finally, the mouth of the Vale of Clwyd and the coastal lowlands were filled with marine and estuarine alluvium of the Flandrian Transgression.

Archaeology

Clwyd has few but important palaeolithic sites: the caves of Pontnewydd, Cefn, Cae Gwyn, Ffynnon Beuno and possibly the Lynx Cave (Fig.11). Examination, by the writer, of the find stratified in boulder clay at Linden Walk,

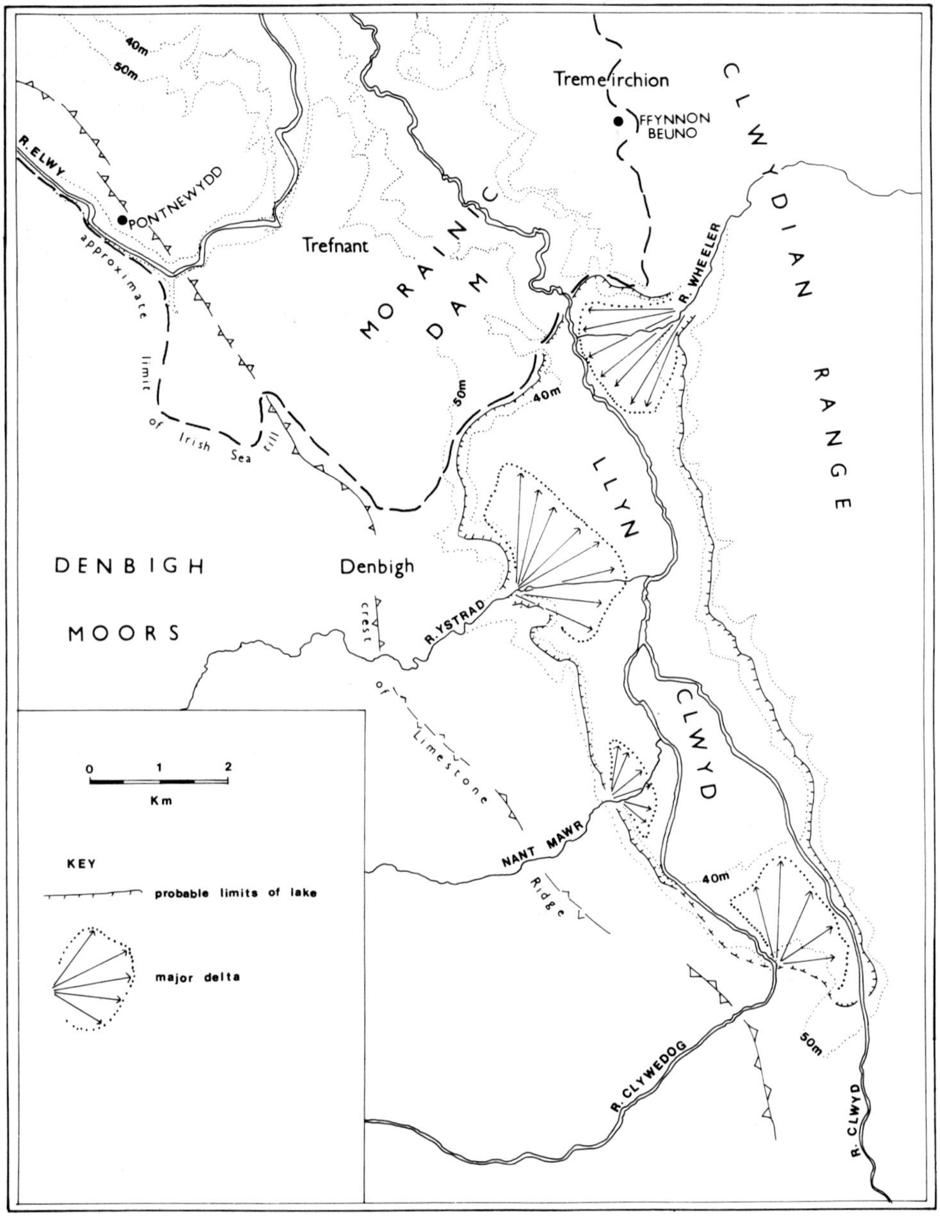

Fig.10 The geomorphology of Lake Clwyd, showing the possible extent of an ancient lake between Denbigh and the Clwydian Hills.

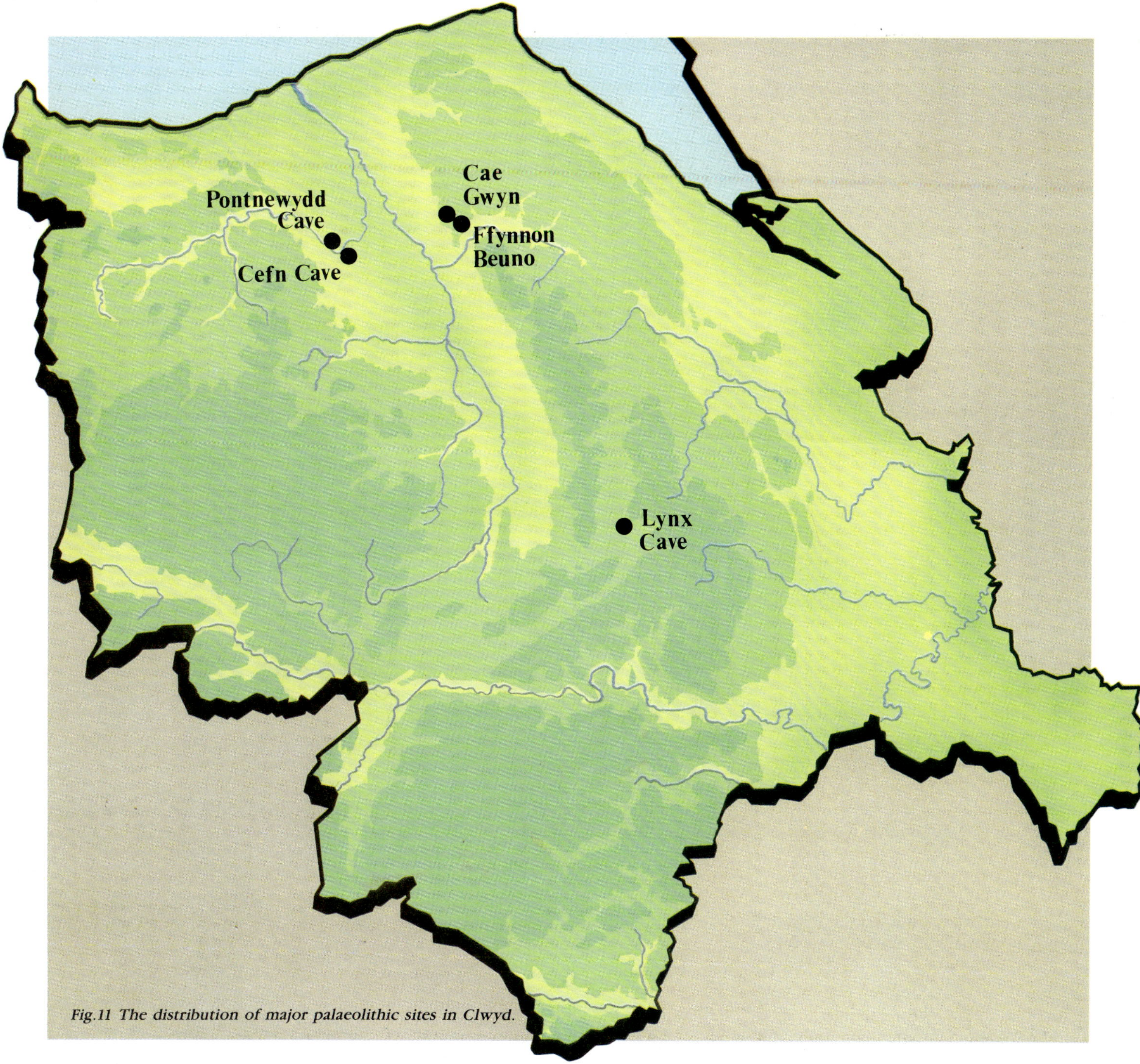

Fig.11 The distribution of major palaeolithic sites in Clwyd.

Prestatyn and described as a fine specimen of a "hand hammer" or "axe",[12] has shown it to be certainly of natural origin. I will turn now to the caves which I will consider in chronological order.

Pontnewydd Cave

The earliest humanly occupied site in Clwyd, indeed in Wales, is Pontnewydd Cave (Figs.12,13,14) in the Elwy Valley.[13] The site is important not only for the antiquity of its occupation, a quarter of a million years ago, but also for the occurrence there of lower palaeolithic stone tools and the fossilized bones of animals and, even, of the remains of human beings themselves. Pontnewydd Cave is one of only two sites in Britain to have produced early human remains and is remote from the main area of earlier palaeolithic settlement in Britain.

The dating of the site is based on uranium-series and Thermoluminescence (TL) determinations on a stalagmitic floor which formed on the surface of the archaeological layers. The determinations give an age of *c.*220,000 years, thus yielding a *terminus ante quem* for the human occupation. A TL age of 200,000 $\pm$ 25,000 BP for a burnt flint core is in general agreement with these results and lends support to the interpretation [14] that the human occupation belongs broadly to the end of the warm stage (Oxygen Isotope Stage 7c) dated to *c.*250-230,000 years ago or to the succeeding cold stage (7b) dated *c.*230,000 years. The overlying stalagmite would have formed during the following warm period (7a).

The cave stratigraphy is complex in detail but the broad outlines and their interpretation are now fairly well understood (Fig.16). A basal accumulation, up to 3 metres in thickness, of sands and gravels contains neither artefacts nor fauna. These layers, which must be older than 250,000 years, were emplaced in the form of debris flows which slumped into the cave. Their importance for the archaeologist lies in the fact that they contain many natural pebbles of the same types of volcanic rocks which were later used as raw materials for implement manufacture by the palaeolithic occupants of the site. Since publication of the First Report in 1984, natural flint has been recognized from the Upper Sands and Gravels in the east passage (find no.D4662) and in the Orange Intermediate layer. Above the basal deposits lie the layers of the Intermediate complex, immediately recognizable visually by their buff, orange and yellow colours. Analysis of the sand and clay mineralogy of these sediments shows them to have undergone the intense chemical weathering characteristic of warm climate conditions; this has resulted in the release of iron followed by oxidation and precipitation of the iron with the consequential formation of hydrous ferric oxides. The Intermediate layers, which are relatively thin and have produced correspondingly few artefacts, were probably emplaced by a series of debris-flow events. They have yielded a range of animals which includes wolf, bear "leopard", horse, narrow-nosed rhinoceros and species of vole and wood mouse; in addition the presence of the characteristically woodland species, roe deer and beaver, suggests an interglacial status (but Currant, [15] has noted the possible occurrence of beaver in temperate phases within glacial periods). Overall, an environment of open woodland is suggested by the fauna. By contrast, specifically warm-climate animals are absent from the overlying Lower Breccia which has produced the bulk of the fauna and artefacts. New species include hyaena, Merck's rhinoceros, wild cattle or bison, and — among the microfauna — the Northern vole and Norway lemming. The presence of the latter two species is suggestive of a climatic deterioration or, perhaps, a change to a more continental climate.

Fig.12 Work progresses on the palaeolithic remains within the confined entrance at Pontnewydd Cave in the Elwy valley.

Fig.13 Meticulous excavation continues outside the entrance to Pontnewydd Cave, in the Elwy valley.

Overall, the species present indicate an open steppe environment.

I would see, then, the early phases of the site as belonging, in all probability, to two successively warm and cold periods.[16] The abundant bear bones, combined with the presence of many deciduous teeth of bear from both the Intermediate and the Lower Breccia indicate that, at times, the cave served as a bear den. Further study of the bones will be needed, however, to attempt to separate human food refuse from carnivore accumulation. The context and the mechanics of the debris-flow emplacements have been discussed elsewhere [17] and need not further concern us here; likewise the upper part of the sequence — the Silt beds, the Upper Breccia and the Upper Clays and Sands — which is very probably of Late Glacial age. Artefacts are present in the Upper Breccia but were derived by natural processes from the earlier deposits.

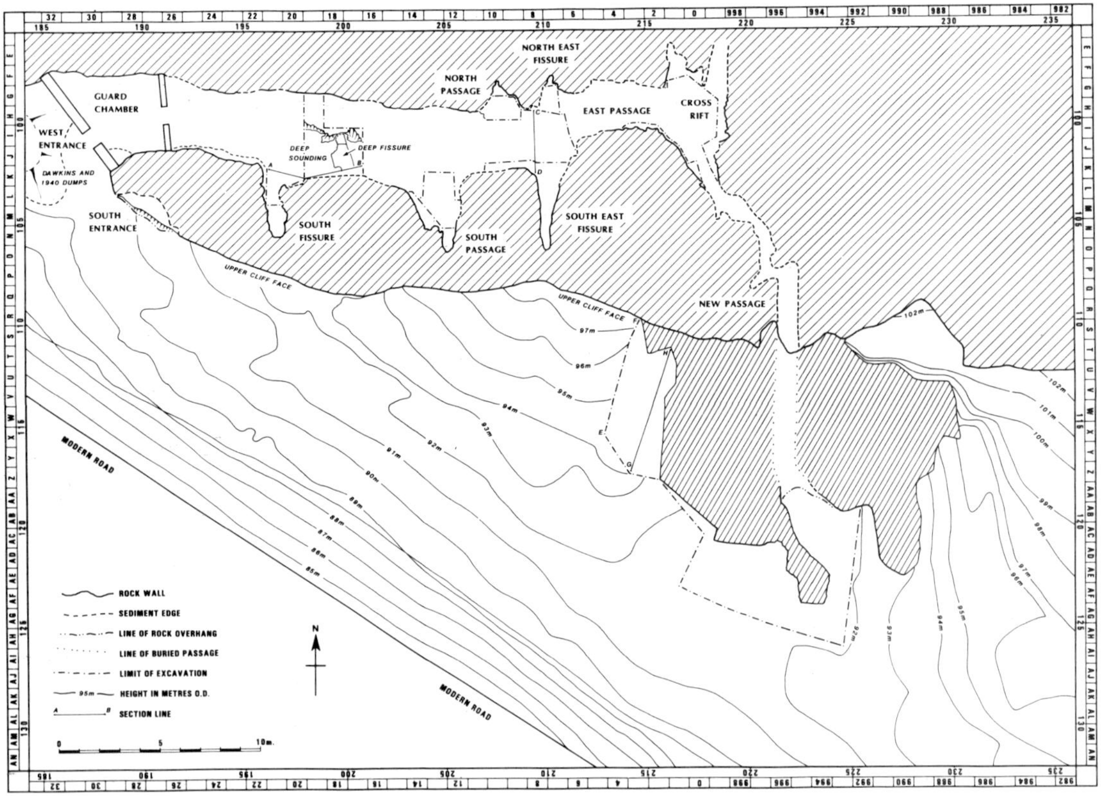

Fig.14 A Plan of Pontnewydd Cave completed during the 1988 season of excavations. Note the new passage to the south, providing an additional entrance to the cave.

	Numbers	**%**
Handaxes	32	9.5
Choppers/chopping tools	2	0.6
Flake cleaver	1	0.3
Scrapers	24	7.1
Notches and denticulates	7	2.1
Naturally backed knives	9	2.7
Mousterian points	1	0.3
Other implements	3	0.9
Levallois flakes and points	36	10.7
Levallois cores	18	5.3
Discoidal cores	12	3.6
Other cores	26	7.7
Flakes (including 66 "pseudo-tools" with natural retouch)	166	49.3
TOTAL	**337**	

Fig.15 Pontnewydd Cave — Analysis of Artefact types [17a]

Analysis of the artefacts has revealed a picture (Fig.15) of an industry dominated by handaxes, scrapers and by the use of prepared-core or "Levallois" technology.

The types and variety of the artefacts, taken with the size and location of the cave, give some clue as to the use made of the site by its human occupants. Excavation at the New Entrance (Fig.14) in 1988 provided clear evidence that the rock face has receded by some distance since the emplacement of the deposit; accordingly, the original form of the entrance area can only be a matter of inference. However, we have no reason to suppose that the phreatic tube which constitutes the main passage of the cave did not

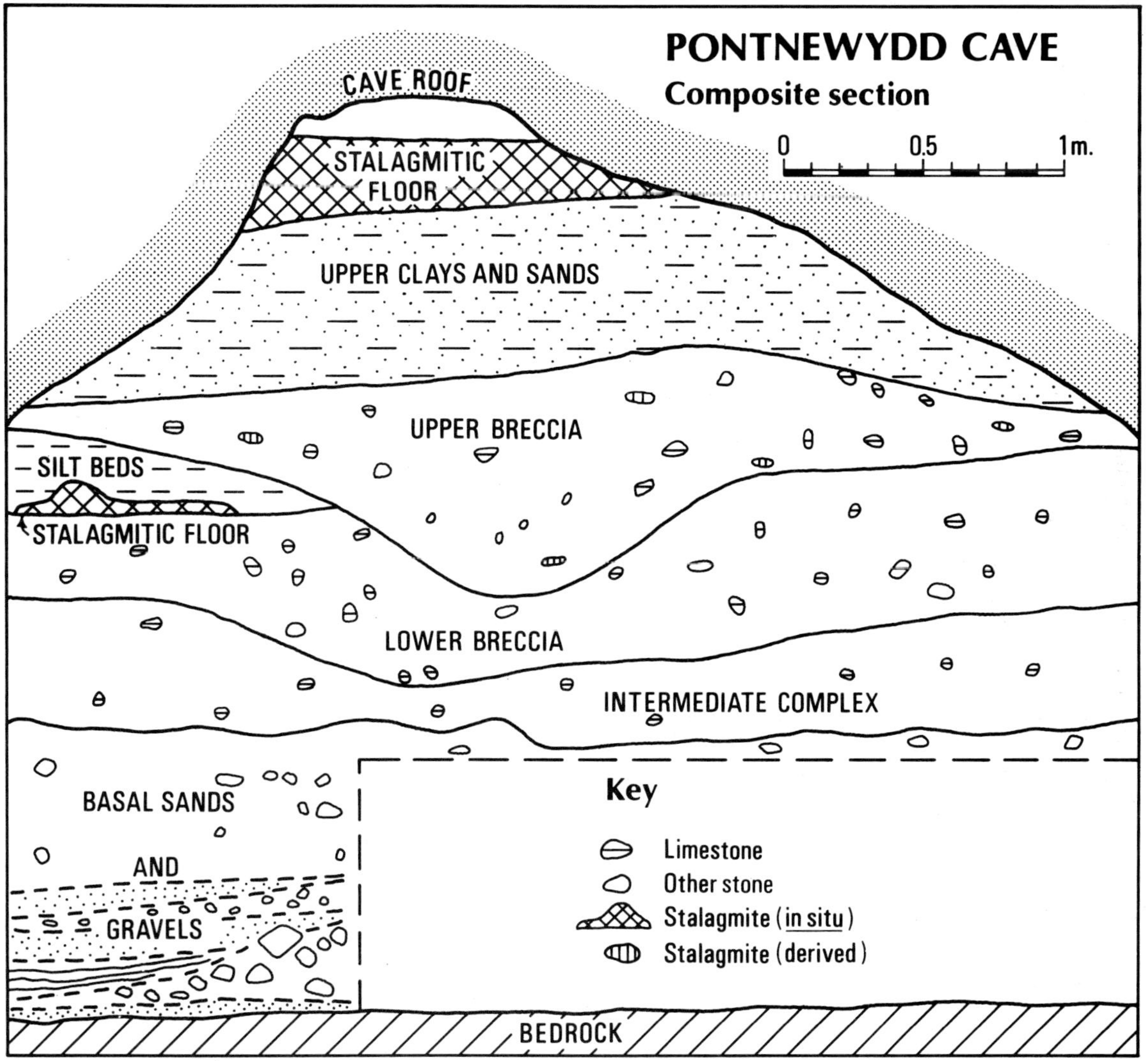

Fig.16 A composite section through the accumulated deposits inside the cave at Pontnewydd in the Elwy valley. Most of the palaeolithic finds come from the Lower Breccia.

once continue in much the same proportions to some distance beyond the present rock face. On this basis, the daylight zone within the overhang is not likely to have exceeded more than about 30 sq m, space for only half a dozen persons or so — although it is perhaps a fair question as to whether the cave may really have represented no more than a convenient temporary shelter and food store for a party encamped along the exterior cliff-face. The discovery of a handaxe in just such a context some 40m east of the entrance during deep excavations of hillslope deposits in November 1986 above the New Entrance, reinforces this suggestion. The site was

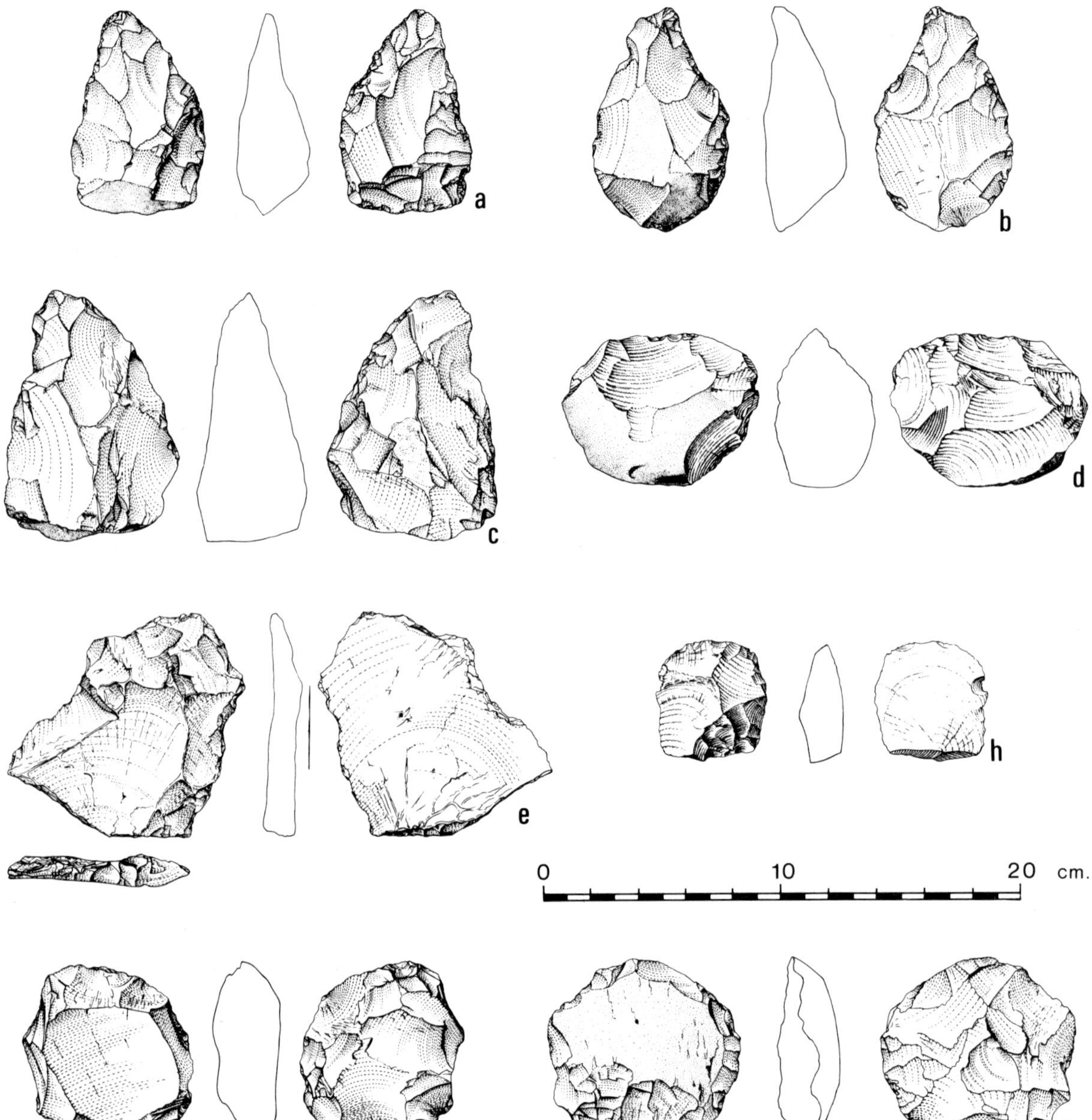

Fig.17 Artefacts from Pontnewydd Cave in the Elwy valley: a-c-handaxes; d-chopping tool; e-levallois flake; f-g-discoidal cores; h-side-endscraper.

Fig.18 A selection of tools dating to about 250,000 years ago found during recent excavations at Pontnewydd cave. The photograph shows (from left to right), top row: handaxe, flake, handaxe; middle row: flake, scraper, handaxe; bottom row: handaxe, core, handaxe; (this last handaxe measures 11.6cms in length).

well located both as a vantage point, giving views of game movements along the Elwy valley, and perhaps as a kill-site for animals driven over the cliff above, although the topography would not favour such a hunting strategy at Pontnewydd. The range of artefacts (Figs.17,18) — with implements, cores and waste flakes all present — demonstrates both tool manufacture and renewal on site and the variety of implements — spearpoints for hunting, handaxes and sharp Levallois flakes for butchering, and scrapers for hide-processing — combine to suggest as incorrect my original view of the site as no more than a "transit" camp.[18] It is clear that a range of activities took place in and around Pontnewydd Cave.

The human beings themselves are known from a variety of finds, mostly teeth and jaw fragments, and appear to represent at least four individuals: an adult and three juveniles, one aged about eight and the two others aged about twelve years. The presence of the characteristic of taurodontism in the teeth of at least two individuals — in which the permanent molars possess an enlarged pulp cavity associated with unseparated roots — has led to the suggestion that the finds may be compared with those of Early Neanderthals.[19]

Cefn Cave

Cefn Cave lies only some 750m to the south-east of Pontnewydd Cave on the same bank of the Elwy (Fig.20). My own excavations at the site have yielded a sequence of debris flow and intercalated stalagmitic floors paralleling, in many respects, the sequence at Pontnewydd.[20] However, the excavations to date have yielded no artefacts and the only examples to come from the site consist of one Late Glacial Creswell point, perhaps *c.*12,000 BP, and three other flints all found in early nineteenth century

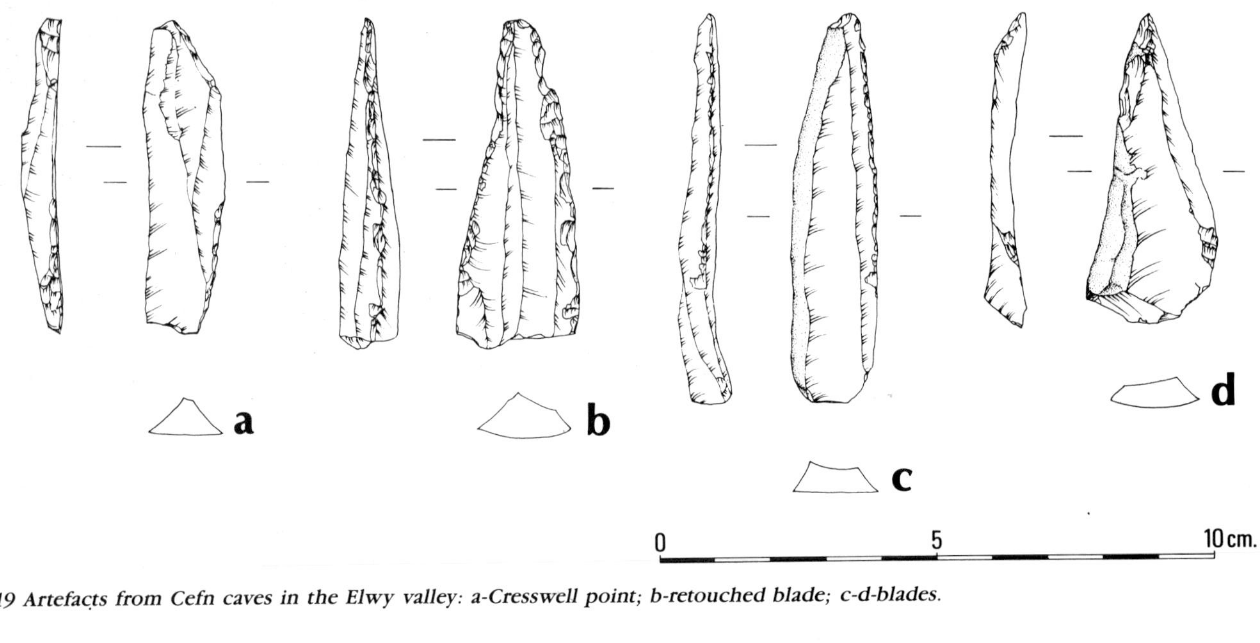

Fig.19 Artefacts from Cefn caves in the Elwy valley: a-Cresswell point; b-retouched blade; c-d-blades.

Fig.20 View of Cefn cave in the Elwy valley. Many caves are formed in limestone through gradual dissolution caused by percolating water over hundreds of thousands of years.

excavations [21] in the west entrance along with bones of "goat, pig, fox and badger, and cut antlers of red deer". The flint artefacts (Fig.19) were clearly in a derived context and nothing can, at present, be said of the nature of the occupation except that the scanty finds do not suggest it to have been other than casual in nature.

Ffynnon Beuno and Cae Gwyn Caves

These two sites are physically contiguous and so must be considered together (Figs.21,22,23). The caves, at heights of *c.*115-125m OD overlook a steep-sided valley — a former glacial meltwater channel — on the eastern side of the Vale of Clwyd. They are situated just north of the Vale of Clwyd moraine complex which rises locally to *c.* 150m OD. The artefacts from Ffynnon Beuno may come from two discrete phases of settlement, the diagnostic types being a large bifacially re-touched leaf point from the earliest phase, *c.* 38,000 BP and an Aurignacian *burin busqué* perhaps representing a later phase, between 30,000 and 28,000 BP. With this latter may belong also an angle-burin, two scrapers (one re-sharpened through its patina) and one worked bone (Fig.24). The supposition of two phases of occupation is however, unsupported by the stratigraphy, all the finds apparently having come from either a single layer of reddish cave-earth or from disturbed contexts. The only hint of two phases of occupation comes from the re-worked scraper but uncertainty as to its precise context renders even this evidence ambiguous. The matter is further complicated by the probability that the finds in the cave were emplaced by some form of debris flow. The evidence is conflicting here but the excavators believed that the cave-earth in the side passage had been reworked by water action "as a considerable amount of a sandy material and some clay with boulders occurred distributed throughout ... and ... [many bones were] in contact with the roof, and others forced into small fissures".[22]

It is relevant here to turn to the discussion of Cae Gwyn Cave (Fig.22). Artefactual finds from this site were rather fewer than at Ffynnon Beuno and comprise a flint blade and a flint end-of-blade scraper (Fig.24.) The statigraphy inside the cave comprised, from top to bottom, a sequence of

Layer 1	Recent loam
Layer 2	Laminated clay with, in places, thin stalagmitic crusts
Layer 3	Sandy clay with pebbles containing Pleistocene bones, a flint scraper and derived stalagmite and stalactites
Layer 4	Gravel consisting mainly of local materials
Bedrock	

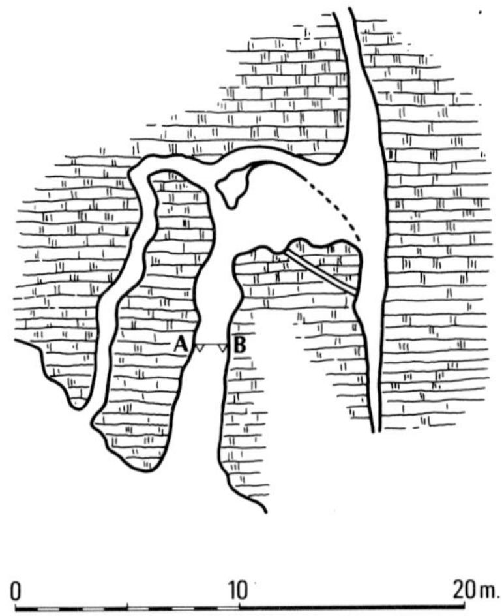

Fig.21 Plan and section of Ffynnon Beuno cave, Tremeirchion, showing the accumulated deposits.

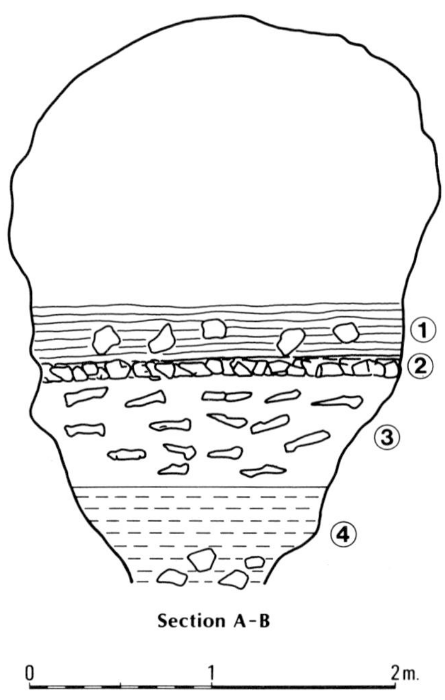

The archaeological level, layer 3, is described as containing pebbles — clearly derived from elsewhere — of felsite, granite, gneiss, quartzite and sandstone and with bones in "inclined and evidently disturbed positions".[23] The layer has the characteristics of a debris flow.[24] Overall, it is tempting to regard these probable debris flows at Cae Gwyn and Ffynnon Beuno as contemporary with the Late Glacial Upper Breccia debris flow at Pontnewydd, dated (on faunal grounds) within the time bracket 15-10,000 BP and arising from the masses of water liberated by thawing ice or permafrost following the end of the Devensian glacial maximum. In consequence, the archaeological layers at Cae Gwyn and Ffynnon Beuno might well contain a mixture of finds covering some thousands, perhaps tens of thousands of years, finally mixed together in one catastrophic debris flow. Thus the radiocarbon age of 18,000 + 1,400/ — 1,200 BP on mammoth bone from Ffynnon Beuno probably signifies no more than a *terminus post quem* for the debris flow event. In these circumstances it seems more than possible that the so-called glacial drift overlying the Cae Gwyn cave [25] is not *in situ* but was redeposited under the peri-glacial conditions of the Late Glacial period. In any event, it would seem that the dated bone came from Ffynnon Beuno and *not* Cae Gwyn — having been selected from the collection still retained by the Pennant family,[26] the former owners of that cave. In consequence, the significance of the 18,000 BP determination for the dating of glacial events in Britain seems tenuous at best and radiocarbon dates from Glen Ballyre on the Isle of Man, only some 100km off the North Wales coast, which show glaciation to have ended by 18,500 BP,[27] may be of greater relevance to the situation in Clwyd, if these determinations are reliable.

Fauna from both caves survives in a number of collections and is in urgent need of re-study.

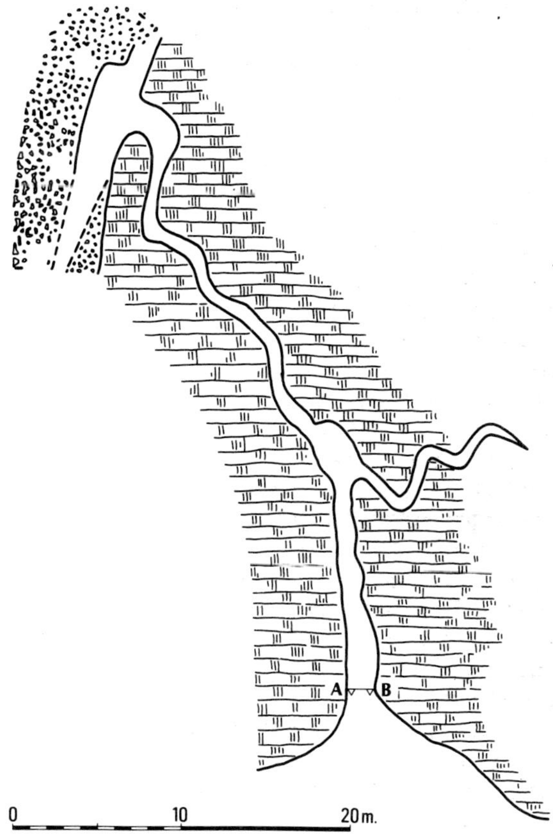

Fig.22 Plan and section of Cae Gwyn, Tremeirchion, showing the deposits filling the cave.

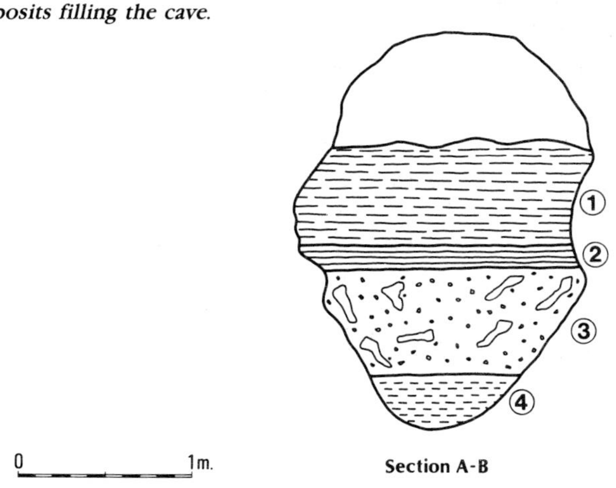

Fig.23 The caves at Cae Gwyn (centre left) and Ffynnon Beuno (centre), Tremeirchion, during the 19th century excavations. The spoil tips and both caves can be clearly seen.

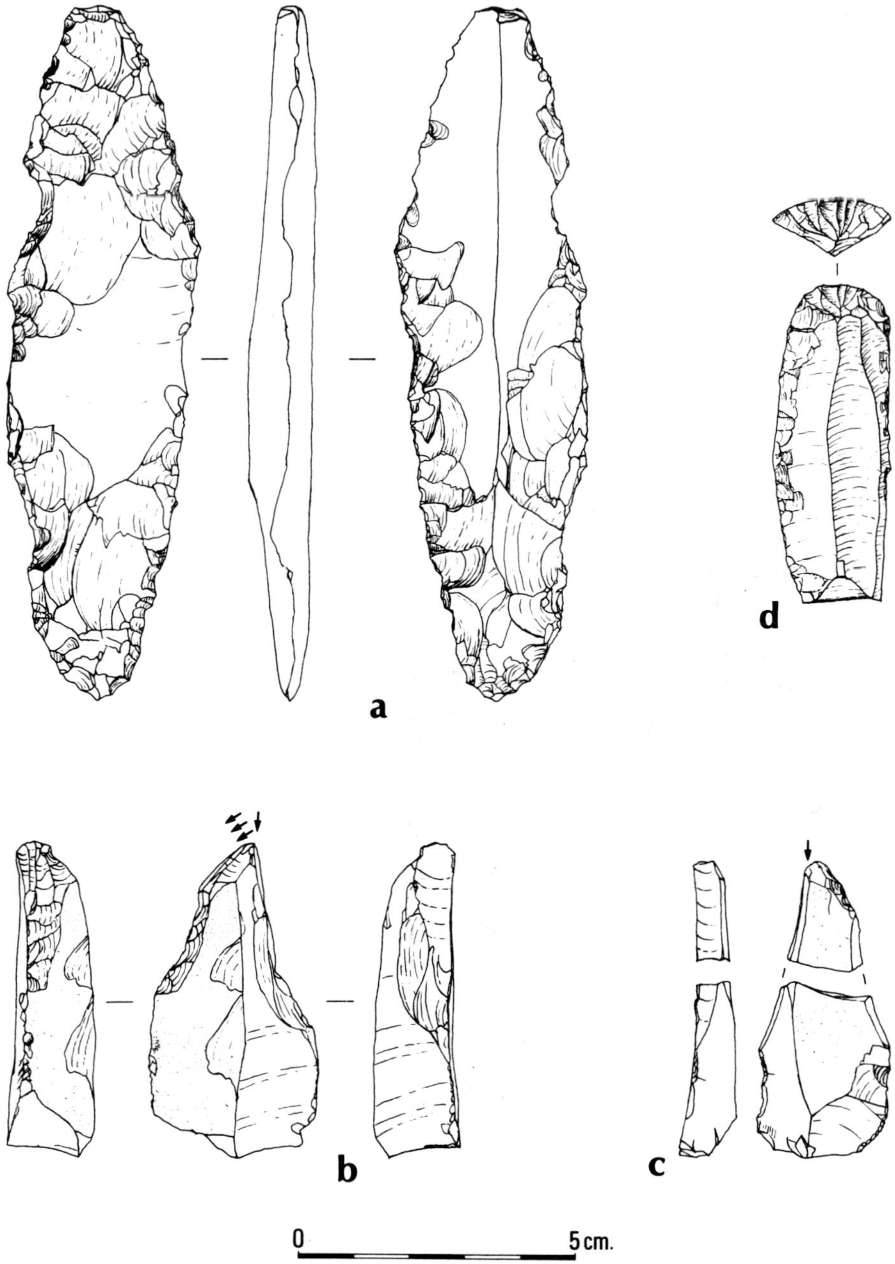

Fig.24 Artefacts from Ffynnon Beuno and Cae Gwyn caves, Tremeirchion: a-c are from Ffynnon Beuno and d is from Cae Gwyn; a-leaf point; b-burin busqué; c-angle burin, d-scraper.

In the published account of the fauna by W. Davies [28] all of the bones from Ffynnon Beuno and Cae Gwyn were listed together. One must presume from this that the species present varied little, if at all, between the two sites. The only difference noted is that the few remains of roe deer came only from Ffynnon Beuno. The carnivore most frequently found is the hyaena, represented by over 200 specimens of jaws, teeth and a few milk teeth; other species, lion, bear, wolf, fox and wild cat are far less common. Of the herbivores, the common species are the reindeer, the horse and the woolly rhinoceros — over 400 teeth of the latter being found. Other animals listed include mammoth, badger, wild boar, bovid, giant deer and red deer.

Recent study of the collections in the Manchester University Museum has, however, revealed a list, dated 19 August 1885 and apparently in Boyd Dawkins' handwriting, of fauna from the two sites. The details are as follows (the dashes are original; it is not clear if they signify a repeat symbol for teeth);

Cae Gwyn

jaws (chiefly hyaena)	20
Horse teeth	34
Hyaena —	26
Rhinoceros —	23
Fox —	3
Bos —	2
Bear tooth	1
C.Hibernicus	1

Ffynnon Beuno

jaws (chiefly hyaena)	50
Horse teeth	545
Rhinoceros —	375
Lion —	6
Bos —	20
Bear —	16
Deer teeth	72
C.Hibernicus teeth	20
Wolf teeth	4

These identifications, all potentially of pleistocene species, make the one addition of *Capra hibernicus* (an archaic term which could signify either the pleistocene ibex *(Capra ibex)* or the Post Glacial domestic goat) to the published lists. The much greater richness of Ffynnon Beuno is immediately striking as is the similarity of the faunal ranges between the two sites. It is clear that the above lists refer only to specimens actually studied by Dawkins, as the document continues with a list of "those animals whose *bones* [author's italics] have been identified, including both Caves" which is identical to Davies's list with the one exception of *"Capra hibernicus"* which seems to have occurred only in the collection studied by Dawkins.

It is quite clear from the frequency of hyaena and the gnawed condition of many bones that the bulk of the fauna is the result of hyaena accumulation. The hyaena, together with the woolly rhinoceros, is not known to have reappeared after the last glacial maximum and these species are unlikely to date later than *c.*18000 BP. The remaining species are consistent with belonging to such an assemblage except for roe deer, badger, wild boar and wild cat which are interglacial species and so are likely to be either intrusive or derived. In the absence of other last interglacial species they are most likely to be of Post Glacial age.

Lynx Cave

Excavations by John Blore at Lynx Cave over the period 1962-1981 [29] have produced a stratigraphic succession of which the basal layers E-G are certainly Pleistocene. Layer E produced one reindeer bone and reindeer was present also in the overlying layer (D) along with Pleistocene bovid and post glacial dog and badger. The finds (Fig.25) include a few pieces which might be of late glacial age, but none is diagnostic nor do

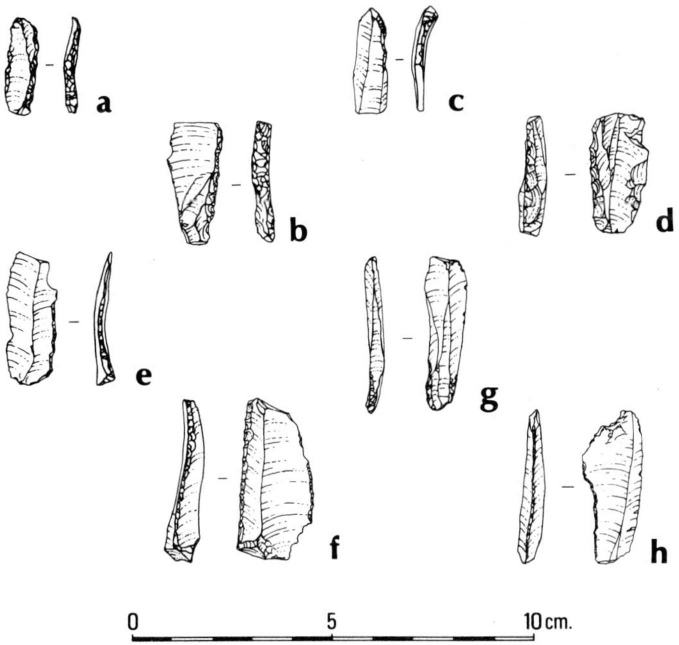

Fig.25 Blades and scrapers found at the Lynx Cave, Llanarmon yn Iâl. Note the careful retouching on the sides of the implements in order to produce a cutting edge.

any come from the Pleistocene layers and so the argument to their age must remain a purely typological one. Nonetheless, they compare most closely with material of late upper palaeolithic age.

Conclusions

The palaeolithic caves and their related quaternary deposits are of pivotal importance for our understanding not only of the progression of the human colonization of the earth [30] - for Pontnewydd Cave is the most north-westerly occupied lower palaeolithic site in Europe - but of a critical phase of human evolution, that of the development of early Neanderthals; and of the chronology of the acquisition by early hominids of technological skills. Much later in time, the twin sites of Ffynnon Beuno and Cae Gwyn are crucial to our understanding of the spread of upper palaeolithic hunters arriving, ultimately, from the North European plain. The very scantiness of the remains from the few Late Glacial sites may suggest that the re-colonization of North Wales after the Devensian glacial maximum was only a fairly brief episode, perhaps reflecting the very remoteness of Clwyd from the "landfall" areas of settlement in southern and eastern Britain.

Acknowledgements

My debt to my co-authors in the Pontnewydd Report [31] — M.J.Aitken, R.E.Bevins, P.A.Bull, C.Clayton, S.N.Collcutt, A.P.Currant, N.C.Debenham, C.Embleton, J.Huxtable, M.Ivanovich, D.A.Jenkins, T.I.Molleson, M.H.Newcomer, H.P.Schwarcz, C.B.Stringer — cannot be overstressed. In preparing the present paper I am particularly grateful to Helen Livingston for her considerable help and advice; Erik Trinkaus for discussion of the hunting strategy of Neanderthals; to Dr. R.M.C.Eager, Keeper of Geology at the Manchester University Museum for access to the Boyd Dawkins collection; to Stephen Grenter for making the Linden Walk find available for study; and to Dr. A.J.Stuart for advice on *Capra hibernicus*. For permission to dig at the caves of Pontnewydd, Cefn and Cae Gronw, I remain in the permanent debt of Sir Watkin Williams-Wynn. I am grateful also to the Clwyd-Powys Trust for releasing Ken Brassil to take part in this work as my Assistant Director. I am pleased also to acknowledge the following grant-giving bodies of their generous and sustained support: Cambrian Archaeological Association, Board of Celtic Studies, Prehistoric Society, British Academy, Society of Antiquaries, the Royal Archaeological Institute, LSB Leakey

Foundation for Research into the Origin of Man. (The drawings are the work of the National Museum of Wales. Illustrators, Colin Williams and Paul Hughes, except where otherwise noted).

The work took place with the sanction of both Cadw and the Nature Conservancy Council, the site being protected by law as a Scheduled Ancient Monument and as a Site of Special Scientific Interest.

FOOTNOTES

1. 1949
2 1960,1970, 1984
3 Arkell 1947
4 Catt 1981
5 Rowlands 1971
6 Embleton 1970
7 Foster 1970
8 Rowlands 1971
9 Peake 1981
10 Coope and Brophy 1972
11 Rowlands 1955
12 Smith 1933
13 Green 1984
14 Green, 1989
15 Currant 1986, 300
16 See Green et al, for a fuller discussion of this question
17 Embleton and Collcutt in Green 1984;
17a Green 1984, 115
18 Green 1981
19 Stringer 1984
20 Green 1986
21 Stanley 1833; Dawkins 1874, 159
22 Hicks 1886, 8-9
23 Hicks 1886, 12
24 *cf* Collcutt 1984, 58
25 Hicks 1888
26 Pers. comm. A.D.H. Pennant, November 1986
27 Shotton and Williams 1971, 146; 1973, 4; 1977, 117
28 in Hicks 1886, 17-19
29 Blore 1981
30 Dennell 1986
31 Green 1984

MESOLITHIC
by Kenneth Brassil

The 4,000 year period traditionally known as the mesolithic or middle stone age witnessed profound landscape changes where hunter-gatherer communities adapted to the expanding forest and wood and the drowning of vast tracts of coastal land. Whilst Clwyd has, through excavation and chance discovery, an increasing and interesting record of human activity during the mesolithic, such evidence can at present provide only a limited view of these mesolithic peoples and the archaeology of this period.

It was the gradually warming climate from 10,000 bc to 6,000 bc which set into motion landscape, vegetational and faunal changes to which man's hunting way of life had to adapt. By 8,000 bc there had been a radical change in the landscape. Pine, birch and hazel woodland was established on the rapidly maturing soils replacing the former open, tundra landscape of Arctic-alpine conditions.

Over a 3,000 year period, from the beginning of the mesolithic, the estimated mean average summer temperatures in this part of the world rose by 5° to 17°C. The attendant changes in the vegetation cover and the warming of the coastal waters broadened the food resources available to these mesolithic groups. Woodland animals, wild ox, red deer, roe deer and pig became the hunter's main quarry; rivers and lakes, estuaries and inshore waters provided fish, shellfish and waterfowl. Hunting techniques had to adapt to the woodland scene. Indeed the type of hunting equipment used is the predominant find on most archaeological sites. This consists of flaked stone tools such as scrapers and knives together with, and characteristic of the mesolithic, small flakes or microliths (Fig 27). Tool-making traditions changed: in the early mesolithic microliths were prepared from broad flakes or blades of stone whilst in the later mesolithic narrower blades were utilised. Whilst it is accepted that microliths were used as the barbs and piercing elements of arrows, it is probable that these slender flakes could also have been part of composite knives, fish hooks or even graters (Fig 28). Larger implements such as flaked stone axes or adzes were probably used for woodworking and the felling of trees. Whilst direct archaeological evidence is rare it is likely that a range of plants, roots, fungi, nuts and berries would have constituted a significant proportion of the food consumed by these mesolithic peoples.

During the earlier mesolithic the coastline of Britain was significantly different from that of today (Fig 29). Dry land linked south-east England with the continent. The Irish Sea was, in part, an extensive plain, drained by the proto-Conwy, -Clwyd and -Dee rivers. The melting of glacial ice had a dramatic effect on sea-level: over a period of perhaps only 200 years around 7,000 bc sea-level rose by as much as 7m creating what is essentially today's coastline (Fig 29). Vast tracts of coastal plain rich in marsh, river and estuary food resources were lost. There was less land for more people. At the same time this isolation of Britain from the continent created a more oceanic weather pattern, warmer, windier and wetter. In response woodlands diversified to include oak, alder, lime, elm and ash, creating a landscape dominated by mixed temperate forest with moorland on the high uplands.

Here in Clwyd our mesolithic archaeology is dominated by stone tools made of flint and chert. The readily flaked flint was collected as beach pebbles, originating in the west of Scotland and carried as far as the North Wales coast by ice. Chert, though a poorer flaking stone, was available in much greater quantity occuring as layers in the Carboniferous

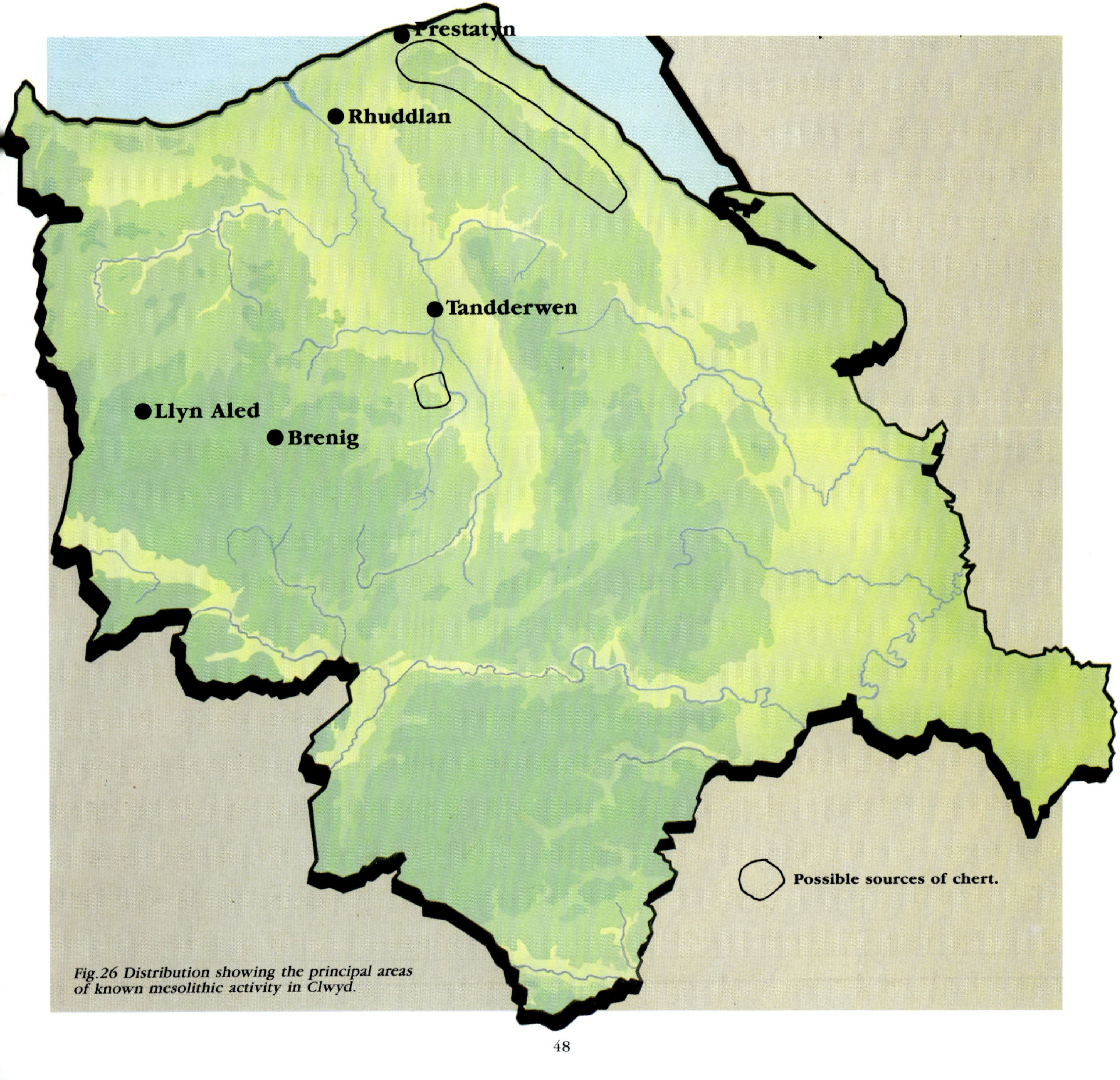

Fig.26 Distribution showing the principal areas of known mesolithic activity in Clwyd.

Limestone in the north-east of the county (Fig 26). Unlike bone or wood, stone has every chance of surviving 6,000 years and more of weathering and erosion. The right kind of conditions, especially waterlogged or peat deposits, are required for the preservation of organic remains whilst bone is best preserved in lime rich soils. Less direct evidence for man's activities — the felling of trees and the clearance of woodland — can be seen in the vegetation record of peats where pollen is preserved. Or, as charcoal horizons in the peat resulting from the burning of woodland. In the Berwyns evidence of such woodland clearance may be due to mesolithic hunters managing parts of the forest, creating glades where browsing animals would concentrate and whose open character could aid the hunter.

Within Clwyd a number of important mesolithic sites have been identified through excavation notably at Rhuddlan, Prestatyn, Tandderwen near Denbigh, Brenig and Llyn Aled Isaf on Mynydd Hiraethog. To these can be added Splash Point, Rhyl; Mia Hall near Trelawnyd; Lynx Cave, Llanarmon and Ffrith, where isolated finds have been made or less extensive evidence has been discovered (Fig 26).

Rhuddlan

Situated on a sand and boulder clay ridge with the River Clwyd and extensive marshes to the west and the nearby estuary and sea providing a wide range of food resources it is not surprising that there is extensive mesolithic archaeology at Rhuddlan. Various sites in the vicinity of the Edwardian castle have, since the late 1960's, produced great quantities of flaked chert and some flint. One site near Ysgol y Castell produced in excess of 12,000 flakes. It is within the layers of sand that have accumulated over the millennia that stone tools have been found. Beginning with a site producing over 2,000 artefacts and associated with a group of pits cut into the sand, there are indications of perhaps lengthy settlement at Rhuddlan during both the early and later mesolithic. Evidence for shelters or windbreaks, seen as stakeholes in the sand and the thousands of flaked stones — most of which comprise the discarded debris from tool manufacture — must represent, in part,

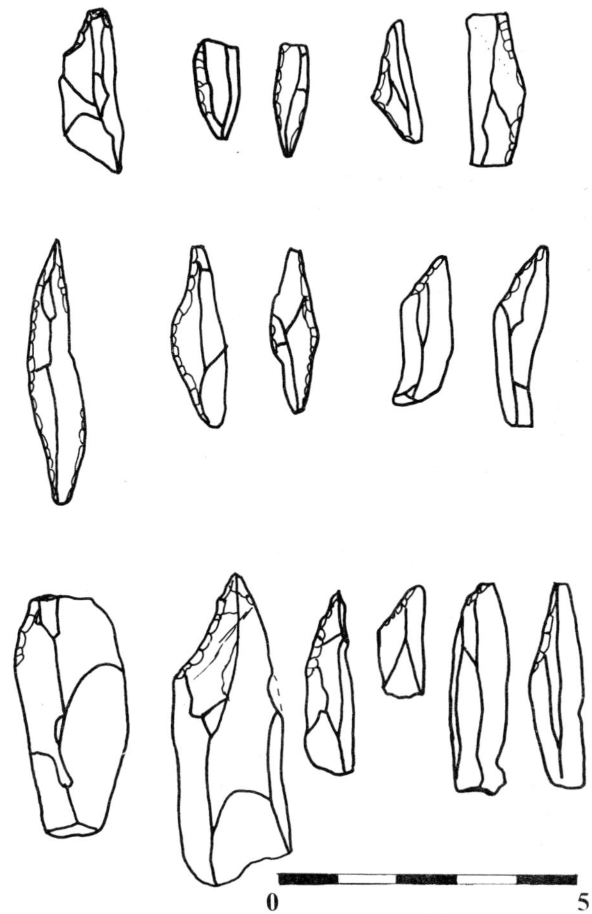

Fig.27 Examples of microliths (small stone tools) found at Rhuddlan, Clwyd during recent excavations.

established settlement and not just occasional, short term camp sites. Of particular interest is the discovery at Rhuddlan of engraved pebbles with various 'fir tree' and flask-shaped patterns (Fig. 31). These artistic representations, whatever their meaning, are very rare examples of mesolithic artwork. Some of the excavated sites have yielded charred hazelnut shells of autumn harvest though indicative, perhaps, of only a small proportion of the edible plants, fruits, berries and nuts available year round to the mesolithic people of Rhuddlan.

Prestatyn

Further along the coast is one of the potentially most interesting of Clwyd's mesolithic sites. Though now covered by the Bryn Newydd estate, tufa or lime-spring deposits are known to occur along the foot of the hills behind Prestatyn. Buried within the tufa is a mesolithic ground surface, last seen almost 70 years ago. Then, the town surveyor, Gilbert Smith, an avid archaeologist, was able to record and excavate parts of this buried layer when service trenches were being laid out for the estate (Fig 32). These excavations produced flint and chert artefacts including microliths of later mesolithic tradition, bone, hazelnut shells, red ochre, shellfish remains, part of an antler tine and a perforated oyster shell. Because of the incomplete excavation records it is uncertain whether all this material is of late mesolithic date or includes neolithic and later remains found on the surface of the tufa. As well as bone the lime-rich tufa has preserved snail shells, many of which lived in and beside the tufa-forming pools around the camp site. These marsh snails and the fossil impressions of leaves and plants provide direct evidence for the immediate environment of the hunter-gatherer site at Prestatyn.

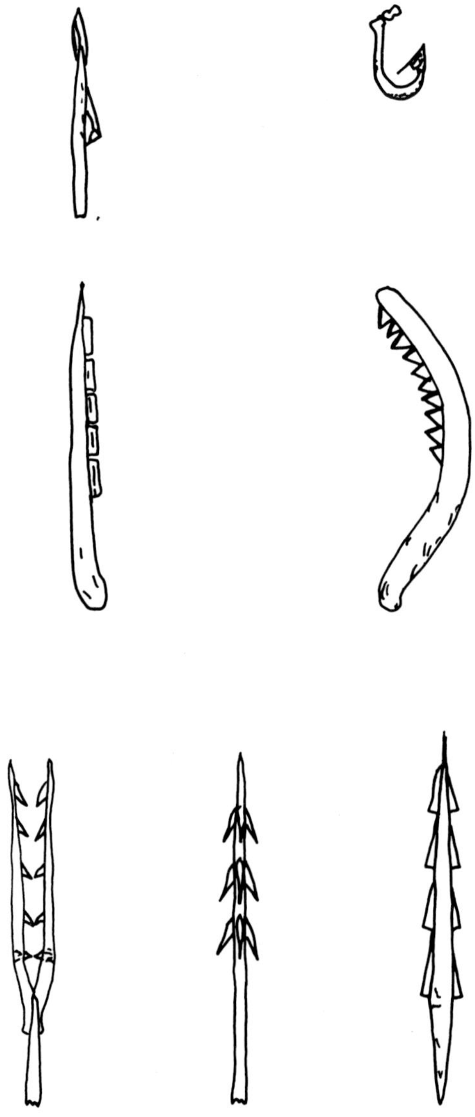

Fig.28 Microliths could have been hafted in wooden handles and used as hooks, spears, arrowheads and various plant processing implements.

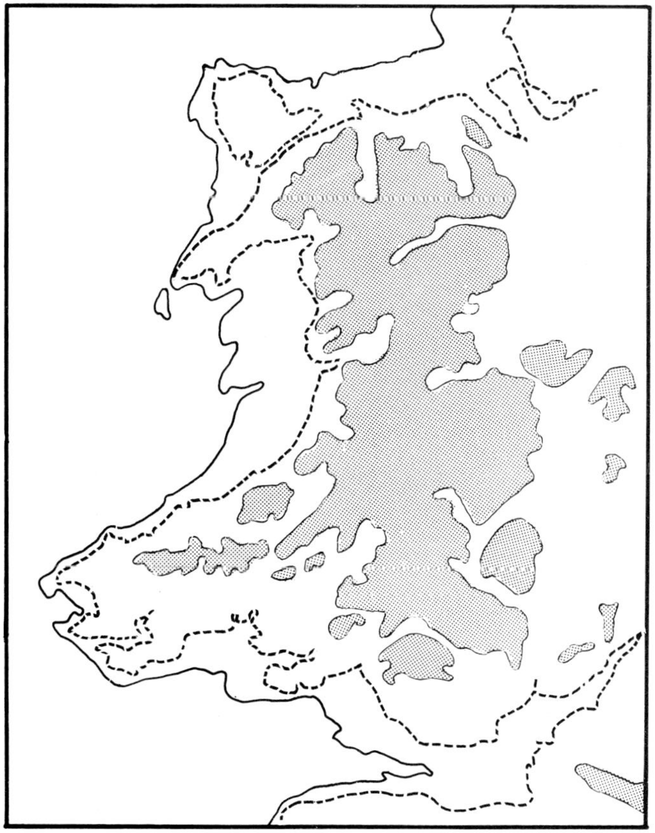

Fig.29 The probable early coastline of Wales, illustrating the extensive coastal plains.

Tandderwen

Although more notable for its bronze age and dark age cemeteries this cropmark site on the floor of the Vale of Clwyd, just east of Denbigh, excavated between 1985 and 1988, yielded late mesolithic chert and flint working-waste (Fig.30) but very few finished microliths. When originally discarded in the course of preparing tools probably for hunting, the stone 'litter' accumulated where a river delta entered Llyn Clwyd — a vestige of the glacial melt-water lake which formerly covered much of the vale.

Mynydd Hiraethog

Also of later mesolithic date as indicated by the character of the microliths are two upland sites located on the Hiraethog moorland and investigated in the 1970s. Rescue excavations at Brenig, which were focused on the bronze age funerary and ritual monuments, uncovered, beneath and between two of the barrows, part of what is likely to be an extensive but disturbed scatter of chert and flint artefacts together with shallow pits, most probably hearths, re-made and re-used a number of times during the sixth millennium bc.

Only limited excavations were carried out at Llyn Aled Isaf during August 1974 - a very dry summer. Indeed it was the drought conditions causing a fall in the reservoir level which led to the chance discovery of this site. The reservoir bed, where the moorland peat was absent, was the surface on which the mesolithic peoples

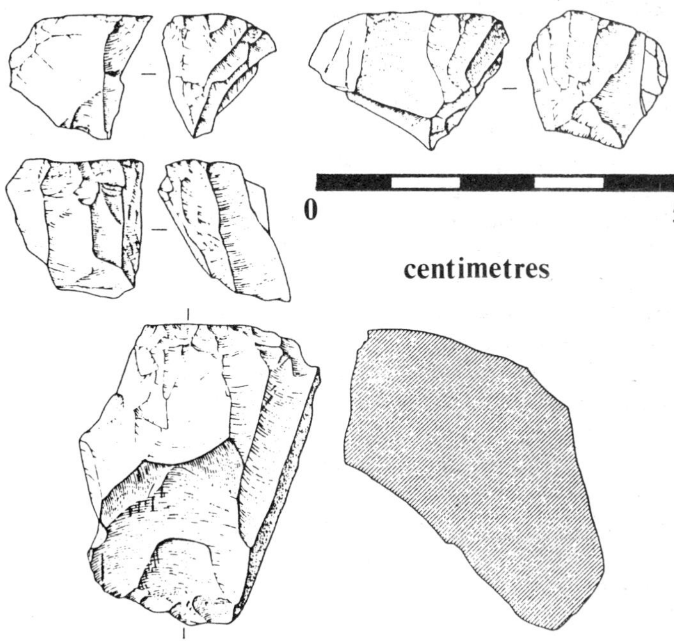

Fig.30 Tandderwen: Chert and Flint cores — from which Blades and Flakes were struck.

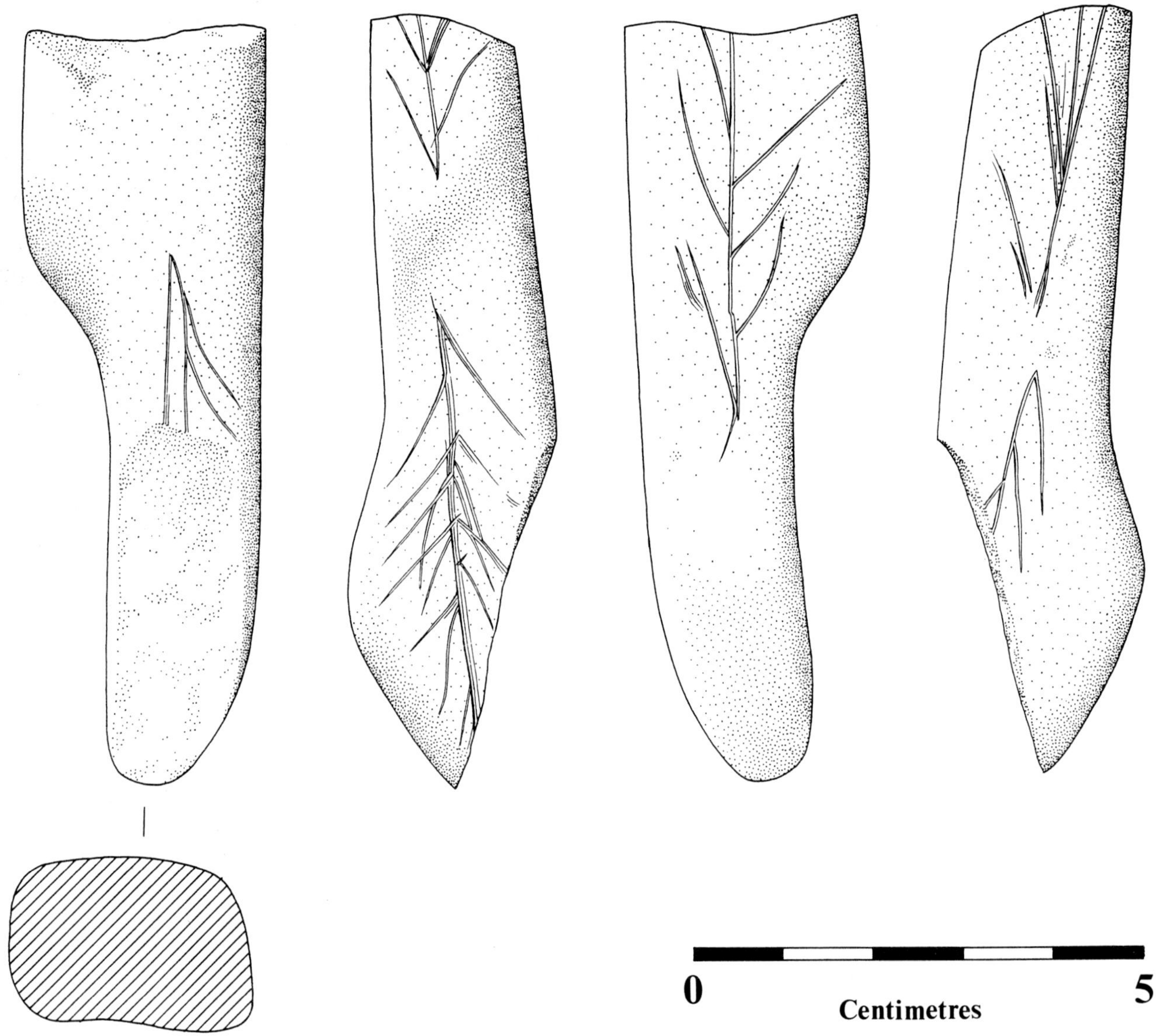

Fig.31 This delicately decorated and engraved pebble from Rhuddlan is the earliest example from Clwyd of the artistic endeavour of hunters and gatherers.

walked: their former presence represented by a very extensive scatter of *in situ* flint artefacts. Possible shelters, seen as stakeholes and shallow grooves in the clay subsoil, also hearths and areas of burnt stone are perhaps indicative of a series of camp sites.

Splash Point, Rhyl

An exceptional chance find is that of a mattock, made of antler and found earlier this century in the estuarine clay - part of the submerged land surface still visible at low tide off the Rhyl promenade (Fig.33). A sample of this heavy duty implement has been recently radiocarbon dated to the fifth millennium bc.

The occasional finds of microliths elsewhere in Clwyd — in the Lynx Cave, or at Ffrith — are a reminder of the wide range of the mesolithic hunter-gatherer's world, a landscape even more extensive before the 'flood'. That loss of land is dramatically seen along our own coast where, beneath shifting sands, lie prostrate trees. In Clwyd we are only beginning to see a pattern of mesolithic life emerge from a very partial and biased record. Are we seeing a permanent home-base camp in late mesolithic Rhuddlan, Tandderwen being the intermediate, hunting-kit preparation site, en-route to the summer hunting grounds of Mynydd Hiraethog? The, perhaps,

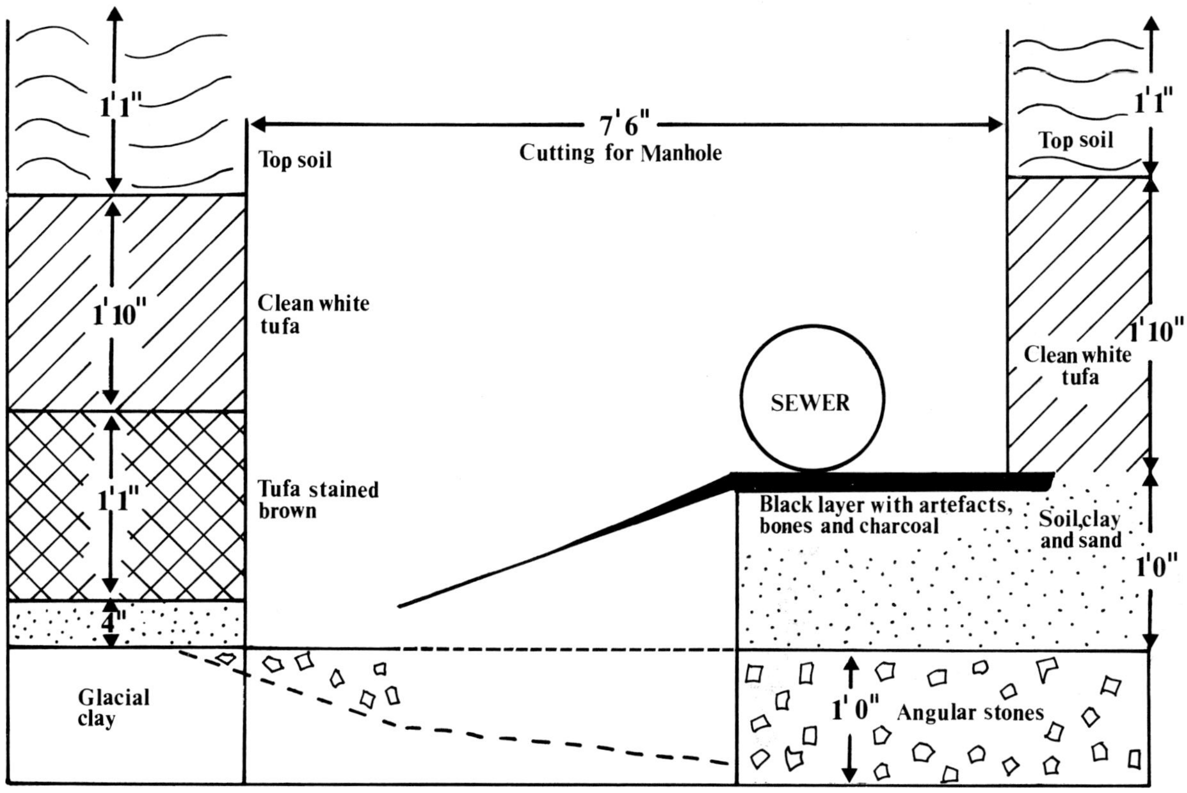

Fig.32 Deposits observed at Bryn Newydd, Prestatyn, in the 1920's during the construction of service trenches for the newly built housing estate.

short-term but regularly used Brenig or Llyn Aled sites do not tell us what was being hunted — we assume red deer, if indeed these were exclusively hunter's camps. No attempt can, as yet, be made to synthesize what is currently such a sketchy view of four millennia. We can anticipate a fuller discussion of individual sites as and when the excavation reports appear in print. In the meantime basic fieldwork should proceed, identifying more upland, foothill, lowland, cave, coastal, estuarine, dune... and what may be now inter-tidal sites. Let's find the food refuse — the meat protein and the vegetarian, catalogue the landscape changes, the dramatic and the subtle and then decide just how good the 'good life' of the mesolithic really was.

Fig.33 The exceptional antler mattock found at Splash Point, Rhyl, dated by radiocarbon techniques to the fifth millennium bc. The function of the perforation is unknown. (Length = 38cms approximately).

Acknowledgements

Thanks to Peter Berridge, Stephen Green, David Jenkins, Helen Livingston, Frances Lynch, Henrietta Quinnell, Chris Smith, Anthony Ward and John Ll. Williams for providing information on various sites.

THE NEOLITHIC
by William J. Britnell

It will be useful to divide the period into an early period from 3,500-2,500 bc radiocarbon years (4,300-3,200 BC calendar years), and a later period from 2,500-1,900 bc radiocarbon years (3,200-2,400 BC calendar years) on the basis of changes in artefact and monument types. The neolithic is conventionally defined by its technology - as the new stone age - but recent work has shown that the social and economic changes are more significant during this period of over fifteen hundred years. The period begins with late mesolithic hunter-gatherer groups, it sees the introduction of farming, and ends with what are clearly already settled, well-structured and highly ordered societies on the eve of the early bronze age.

Settlement Sites

Excavation and fieldwork during the first half of the century have brought to light a concentration of probable neolithic hilltop settlement sites in Rhuddlan and Delyn, represented by arrowheads (Fig.39), sherds of pottery, axe fragments and working debris - Dyserth Castle, Bryn Llwyn (Gwaenysgor), Craig Arthur (Newmarket) Moel Hiraddug, and Prestatyn - although the distribution of chance finds throughout the county clearly shows that settlement was more widespread (Fig.34). Little of the material from these sites is securely stratified, however, and the nature of the settlements is uncertain.

The most recent, and potentially the most important evidence comes from a further hilltop site in Delyn, within the iron age hillfort of Moel y Gaer, Rhosesmor. A possible neolithic long house, of a type known elsewhere in Britain and Ireland, may be represented by a group of postholes and a stone-packed gully underlying iron age round-houses more or less at the summit of the hill (Fig.36). The slot, dated by associated charcoal to the early neolithic - (2994 ± 40 bc), might form an end wall; it defined an area of flint knapping represented by small chips of flint. Some of the chips, made of yellowish flint, closely match several neolithic leaf-shaped arrowheads from the hill. There are several nearby shallow pits which have produced fragments of early neolithic pottery, and later neolithic activity, possibly of a ritual nature, is suggested by a pit holding fragments of an Ebbsfleet bowl which was found beneath the iron age defences.

Whilst the interpretation of these features at Moel y Gaer must be regarded as highly speculative, it bears a similarity with the plan of possible neolithic houses found elsewhere in Britain, as for example at Buxton, Derbyshire and Ballyglass, Co. Mayo, and represents the kind of evidence that would be expected of a site of this kind.

The site is important in helping to construct a model of early neolithic settlement in the region. The possible timber building lies in a relatively large excavated area, and it is fairly clear that if it does represent a building, it is an isolated one. This conforms to a pattern of isolated farmsteads seen elsewhere in the early neolithic in Britain. It is also clear from the extensive work that has been carried out at the site that it was undefended at this period. It is only a single site, but it throws into doubt suggestions that some of the other hilltop sites in Rhuddlan and Delyn were defended in the neolithic period.

A general pattern of settlement in the county is suggested by the distribution of distinctive neolithic artefact types - polished stone axes, leaf-shaped and oblique arrowheads, and some forms of macehead. Few of these are closely datable, however, and are inadequate in helping to give us the dynamic picture of land clearance

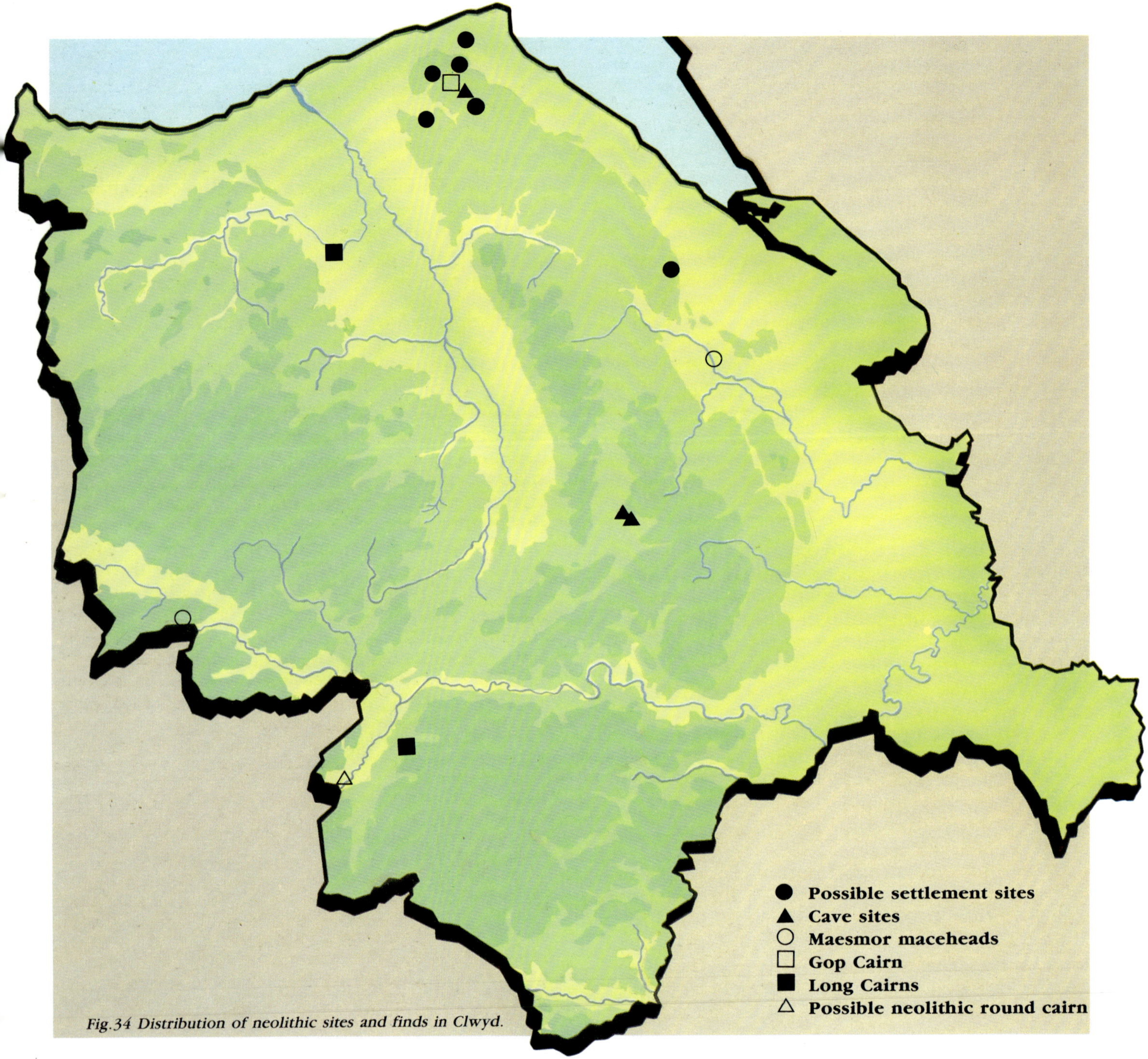

Fig.34 Distribution of neolithic sites and finds in Clwyd.

and settlement that is likely to have been carried out during the period. The distribution of finds will no doubt to some extent reflect the activities of modern collectors, but it gives us the best idea we have of the scale of settlement during this period, and suggests that a wide range of ecological zones were being exploited. The concentration in Rhuddlan and Delyn — one of the densest in the whole of Wales — coincides with the area in which settlement sites are known, but finds have also come from coastal foreshore at Rhyl and Colwyn Bay, low-lying land in the Vale of Clwyd and the Dee valley, and right up to 300m above sea level on the south-eastern side of the Berwyns and the northern and western edge of Mynydd Hiraethog.

A rise in sea level has since submerged part of the neolithic coastline, and climatic changes have made some upland areas less usable; indeed tree clearance by early man in some upland areas, combined with climatic deterioration may well have led to irreversible soil changes which promoted the formation of blanket peats and heathland.

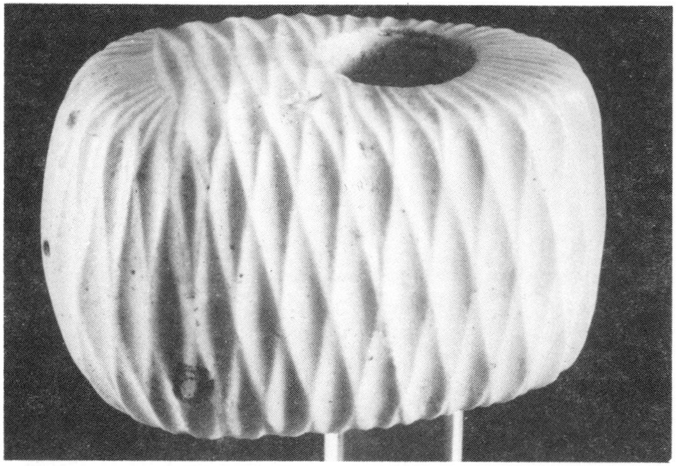

Fig.35 An elaborately fashioned macehead with a laboriously ground central perforation found in 1840 on the Maesmor Estate, Llangwm, Corwen. The perforation presumably housed a wooden shaft or handle.

Economy

There is little reliable evidence of the nature of the neolithic economy in the region, but such a wide range of terrain appears to have been utilized that we should think of an equally broad range of different or interdependent economies, possibly continuing the patterns of exploitation in both upland and lowland which evidently begins in the mesolithic period. There is as yet no reliable evidence of the extent of land clearance, and none of the settlement sites have provided reliable evidence of the nature of arable agriculture, but herds of domesticated animals are suggested by bones from some of the tombs and cave sites mentioned below. The wild ancestors of the domestic crops and animals known from neolithic Britain were not native to the country, which implies some element of colonisation from abroad, but the nature of the transition between late mesolithic and early neolithic cultures in the region is unclear at present. The supposed relationship of mesolithic and neolithic industries at Gwaenysgor and Gop Cave, for example, must be questioned due to uncertainties of stratification. About 80 complete flint or stone axes or fragments have been found in Clwyd, of which a majority are chance finds. They were made in a variety of shapes and sizes, and hafted in wooden handles would have been suitable for carrying out a wide range of tasks, including carpentry, tree-felling, and other agricultural uses. Most of the axes are of rock types which are not native to Clwyd, about 10% being of flint or chert and the remainder of hard stone, which have been ground and polished to form an efficient cutting edge. Though some might be made locally of suitable exotic rocks brought here by glacial action, systematic petrological examination of thin sections taken from them has helped to identify a number of distinctive groups whose sources have been located in various parts of the country, suggesting that many were transported by way of trade or exchange.

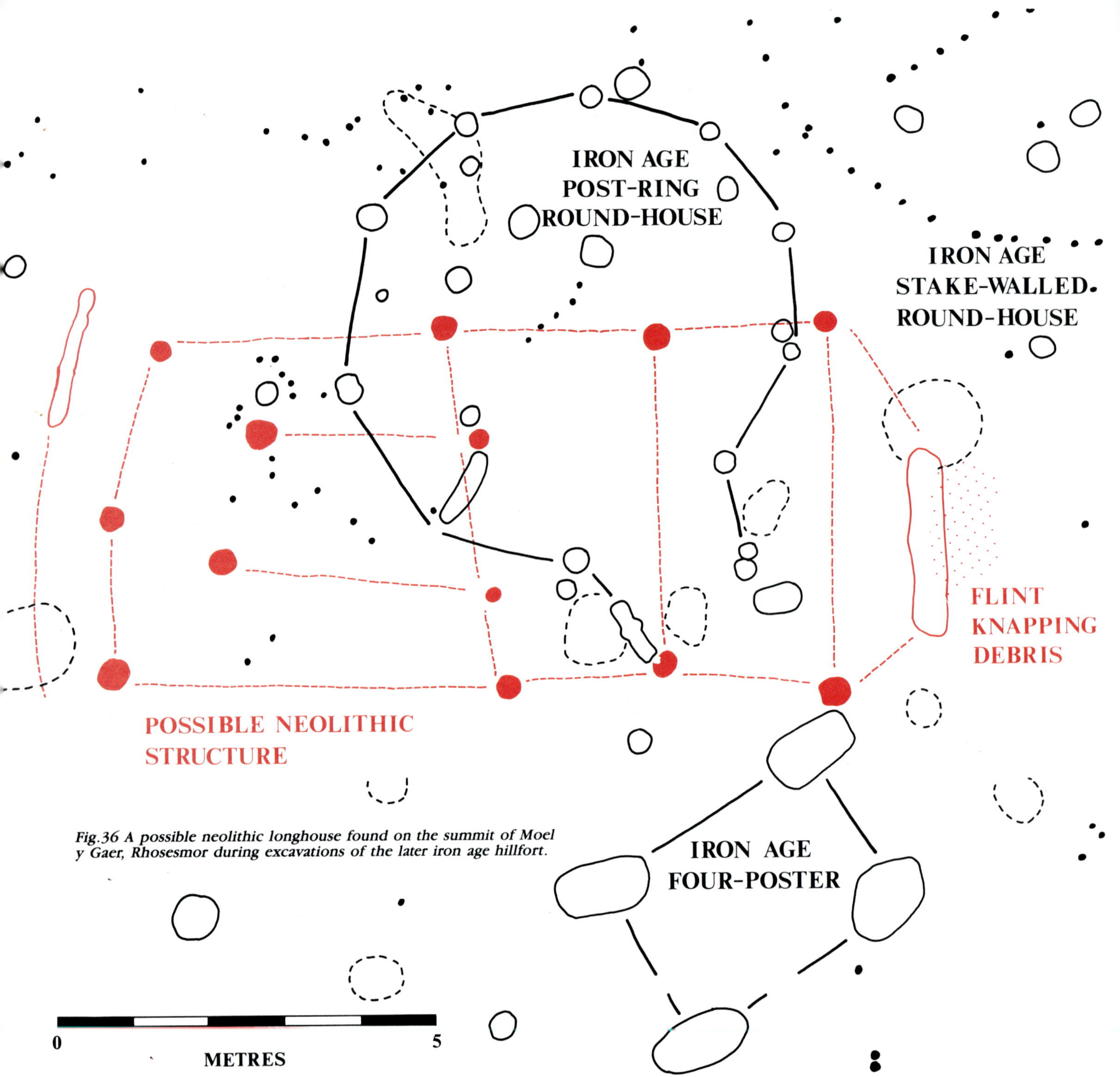

Fig.36 A possible neolithic longhouse found on the summit of Moel y Gaer, Rhosesmor during excavations of the later iron age hillfort.

It is questionable whether coastal flint from the Irish Sea drift would have been suitable for the production of flint axes known from the county, and a source in the chalk areas of England is probable. A high proportion of the *stone* axes are thought to originate from an 'axe factory' at Graig Lwyd, Penmaenmawr, only 25km from the mouth of the Clwyd, which appears to have been a centre of production during the middle and late neolithic. Apart from dominating a local market, examples were widely distributed throughout the country - the Midlands, South Wales, Wessex, and as far afield as Land's End. It is possible that roughouts made at source were finished elsewhere, and several of these are known from Clwyd, including one from near the entrance to the north-west cave at Gop. The settlement sites in Rhuddlan and Delyn are amongst the closest known to the source, and geography suggests that neolithic communities in this area will have exercised some form of control over the distribution to other areas of the country.

Various types of flint arrowhead are known from the county, with notable concentrations again on the Rhuddlan and Delyn plateau, including both early and late neolithic forms. Most are leaf-shaped, and predominantly of the small squat form common to Wales and other areas of western Britain where sources of naturally occuring flint are rare or non-existent. Five maceheads are known from the county, and although the dating of some is uncertain, two fine examples, one from Maesmor (Fig.35), near Corwen, and one from Mold are of a distinct and relatively uncommon late neolithic ovoid form, known as the 'Maesmor Group'. The example from Maesmor is very similar to other facetted examples widely distributed across the country - Quarnford (Staffordshire), Airdens (Sutherland), Urquart (Moray), and the even more remarkable one from the eastern tomb of the passage grave at Knowth, in the Boyne Valley, Ireland. These are all made of flint, and have been partly flaked, and partly ground and polished into the intended shape. The example from Mold is made of quartzite. They have rightly been considered to denote prestige and status - to be symbols of power. Maceheads are not abundant in North Wales, and yet two examples of the Maesmor group have been found here. Like the early bronze age gold cape from Mold they stand out, and point to powerful elites which might otherwise be unexpected from the local archaeological record.

Ceremonial Sites: Long Cairns

At least two neolithic chambered tombs are known in Clwyd - Tyddyn Bleiddyn in the Elwy valley and Tan-y-coed in the Dee valley, but the history of these sadly neglected monuments suggests that others have been totally destroyed: Tyddyn Bleiddyn was fortuitously saved from destruction in 1869 when the removal of a limestone cairn for road-mending revealed capstones of a chamber containing a deposit of human bone. Tombs of this kind were often sited within or on the margins of the more intensely farmed areas, and have commonly been subject to damage of this kind.

The plan of neither tomb is well known, but the shape of the cairns and chambers, like Capel Garmon at the head of the Conwy valley, and others in Ardudwy, north-west Wales, show the influence of ideas from south-west England and south-east Wales. The cairn at Tyddyn Bleiddyn (Fig.37) has been much damaged, but appears to be about 26m long, 12m wide and 0.8m high and contained at least two chambers and passages made of large limestone slabs entered from the northern side of the cairn. The only visible chamber today is one investigated by Boyd Dawkins in 1869. He describes it as consisting of a passage about 1.8m long and 0.6m wide, leading to a wedge-shaped chamber 2.7m long and up to 1.5m wide. Between the passage and the chamber was a partition with

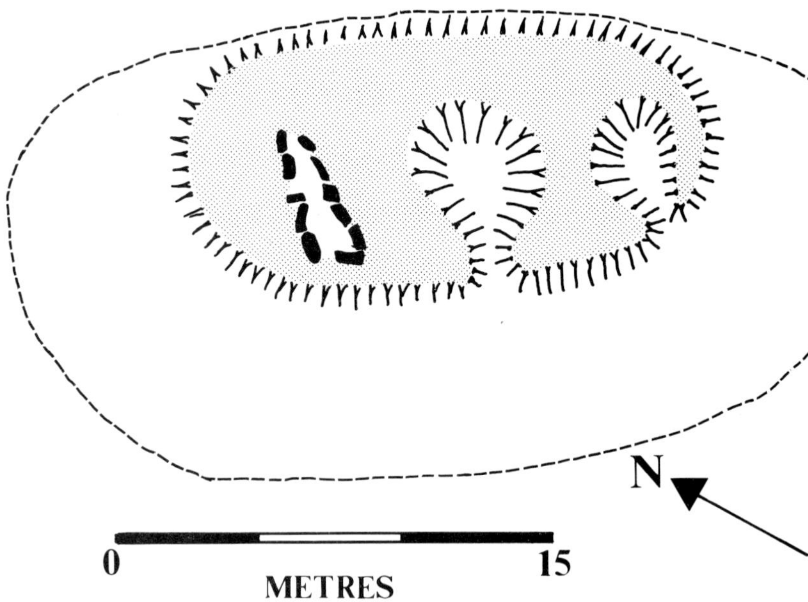

Fig.37 A chambered tomb at Tyddyn Bleiddyn, near St.Asaph, discovered, but saved from destruction, during the removal of limestone for road-mending in 1869.

transverse jambs, and a sill slab 0.45m high. Human bones were found in both the passage and the chamber, representing at least 12 people, including both infants and adults. One of two hollows visible to the south-east of the chamber must represent the second chamber found in 1871, which probably lay roughly parallel to the first, and between 3m and 4.5m away. This second chamber was said to have been roughly triangular in shape, about 3m long, 1.8m wide, and similarly partitioned from the passage by transverse slabs. The passage was 3m long by 0.7m wide, and was again entered from the northern side of the cairn. Human remains were again found in the chamber and passage, as well as the bones of roe deer, goat, dog and pig. The visible chamber is similar to two opposed chambers at Ty-Isaf, southern Powys, and two adjacent chambers at Penywyrlod, Talgarth, southern Powys, as well as those at other sites in south-west England.

All that is now clearly visible at Tan-y-Coed, is the roof of a chamber - a large capstone, 3.6m long, 3m wide and 0.45m thick, supported by at least one standing orthostat. This is embedded in a cairn about 30m long, and there is the suggestion that the chamber was again entered by a passage about 3m long from the side of the cairn. (Fig.38).

Similar tombs in south-east Wales and south-west England were in use from about 3,000 bc until about 2,500 bc or later. There is no dating evidence for the Clwyd tombs, but the discovery of sherds of beaker pottery in the passage to the chamber at Capel Garmon suggests that some remained in use until a relatively late date.

The number of certain neolithic tombs in the county is small, but the disparity between their distribution and the densest concentrations of neolithic finds implies that they cannot be used as an index of settlement density. Few if

Fig.38 The impressive remains of a megalithic tomb from Llandrillo, in the Dee Valley.

any are known in adjacent areas of mid-Wales or on the Cheshire Plain, which must surely have been occupied at this time, and unless they are mere accidents of survival it suggests either that other forms of monument were built, possibly using timber, which have not survived, or that they were only built in some areas. Siting of tombs at the periphery of main settlement areas has been noted elsewhere, and they may relate to areas where competition with other groups or the forces of nature was more severe. It has been suggested that as well as providing a place for burial, the construction of monuments containing the bones of ancestors may have been a way of establishing a community's claim to the resources which they were controlling.

Round Cairns

It is interesting to note the absence of portal tombs known in the Conwy valley further west in Gwynedd. There are other types of tomb in the county which might be neolithic, but this can only be determined by excavation. One example is Branas-uchaf, near Llandrillo in the Dee valley, where the remains of a megalithic chamber (Fig.38), about 4.5m long and 2.5m wide, lies at the centre of a circular cairn 27m in diameter and 1.5m high.

In this context we must also seriously consider the date of the Gop cairn, near Prestatyn, at the heart of one of the apparent core areas of settlement (Figs.40,41). The giant cairn, 8-14m high and 70-100m across - the largest in Wales - dominates the surrounding plateau. It was investigated by Boyd Dawkins at the end of the last century. He sunk a shaft down through the centre and then drove two tunnels along the surface of the bedrock at right-angles to each other, but failed to find any burial or burial chamber. It has often been thought to be bronze age, but it would fit just as happily with a range of middle to late neolithic mounds - the passage graves of the Boyne Valley in Ireland, and very large round mounds in Yorkshire and the Pennines (eg Howe Hill, Duggleby) and even Silbury Hill, Wiltshire (dated to a little after 2145 $\pm$ 95 bc).

There is no evidence that the Gop cairn covered a passage grave, but it is clear from the tombs of this type known at Barcloddiad y Gawres on Anglesey, and the now largely destroyed Calderstones, Liverpool, that the form would have been familiar to groups living in the

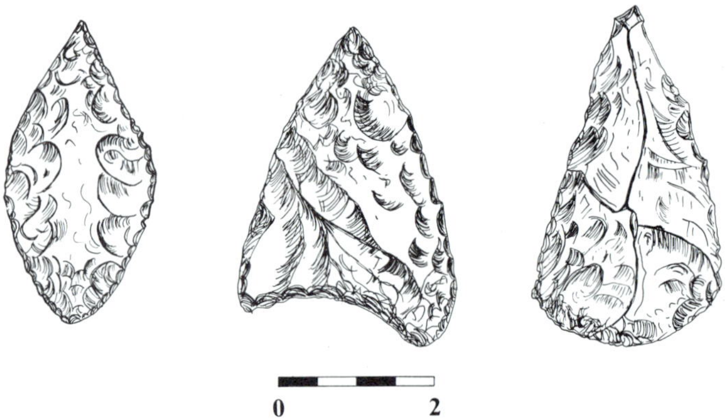

Fig.39 Neolithic arrowheads found on Gop hill, Gwaenysgor, close to Gop cave. These flint arrowheads would have been fitted to the ends of wooden arrow-shafts.

region. Recent disturbances around the southern base of the Gop cairn have revealed limestone revetment walling, which may well be original, and it is interesting to note that Silbury Hill was built with concentric retaining walls of chalk blocks.

Finally, we must suppose that some of the nominally bronze age barrows are of neolithic date, as elsewhere in the British Isles. Recent excavations in the Upper Severn valley have revealed several multi-period monuments which began life during the middle and late neolithic. It may be significant that late neolithic Peterborough pottery was found during the excavation of a beaker barrow at Ysgwennant, Llansilin.

Fig.40 Gop Cairn, Gwaenysgor. The most substantial prehistoric man-made mound in Wales, and the second largest in Britain. (Silbury Hill, Wiltshire, is, of course, the largest).

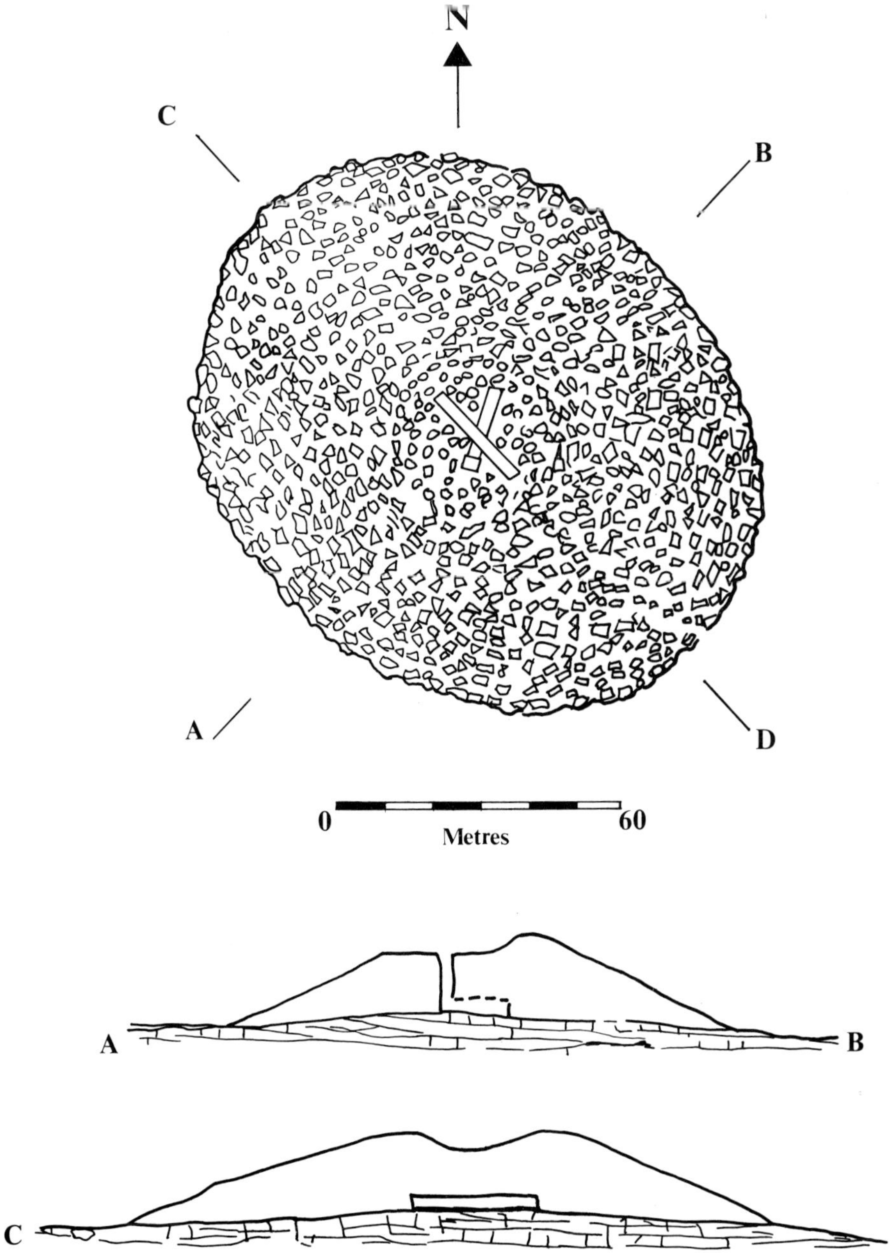

Fig.41 Plan and sections of Gop Cairn, Gwaenysgor, showing the extent of excavations carried out by Prof. Boyd Dawkins of Manchester University in the late 19th Century.

Caves

Late neolithic burials are known from cave sites in Clwyd. The rock shelter just to the south of the Gop cairn was also examined by Boyd Dawkins before the turn of the century. In this case he found the burials of about fourteen individuals buried in a rough stone enclosure or chamber about 1.5m across, built against the back wall of the cave. The burials appear to represent successive inhumation burials, placed in a crouched position. Other crouched burials which have also been thought to be of neolithic date have been found in various other cave sites in Clwyd, including Perthi Chwarae, Llanarmon, and Rhosddigre, Llandegla, both in the Alyn valley. Rhosddigre produced a Graig Lwyd axe, fragments of others, and sherds of neolithic pottery, but the significance of these finds and their relationship with human remains is open to question. Only in the case of Gop cave is there reasonably secure dating evidence for the burial deposit, which has been classed as sub-megalithic in character. The finds consist of a sherd of Peterborough pottery, two jet 'belt sliders' and a polished flint knife. These all indicate a late neolithic date for the burials, and fall into a pattern of late neolithic cave burials known elsewhere, particularly in Derbyshire. The subsequent discovery of another narrow cave running off the open shelter at Gop revealed further scattered human remains, some of which are said to have been sealed by rough walling. The supposed association of material from the cave, which includes mesolithic flint and chert types as well as a roughout of a Graig Lwyd axe, is open to question.

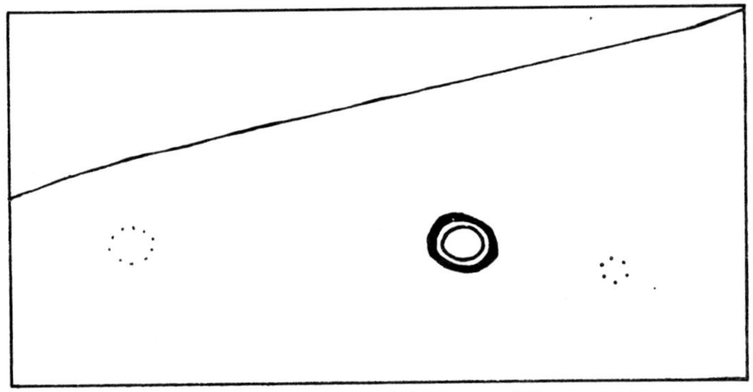

Fig.42 A possible henge, discovered during aerial reconnaissance near Llanrhaeadr-ym-Mochnant in the Tanat valley. Note the two outlying circles of pits or post-holes, perhaps indicating timber circles.

Henge Monuments

The last class of monument known from Clwyd which might be of late neolithic date is timber circles known from aerial photography near Llanrhaeadr-ym-Mochnant in the Tanat Valley in southern Clwyd. Circles of pits to either side of a probable ploughed-out round barrow - one of six pits forming a circle 6m in diameter, and the other of ten pits about 10m in diameter - may represent timber circles. Again, only excavation can tell us their date, but they bear a strong resemblance to late neolithic timber structures loosely classed as henges. Their dimensions are similar to the timber structure in the henge monument at Marden, Wilts, and timber circles underlying the stone circle at the Sanctuary, Wilts.

THE BRONZE AGE
by Frances Lynch

It is in the centuries on either side of 2,000 bc, the late neolithic of our traditional terminology, that the archaeological record of Clwyd begins to fill out and the pattern of occupation then becoming apparent is continued in the bronze age. In this part of the world the new technology does not mark a serious break in the economic life of the region; the new departures in terms of expansion of settlement and population had already been made. On the other hand, because of the paucity of neolithic evidence, it is difficult to know how great were the social changes at this time. Clwyd becomes far more clearly integrated during the bronze age into the culture of neighbouring regions to the west and north-east, sharing with them traditions of burial and ceremony and partaking in the same marketing networks. But despite this integration, however, variations can be recognised within the county which suggest differences in the history of communities which archaeology is not subtle enough to elucidate fully.

The economic shift in settlement patterns and their general expansion in the late neolithic may be exemplified by the building of the 'marker cairn' (Brenig 47) on the pass between Nantglyn and the Brenig valley. This cairn covered no burial and has been radiocarbon dated to 2,140 $\pm$ 70 bc. This is several centuries before the building of the bronze age cemetery in the valley below, but it foreshadows two important themes of bronze age life in this region, both having their origin in this crucial period at the turn of the millennium. The first is the reappearance of man in the uplands, virtually unoccupied since the mesolithic and the second is the tradition of building circular monuments, whether for burial or other related rituals (Fig.43).

Today the view from Brenig 47 encompasses two landscapes, one the wooded and fertile valleys of the Clwyd and its tributaries and the other the bleak moorland of Hiraethog with Snowdonia beyond. When the mound was built the view must have contained a similar but perhaps less sharp dichotomy. After well over a thousand years, agricultural use of the valleys may have reduced their fertility while a small improvement in average temperatures may have made the higher ground more attractive to farmers. The extent to which the uplands were forested at this time is still a matter of dispute but the pollen analytical work from the Brenig valley, an area typical of the Clwyd uplands, suggests that the landscape was open, a grass and sedge moorland which could provide useful pastures. However, even by 1,700 bc there were signs of incipient podzolisation, perhaps due to overuse, perhaps to an increase in rainfall which by the end of our period was to drive communities down off these moors to concentrate settlements once more on the central valley and its immediate margins. In the earlier bronze age, however, the uplands obviously provided a reasonable living, not only for pastoralists but also for arable farmers, for the pollen in the turves used to build the monuments of the Brenig cemetery suggests that cereal crops were growing on the land from which these turves were cut, land which cannot have been too far away from the cemetery in the head of the valley.

Settlements

The discovery of evidence for crops must suggest the proximity of farming settlements but the farm sites themselves remain tantalizingly elusive. One of the reasons for this, is that many houses were almost certainly built of wood, though the level platforms on which such houses stood should be recognisable and the

Fig.43 The distribution of scheduled bronze age barrows and major find spots in Clwyd.

presence of their fields might be indicated by cairns of cleared stones or meandering walls. In many parts of upland Clwyd the foundation of the walls would have been of stone which should make their recognition easier and indeed some round huts of a general type which in other parts of Britain have been shown to be bronze age have been found in the hills north of Cerrigydrudion. In the early years of this century Canon Ellis Davies recorded the remains of several round stone huts at Cefn Bannog which he thought might be of bronze age date. Unfortunately the area is now covered by the Clocaenog forest and very little of the settlement can be recognised. More recent work on Mynydd Poeth and Bryn Helen has revealed several huts and enclosures, but without excavation it would be unwise to claim them all as bronze age. However, recent excavations by John Manley at just such a site, Pentre Llyn Cymmer, have produced radiocarbon dates in the late bronze age (Fig.53). In Ardudwy stone huts of a similar type have been shown to belong to the iron age and North Wales, for all its prolific remains of upland huts and fields has yet to produce one that is convincingly dated to the early bronze age.

Further evidence of agricultural settlement might be sought in the cairnfields — groups of small clearance heaps which must indicate an effort to improve the land, for pasture if not necessarily for ploughing. Cairnfields of this type have been found in the Cerrigydrudion district and on the slopes of the Berwyns above Llandrillo. Both are likely areas for bronze age settlement but, as the excavation of the cairnfield in the Brenig valley has shown these features are even more difficult to date than the stone huts.

Where caves exist they have always been attractive to man as ready-made shelters, but the bronze age is the one period which is virtually unrepresented amongst the material from Clwyd's numerous limestone caves. These shelters saw notable use in the neolithic and have produced finds from the iron age and romano-british periods, but the only material of bronze age date is a single sherd of possible Food Vessel from Nant y Fuach, near Dyserth and a barbed and tanged arrowhead from a cave at Llanferres. The wooden houses mentioned at the beginning of this section leave scant evidence and their presence is discovered only accidentally during the excavation of more obvious features or by modern disturbance of the ground. The scatter of charcoal, flint implements and beaker potsherds beneath the cairn at Brenig 51 on the eastern side of that valley, the finds from Dyserth Castle which include a sherd of bronze age pottery and the flint implements turned up by the plough beside a hearth at Maesol, Llangernyw are instances which serve to point up both the potentially large number of such sites and the difficulty of finding them.

Burial and Ritual Monuments

In searching for a general picture of the distribution of man and his activities in the bronze age, therefore, we are forced to look, not at his villages and farms, but at the more formal evidence, the burial and ritual monuments which he intended to leave as visible reminders of his presence, and at the accidental evidence, the tools and belongings lost in everyday use. This evidence combines to indicate the Delyn plateau, north of the Wheeler valley, as the area of densest occupation where earthen round barrows still survive in impressive profusion.This fertile limestone plateau has been the focus of occupation in the region in most periods so it is not surprising to see that it is the richest area in the bronze age. The higher land to the south, the Clwydian hills, the moorland

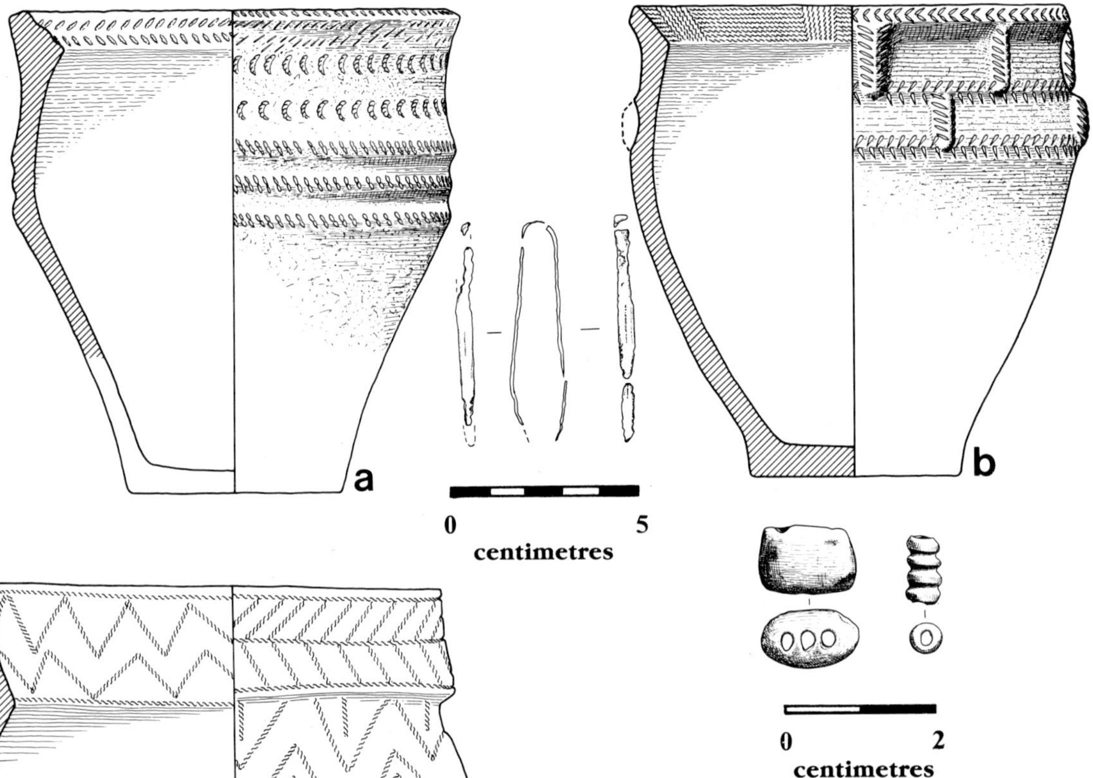

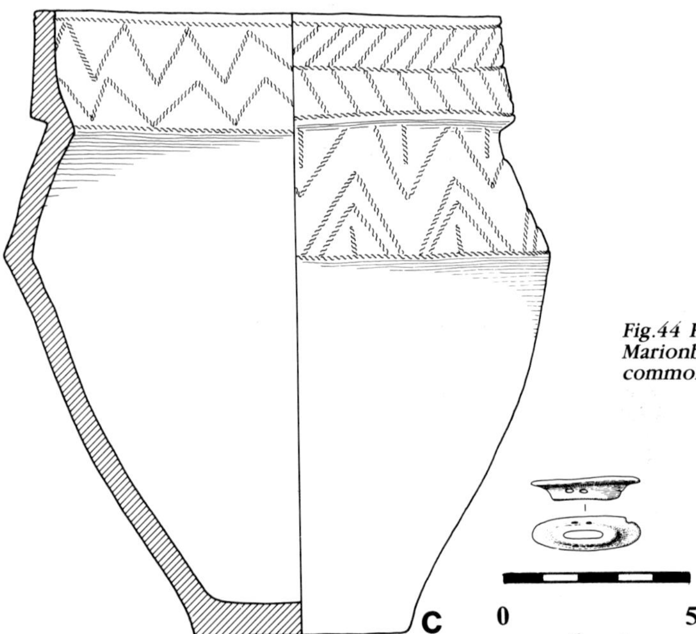

Fig.44 Pottery and finds from a) Clocaenog; b) Brynford and c) Marionbach. Vessels such as these were used for burials and commonly contained cremations.

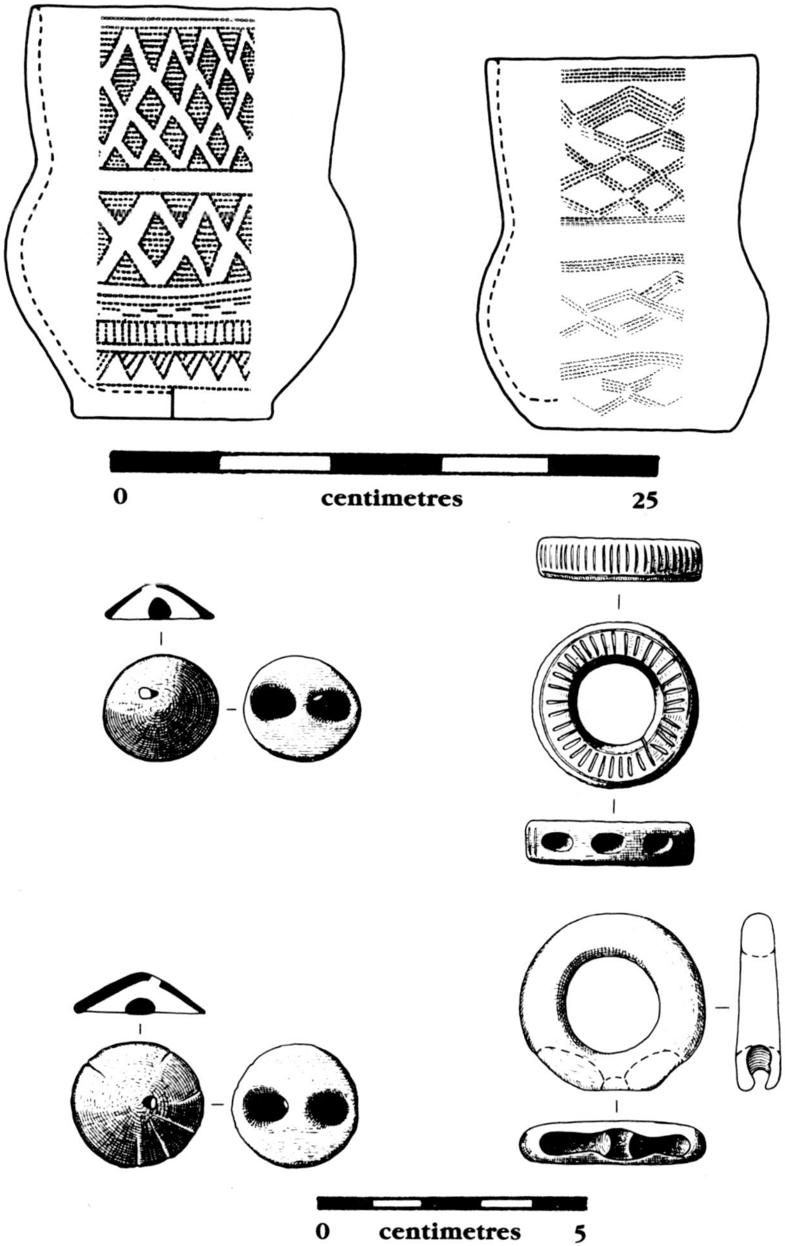

Fig.45 Beaker pottery and jet objects found during the excavation of the burial mound of Ysgwennant at Llansilin. The perforated circular buttons are typical of this period.

above Ruabon and Llangollen and its extension across the Dee to the northern end of the Berwyns and the great mass of Hiraethog which has been mentioned previously, are all classic upland environments which must have been almost virgin territory when man first came there in the late neolithic and early bronze age to exploit the grazing and lay claim to the land through the burial of his patriarchs.

The occupation of the Clwyd valley itself is something of an enigma. It is easy to believe that subsequent occupation and agriculture will have removed many monuments and the broken urn found during road works at Llanrhaeadr and barrow ditches showing as cropmarks at Tandderwen (CAR 1755, 1757) and Llandyrnog (CAR 1455) demonstrate that this is in part true. However the record of finds from the valley is not great except at the traditional crossing point at Rhuddlan at the end of the coastal marshes and at the head of the main valley, around Llanfair Dyffryn Clwyd. At this point the river enters a narrow defile and it is interesting that finds should be concentrated here at the junction of the steep, narrow upland valley and the broad open vale. Archaeological work at this boundary might be particularly rewarding. It is interesting to compare the relative paucity of finds in the broad, perhaps marshy, valley of the Clwyd with the quantity of evidence which is emerging as cropmarks in the Tanat valley (CAR, 997, 1005, 1432-3, 1706-7, 1715, 1759-61) and which may be seen in finds and eroded barrows along the lower reaches of the Alyn valley. These lowland finds, together with the material from the Wrexham area, demonstrate that, though it is indeed true that this period sees a shift of settlement into the upland, the lower ground was by no means deserted, at least on the eastern edge of our region.

The ubiquitous round barrow, built of earth, turves or stone, is undoubtedly the commonest relic of the bronze age surviving in Clwyd today and it is from the burials beneath these mounds that most of our knowledge of the life and attitudes of their builders is derived. The pattern of excavation among the five hundred and forty-seven barrows of Clwyd has not been a consistent one so the detailed picture of burial systems, pottery styles and trading links is not entirely satisfactory. Barrows have been excavated in Hiraethog, at Brenig (Figs.46,54) and Clocaenog but there is only the brief record of the early excavation at Henllan to represent the northern part of Denbighshire. Cefn Goleu on the Clwydian hills has been excavated and there is a record of another cemetery mound at Llanarmon yn Iâl but there is very little information from the numerous cairns above Llangollen and from the Berwyns south of the Dee where only the mound at Ysgwennant (Fig.45) has been reported on. From the Alyn valley there are some notable finds but the information about the graves from which they came is very thin. The Delyn plateau with its profusion of barrows contains several excavated sites, such as those near Ysceifiog, the group at Bryn Gwyn Hall, Ffridd y Garreg Wen, Pant y Dulaith, Marion Bach (Fig.44) and Brynford but few of these excavations have been published fully.

The building of these round mounds marks a considerable change from the collective burial traditions of the earlier neolithic period in most parts of the country. In the bronze age burials become more individualistic; the monuments may be smaller and simpler in construction but they were often erected for one man and the dead took with them personal belongings which reflected their status and aspirations in life, these aspirations often being war-like. Such fundamental changes must obviously have wide-ranging and complex roots, springing perhaps from both internal and external stimuli. One external factor which looms large in the

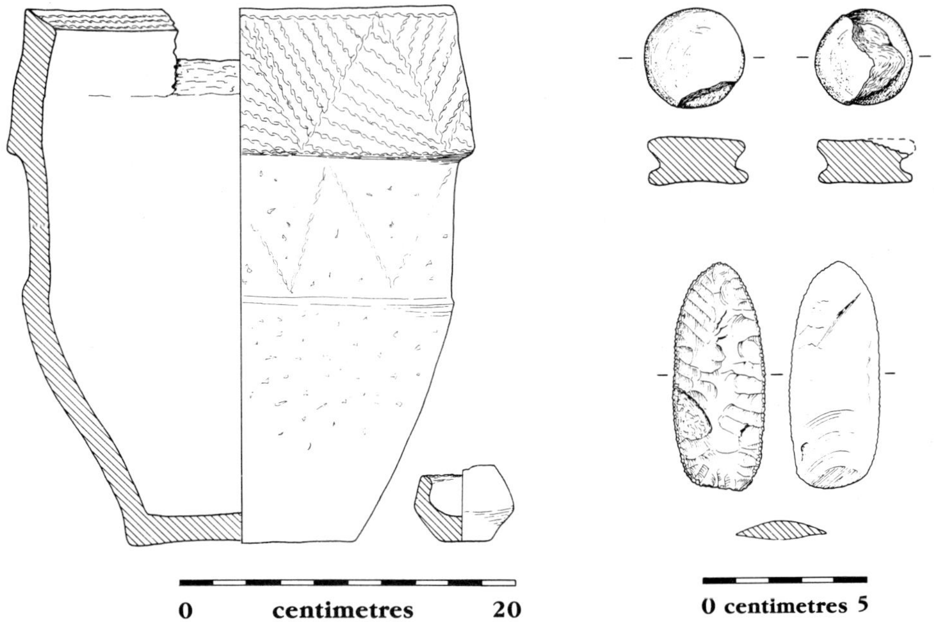

Fig.46 Cremation vessel and finds found during excavations prior to the construction of Llyn Brenig on the Denbigh Moors.

archaeological record of the period is the appearance of a new style of pottery, already widespread on the Continent. This beaker pottery has been traditionally associated with ideas of 'invasion' — the Beaker People setting themselves up as new warlords, their superiority guaranteed by their knowledge of metallurgy and the weapons it could make. This single explanation for the complex developments of this troubled period in Europe is undoubtedly too simple, but it is true to say that this distinctive pottery, whether brought by foreign invaders or used by local leaders adopting foreign fashions or cults, is often to be found with the new elements, copper weapons and individual burial under small round barrows or cairns.

When individual burials first became popular inhumation was the system used. At first a beaker pot was placed beside the body, as at Henllan and Ysgwennant where the dead man was dressed and carried his fire-lighting equipment in a jet-decorated pouch at his waist. Eventually the beaker was dispensed with but inhumation remained the norm, sometimes in wooden coffins like those found at Clocaenog and perhaps Llong where the young girl's jet necklace was dropped down among the stones which covered the grave. In all these instances later burials were added to the same monument and normally these later bodies had been cremated, a change in burial rite which appears gradually all over the country without apparent social disruption. In some cases, such as Clocaenog and Llong these secondary burials were simply dug into the existing mound; in others, such as Ffridd y Garreg Wen near Holywell, the monument was enlarged for each additional burial.

Most of these monuments were originally designed to cover a single burial, stressing the individuality which is such a mark of the bronze age. But the appearance of secondary burials, often several secondary burials, in the same mound blurs this concept and brings us perhaps closer to the older family burial traditions. There are even bronze age barrows in the north and west of Britain which were designed from the start to cover several bodies buried in what was probably a single funeral. Such 'Cemetery Mounds' suggest that in those parts of the country, where neolithic traditions had survived longer, the family group remained the basis of social power. This situation contrasts with that exemplified by the early bronze age graves of the south of England which contain the burials of rich chieftains suggesting a sharply stratified society in which the warrior was the admired model. In the full early bronze age, therefore, we can see some profound regional differences emerging. Although much of the country shared fashions in jewellery and luxuries from abroad and used pottery of a broadly similar kind, differences in social attitudes may have run deep and may have divided even quite small regions.

In Gwynedd, with a long tradition of collective burial in megalithic tombs, the cemetery mounds predominate. In Clwyd the picture is less clear and the mixture of single burial monuments, such as the barrows of the Brenig cemetery, and those covering multiple burials, like those at Cefn Goleu and Gledlom to the east of the river, may reflect the mosaic of new and old occupation areas which resulted from the expansion of settlement mentioned earlier.

At both single and multiple burial sites some of the barrows may be quite complex in construction though the complexities were finally concealed beneath the mound. At Cefn Goleu and at Pant y Dulaith there were stone cairn rings surrounding the central graves and at the latter site there had also been a wooden ring of stakes and planks. In the Brenig cemetery several rings of stakeholes were found beneath the turf mounds; some were entirely functional fences erected to mark out the site some years before building began, others had no practical purpose and must be ascribed some ceremonial functon during the rituals of burial. In all cases the circular shape may be explained by the almost universal obsession with circular enclosures at this time, epitomised by the monuments which we know simply as Stone Circles and whose ceremonial use we know so little about.

The Stone Circle as a ring of upright stones is a rare phenomenon in Clwyd, in fact only two are known, one in the group of circles at Capel Hiraethog and the rather dubious example in Penbedw Park, Nannerch, but other designs of circles, either Ring Cairns or Kerb Circles, are rather more common although having an uneven distribution. These monuments, in which are found enigmatic deposits of charcoal carefully buried in deep pits and also some more readily understood human cremation burials, seem to have played some ancillary role in funerals for they occur in cemeteries such as that at Brenig and on Eglwyseg Mountain; but since they also stand within sanctuaries they may form a link between the strictly funerary and the more cosmological aspects of the religion of the day. It is interesting that a Ring Cairn should occur in the Brenig cemetery (Fig.52) with its rather southern-looking single grave barrows since the Ring Cairns belong to a western and northern cultural province where cemetery mounds are the norm. These Variant Circles are a feature of the southern half of Clwyd with examples on Hiraethog, in the area between Corwen and Bala and on Eglwyseg Mountain above Llangollen. In spite of the presence of concealed circular features at Pant y Dulaith and possibly other Delyn sites, the open Ring Cairn has not been recognised among the numerous barrows of the

Fig.47 Magnificent gold cape found on the outskirts of Mold in the 19th Century. Buried about 3,500 years ago with the skeleton of a man, it is the finest piece of decorated sheet gold work of its time from Wales and arguably from Europe.

plateau. The single standing stone, alone or occasionally in pairs, would seem to be a preferred ritual monument in north-east Clwyd, especially in the Alyn Valley. Unfortunately no excavation, either here or elsewhere in the country has provided any universally applicable explanation for the erection of these memorials, though deposits of pottery have indicated a bronze age date.

Personal Possessions

One of the most interesting aspects of bronze age burial customs is the glimpse into economic lives and social aspirations afforded by the personal possessions buried with the dead. In some areas it is obvious that the dagger is the symbol of status and power and in such areas a sharp stratification of society may be inferred. In Wales as a whole and in Clwyd in particular such interests do not seem to be paramount. Only the lost blade from Yr Orsedd Wen, Selattyn, is large and fine enough to be considered a dagger, the others, such as that from Ffridd y Garreg Wen should be classified as knives and no doubt had a role no more threatening than the modern penknife. In bronze age terms they were only one step up from the ubiquitous flint knife which must have been in most people's pockets, for many have been burnt on the pyre and gathered up with the bones. Although social attitudes varied from region to region there is across Britain a veneer of similarity deriving from the fashions in beads and decorations, especially those in imported materials, in which the wealthy aristocracy of Wessex led the way. The most exotic of these materials was faience originating in Egypt but eventually made in Britain as the unusually shaped bead from Brynford demonstrates. Those from Llangwm are more typical of the imported type. Amber from the Baltic was found in the exceptional grave at Mold but the more common material for buttons and beads was jet (found at Ysgwennant and Llong and as a rough lump at Brenig) which must have come from eastern Yorkshire. A number of other fashions and practices, such as the use of special funerary knives with fine bone pommels, link North Wales with this northern province, the trade routes running from Clwyd, across the Cheshire plain to the southern end of the Pennines.

The excavations in the Brenig valley have shown that it was not only luxuries that were imported. There is no good flint in Wales and people had to make do with the flawed material washed up on the coasts, but in the late neolithic and bronze age much better quality flakes are used which must have been brought in from some distance. Analysis of clays has suggested that even the pottery was produced far away from the valley, so we may conclude that some system of trade was operating over a wide area and penetrating even remote communities whose level of wealth was in no way outstanding.

The one exception to these comments on the low key nature of economic life and social aspirations is the astonishing gold cape, the largest piece of prehistoric goldwork from Britain, found beneath a barrow beside the River Alyn at Mold. This garment (Fig.47) of thin gold sewn to a leather backing covered the chest and shoulders of a young man without weapons or other symbols of power. As a spectacular but constricting garment it may be interpreted as a priestly vestment. At present it is unique, and as such is difficult to interpret and date, but what may have been a similar "corselet" is recorded from Wrexham. Together they raise many questions about the nature of society in this eastern part of the county. On the question of date one may suggest the earlier bronze age on the basis of the associated amber beads and the inhumation rite, but it is tempting to suggest

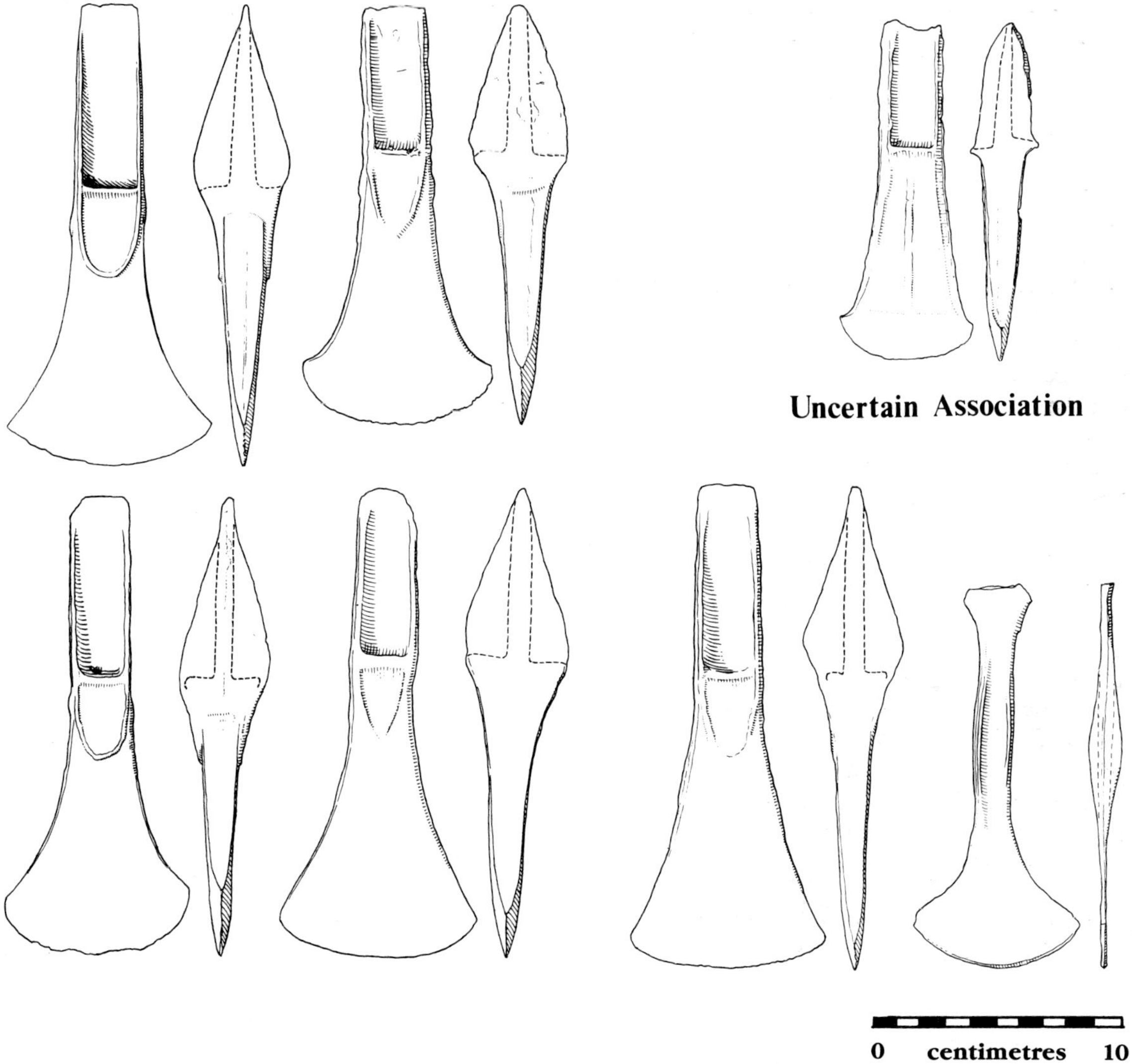

Fig.48 The Acton Park hoard of bronze axes or palstaves. Found in Wrexham, this hoard has given its name to a local prehistoric industry typified by effective design and competent mixing of metals.

that the level of wealth implied has something to do with local developments which reach their climax at a slightly later date.

In the neolithic, communities could have been essentially self-sufficient, but even then tools with particular qualities were traded over long distances. With the introduction of metal, at first for rare, status-enhancing purposes, later for everyday tools as well, trade becomes a necessity and, as we have seen, a great number of quite common goods were brought in from a distance.

Metalworking

The working of copper may have begun rather earlier in Clwyd than elsewhere in southern Britain for the only hoard of flat axes, one of the earliest and simplest tools made, from this side of the Irish Sea was found on Moel Arthur. Moreover analysis of a similar axe from Halkyn has suggested a local source for the ore. Recent finds of two flat axes and a halberd (Fig.49) from Clwyd reinforce this picture of an important metal working region. The earliest axes were simple in shape but difficult to haft satisfactorily and, with the technological advance of the two-valve mould, design changes appear which attempt to solve these problems of attachment. The group of unusual flanged axes or proto-palstaves from Moelfre Uchaf, Betws yn Rhos (Fig.50), shows an interesting stage in that development and the number of such intermediate forms in north-east Wales suggests that local bronzesmiths were in the forefront of experimentation. The final form, the shield pattern palstave appears in the Acton Park hoard (Fig.48) from Wrexham which has given its name to a strong local industry which shows initiative in design and appears to have contacts ranging as far as Brittany, the Netherlands and north Germany. This industry is recognisable not only for its effective design but for its unusually competent mixing of metals to produce a tin-

Fig.49 Part of a halberd, found on top of a sandstone outcrop at the east end of the Dee estuary at Shotton. The three rivets are typical of this type of tool, which was hafted at right angles to its handle. The remains of this halberd are 16cm long.

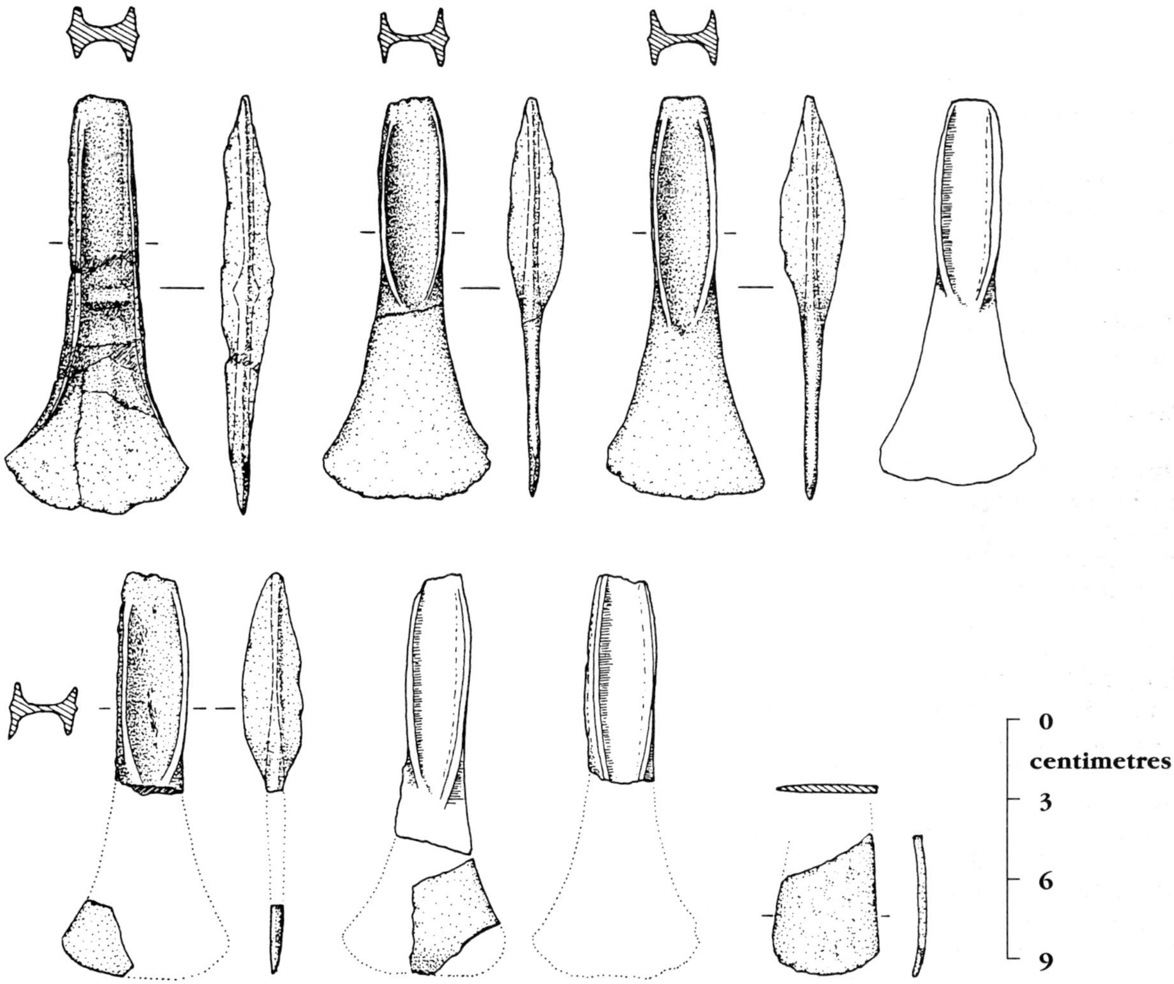

Fig.50 A group of unusual flanged axes or proto-palstaves from Moelfre Uchaf, Betws yn Rhos, Colwyn.

bronze with a small proportion of lead. This particular recipe no doubt reflects the resources available within the local region. Products of this Acton Park Complex are to be found right across North Wales and it may not be too fanciful to link this successful and lively industry with the wealth displayed in the Mold Cape.

After this high point at the beginning of the middle bronze age the North Welsh industry seems to have lost initiative and by the succeeding Cemmaes Phase both the designs and the metallurgical techniques have become derivative. The products of these later industries are quite common in the county, but there are no merchant's or production hoards. The last flicker of originality appears at the end of the middle bronze age in the extraordinary socketed palstave from near Abergele and the recently found cylinder-socketed sickle from Pentre Halkyn. In the late bronze age a new element appears in the trading pattern when Clwyd forms a link in the exchange of Irish and European decorative bronze and goldwork — ornaments for both men and horses. The heavy twisted gold neckring (torc) from Bryn Sion near Ysceifiog is an Irish product and marks the beginning of this traffic. Two similar gold torcs from Tan y Llwyn near Llangollen have been lost. The harness hoard from Parc y Meirch with its Scandinavian jangles and buckles and strap junctions represents the other end of the trade and reflects the value of the horse as a status symbol at this period. The origin of the shale bowl in the form of a small boat (Fig.51) bobbing on a choppy sea is less certain, but the gold foil which covers its rim is decorated with compass work in traditional north European style. It was found in the bog at the foot of Caergwrle Castle rock and it is perhaps significant that both these rich finds have come from beneath hilltop sites which later became important defended settlements.

The distribution of other late bronze age metalwork reveals two interesting distinctions. The first concerns the type of axehead preferred; in the east and in the Dee valley the newer socketed axe in various designs is found; in the west of the county the population remained faithful to the palstave. However the recently discovered hoard of four palstaves, two socketed axes and a mould for a socketed axe from Gwernymynyd near Mold demonstrated that some metal workers supplied both groups.In these preferences or market availabilities, we may perhaps see a faint foreshadowing of the tribal areas indicated by Roman writers. The second concerns their distribution. By and large these late tools are found in the lower ground and in the river valleys. In contrast the weapons of the period are found on the moorland and often in the peat which was advancing over the agricultural areas which had supported the barrow builders some centuries earlier. Some of the spearheads may have been lost during hunting but others may have been deposited deliberately to propitiate the water gods in a period when increasing rainfall was threatening the livelihood of many. Although the religious

Fig.51 This beautiful gold-foil decorated shale bowl (c.18cm across the rim) found in a bog at the foot of Caergwrle Castle Hill, appears to be a rare representation of a prehistoric boat.

Fig.52 Reconstructed ring cairn at the northern end of Llyn Brenig. The ring cairn, a ceremonial rather than burial site, was in use throughout the 400 year history of the Brenig cemetery. It was originally on the side of a shallow valley, which has now been flooded by the construction of a reservoir in the mid-1970s.

Fig.53 Excavations in progress at Pentre Llyn Cymmer, Cerrigydrudion revealing a small hut (top left of photo) and enclosure wall (bottom-right) dated by radiocarbon technique to the late bronze age.

nature of these deposits is by no means certain, in these centuries after 1,000 bc we have no alternative religious sites. The long tradition of death-oriented ceremonies seems to have come to an end and burial mounds and circles are no longer regularly built. Since such watery deposits may be confidently recognised in the iron age as religious, to suggest that the origin of the tradition lies in the late bronze age is not unreasonable. Moreover the idea is supported by the nature of some of the other bog finds, like the Caergwrle bowl mentioned above.

Settlement in the later bronze age is in many ways as elusive as it was in the earlier part of the period. Moreover we know less of the pottery and small tools used, so the recognition of find scatters becomes more difficult. Only at Rhuddlan, the traditional river crossing point, have any finds been made which would confidently indicate an open settlement of this date. However radiocarbon dating has, over the last decade, revealed that several hilltop enclosures, normally thought to belong to a later period, may have originated as protected settlements in the first centuries of the first millennium bc. Such developments — the concentration of settlements, the retreat from the central uplands towards the flanks and the definition and protection of the living space are all trends which may stem from a deteriorating economic situation and the resultant stresses and strains which this must have caused.

Fig.54 Excavations in progress at Brenig — during the 1970's.

THE IRON AGE
by Fiona Gale

Perhaps the most tangible evidence of the iron age in Clwyd, as in many other counties in Wales, is the hillfort. There are over 30 hillforts in Clwyd (Fig.56), of which perhaps the best known lie along the Clwydian range. These include Moel Hiraddug, Moel Arthur, Moel Fenlli and one of the largest hillforts in Wales, Penycloddiau (Fig.55). During this century several hillforts have been extensively excavated. Dr. Willoughby Gardner excavated at Pen y Corddyn in 1905, and a few years later at Dinorben, both near Abergele. Dinorben was again excavated in the late 1950's and 1960's by Dr. H.N. Savory when there was a threat from quarrying. Moel Hiraddug, too, has suffered the ravages of quarrying and a series of rescue excavations were carried out between the mid 1950's and 1980. Firstly in 1954-55 under the direction of Mr. C.H. Houlder, who examined the north-west gateway and then by Mr. Bevan Evans excavating during the 1960's. Excavation re-started in 1969 under the direction of Mr. Bevan Evans and Dr. J.L. Davies who continued alone from 1970-72. Finally the Clwyd-Powys Archaeological Trust took over excavation in 1979-80 under the direction of K.S. Brassil. By the time excavation ceased in 1980 a large part of the northern area of the hillfort had been destroyed by quarrying. Another hillfort in Clwyd to undergo extensive study and excavation is Moel y Gaer, Rhosesmor. An area excavation directed by Graeme Guilbert began in the early 1970's prior to the construction of a 500,000 gallon storage reservoir and associated pipelines.

Fig.55 The hillfort of Penycloddiau, in the Clwydians, is one of the largest in Wales. Its defences enclose an area of some 21 hectares.

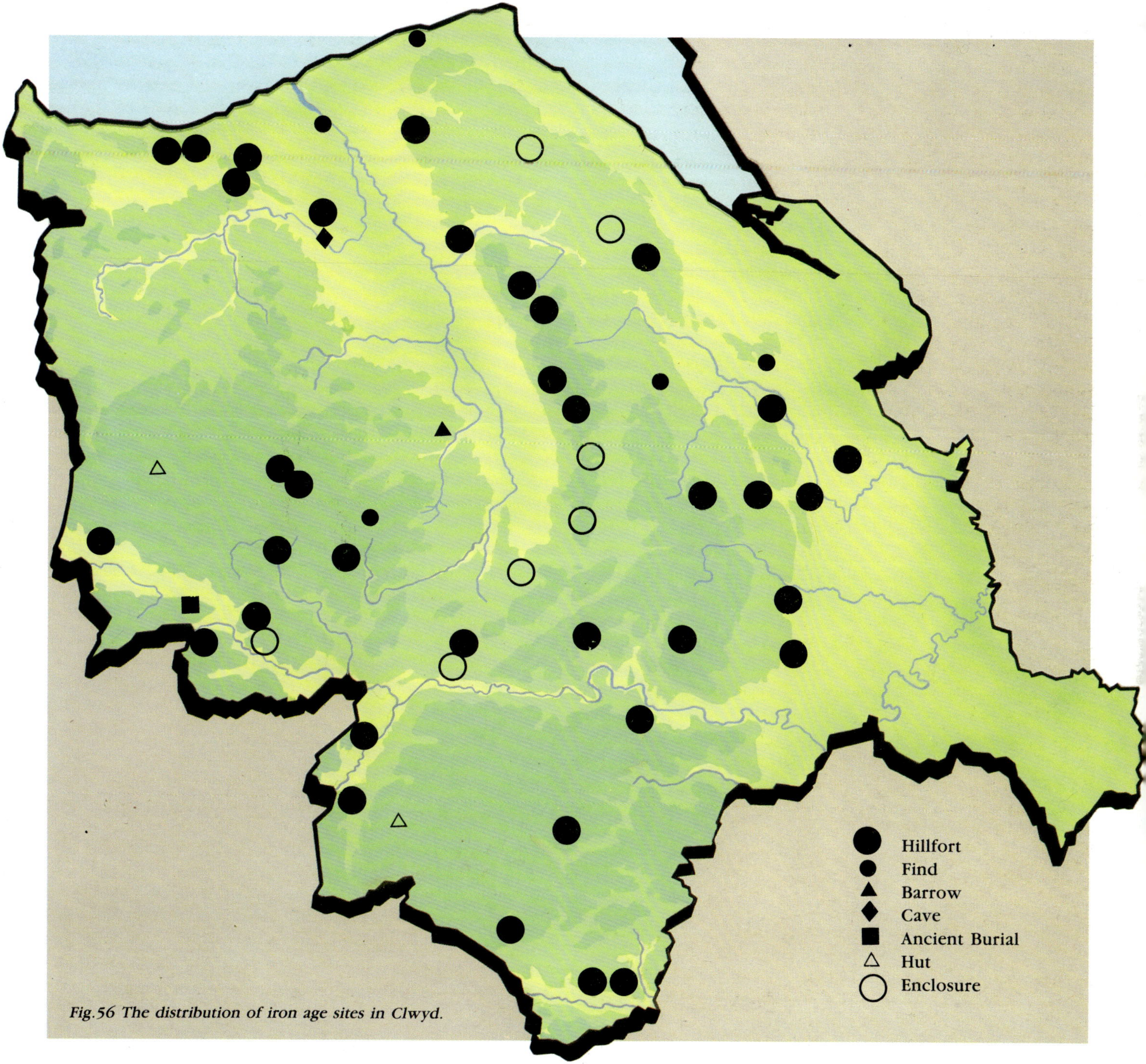

Fig.56 The distribution of iron age sites in Clwyd.

Hillfort excavations

Through the eyes of these excavators spanning 70 years of the 20th century we can see ideas concerning the construction and function of hillforts change. The earliest ideas were put forward by Dr. Willoughby Gardner and later by Dr. Savory. They saw the hillforts as largely defensive and considered that hillforts had been built to defend the local population from invaders. In his presidential address printed in *Archaeologia Cambrensis* in 1926 Dr. Willoughby Gardner paints a vivid picture of an assault on the hillfort of Moel y Gaer, Llanbedr (Figs.57,58), a hillfort on the Clwydian range which has a complete double circuit of ramparts and a third rampart on its northern side. According to Willoughby Gardner the second ditch and slope are *"Set with a 'chevaux de frise' of sharp pointed stones firmly inserted in the ground"*

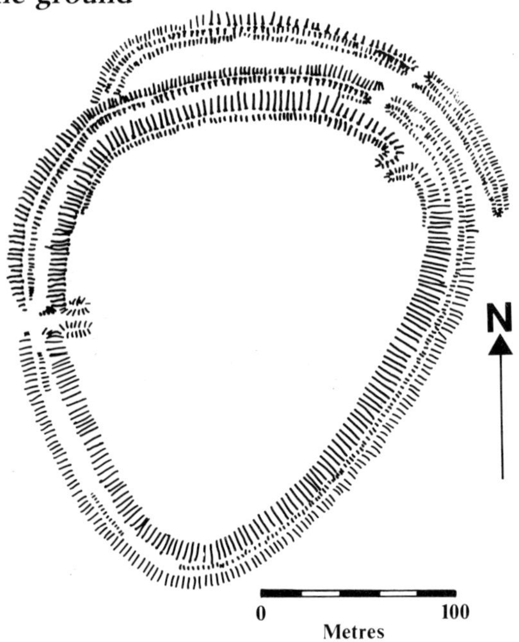

Fig.57 Plan of the defences at Moel y Gaer, Llanbedr.

There follows a vivid description of the course of an attack on this hillfort.

"Let us picture to ourselves an assault upon the south-west wall of this hillfort. The attacking horde would first charge across the little obstacle ditch, and, rushing on the "glacis" they would be brought to a halt by the first row of spiked stones inserted on its edge. Then for a distance of forty-five feet or more up the "glacis" slope they could but slowly pick their way among the bristling points protruding out of the ground on every side. By these they would be badly bruised and cut if they tripped or were struck down by the staves or slingstones and other missiles poured down upon them from the rampart above. Those who survived this ordeal would renew their rush across the next ditch and scramble up the steep scarp in front which was very probably made still more difficult by being covered with slippery scree upon its lower half. When they reached firmer ground, another charge would be made to cross the next ditch. But here an unseen and terrible reception was prepared for them in the form of a seven foot belt of sharp stone stakes lining the bottom of the ditch; on these they could hardly help but fall with the impetus of their dash over the last banks and the pressure of the throng behind. All this time the shower of missiles from the ramparts above would doubtless continue; and one can well imagine that but few of the host that started on the "rush" would survive to climb the last bank and to cross the final ditch and thus reach the foot of the great stone rampart."

That slingstones must have been used is testified by 'caches' of stones found during excavations at Moel y Gaer, Rhosesmor; they were stored just inside the ramparts ready to rain down upon the enemy. Hillforts must have been an effective form of defence for they are mentioned by Juvenal writing in Rome during the time of Nero. A father is urging his son to go into the army and to persuade him says *'wake up! Prove your valour, either by going to fight against the Moors or by tearing down the forts of the Brigantes'* The Brigantes lived in the north of England to the north of the Deceangli in Clwyd.

Savory and Willoughby Gardner when interpreting the results of excavations at Pen y Corddyn and Dinorben (Fig.59) saw the construction and destruction of successive ramparts as a reaction to the influx of new peoples into the area. Hut platforms and evidence of occupation have been found at these two sites. The earliest settlement at Dinorben consisted of a large number of medium sized round-huts and Savory noted what appeared to be groups of similar huts at Moel Hiraddug and Moel Fenlli on the Clwydian range. He argued that these timber framed huts represented an adaptation of early iron age culture which occurred as it moved northward and coalesced with local groups who perhaps led a more pastoral life. The larger hillforts have sometimes been seen as cattle corrals for the local pastoral community.

Fig.58 Aerial view of Moel y Gaer, Llanbedr. Defended by a double circle of ramparts on the west, east and south sides, it is further strengthened by a third line of defences on the north side where the gentle gradient offers little in the way of natural defence.

Willoughby Gardner in his presidential address said that the native Celtic population *'dwelt permanently in these elevated strongholds'*. At Moel y Gaer where a large area of the interior was excavated prior to the building of a reservoir, a complex sequence of huts emerged (Fig.60). The success of the excavation depended on excavating a large area; had smaller areas been opened up the

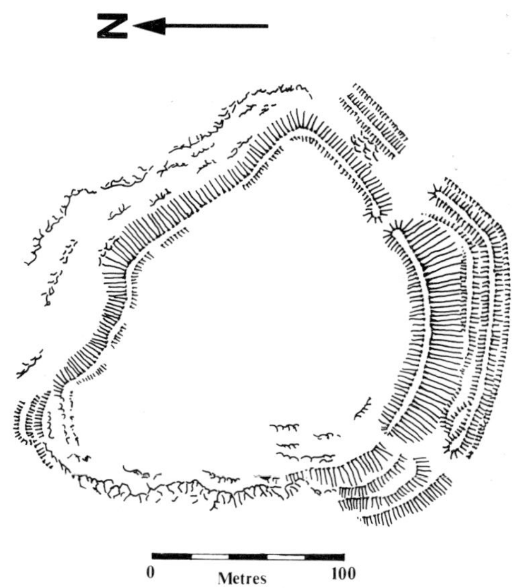

Fig.59 Plan of the hillfort of Dinorben, Abergele. This hillfort has now been largely destroyed due to the extraction of limestone.

significance of many of the post-holes and timber slots would have been lost. At Moel y Gaer it would seem that occupation began with a few post built round-houses. These spread to form a group of closely packed round-houses with no apparent organised system of roadways between the buildings (Fig.61). This phase was followed perhaps by the building of the defences, and a new style of round-house with walls made from stakes, was constructed. The settlement took on much more of a 'plan' with rows of round-houses and a neat grid of four-post structures (Fig.62). The final phase at Moel y Gaer is characterized by timber framed rectangular buildings. Why the nature of settlement changed is harder to explain, particularly the differences between the two round-house types. Do we see new ideas representing new peoples, or the same people taking on board new ideas? That there is an element of planning to be seen in the second phase is inescapable; here we see the work of the Celtic town planner, organising the 'village' not only into a 'street' pattern but also allocating specific areas for buildings with different functions. Perhaps we can interpret the four post structures as granaries and the circular huts as dwellings. This paints a very rural view; Celtic peoples quietly living on the hill, storing their grain. The hillforts may also have acted as redistribution centres for produce from the surrounding area, and as centres where itinerant metal-workers and craftsmen came, and where farmers occasionally sought security during outbreaks of hostilities. We must not lose sight of the fact that all these hillforts had massive defences (Fig.63), far larger than were needed purely to mark out a village boundary or keep cattle enclosed at night. There must have been a need for such defences.

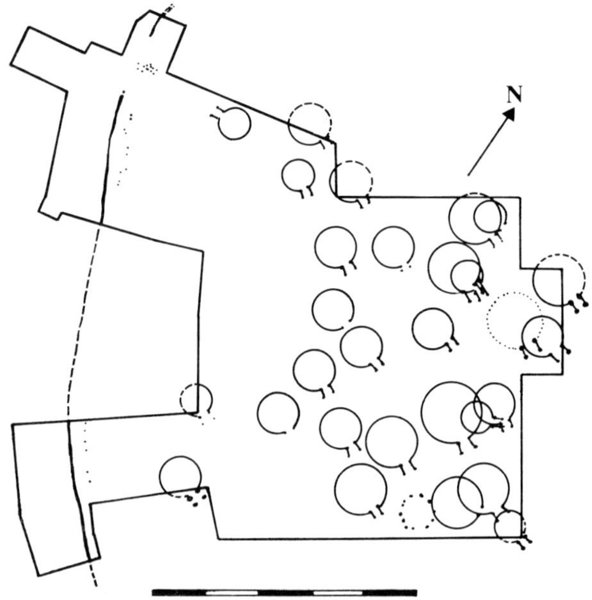

Fig.61 The earliest phase of iron age occupation at Moel y Gaer, Rhosesmor, reveals a group of round-houses enclosed within a timber 'palisade'.

Fig.60 Plan of Moel y Gaer, Rhosesmor, prior to the construction of a reservoir in the early 1980s.

At both Pen y Corddyn and Dinorben relatively narrow sections were cut through the defences which revealed in both cases stone-faced ramparts. Willoughby Gardner stated that

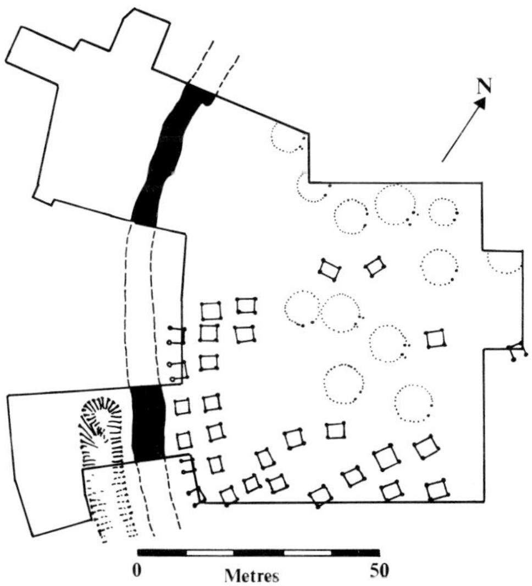

Fig.62 By the second phase of iron age occupation at Moel y Gaer, Rhosesmor, the defences had been built and the 'village' took on a much more orderly, 'planned' appearance. Note the concentration of four-post structures, thought by many to be granaries.

Fig.63 Aerial view of Moel y Gaer, Rhosesmor, during the construction of the reservoir. The circuit of iron age defences is clearly visible.

in Gaul the Celtic tribesmen built ramparts of stone reinforced with great logs in order to withstand the Roman battering rams, but that such constructions had not yet been identified in Britain. At Dinorben (Fig.64) a succession of ramparts were identified which allowed Willoughby Gardner to identify 5 phases of building and occupation of the site. Savory returning to dig the same site found evidence of burnt timber within the ramparts (Fig.65) of Period II and a previously unknown palisade trench which surrounded the earliest occupation on the site. At Moel Hiraddug in 1979-80 the multivallate section of the north-eastern defences came under threat from quarrying. It was decided to excavate a 10m wide section through the ramparts. Previous sections through ramparts in this and many other sites were very narrow, perhaps only 2-3m wide, providing a minimal view of the rampart construction. At Moel Hiraddug the base of both the outer and middle ramparts were shown to have been divided transversely by lines of stones as part of a cellular construction.

At Moel y Gaer, Rhosesmor, a 15m wide trench was cut through the defences. Two successive ramparts were found, built along the same line. Rampart A had a front face which was a combination of vertical timbers and drystone walling. We can perhaps envisage on

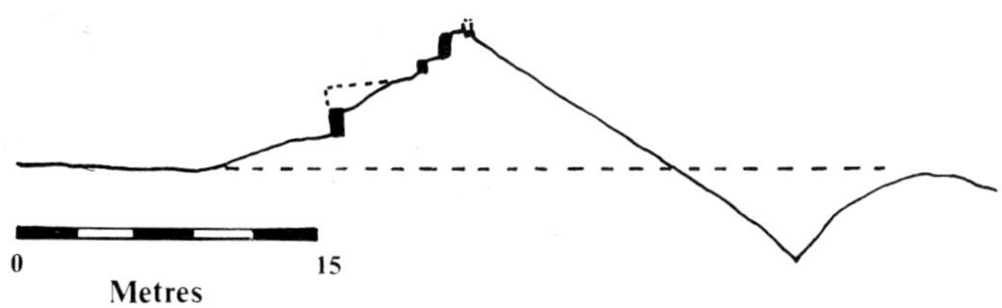

Fig.64 A section through the rampart at Dinorben as interpreted by Willoughby Gardner.

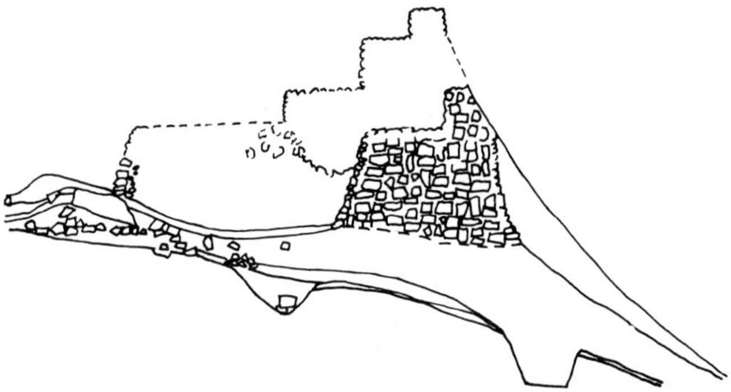

Fig.65 A section through the rampart at Dinorben as interpreted by Hubert Savory.

top of this a wattle breastwork behind which the inhabitants patrolled on the look out for marauders. From the post holes found, it appears that Rampart A is of a timber framed construction. This rampart was succeeded by B (Fig.66), built on top of A, and was wider and higher than its predecessor. Evidence for timber lacing was found in the construction of the ramparts — betrayed by a series of transverse breaks in the stone at intervals of 1.0 to 1.2m. In a narrow excavation a lot of this information would go undetected.

Hillforts needed entrances (Figs.67,68,69). These were an obvious weak point in the line of defence. In the late prehistoric period complicated forms had evolved incorporating guard chambers and bastions. As early as 1926 Willoughby Gardner compared the south-east entrance of Dinorben to the north-east entrance at Pen y Corddyn, both with two guard chambers and recessed post-holes. He posed the question *'was this the work of the same designer?'*. More recently Graeme Guilbert has compared the main inner gateway at Moel Hiraddug with the south-east entrance at Dinorben. In both cases an earlier simple entrance was blocked with debris and replaced. In both cases the new gateway involved the use of inturned rampart terminals which incorporated drystone-lined guard chambers. In both cases the new entrance was placed to the left of its predecessor thus allowing the old entrance to remain in use until the new one was completed. In this context is it fanciful to suggest a 'professional' hillfort architect travelling from hillfort to hillfort much as the metal worker or tinker might to sell his goods to the residents?

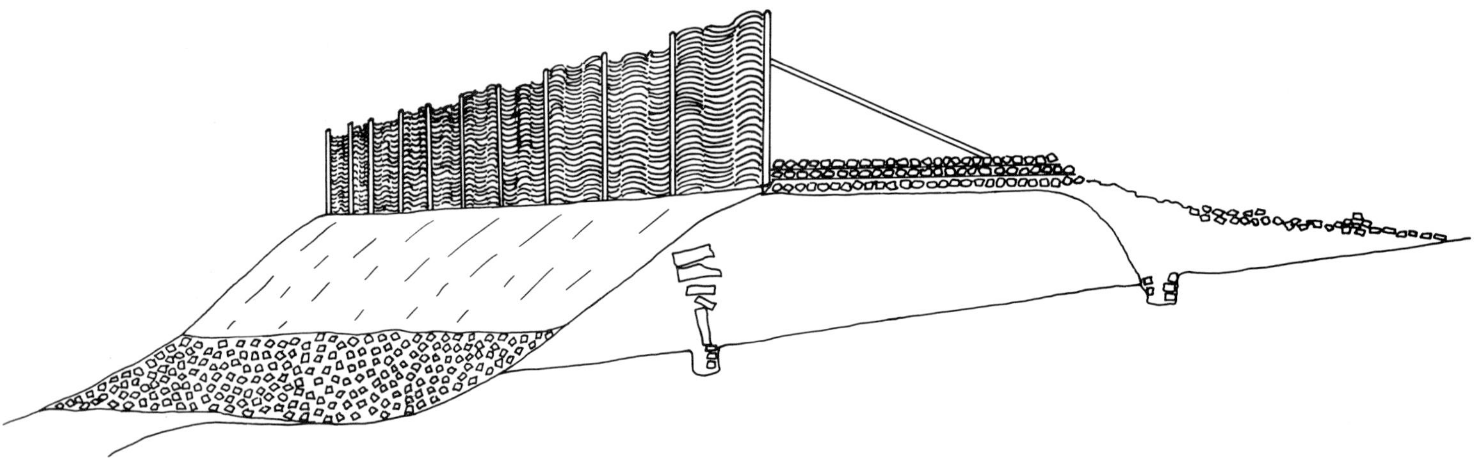

Fig.66 The latest iron age rampart at Moel y Gaer, Rhosesmor, as reconstructed by Graeme Guilbert.

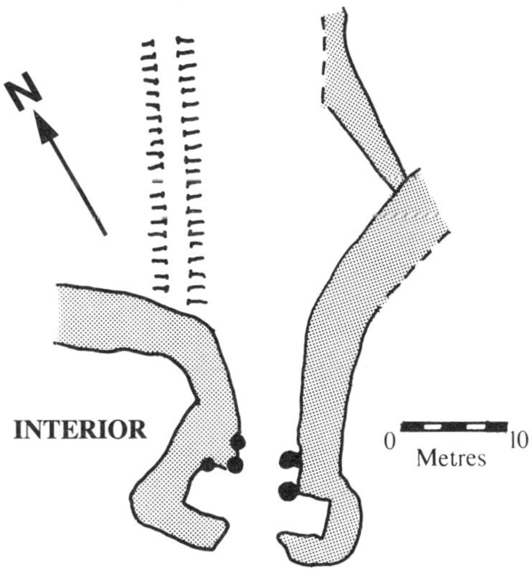

Fig.67 The north-east entrance of Pen y Corddyn, near Abergele. Note the paired guard chambers flanking the entrance in this gateway and the others on this page.

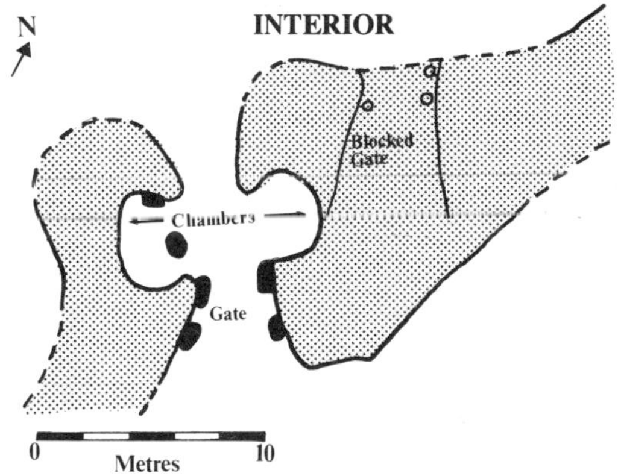

Fig.68 The main inner gateway at Moel Hiraddug, Dyserth.

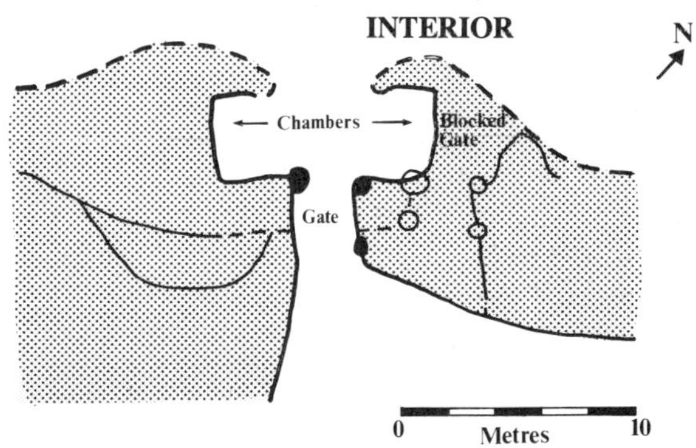

Fig.69 The south-east entrance at Dinorben, Abergele.

Returning to the function of hillforts were they defensive settlements or purely pastoral enclosures? The truth must surely lie somewhere in between; that they were important collection and redistribution centres cannot be doubted. There is much evidence for food collection, storage and processing. Emmer and spelt grains were found at Dinorben and we have already noted the possible granaries at Moel y Gaer. There is plentiful evidence of weaving in the form of spindle whorls, and cloth would have been made from the fleeces of sheep roaming the surrounding countryside. From the many animal bones found (eg Moel Hiraddug; Dinorben) we can surmise not only the processing of carcasses but also leather-working. At Dinorben there is evidence for local small-scale metal-working mainly of iron, although the working of copper/bronze is hinted at by the discovery of a copper bun ingot. In all these cases we might picture a busy village with some functions carried on by members of the community, such as food processing and weaving, while others were carried out by itinerants like the metal worker or salt purveyor.

Hillforts also served an important defensive rôle. The huge defences, elaborate gateways and signs of burning and destruction during their history indicate that life in hillforts could be turbulent (Fig.75). Skeletons have been found under the trackway through the main inner gateway at Moel Hiraddug. Do these indicate the slaughtered enemy or sacrifices to appease the gods and ward off attack? In a similar vein remains of a human lower jaw have been found at Dinorben on the road surface of the south-east entrance. Does this hint at the use of gateways and ramparts to display human heads as a warning to future assailants? Fragments of heads were also found on several hut floors during excavations in the late 1950's, perhaps indicating the practice of exposing the heads of enemies. Strabo talks of Celtic headhunters and the cult of the head. Examples of stone heads have been found in Clwyd; six carved stone heads had until recently stood outside a local farmhouse at Llandegla. There is no information as to where they originated but it is tempting to see them coming from the nearby ancient well site of St. Teila at Llandegla. Stylistically they could be iron age and are very similar to groups found in France but until they are studied more closely we cannot be certain. However even if they themselves do not date from the iron age they embody a Celtic tradition of reverence for the head.

Where should we look for the origins of the iron age in Clwyd? In the earlier part of the century when Willoughby Gardner was excavating he suggested that what we were looking at was a transition from the bronze age, with the people remaining the same or very similar but absorbing the ideas from other groups with whom they came in contact. But why should the nature of settlement and more particularly burial customs change so dramatically? We do not see hillforts or their equivalent in the bronze age, where instead we have smaller settlements and their associated field systems. Perhaps we can see hillforts emerging against a background of a deteriorating, wetter climate. More land became marginal and unable to be cultivated as a result, thus the same number of people had a smaller area to exploit. Nucleated settlements with specialised functions developed. The form of settlements may therefore change as a reaction to changing density of population.

In the bronze age we have ample evidence of burial customs seen in the many barrows throughout the county. In the iron age no cemeteries have been discovered in Clwyd. The only human remains found are those mentioned already from Moel Hiraddug (Fig.70) and Dinorben and it is unlikely that these represent the everyday treatment of the dead. The Cerrigydrudion hanging bowl, found in 1924 and often regarded as one of the earliest Le Teñe objects in Britain, was found in association with a cist which lay about 50cm below the surface. No trace of bones or ashes were found although it is still possible that a burial of some type is represented. Indeed recent work on the reconstruction of the bronze fragments found at Cerrigydrudion call into doubt the function of the object. As a hanging bowl it is unique in a Le Têne context and work by Ian Stead, prior to an exhibition at the British Museum entitled 'The Gauls', indicated that it could perhaps be a lid of a vessel, or possibly two vessels, as differences in the pattern hint at the possibility that two objects may be represented. A burial in association with such a fine object is not perhaps representative of the general population. The burial customs in the iron age represent a large gap in our understanding of Clwyd. It is possible that the iron age sees the disposal of the dead either on above ground pyres (much as one sees in India today), or perhaps exposure of the dead in certain 'holy places' as practised by North American Indians. This gap must be filled by future discovery and investigation.

There is little further evidence in Clwyd for settlement sites other than hillforts. This does not mean that other sites did not exist, rather that we have not yet found them. Hillforts after all are very obvious; undefended lowland settlements of timber framed houses leave little trace. It is largely due to luck that some have been discovered. This is certainly the case at

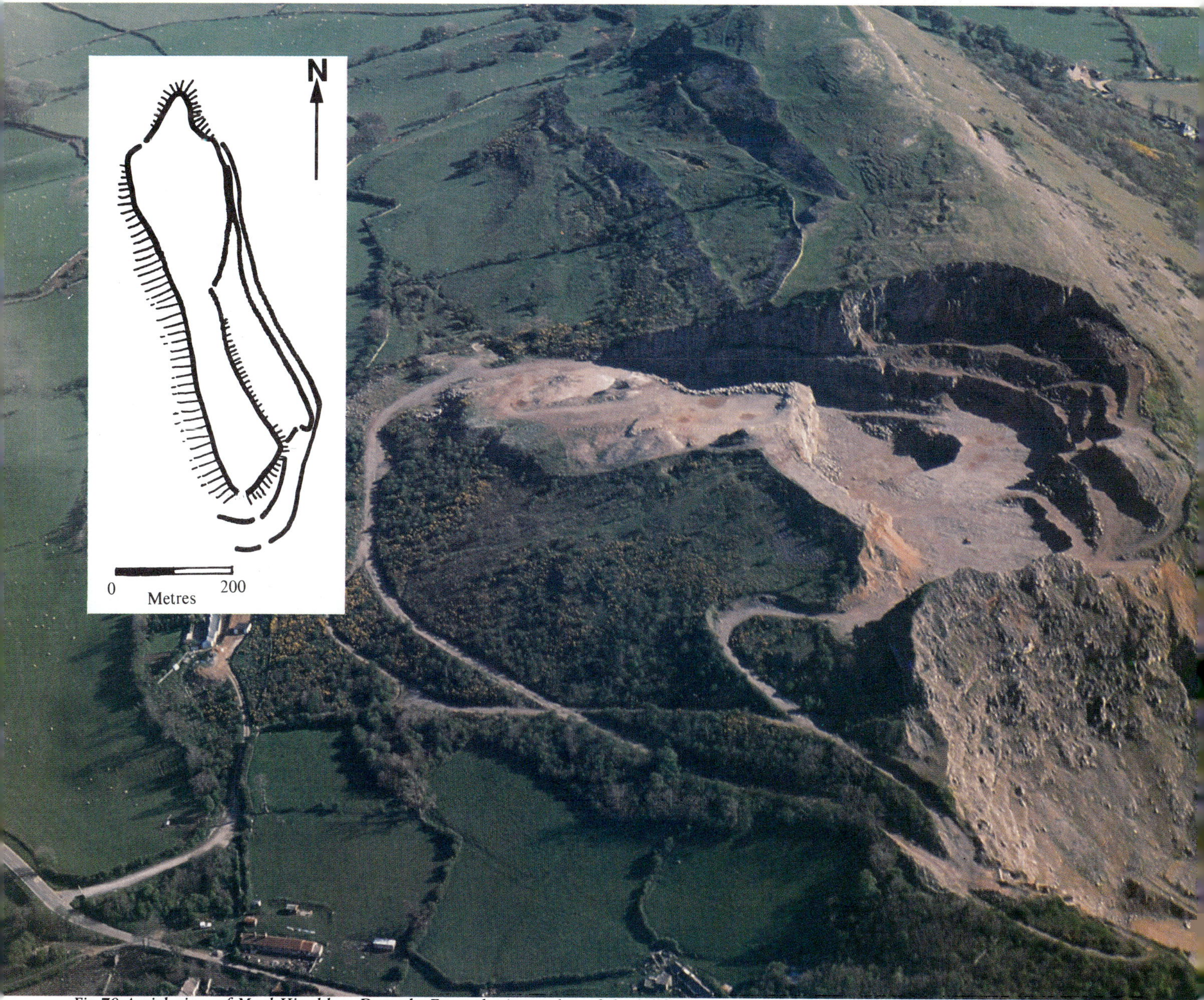

Fig.70 Aerial view of Moel Hiraddug, Dyserth. From the inset plan of the hillfort it is possible to see the extent of the destruction caused by modern quarrying.

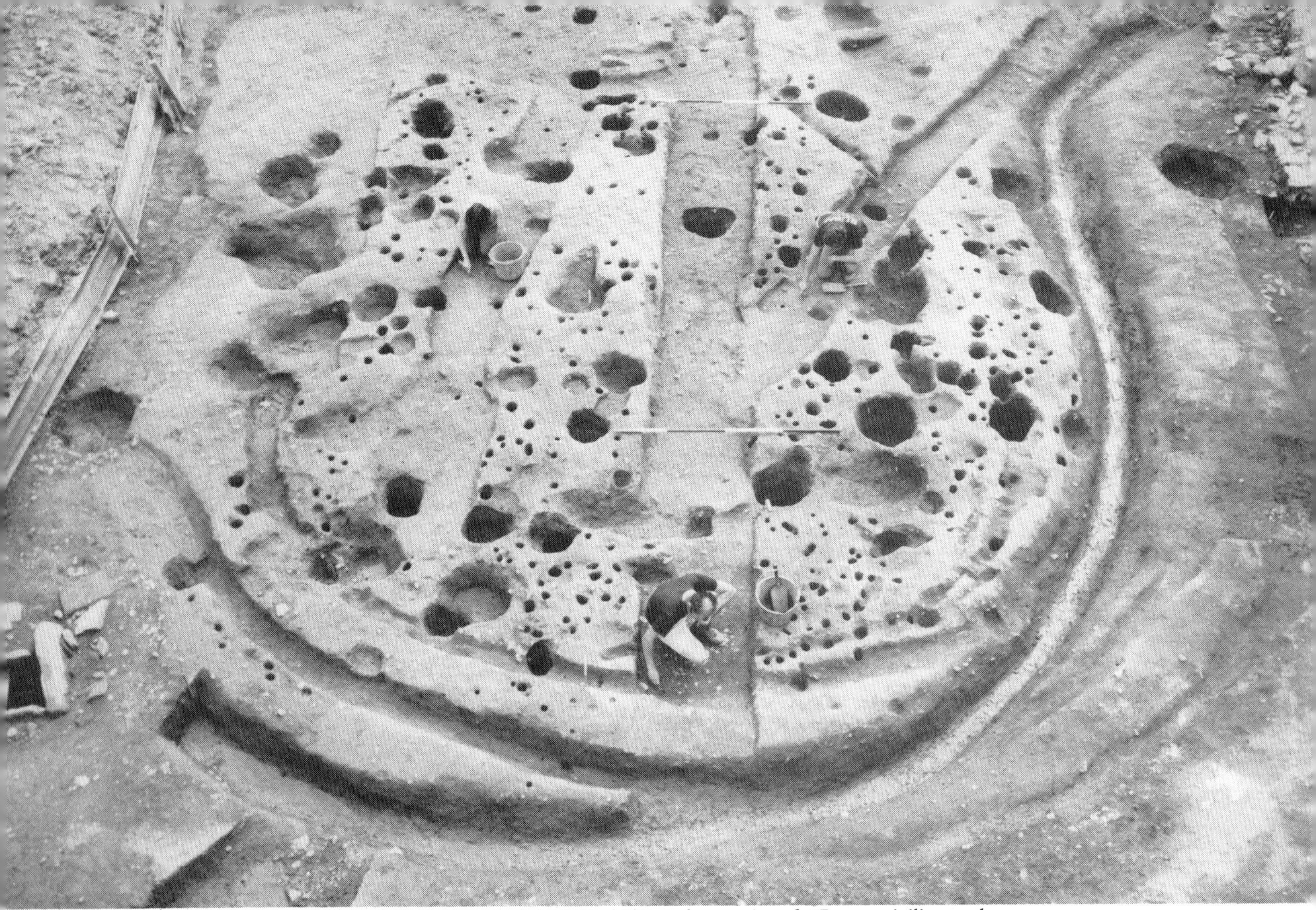

Fig.71 This iron age round-house was discovered at Prestatyn underlying the remains of a Roman civilian settlement.

Prestatyn where a Roman civilian settlement was excavated by the Clwyd-Powys Archaeological Trust in 1984-85. Here towards the end of the excavation remains of an iron age round-house were discovered (Fig.72,74). It probably existed during the final decades of the 1st century BC. It is unclear whether this round-house, and a similar one nearby, form part of a single farming complex, or part of a small village. We can assume that there were settlements outside the hillforts on the lowland, more fertile, areas, for it is here that a good deal of the grain needed by the local population was grown and their animals tended. In addition some of the small enclosures surveyed by John Manley may have been defended farmsteads of the iron age.

The Finds

As well as using settlement sites, houses and fortifications to build up a picture of iron age people living in Clwyd we can turn to their artefacts some of which have survived. From these we can try to get more information about the type of life the people led, their economy and social structure.

People in Clwyd during the iron age seem not to have used pottery. The majority of pottery found on hillfort sites is Roman. This is one reason why early excavators like Willoughby Gardner saw the iron age as starting late and continuing on into the period of Roman occupation. What native pottery exists, is largely the type known as VCP and this has recently been linked with the production of salt at inland sites. This type of pottery was used as a container in the production of salt and for its distribution. Two centres of production have been put forward, one identified in the Droitwich area of Worcestershire, the other, somewhere in the Nantwich/Middlewich area of the Cheshire basin. It is from this latter source that any VCP in Clwyd originates. A source in Cheshire has been postulated from the petrology or mineral content of the pottery fabric. The fabric contains small stone particles transported by the glaciers of the Ice Ages. However it must not be forgotten that this ice sheet merged with one from Snowdonia somewhere in the area of the North Wales coast, thus a source in this area cannot be entirely ruled out. Whatever the origin, VCP does indicate movement of what must have been a very vital commodity.

We can only assume that containers of material other than clay were used for many everyday domestic tasks and for transporting goods. These materials would be organic, perhaps animal-skin, wood or bark, and would not usually be preserved. At Moel y Gaer where the most systematic internal excavation has taken place the nature of the soil is so acidic that little survives. Both bone and metalwork disintegrated many centuries ago. At Moel Hiraddug and Dinorben a quantity of antler and bone artefacts have been found, perhaps reflecting the number of deer still roaming wild

Fig.72 A reconstructed iron age round-house built at Butser Hill in Hampshire.

in the Vale of Clwyd. Antler was used for a number of different objects. A great many served as handles for tools, while others were used as fastenings for clothes. There are many examples from Dinorben, Moel Hiraddug and other sites in Britain of perforated antler tines and it has been suggested that these are from horse fittings used as part of a bridle. At Dinorben particularly, many antler pieces were either unfinished or waste pieces, so we can assume that manufacture of antler articles took place on site. Whether someone was a full time manufacturer or whether it was something that everyone could do if necessary is impossible to tell. The same question can be posed regarding metal-working. Once again at Dinorben there is evidence for metal-working on site. Iron slag has been recovered and a fragment of copper bun-ingot generally associated with copper or bronze-working. Perhaps metal-working is a more specialised skill than bone or antler-working; indeed analysis of a piece of slag from Dinorben suggests it is a bloom of carbon steel which had been water-cooled and reheated after smelting in a primitive furnace. Did the settlement support it's own metal worker or are we seeing the remains of an itinerant craftsman moving from site to site 'selling his expertise?'

The importance of agriculture is reflected in the finds recovered from the sites in Clwyd. Dinorben has a collection of iron tools adapted for agricultural use. Stone quern and quernstones have been found at Dinorben, and Moel Hiraddug. These were used in the processing of grain. Spindle whorls have been found, generally of stone, and were used in the spinning of fleeces to make clothing.

Larger and more dramatic finds of metalwork may be interpreted as a sign of wealth and power, and as an indicator of social status. The chiefs, or influential people who possessed them, organised the building of defences, the collection and redistribution of foodstuffs and the movement of 'goods', between settlements. They would also, of course, rally support when either defending a settlement or maintaining an offensive on a neighbouring rival.

At Moel Hiraddug a large hoard of metalwork was found in 1872 during the making of a road through the eastern defences. The objects were found lying in or near the bottom of the rock-cut ditch covered by the debris of the collapsed rampart. The hoard contained parts of an iron sword blade, a bronze curved sheath, a bronze crescent shaped plate, both ornaments from a shield, a square bronze plate with triskele pattern, and a three cornered plate of bronze (Fig.73). The circumstances of their discovery mean we have a very limited idea of how they relate to the site. They are thought to fit into the later part of the iron age, perhaps the 2nd or 1st century BC. This contrasts with other metal objects found at Moel Hiraddug during the 1960's, particularly a fibula or brooch, a swan's head pin and an open work disc of iron. These all date to around 400 bc. The bronze brooch, the first of its kind to be found in North Wales, is so well preserved that the pin can still be

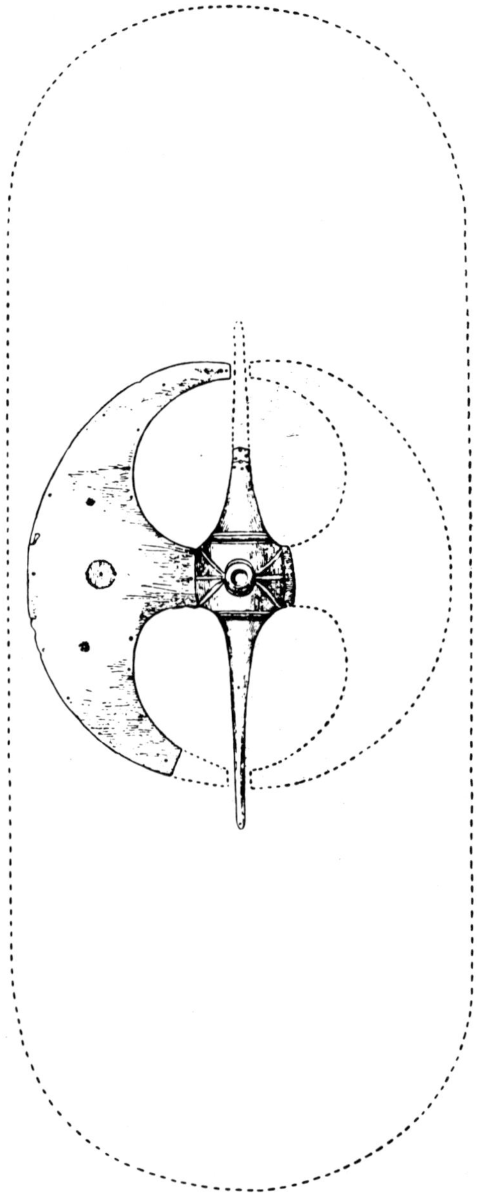

Fig.73 The remains of the Moel Hiraddug shield were discovered with a large hoard of metalwork in 1872 during the making of a road through the eastern defences of the hillfort. (Length of shield is approximately 1.3m).

released from the catchplate. It shows signs of wear and was obviously a much loved object. It is possible that originally it had an inlay, perhaps of coral but more likely of tufa which is readily available in this area of North Wales. The iron cup-headed pin, found in 1960, also originally contained some kind of inlay. When Professor C.F. Hawkes saw the object in 1961 he commented that it had some sort of 'decorative substance' attached to it which had the appearance of tufa.

The iron openwork disc, found at Dinorben in 1962, may have been part of a bridle bit. Other horse fittings form part of the Abergele hoard, found in 1868 at the foot of the cliff around Dinorben. Traditionally this hoard had been seen as belonging to the bronze age but there are one or two items that definitely belong in the early iron age. It is intriguing to know how such 'hoards' were lost. Were they deliberately buried to be collected at a later date? Or can we picture a more dramatic situation — with the hoard, accompanied by it's owner, crashing down the cliffs of Dinorben in a vain bid to escape whatever lay in the hillfort? No metal-work was recovered from Moel y Gaer due to the acidic nature of the soil. We cannot speculate as to the finery or otherwise of people living there. As already mentioned the fragmentary remains of a very fine 'hanging bowl' were recovered from a cist in Cerrigydrudion in 1924. The 'bowl' is extremely well decorated and it may have had a ritual function.

At Ffynogion farm near Ruthin, during construction works for the Denbigh-Corwen railway in 1861, two spoon-shaped bronze objects were found (Fig.74). The spoon-like objects have a large bowl and short handle. One has two lines on the bowl which cross at the centre, the other has a perforation made at the edge. Other examples have been found in the British Isles sometimes associated with a skeleton. The spoons are said to contain a high proportion of copper.

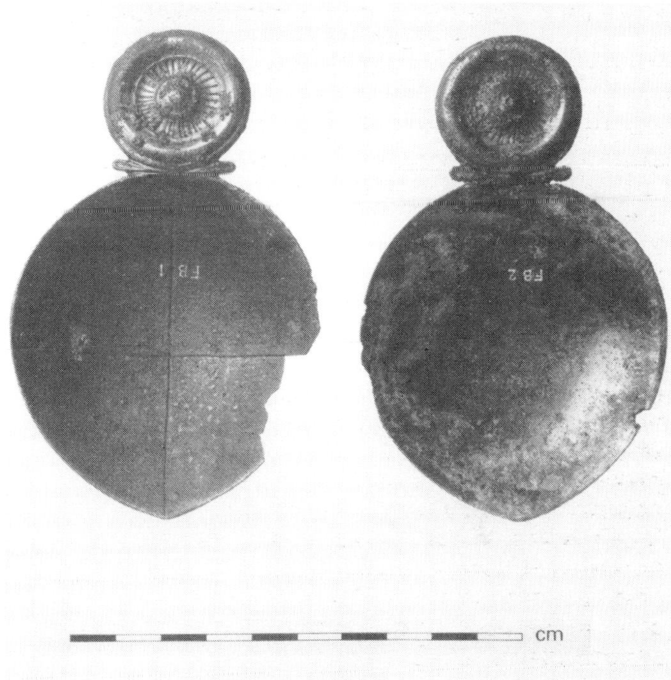

Fig.74 Two spoon-shaped bronze objects, found at Ffynogion near Ruthin.

Problems of Interpretation

We find difficulties when trying to get some idea of the population density of Clwyd in the iron age. There are problems of the evidence perhaps not being a representative sample. It is biased towards evidence from hillforts since these features have survived, as against lowland settlements, about which, with the exception of Prestatyn, we can only conjecture. But also there are problems associated with our interpretation of the evidence. This has been succinctly put forward by Graeme Guilbert. Are all our assumptions correct? Do all round-houses represent dwellings? Do four-post structures represent food/grain stores? If so were all the 'dwellings' occupied at the same time? How many people do we assume lived in each dwelling? Were family units the norm, or was

Fig.75 The impressive hillfort at Caer Drewyn, Corwen, recently purchased by the County Council. The site will undergo a management scheme to interpret it to the public.

society divided up in a different way, more like the early kibbutz? And who lived in hillforts? The chiefs, the priests or Druids, the craftsmen, the warriors or the ordinary people? And did they live there all year round, or only in summer? We run into even more queries on sites that are unexcavated but have obvious platforms terraced into their surfaces. These are generally interpreted as 'hut platforms' and taken as an indication of occupation on the sites as indeed they may be. Examples from unexcavated sites can be seen at Moel y Gaer, Llanbedr, although they are also present at Moel Hiraddug and Dinorben where excavations have taken place. At the recent excavation at Dinorben an area which appeared to have many 'hut platforms' was cleared and investigated. Remains of post-holes were found but they did not appear to correlate closely with the rock-cut platforms — the 'hut' platforms. On the other hand we must not lose sight of the fact that some structures such as timber buildings on a timber sill-beam or perhaps turf built buildings, may leave virtually no trace for the archaeologist to find. In view of these many uncertanties it is unwise to attempt a guess at levels of population in iron-age Clwyd until we have a more balanced view of both settlement types and burial practices during the period.

SMALL SETTLEMENTS
by John Manley

The aim of this article is straightforward: to present an inventory of some putatively iron age and/or romano-british small settlements in Clwyd (Fig.76). The forms taken by these small settlements vary considerably but can be subsumed under the heading 'small enclosures'. The means to achieve this aim however, need to be quite circumspect: all the sites are undated, none has been excavated to adequate standards; most lack a measured ground plan; more will be discovered (and probably have been by the time this account is published).

Faced with such a diverse collection of data it may seem prudent not to anticipate the slow progress of research which, given time, might reveal some homogenous attributes to group or divide this selection, both more meaningfully and assuredly. Yet the lack of any previous published consideration makes the present survey more imperative. Suffice it to say that if we set out with the intention of simply reviewing the evidence and remain content with prompting questions rather than pursuing too many conclusions the undertaking may not be completely without value. The general assumption underlying the following presentation, therefore, is that many of these sites were probably agricultural settlements or activity areas of one kind or another.

Introduction

Clwyd is a county that straddles the transition between lowland and upland. The principal lowland elements — the Vale of Clwyd and the Maelor — are physiographically an extension of the Cheshire Plain into Wales; the uplands — the Denbigh Moors, the Clwydian Range and the Berwyn Mountains — comprise the more anticipated topography of North Wales. In between lie the limestone slopes of Halkyn Mountain and the less elevated coastal hinterland.

Not unnaturally, some of the archaeology tends to reflect this fundamental dualism. In the iron age the known settlement pattern groups the major developed hillforts, whose affinities stretch southwards down the Marches and spill into south-central England, with smaller fortified sites which might be considered as an eastwards extension of the typical south-west England and west Wales settlement form. The later prehistoric landscapes of Gwynedd, comprising extensive tracts of stone enclosures, 'huts', field-systems and cairns, scarcely appear in western Clwyd. Similarly, in the medieval period, those characteristically lowland and predominantly English earthworks — the moated sites — intrude in any numbers only in the Maelor and the Vale of Clwyd. Topographically a hybrid, north-east Wales consequently lacks a diagnostic, clearly defined small settlement 'personality' in the iron age and romano-british periods to match those of the other Welsh regions. The twinning of enclosed stone farmsteads with Gwynedd, of small fortified settlements with Dyfed and of hilltop, hillslope and (increasingly) vale-bottom enclosures with the upper Severn finds no corresponding association in Clwyd.

The known archaeology of north-east Wales in the period 500BC to AD500 is characterised by imposing hillforts of the iron age and the less-understood centres of Roman occupation. Such a rudimentary reflection of the history of a millennium is a direct result of the greater likelihood of some sites to survive and be recognised. Large earthworks on remote hilltops have usually escaped the attentions of the plough (though not always the quarryman), while lowland Roman centres owe discovery to the relative quantity and endurance of their physical characteristics. This paper is based on

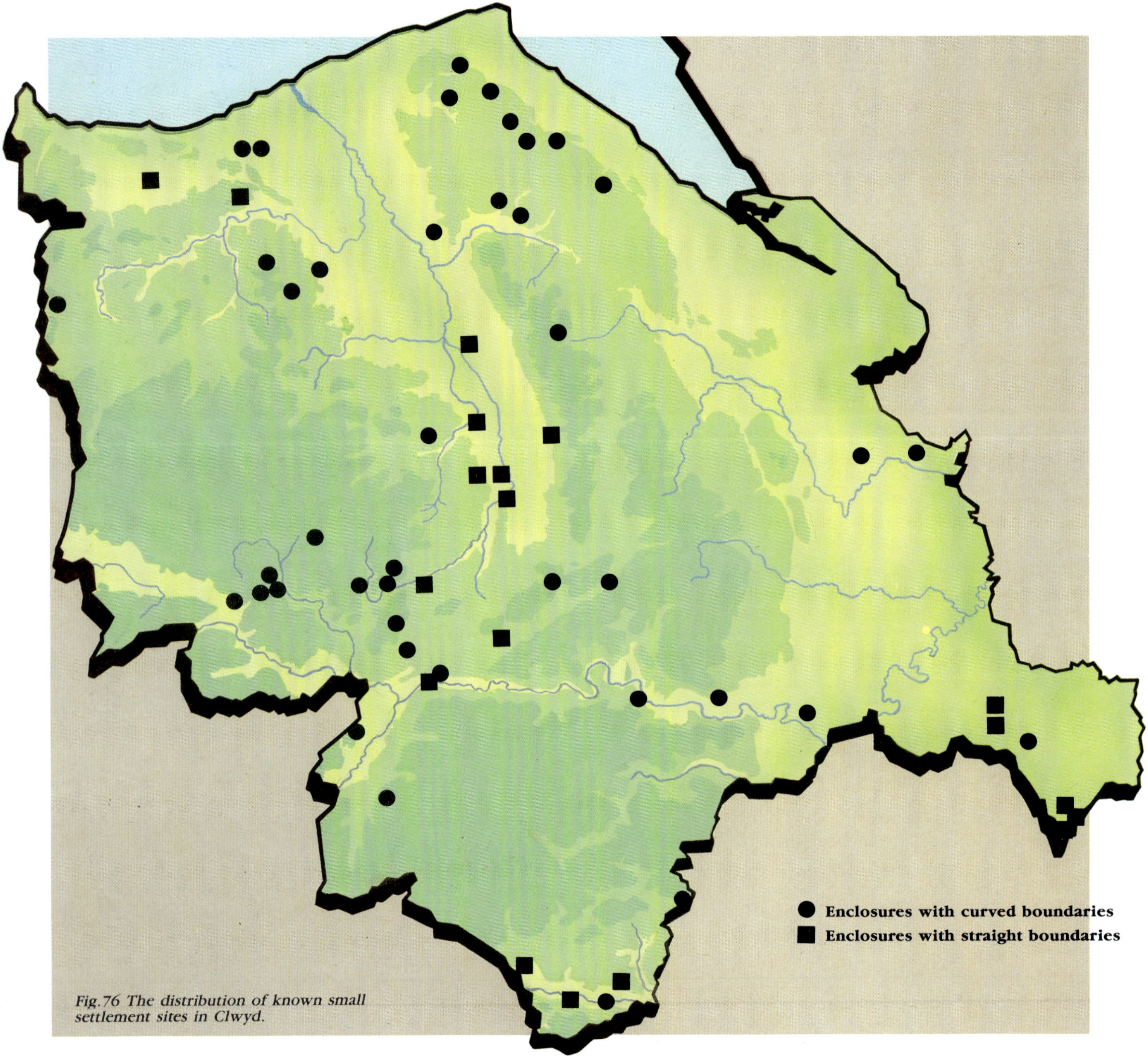

Fig.76 The distribution of known small settlement sites in Clwyd.

the premiss that smaller agricultural settlements must have existed in numbers during this millennium constituting *at least one* lower order of site in a settlement hierarchy. Some of these farms, villages or hamlets may be found among the 'small enclosures' which are the subject of this paper, although the possibility remains that unenclosed emplacements, like the unenclosed round 'houses' beneath the Roman site at Prestatyn, may have constituted others; the latter, of course, stand even less chance of survival and recognition than the former. It is essential to understand the important rôle played by such lesser centres, not only in their own right but also in their collective function in providing the context in which the larger centres operated.

There is an imminent danger in this premiss, however. We see in the modern landscape of north-east Wales a 'logical' hierarchy of towns, villages, hamlets and dispersed farms. What could be more obvious and less unexpected than to seek, find, order and interpret iron age or romano-british antecedents to our current situation? In essence, therefore, this methodology is a backwards projection of our contemporary perspective. It conditions our acceptance of the 'reality' of an iron age or romano-british 'economy' separate from social organisation and it relegates to the periphery the social considerations that may have influenced the settlement patterns of later prehistoric and early historic communities. We must be wary of seeking the present in the past.

How then should we justify the basic premiss that numerous small agricultural settlements existed in north-east Wales? At best only an incomplete justification can be provided. Firstly there has been a steady rise in the number of small enclosures discovered in the area, either through aerial photography (CR Musson; JKS St Joseph; GDB Jones) or field-walking (JFM *et al*). On analogical grounds many of these resemble sites in other areas (eg Dyfed; Severn Valley; Cumbria and Wessex) usually ascribed to the iron age and/or romano-british periods. Secondly there has been a re-evaluation of hillfort functions, a shift from 'military' interpretations or the independent 'village' hypothesis espoused for Herefordshire, for instance, by Stanford to the territorially dependent redistributive rôle favoured by Cunliffe. Such a reappraisal owes as much to anthropological classifications of ranked societies or chiefdoms as to the inherent promptings of archaeological data. Indeed, Bradley's recent attempt at a social interpretation of prehistoric Britain questions the redistributive rôle of hillforts and instead argues for a more orthodox militaristic explanation. Which of the several hypotheses are favoured is incidental to our argument; all seek to interpret a landscape of hillforts and smaller settlements, peopled either by redistributors and recipients or protectors and the protected. Thirdly, the influence of Pax Romana, especially in the military zone, seems increasingly circumscribed by recent studies. Greater emphasis is laid on the continuity of settlement, population and socio-economic practices across the prehistoric/historic divide.

Finally, how can sites later than the romano-british era be excluded from our sample? Dark age settlements have been so rarely forthcoming throughout Wales that it is unlikely that the present sample conceals an unsuspected and significant early medieval sub-set. The fact that a diagnostic settlement form for a conjectural dispersed later medieval farmstead has not yet been recognised in Clwyd encourages caution, however. Outside of major urban sites, the few deserted villages (eg Llandrillo, Caerwys) and the atypical moated sites, the anticipated farm or hamlet has escaped recognition. Some fugitive traces may lie beneath the collection of post-

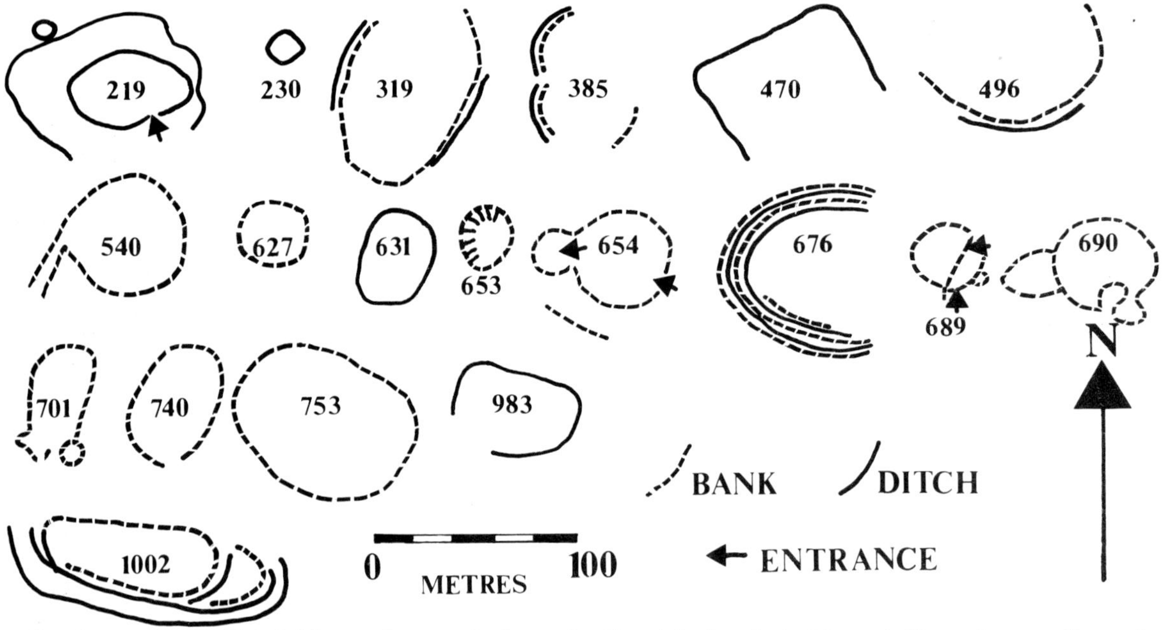

Fig.77 Plans of enclosure sites in Clwyd. The numbers used refer to the Clwyd Archaeological Record. These sites usually survive as slight earthworks or as crop-marks visible from the air.

medieval villages and farms. Knowledge of the commonest form of medieval settlement, therefore, is almost entirely deficient. Suitably forewarned of the considerable unresolved problems in this field let us proceed to the survey.

The Survey

A summary review of the existing documentation on small enclosures in Clwyd revealed a considerable degree of divergence in the quality of record for each site. The better examples usually comprised surviving earthworks discovered earlier this century; these had been described in one of Davies' volumes and possessed an Ordnance Survey card and plan at a scale of 1:2500. At the other end of the spectrum were references to vague 'enclosure marks' on aerial photographs; the latter, on examination, could often not be verified in the field since the site had been subsequently destroyed, with no plan ever having been made. In a few cases, even the aerial photograph could no longer be traced. It was apparent that there could be no objective criterion with which to distinguish likely antiquities from more spurious or enigmatic evidence. The aim of the survey was not only to present an inventory of putative iron age/romano-british small settlements, but also to be fairly conservative in selection, rejecting any truly ambiguous sites. Therefore a few enclosures, documented by other workers, have not been included. The end result is a considered but undeniably subjective group of 70 sites, divided by the reliability of the evidence into 60 'probables' and 10 'possibles'. Despite careful selection, the quality of data for each of the 60 'probables' still varies considerably. Well preserved examples will be represented by complete, upstanding earthworks, sometimes with internal 'hut' platforms and external associated field-systems.

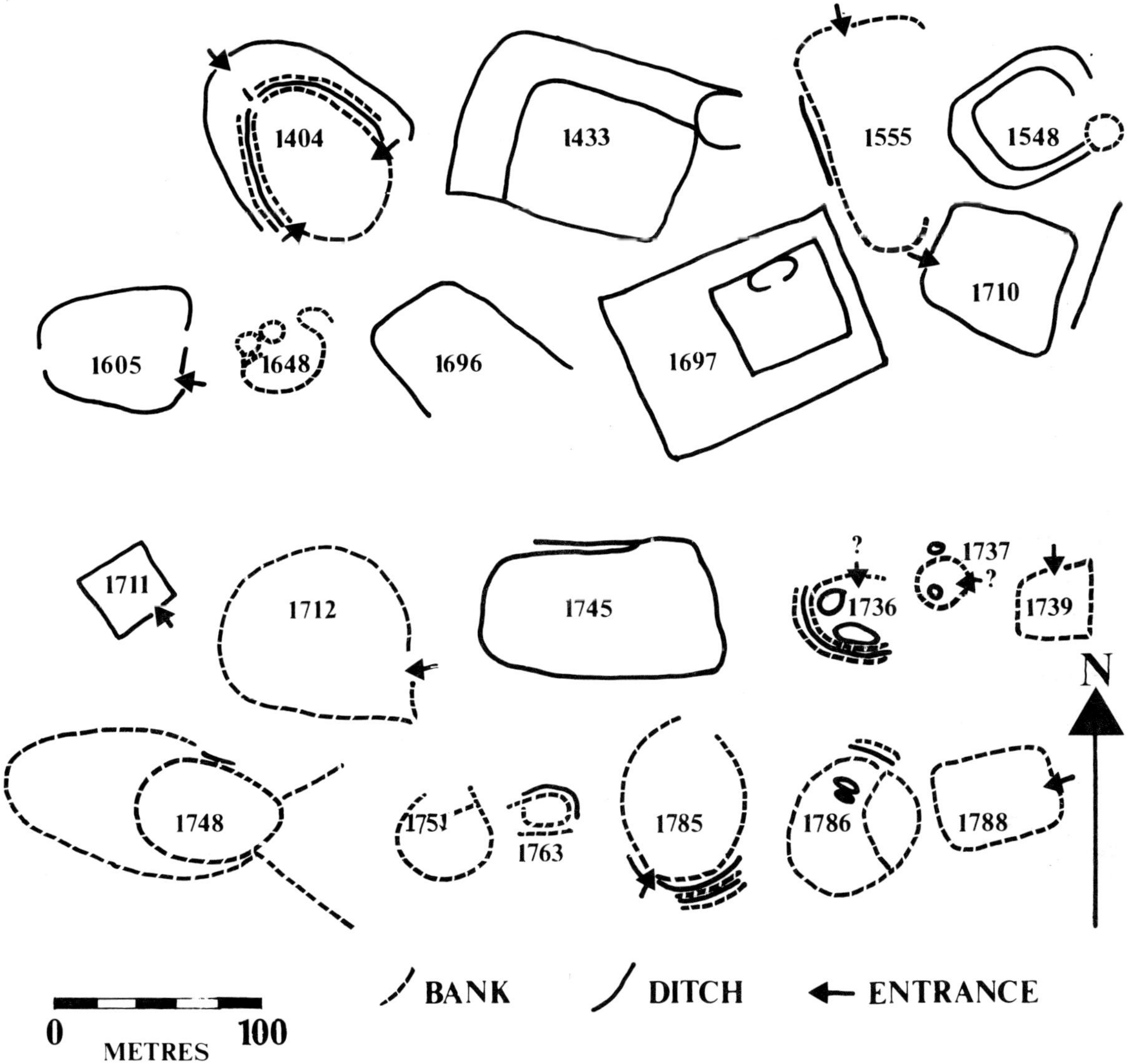

Fig.78 Plans of enclosure sites in Clwyd. The numbers used refer to the Clwyd Archaeological Record. Note the enclosure 1748 with its attached field boundaries.

Poorly preserved sites will be indicated, perhaps, by no more than an incomplete cropmark. Analysis in the subsequent section is perforce constrained to the available evidence and the current absence of a particular attribute does not necessarily imply an original absence of the same. Any analysis in this paper, however, will be restricted to the sample of 'probable' sites. Thus, of the 60 sites, 38 are here planned (albeit in 'sketch' form only) for the first time (Figs.77,78,79).

An element of subjectivity was also unavoidable in defining a 'small enclosure'. The basic connotation used here has been 'an area defined by an enclosing perimeter, large enough to *contain one or more buildings*'. Difficulties arise where some large enclosures may overlap with small hillforts and conversely where very small enclosures may be indistinguishable from large hut-circles. Similarly, as our requirement was a statement about small settlements, those sites that are morphologically small enclosures but functionally not thought to be settlements (eg large ring cairns) have been excluded.

Another factor clearly affecting the quality of the evidence is the varied amount of field walking or aerial survey carried out in the county, which must, in part, determine the quantity and distribution of known sites as shown in Fig.76. The concentration of enclosures at the north-western end of Halkyn Mountain may owe something to Davies' residence at nearby Whitford; the overall number in the Tanat Valley and the southern part of the Vale of Clwyd undoubtedly reflects Chris Musson's usual flight-range from his base in central Powys. Conversely, a paucity may reflect areas (eg the Maelor) where, owing to a combination of intensive agricultural practices in the past and the unresponsive nature of heavy soils in terms of cropmark formation, small earthworks are less likely to survive or be detected from the air. Lack of sites, therefore, is

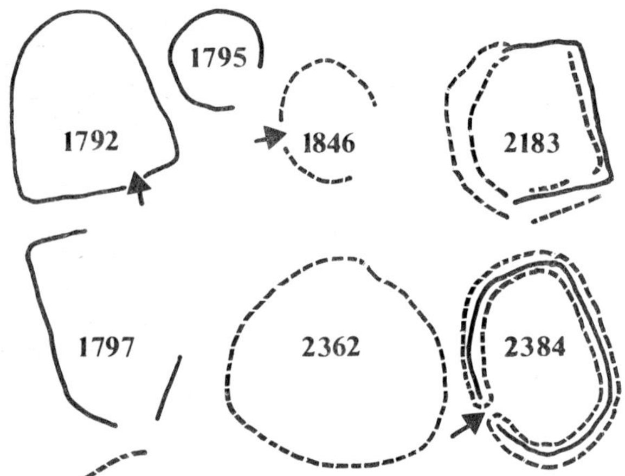

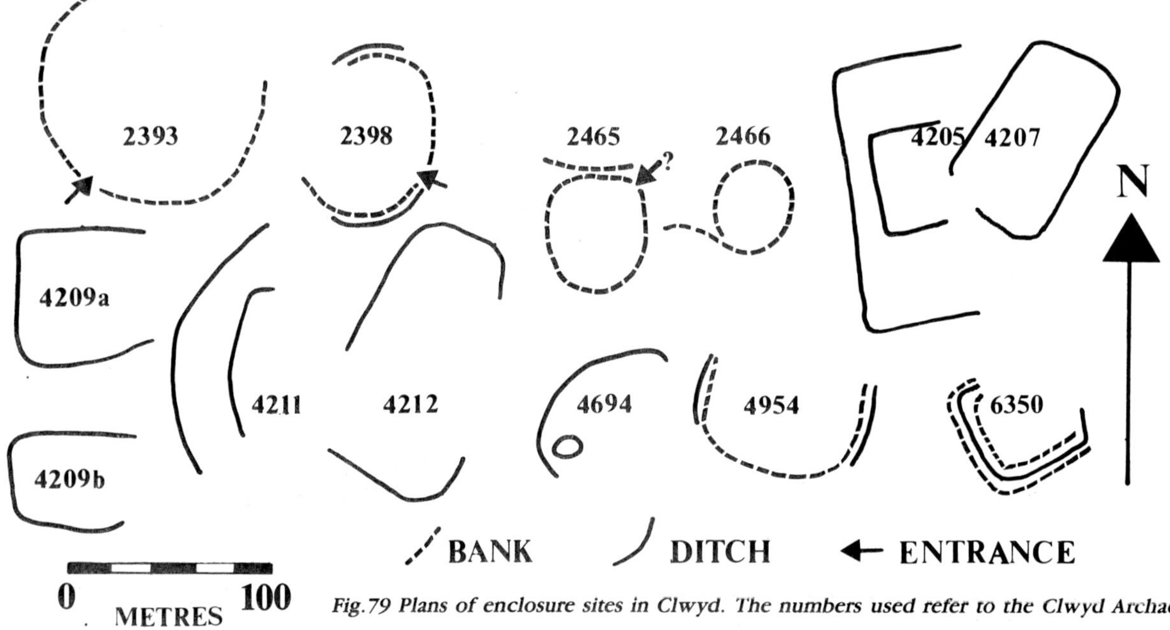

Fig.79 Plans of enclosure sites in Clwyd. The numbers used refer to the Clwyd Archaeological Record.

just as likely to indicate lack of survey or survival as lack of settlement.

The methodology of the survey was straightforward. All 70 sites were visited, described and provided with a 'sketch' plan measured by pacing, where no other published plan was available. (In practice many more sites were visited but were subsequently excluded from consideration for a variety of reasons). Sometimes 'sketch' plans were produced from aerial photographs or a combination of previously published plans and more recent photographs. The distribution of sites is shown in Fig.76 and individual plans in Figs.77-79. It is important to stress that none of the site plans made by the author is an accurate measured drawing. The conventions used on the plans follow those employed recently by the Royal Commission in England. Fuller site descriptions and aerial photographs have been lodged with the Clwyd Sites and Monuments Record, held by Clwyd County Council at Shire Hall, Mold.

Analysis

The sample of 60 small settlements can be considered with reference to a variety of variables. While not claiming any statistical validity for the following exercise the categories do provide some approximate descriptive parameters within which the nature of the data can be more easily appreciated.

Altitude: The contrasting altitude of small enclosures, hillforts and Roman sites in Clwyd are presented in Fig.80. The enclosures show little altitudinal preference within the band 0-400m OD. The hillforts (37 in number) likewise show no overall preference for a particular altitude. Comparison with the enclosures, however, does reveal a slight difference. Whereas the enclosures are contained entirely within the band 0-400m OD, the hillforts occupy a slightly more elevated niche,

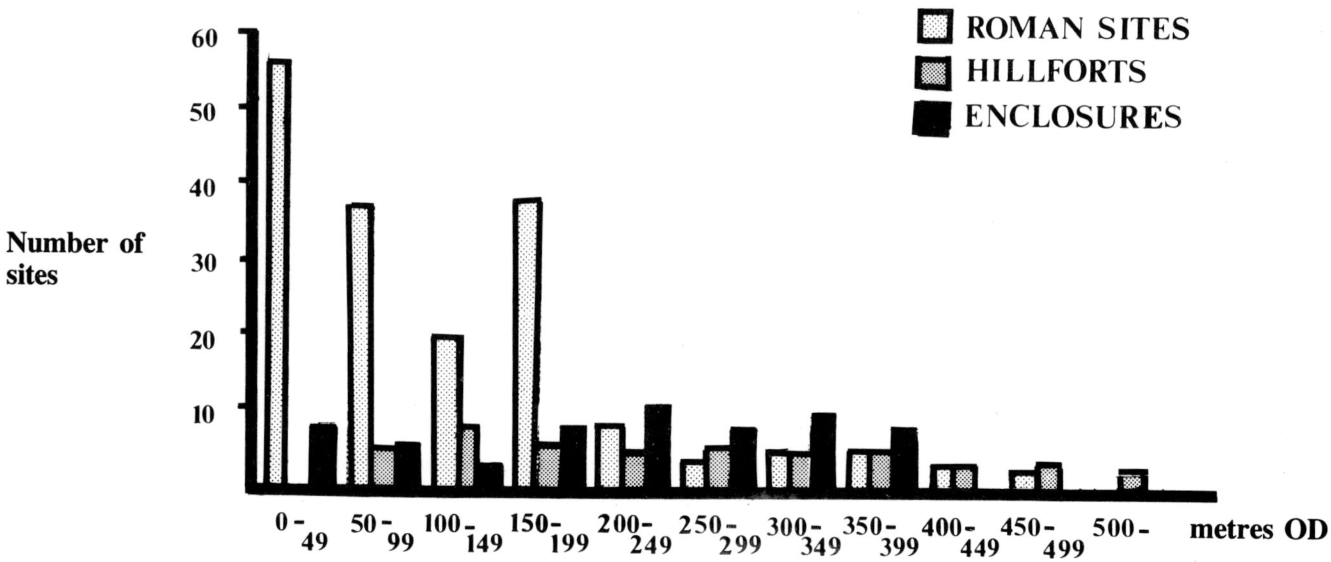

Fig.80 This diagram illustrates the contrasting altitude of Roman sites, hillforts and enclosures. Roman sites are predominantly low lying, while enclosures lie at altitudes more similar to those of hillforts.

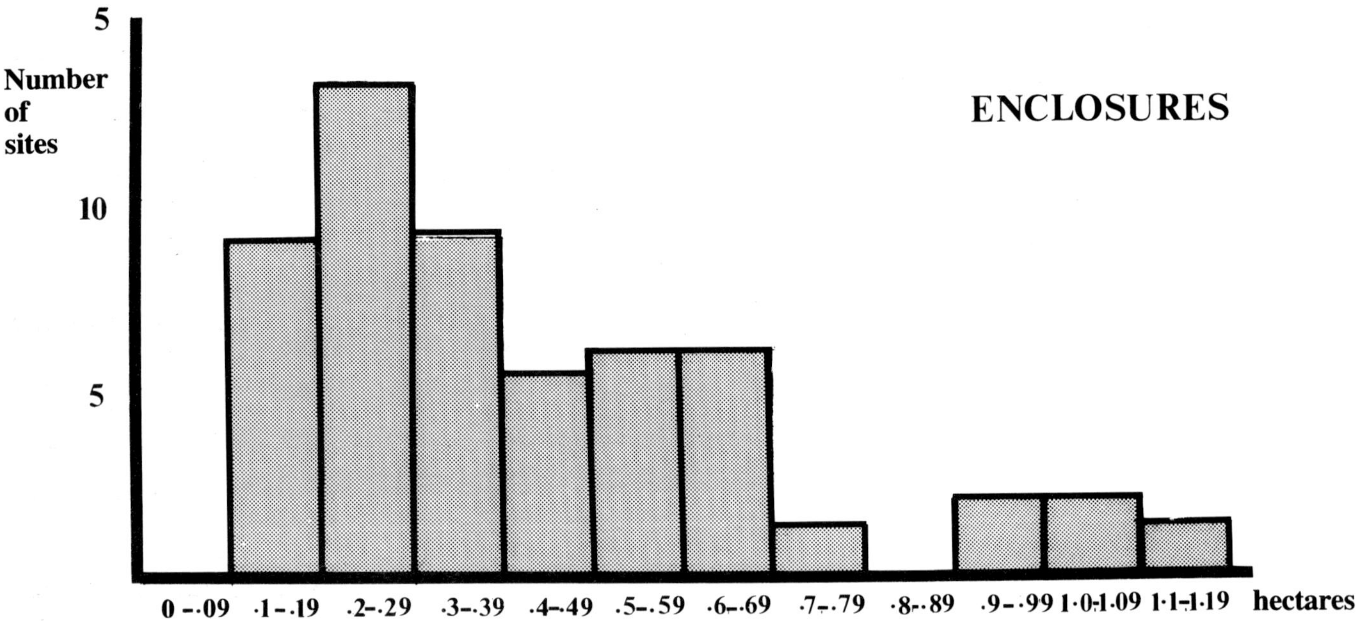

Fig.81 This diagram shows the internal area of the small enclosures studied. The majority of enclosures are 0.5 hectares or smaller.

between 50 and 500m OD; (the highest place in Clwyd is Moel Sych, on the Berwyns at 827m OD). The Roman sites, on the other hand, provide a not unexpected complete contrast; the majority are below 150m OD, reflecting the predominant bias towards a coastal or valley-floor distribution. With regard solely to altitude, the small enclosures show greater affinity with the hillforts than with the Roman sites.

Area: The internal areas of the small enclosures are presented in Fig.81. (Where the enclosure is defined by more than one boundary the area is calculated to the inner perimeter). Clearly the distribution is skewed towards the smaller end of the range, with the majority of examples below 0.5ha in size. Comparison with the areas of Roman sites is not feasible since hardly any site is sufficiently well known to permit area calculation with any certainty. A limited comparison can be made, however, between the small enclosures and the areas of a sample of hillforts in Clwyd (31 of the latter allow area-estimation). There is an obvious separation; no hillfort is smaller than 0.5ha and indeed the majority fall between 1 and 5ha.

Shape: The shapes of the small enclosures are indicated on Figs. 77-79. Clearly a variety of configurations is represented, although it is wise to avoid an overly complex attempt to define specific groups. It is perhaps simplest to separate those examples whose perimeter is largely formed by *straight* boundaries from those formed by *curved* boundaries. Using this distinction 19 of the small enclosures fall into the former category, 41 into the latter.

Position: The defensive possibilities of the topographic situation of each enclosure are obviously of some importance. A non-defensive position is defined as one which is overlooked by adjacent, higher ground. According to this definition 41 of the examples are non-defensive. Of course, this may not accurately reflect the number of defendable enclosures, since the size of any man-made defences can more than compensate for a disadvantageous location (eg CAR 2384) while, conversely, not all well-sited enclosures may have made proper use of the terrain for its defensive possibilities (eg CAR 1736).

Form: The surviving forms of the monuments can be grouped under the headings earthwork, cropmark or stonework. In some cases these may be rather artificial distinctions, owing more to the present than past appearance of the site. Thus cropmarks can be near-destroyed earthworks, earthworks can mask underlying stoneworks and stoneworks may be denuded earthworks. Of our sample of enclosures, 32 can be classed as earthworks, 23 as cropmarks and 5 as stoneworks. It comes as no surprise to realise that form is partly determined by local geography and land-use. Cropmarks predominate in the cultivated lowlands, earthworks in the pastoral uplands and stoneworks cluster in the south-west of the county, where glacially-derived surface stone is plentiful.

Ancillary Features: Two aspects of the enclosures are considered under this heading, namely the presence of 'huts' or, in their absence, 'hut' platforms, and the existence of possibly contemporary field-systems. 'Huts' or 'platforms' have been noted at 15 sites. The clearest example of 'huts' is in the stonework CAR 1648 and of 'hut platforms' in the earthwork CAR 1748 (Figs.85,88). There are several uncertainties when considering these features, not the least of which is whether the 'hut platforms' actually supported 'huts'. On a more positive note, it seems that 'hut platforms' can be either internal (eg CAR 1404) or external (eg CAR 654).

Field systems that *may* be contemporary with the enclosures have been noted at 13 sites (Fig.89). Since it is apparent that many of these small enclosures have been damaged or destroyed (see below) the likelihood of attendant field-systems suffering a similar fate would seem considerably greater. Fields are, therefore, considerably under-represented. It was not within the resources of this study to plan such field systems. However, it is worth remarking that only in isolated examples (eg CAR 654 and CAR 1748) is there reasonable evidence for claiming contemporaneity between enclosure and field-system.

Rate of Discovery: It is interesting to note the increased rate of discovery of small enclosures in Clwyd. Taking the year 1978 as our reference point, 35 sites had been found up to and including that year, while 25 enclosures have come to light since. Of the latter, 12 are earthworks while 13 are cropmarks. The more rapid discovery rate over the last few years seems entirely a product of greater archaeological resources, both professional and amateur, that have been deployed in the county. Most of the 'new' sites have been located by aerial photography (eg Fig.87), although the presence of a considerable number of 'new' earthworks (eg Fig.86) indicated that these sites could still be found by the more traditional method of field walking.

One of the advantages of field walking in the 'highland zone' is the promise of 'new' earthwork or stonework discoveries which provides some compensation for the rather more restricted opportunities to fieldwalk ploughed fields for find-scatters. Indeed, the juxtaposition of hill and vale sometimes allows detection of a cropmark by the earth-bound archaeologist (eg CAR 219).

Condition: For the purpose of this analysis an attempt was made to describe the condition of the enclosures with respect to three rudimentary divisions — intact, damaged and near-destroyed. The first two terms each cover a considerable latitude. 'Intact' may refer to complete earthwork enclosures whose perimeter bank may survive to an impressive height or just a few centimetres — the 'intactness' here refers to the *complete circuit* of the enclosure rather than the degree of preservation of its boundary. 'Damaged' can encompass both large-scale disturbance on a small site and small-scale disturbance on a large one. 'Near-destroyed' tends to be applied to former earthworks that have now disappeared from the visible landscape and whose form is usually represented by an aerial photograph.

Of our sample of small enclosures, 14 are intact, 18 damaged and 27 near-destroyed (Fig.82). Such damage and destruction seems in part caused by the low priority these sites have enjoyed for scheduling as ancient monuments — only 14 of the 58 are legally protected (*c* 25%). A contrast with a sample of 33 hillforts in Clwyd is revealing: 12 are intact, 18 damaged and only 3 destroyed or near destroyed; 27 of these hillforts are scheduled, however (*c* 90%). Clearly a representative selection of both these types of monument is not being preserved. Small enclosures seem to merit less protection perhaps because they are relatively insubstantial and because they cannot be so easily dated or classified by diagnostic morphology. They also survive less well since some of them are situated on agriculturally productive land where the destructive effects of cultivation are most marked. We may legitimately ask, therefore, whether the low rate of scheduling *reflects* the poor state of preservation or whether preservation is determined by the rate of scheduling. These two causal relationships are not mutually exclusive however, and the truth probably lies in a simultaneous interplay of the two factors.

Subdivisions: If more than one variable is considered (eg shape, size and form) obvious similarities appear between some of the sites.

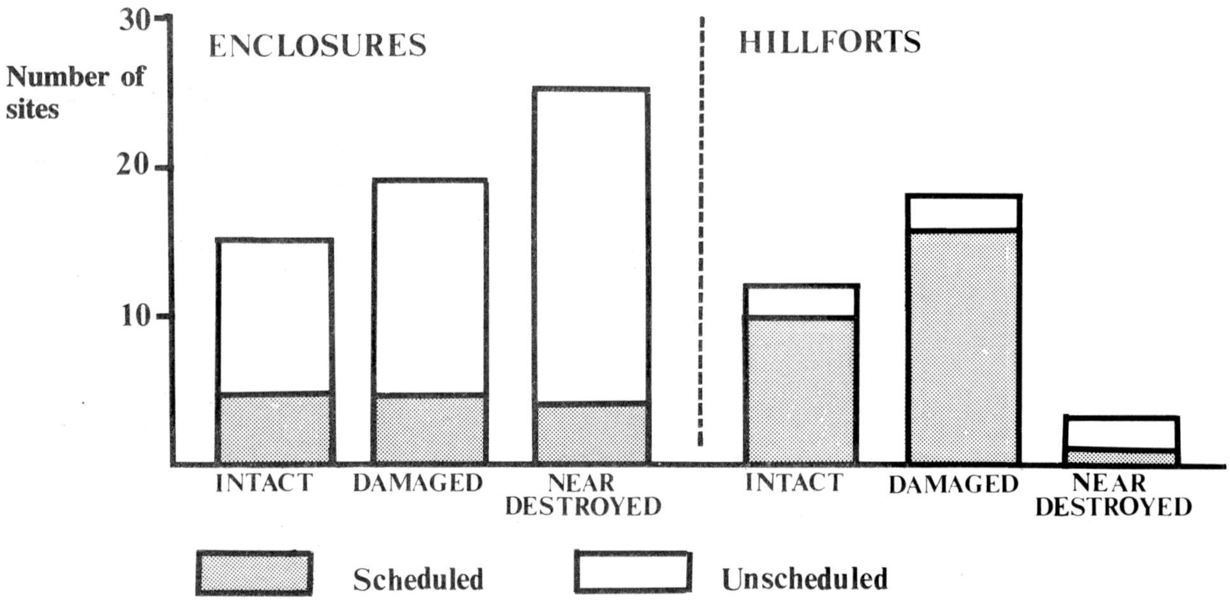

Fig.82 These diagrams graphically show the low rate of scheduling of enclosures contrasted with that of hillforts, and their poorer state of preservation.

Very rectangular, double-perimeter enclosures are represented by CAR 1697 and 4205. Less rectangular double perimeter examples can be seen in CAR 1548 and 1433. Oval inner and outer enclosures, the former eccentrically placed within the latter, are in evidence in CAR 1404 and 1748. Peripheral stone 'huts' associated with stone enclosures are found at CAR 689, 690, 701 and 1648. Whether these subdivisions have any other than taxonomic value is problematic.

Discussion

Still holding (for the lack of any evidence to the contrary) to the premiss that the majority of our sample belongs in the iron age and romano-british periods, some tentative discussion can be pursued by two distinct approaches. The first is to contrast the distribution of enclosures in Clwyd with the iron age and romano-british settlement patterns as established by *other* forms of archaeological evidence. The second is to compare our enclosures with those in other areas of Britain.

Accepting the assumption concerning the likely date of the majority of the 60 enclosures it follows that all or most of the sites could be either iron age or romano-british or, indeed, through lengthy occupation, belong to both periods. There seems little reason to anticipate that a makeshift comparison between Fig.76 and either Fig.83 or 84 will provide significant and previously unsuspected dimensions to this study. Yet there are assertions that both large iron age centres and Roman sites can affect the spatial distribution of contemporary smaller settlements. These claims provide some justification for the following exercise.

The iron age map (Fig.83) is dominated by hillforts. With such substantial sites we can have some confidence that the present distribution reasonably reflects the past, since total hillfort destruction would appear to be an infrequent occurrence (with the exception of Dinorben — CAR 2037B) while the very size of such sites facilitates their recognition. Topographically, hillforts are generally situated close to the upland/lowland divide and central to neither, their locations seem to effect a compromise between the need for a defensive vantage point and access to lowland agricultural zones as well as upland pasture. Predilection for valley-side positions are attested by the sites lining the Tanat Valley and the vales of Llangollen and Clwyd. This tendency is no more clearly demonstrated than by the hillforts of Caer Ddunod — CAR 620 and Cerrig Gwynion — CAR 926, both of them adopting identical situations — the principal access route into an upland massif.

Turning to the respective locations of hillforts and enclosures, the limited number of both types of sites only permits the most simplistic of comparisons. We can but ask, therefore, whether there is a positive, neutral or negative spatial correlation between the two. The answer can only be hedged with qualifications. Some hillforts (eg Moel y Gaer — CAR 265D) are considerably distanced from the nearest enclosures while some enclosures (eg Glol — CAR 2362 — *et al*) are some way from neighbouring hillforts. Conversely, in certain cases, it is tempting to see an association. In particular, hillfort-enclosure(s) pairings may emerge (eg CAR 643-1748 *et al*; 761B-1788, 1404; 1101A-1785; 999-1002; 2300A-219; 2087A-1712; 2037B-1736, 1737). Of course, it is not sufficient to simply note an apparently positive spatial correlation, at least for a proportion of the sites. The critical questions concern the reason(s) for such a pattern. It would be entirely misleading, in the present light of our knowledge, to conjure up some socio-economic relationship between contemporary hillfort and enclosure as the

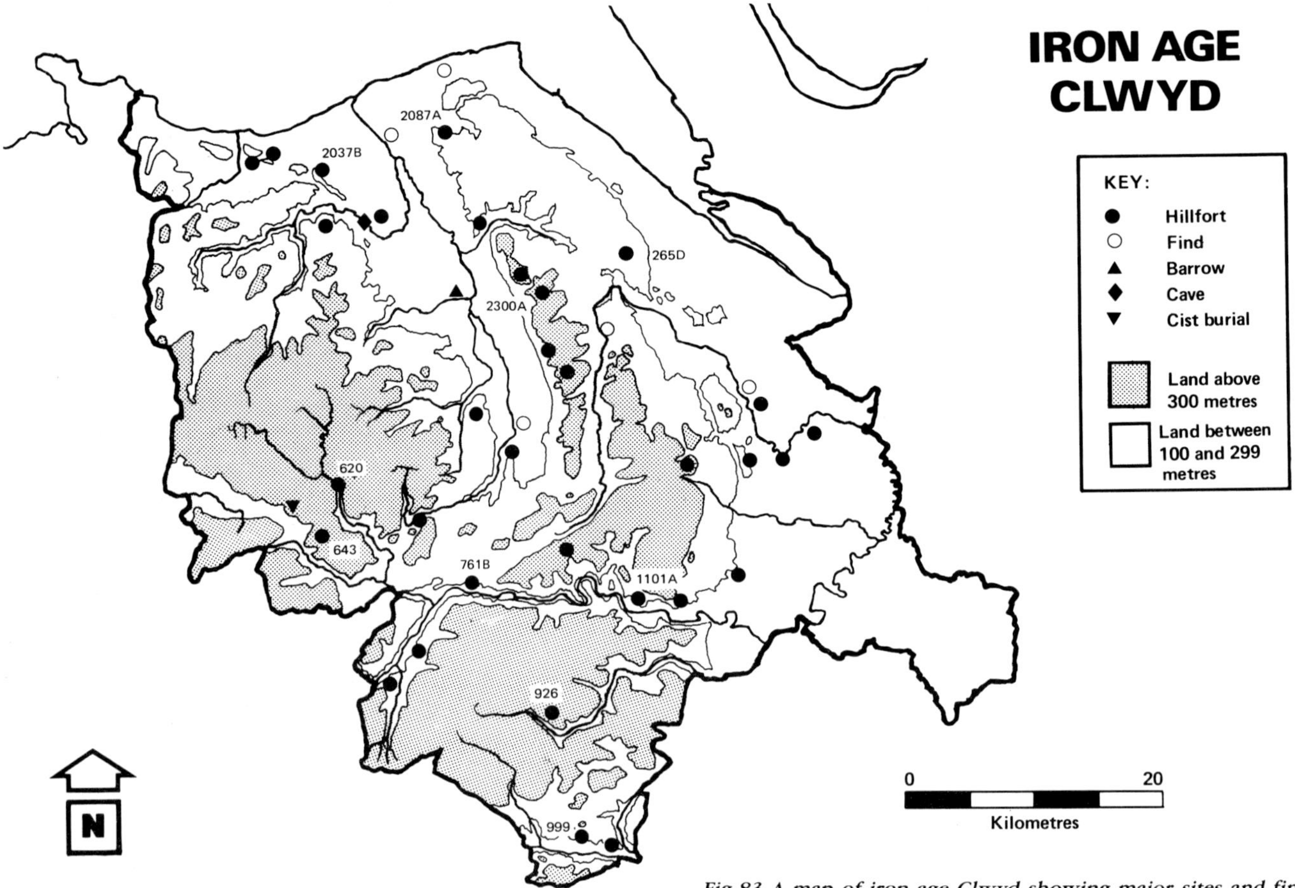

Fig.83 A map of iron age Clwyd showing major sites and finds.

accounting factor. Both hillforts and enclosures were seemingly attracted to locations within or peripheral to good agricultural land. It may well be the amount of the latter that is the common, unifying variable.

As a portrayal of the original spatial extent of activity during the romano-british period Fig.84 is not to be trusted. What it does portray reasonably accurately is the extremely circumscribed nature of our information and the limited amount of research and excavation that has hitherto taken place. The majority of known sites comprise find-spots of portable artefacts; most of these are chance finds which, owing to the circumstance of their discovery and the restricted data that they can convey *per se*, furnish few indications of the character of the sites from which they may have originated (eg CAR 2213). Nevertheless, the majority of finds display a bias towards the coast which may well reflect the real intensity of Roman activity along the seaboard, while the occurrence of artefacts within former iron age hillforts probably tells us more about continuing 'native' presence rather than an upland penetration of Romanised citizenry.

The more substantial centres of Roman activity are only understood in parts: Holt (CAR 1177) as a tilery for the XXth legion: Ffrith (CAR 19) as an industrial? complex; Flint (CAR 115) as a lead working/management depot and Prestatyn (CAR 2228) as presumed port and industrial site, again perhaps associated with the exploitation of nearby mineral resources. The known emphasis is clearly on the military locations and metal industries rather than any flourishing civilian sector, whether urban or rural. The influence of these major Roman centres on the distribution of small enclosures seems marginal; none of the four complexes has significant concentrations of enclosures in its immediate vicinity in contrast to the concentrations near the forts at Caersws and Forden Gaer. On the other hand there are specific clusters of small enclosures (eg CAR 1748 *et al*) which are quite removed from the nearest Roman site. There are some apparent correlations between enclosures and Roman finds (eg CAR 1710, 1745, 4205-810, 821, 4525) but the uncertainty surrounding the significance of the Roman material precludes any useful discussion. The road network during this period in north-east Wales is only partially known, and is not shown on Fig.84; its relationship to small enclosures cannot readily be ascertained. Indeed, the recently reviewed line from **Varis** to **Canovium** effectively by-passes most of the known Roman sites in this area of the county.

In pursuing our second approach it is possible to review briefly the evidence from small enclosures in Wales and select regions of England, and ultimately to compare and contrast the wider situation with this aspect of the archaeology of present-day Clwyd. A similar survey to the current one was carried out in the upper Severn in Powys. There, 53 enclosures were described (although a quarter of these could be termed hillforts). Of 45 sites tabulated, more than half (23) were less than 0.4ha in area. Apart from two exceptions all were close to arable land and a general tendency to cluster in the vicinity of hillforts was observed. A continuum of occupation from the iron age to the romano-british period was envisaged. The quantity of such sites in this area has been considerably increased through aerial photography although the same fundamental imponderables, such as date and function, remain. Where small enclosures have been excavated important evidence has been forthcoming. The complete stripping of the interior of the hillslope enclosure at Collfryn, in north Powys, has revealed iron age occupation followed by internal ditched divisions, not necessarily reflecting settlement, between the second and fourth centuries AD. Small-scale excavation of a double-ditched enclosure at Arddleen indicated occupation during the earlier Roman period. A remarkable concentration of undated enclosures lies immediately to the north of the Roman auxiliary fort at Forden Gaer. To what extent such a proliferation is a product of a combination of optimum viewing conditions and repeated flying, rather than a Roman phenomenon is difficult to judge.

In Glamorgan 22 sites are described by the Royal Commission as 'univallate enclosures in positions unsuited to defence'. All are small, ranging from a little over 0.2ha in area down to about 0.05ha, and although now ringed by slight enclosing earthworks, excavation has shown that, in some cases, the ramparts were much more substantial (eg Llwynheiernin). 'Hut platforms' can sometimes be observed (eg Hardings Down North). Most of the sites were probably farmsteads although specific functions and dates are largely unknown. In addition, it is possible to cite the 11 'multivallate enclosures with wide-spaced ramparts' as examples of a distinctive type of small enclosure, the inter-rampart space being traditionally interpreted as a

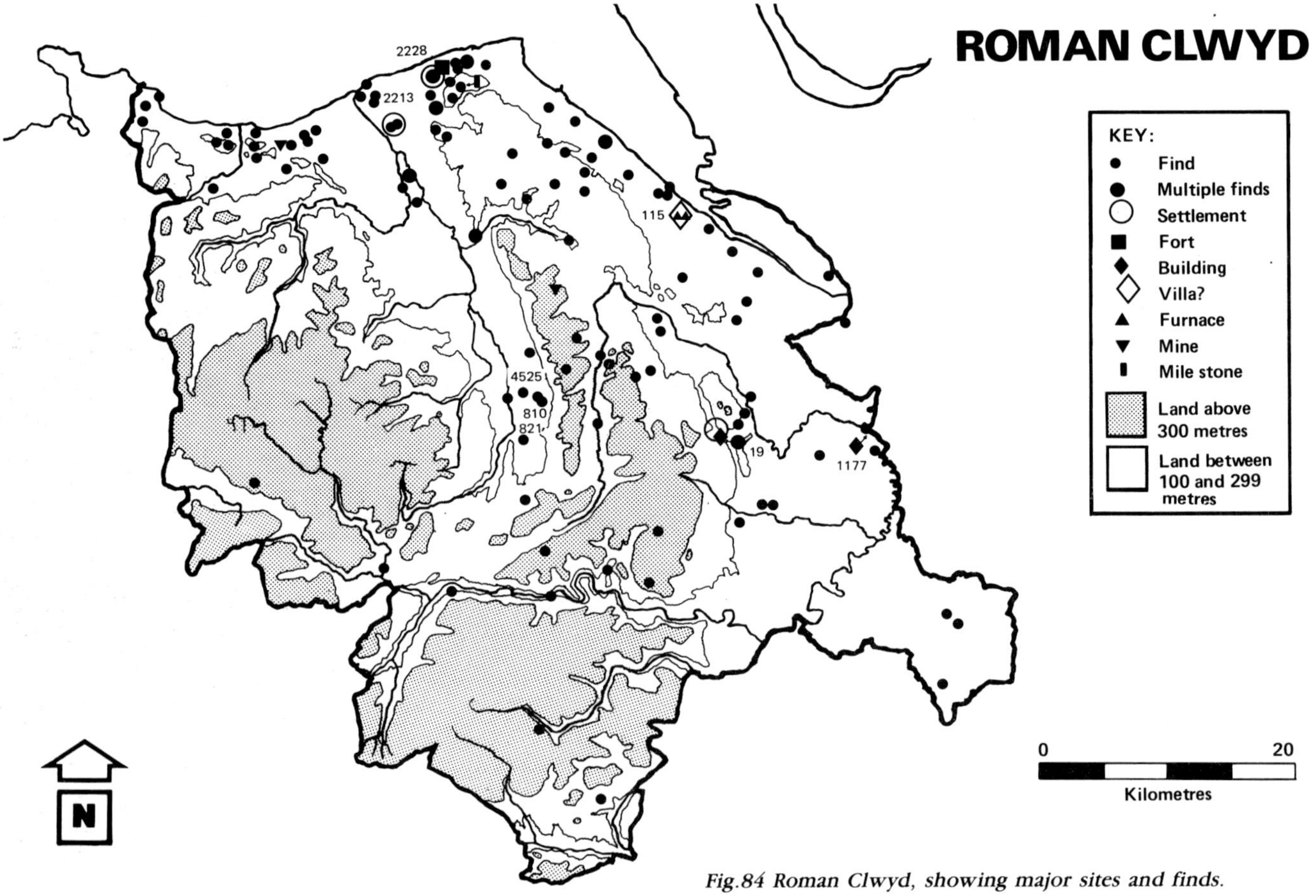

Fig.84 Roman Clwyd, showing major sites and finds.

livestock corral. A variety of shapes is represented in the total of 33 examples; most, however, occupy a zone sandwiched between the coast proper and the upland interior. While all of the previous enclosures are described by the Commission in the iron age section of its volume, an enclosure in the Roman part of the publication, Whitton Lodge, provides the most illuminating evidence. Here a timber farmstead of the first century BC sat within a small, approximately square enclosure. In the early second century AD the interior of the site was transformed into ranges of rectangular stone buildings around a central courtyard, a rather typical Roman 'villa'. Similar sequences demonstrating the transition from iron age to romano-british settlement have been attested at Caldicot and Biglis.

In south-west Wales the general context of small enclosures is quite different from the south-east. In the south-west both the iron age tradition of large hillfort construction and the influence of Roman civilian settlement are considerably less in evidence and, indeed, the further west one goes the more evident this pattern appears. In the old county of

Fig.85 An aerial view of the enclosure 1748 at Bryn Teg, Cerrigydrudion. It is possible to see contemporary field boundaries associated with the perimeter of the site.

Carmarthenshire the majority of non-defensively situated enclosures have been described as hillslope ring-works. These are generally small, univallate and weakly embanked; oval or circular plans are most common, although sub-rectangular plans are also found. It is possible that such a proliferation of small enclosures occurred during the later phases of the iron age. Defensively sited single enclosures ('small hillforts') are more variable in date, size and vallation but the smaller examples show affinity with their non-defensive counterparts. The majority of sites which have produced evidence of romano-british occupation are the defended enclosures, although there are reasonable grounds for suspecting that most of these may be pre-Roman in origin. Indeed most of the small enclosures excavated as part of a thematic project by the Dyfed Archaeological Trust show continuing occupation or use into the Roman period (eg Drim; Castell Henllys; Woodside Camp and Dan-y-Coed). Such 'Romanised' phases

Fig.86 Aerial view of Gwaenysgor enclosure near Prestatyn.

Fig.87 Plas Uchaf enclosure, Llangedwyn, Clwyd.

Fig.88 An artist's reconstruction of life 'down on the farm' for an iron age extended family over 2,000 years ago. The reconstruction is based on the Bryn Teg enclosure.

at typologically 'native' sites should not necessarily be taken as an indicator of settlement continuity. A panoply of episodic periods of disuse or functional change with possible concomitant alterations and dislocations of personnel is perhaps nearer reality, a reality still largely resistant to the increasingly sophisticated gamut of archaeological detection. Conversely, the paucity of finds from excavated enclosures of south-west Wales makes it hazardous to dismiss occupation or use of the site on the evidence of a lack of relevant small finds (cf Woodbarn Rath).

The preponderance of small stone enclosures with associated stone structures in Gwynedd is the characteristic feature of the archaeology of north-west Wales. These have been studied, surveyed and examined by a variety of workers and by the Royal Commission. That most of them were small farming establishments seems a reasonable assumption although the period(s) and duration(s) of such activity are still largely uncertain. The conventional view was that most of these sites represented native agricultural undertakings during the Roman occupation, with qualifications of putative earlier or later phases. Griffiths saw some of the upland variety as possibly bronze age in date, while recent excavations on the Holyhead Mountain hut-circles at Tŷ Mawr indicate a principal phase of occupation in the iron age. Pant-y-Saer, of course, has for a considerable time been held as an example of a sub-Roman or dark age stone enclosure, although reservations are now frequently expressed about the certainty of such

Fig.89 A bird's-eye view of an enclosure and associated fields at Craigfechan, Llanfihangel Glyn Myfyr, Clwyd.

a date. Recent excavations at Moel y Gerddi and Erw Wen, both circular enclosures with centrally placed circular huts, have produced evidence of occupation confined to the iron age, while the more substantial rectangular enclosure at Cefn Graeanog indicates activity continuing into the romano-british period and possibly beyond. Some earthwork enclosures do exist in the area (eg the rectangular enclosure at Llifad and the small circular earthwork in the same parish, in a field rather unimaginatively called Cae Trenches — both on Anglesey); but these are generally undated and can add little to our present discussion.

It remains, briefly, to consider similar evidence beyond Wales. One region that has been well served by surveys is Wessex. In a study area of some 4,050 sq.km, 437 enclosures were identified and divided into four basic shape-types: curvilinear, D-shaped, rectilinear and polygonal. With respect to internal area there was a distinct clustering of sites below

0.4ha, with a gradual spread up to 0.9ha, followed by an evenly distributed scatter beyond. In an interesting attempt to extract more detailed information from aerial photographic data, Palmer tried to distinguish settlement from non-settlement enclosures, using the criterion of the presence or absence of internal pits, 'splodges', hut-traces or minor ditched features. Following this exercise a model was suggested of settlements at 600m intervals, with each major site having a number of non-settlement enclosures in its catchment, the latter being likened to 'farm outbuildings'.

Chronologically, rectilinear sites were seen as early and late iron age, while D-shaped and curvilinear examples occurred both during the iron age and romano-british period. The number of unenclosed settlements identified by Palmer is probably an underestimate since this type of site is much more difficult to locate from the air. However, they do serve as a salutary reminder that the small settlements dimension may not solely be restricted to small enclosed sites. Lastly, Cunliffe has attempted to determine what section of the populace lived in, and farmed from, small enclosures. Using the analogy of Celtic society in Ireland during the first millennium AD — which basically depicts a tribal population differentiated by occupational rôles but linked by clientship — freemen are suggested as the likely occupants. The latter may have supplied an agricultural tithe to the nobles and chief within the neighbouring major hillfort in return for military protection, exotic artefacts and religious services. Further to the west, in Cornwall, the study of small enclosures, as in Clwyd, is in its infancy. An impressive recent survey, which justifiably concentrated on presenting the basic evidence rather than formulating conclusions, identified a total of 630 defensible enclosed settlements from the iron age and romano-british period, covering a wide variety of types.

Postscript

The approach adopted in this paper has been a conservative one: to collect, arrange and display the currently available data on small enclosures rather than to attempt much by way of analysis. It might have been possible to pursue the chronological attribution of some sites a little harder — perhaps suggesting CAR 4205 and 1697 as Roman and 1748 and 1404 as iron age — but our overall gain in understanding would have been minimal. One comparative statistic that does emerge from the study is the large number of small enclosures, less than 0.5ha in area, in Clwyd, the upper Severn, Wessex and no doubt elsewhere. We can be increasingly certain, however, of three factors. Firstly that many more small enclosures remain to be discovered. Secondly that many of them will provide evidence of use both in the pre-Roman and Roman periods. Thirdly, that the impact of Roman rule in the largely military zone of Wales did not produce extensive small settlement dislocation, although its effect on the movement of people is much harder to determine. Small enclosures, then, are likely to represent a 'native' or indigenous stable element in the overall settlement pattern. If we are to proceed further — from data to analysis, from evidence to interpretation — some of the enclosures in Clwyd need to be adequately excavated, and more need to be discovered so that our distribution plans are more reliable. The Dyfed Archaeological Trust, through its small enclosure project, has already demonstrated the value of a thematically conceived research-within-rescue approach, and it is obvious that such an exercise in Clwyd could produce similar gains. Only by such application can we begin to get a more balanced view of the iron age and romano-british period in north-east Wales.

Acknowledgements

This survey was largely based on information extracted from the Clwyd Sites and Monuments Record. I am grateful to Stephen Grenter, the Clwyd SMR Officer, for assistance in the initial selection of sites and for the computer drawn distribution maps that formed the template for the hand drawn Figs.76, 83 and 84. I owe special thanks to Charles Evans-Gunther who drew all the figures. Chris Musson and George Williams kindly offered comments on a first draft of this paper.

THE ROMANO-BRITISH PERIOD
by Kevin Blockley

Few large-scale excavations have been undertaken on romano-british sites in Clwyd and the known sites may be counted on the fingers of two hands. The vast majority of the finds have been made along the north coast (Fig.90), with a scatter of finds in mid-Clwyd. Upland areas, west of the Vale of Clwyd and south of Corwen are virtually devoid of archaeological finds of a Roman date.

This paper will summarise what is known of Roman Clwyd, especially from recent excavations, and put forward some general conclusions and suggestions for future work in the area.

Historical Background

The iron age tribe governing the area of northern Clwyd, the Deceangli, controlled a territory which extended eastwards as far as the river Dee and westwards to the river Conwy. The remaining southern area of Clwyd may have lain in the northern section of land occupied by the Ordovices.

A Roman campaign of AD 49, led by Ostorius Scapula, was devoted to an attack on the Deceangli, but this was halted to attend to a Brigantian revolt. Two campaigns by Suetonius Paulinus in AD 58-9 are presumed to have been fought against the Silures, and Ordovices or Deceangli. A later campaign in AD 60, capturing Anglesey, certainly suggests that the Deceangli were no longer a threat at that time. To the south, the Ordovices rebelled in AD 78 but were suppressed by forces under Julius Agricola.

Military Occupation

No Roman forts are known in Clwyd, although perhaps two or even three await discovery. Strategic sites where forts may be expected are St.Asaph, Corwen and Ruthin.

The first, St.Asaph is suggested as the site of **Varis**, mentioned in the *Antonine Itinerary for Britain*, under Iter XI. Excavations by Dr. J.L. Davies in the grounds of Old Canonry, St.Asaph, failed to locate any romano-british occupation, but pottery and tile fragments have been found west of the A541 (SJ 045 731) and to the south near Bryn Polyn. It seems likely therefore that the location of **Varis** should be sought near H.M. Stanley Hospital or Bryn Polyn, on the summit of a ridge between the rivers Clwyd and Elwy.

The Corwen area is a further strategic location — a fort may have been situated where the Caer Gai to Chester **(Deva)** and St.Asaph to Corwen Roman roads converged to cross the river Alwen some 1500m west of Corwen. A fragment of a Twentieth Legion antefix tile and supposed Roman building have been found at Corwen.

The third possible site for a fort is at Ruthin. Several sherds of pottery were found at Ruthin Hospital, representing at least two small jars (Fig.91) — probably produced at the Holt depot. The vessels are datable to the late first-to-mid-second century AD and are indicative of a grave group in a cremation cemetery. Dr. Davies has argued that such cremations must, in a Welsh context, be military and has postulated that the site of a possible fort lies 400m north-east of the findspot on raised ground now occupied by Ruthin School and its grounds. Excavations in advance of development at Brynhyfryd Park, east of Ruthin Hospital, have produced further Roman pottery.

One probable marching camp is known at Penrhos, west of Corwen. The north, east and west sides of the camp are recorded, measuring some 312m by 440m. No finds are known but it is likely that the camp was built in the Scapulan campaign of AD 49.

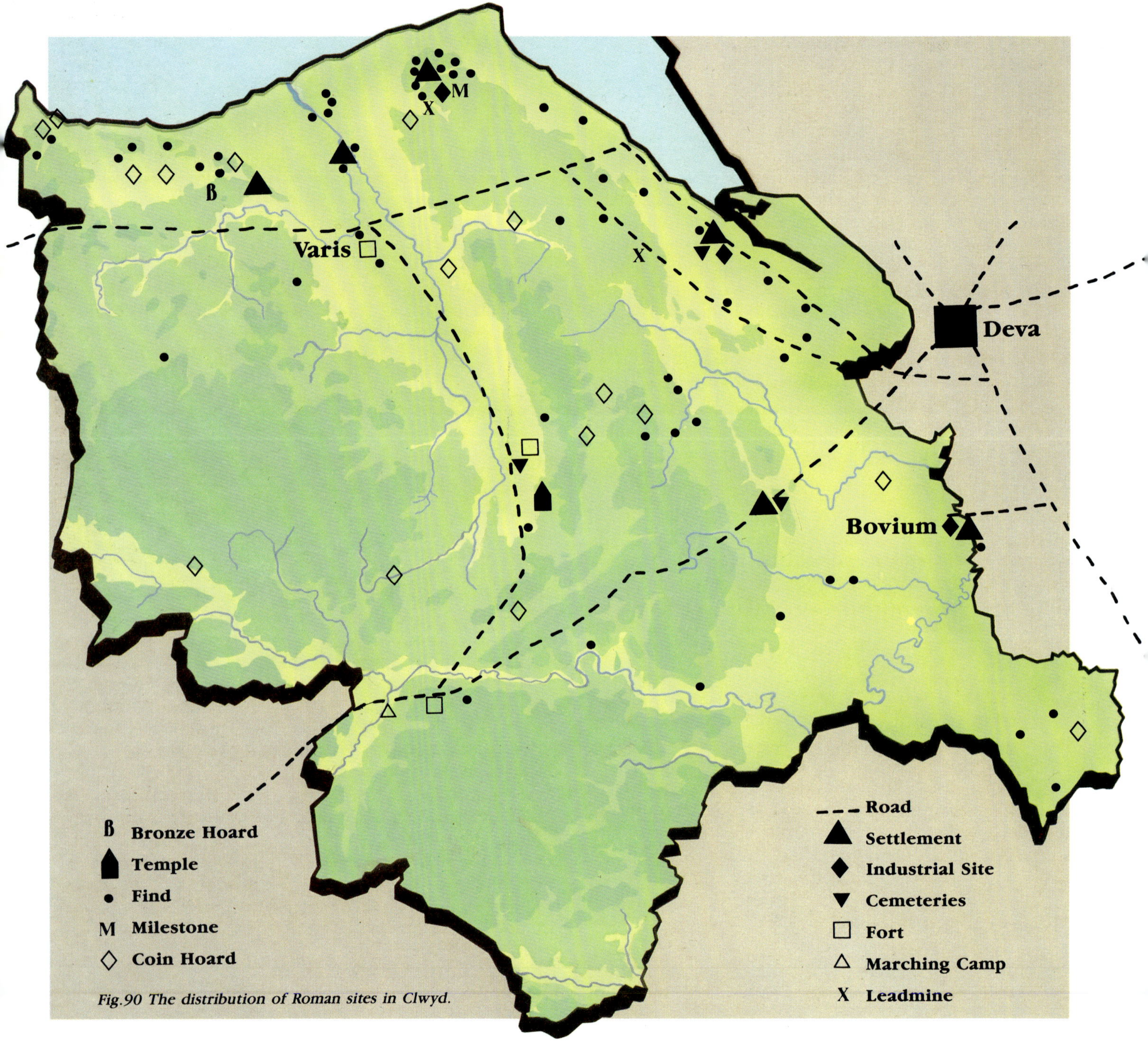

Fig.90 The distribution of Roman sites in Clwyd.

A number of sites have produced stamped tiles of the Twentieth Legion, which was based at Chester from *c* AD 88, and indicate military activity, but not necessarily the sites of auxiliary forts. Such tiles have been found at Corwen, Ffrith, Flint and Prestatyn, but only one of these sites (Corwen) is thought to be near the site of a fort.

Legionary Works depot at Holt

The Legionary works depot at Holt **(Bovium)** was situated on the west bank of the river Dee. It was noted in the *Antonine Itinerary for Britain* under Iter II ten Roman miles from Chester. At least one auxiliary unit, Cohors I Sunicorum, used the depot.

Excavations conducted by the late Mr. T.A. Acton between 1907 and 1915 revealed an area of workshops, drying sheds and kilns for the production of pottery and tile, and a group of domestic buildings largely situated inside a walled enclosure. The depot was producing ceramic roofing tiles and pottery from *c* AD 90 to *c* AD 125 in a number of kilns. Two workshops were identified — one a throwing shed, the other a drying shed with store room.

The latter lay adjacent to a rectangular double-flue kiln. South-east of this group was a bank of seven rectangular kilns, six of which were fired from a common stokehole. An eighth kiln, circular in plan and probably producing pottery, was added when one of the rectangular kilns went out of use. Products ranged from the roofing tiles, some bearing the stamp of the Twentieth Legion (LEG XX VV), to coarse pottery such as mortaria, jars and bowls and fine wares with mica-dusted or glazed surfaces.

Domestic accommodation in the walled enclosure comprised three barrack blocks, one with centurion's quarters at the east end — perhaps for a legionary officer. Stephens has argued that the barrack block with centurion's quarters was for *c* 80 men whilst the smaller ones may have been for slaves. A further possible explanation is that one of these buildings may have been a stable block — undoubtedly a necessity for the distribution of the finished products. Also inside the compound were probable store buildings and a latrine. Two buildings just outside the compound were interpreted as a bath-building and a supposed dwelling house. The latter is now thought to have been a second bath-house.

Fig.91 A Roman pot found at Ruthin; it was probably made at the Roman potteries at Holt. The vessel originally contained a cremation, perhaps of a Roman soldier, who died in the first or second centuries AD.

Roman Roads

The Roman road system was undoubtedly developed by the military to link auxiliary forts in North Wales. Three roads are known, one linking Chester with Caernarfon and mentioned in the *Antonine Itinerary for Britain* under Iter XI. The other roads link Chester with the fort at Caer Gai (Gwynedd), and the Holt depot with Watling Street. A further postulated road is suggested along Halkyn Mountain to Holywell, where it probably joined the coast road, and may perhaps be seen as an early access road to the lead mines. These are considered in detail by Margary and need not be discussed here.

Several years ago the course of a possible Roman road was noted in the Vale of Clwyd, but this has still to be verified. It is, however, likely to be a sound hypothesis, since such a route would have been needed to link the postulated forts near St.Asaph and Corwen.

A Roman milestone was found at Gwaenysgor in 1956. It is 1.1m long and 0.3m wide and may be dated to AD 231-5. The stone is assumed to have come from the Roman road 6km south of its findspot.

Lead Mining and Processing

Halkyn Mountain was rich in veins and cross-courses of galena (lead ore) and these deposits were no doubt worked in Roman times. It is, however, difficult to prove which of them were Roman workings because of later mining. Romano-british objects have been found in the Talar Goch mine in Meliden, Dyserth, and it is likely that a number of mines were situated along Halkyn Mountain. Graham Webster has considered at length the subject of lead mining in North Wales and more recently Clement Whittick has reappraised the evidence.

The earliest lead ingots or pigs from Clwyd are dated AD 74 and it is highly unlikely that lead ore was being processed in Clwyd before the area was under military control around AD 60. Of the eight pigs noted by Webster, five were cast in the time of Vespasian, one under Domitian and two are undated. One of the undated pigs, found at Carmel, bore the name C. Nipius Ascanius (C. NIPI. ASCANI) indicating a private lessee was working in the area. It is possible that the Carmel pig was produced in the mid-60s before the imperial control of the mines was organised (Fig.92).

Fig.92 An undated lead 'pig' or ingot found during the construction of Carmel School, Holywell. It was possibly produced in the mid-60's AD, prior to the imperial control of the mines. The name of Nipius Ascanius indicates a private leesee. Ascanius is the first named historical figure from Clwyd.

Processing of the galena was certainly undertaken in the Pentre-Oakenholt area of Flint. Here several smelting furnaces have been excavated since 1840. Parts of at least three masonry buildings lay adjacent to the furnaces, but they need not all have been industrial. One building in particular yielded fragments of painted wall-plaster and box-flue tiles. Pottery found on the excavations indicates that occupation was continuous from *c* AD 85/90 to the late second century. Limited occupation of the late third/early fourth century and late fourth century is indicated by the pottery. A variety of interesting copper-alloy personal items have been found including toilet implements, brooches, finger rings, keys and two seal-box lids.

An extensive building complex was excavated at Pentre Farm, Flint in 1976-7 and 1981 (Fig.94). A sequence of timber structures constructed around AD 120 was revealed comprising three ranges divided by alleys and verandahs. An ornamental pond lay in an enclosed courtyard in the heart of the complex. These buildings underwent a number of structural changes before being partly rebuilt in stone in the mid-second century to a different plan. A bath suite was added to the masonry complex which went out of use around AD 240.

The complex has been interpreted as the residence of an army officer responsible for the management and policing of the local lead industry. Stamped tiles of the Twentieth Legion certainly support a military connection, whilst the painted wall-plaster, a dressed stone bench leg, Holt fine wares and continental imports indicate an above average lifestyle for the complex. That at least one inhabitant was literate is proven by the presence of a seal-box lid, inkwell lid and stylus. The evidence certainly suggests that the complex was the residence of an official and his attendants — not necessarily an army officer but perhaps an imperial official.

The plan of the timber complex shows three ranges of buildings (probably four existed originally) The central (south) range was the most prominent, with a courtyard behind, and most likely to have been the main residence.

Bronze Smithing

A bronze-smithing site has recently been excavated by the author at Prestatyn to reveal three small workshops producing a variety of goods. Trumpet brooches were produced in Building 1 and here was found a complete unused two-piece mould for such an object, whilst Building 2 was used for manufacturing pony-harness bridle-bits and terrets in native style. Hundreds of pieces of pattern and investment moulds were found — they had been broken to get at the marketable goods inside — but some are so small that no surface impressions survive to enable a positive identification of the items being cast. Numerous brooches decorated with multi-coloured enamels (again a native decorative trait) were recovered, many of which were probably manufactured on the site. The workshops date from *c* AD 90/100 to *c* AD 160. A rare find was an iron brooch inlaid with red enamel.

Other evidence of industrial activity is the presence on site of waste products of iron smithing, and galena and lead waste perhaps intended partly for inclusion in the copper-alloy, for ease of casting, and also for the plumbing of a nearby bath-house. Worked bone and antler waste indicate that these materials were also utilised on the site.

The masonry bath-house was excavated in the 1930s and more recently in 1984-5 to establish more precisely its chronological development and relation to the bronze-smithing workshops (Figs.95,96,97). It is now known that the Prestatyn baths were built in two stages, the initial one being constructed by the Twentieth Legion (stamped tiles being found in the walls and heating system of the building) around AD 120. The addition of a cold room and plunge bath, with timber aqueduct feeding it, dates to the mid-second century. Two other masonry buildings were found in the 1930s and indicate that the main part of the settlement may lie under the Meadows Estate west of the bath-house. A number of lathe-turned column fragments were found during the construction of the estate in the early 1970s.

Earlier excavations had erroneously interpreted a ditch up slope of the buildings as part of a Roman fort lying under the Ysgol Y Llys playing field. Recent trial excavations and geophysical survey have shown this to be false. A more reasonable hypothesis, in the light of the recent excavations, is that the ditch was a boundary to the civil settlement or vicus to the south. Professor G.D.B. Jones has also drawn attention to a possible harbour at Prestatyn in Roman times when the water table was several metres higher than today. Such a harbour may lie at the junction of the Meadows Estate and Ffordd Isa where a small stream now runs through a silted inlet.

Interpretation of the Roman site at Prestatyn is fraught with problems, but it would appear that the site was established by the Twentieth Legion possibly as a harbour site for the shipment of lead from the nearby mines. Native blacksmiths, bronze-smiths and enamellers were attracted to the site to provide for the inhabitants and traders who used the harbour. The decline of the settlement probably came when the lead veins became unprofitable, although the site was reoccupied, on a small scale, in the late third and early fourth centuries.

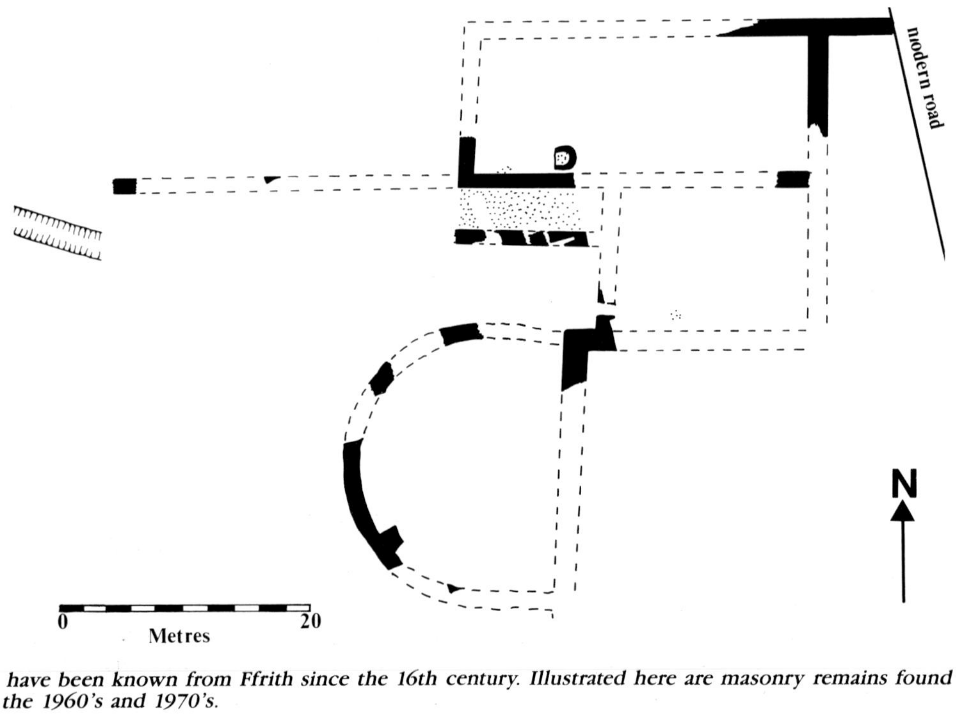

Fig.93 Roman finds have been known from Ffrith since the 16th century. Illustrated here are masonry remains found during excavations by Mr. Bevan Evans in the 1960's and 1970's.

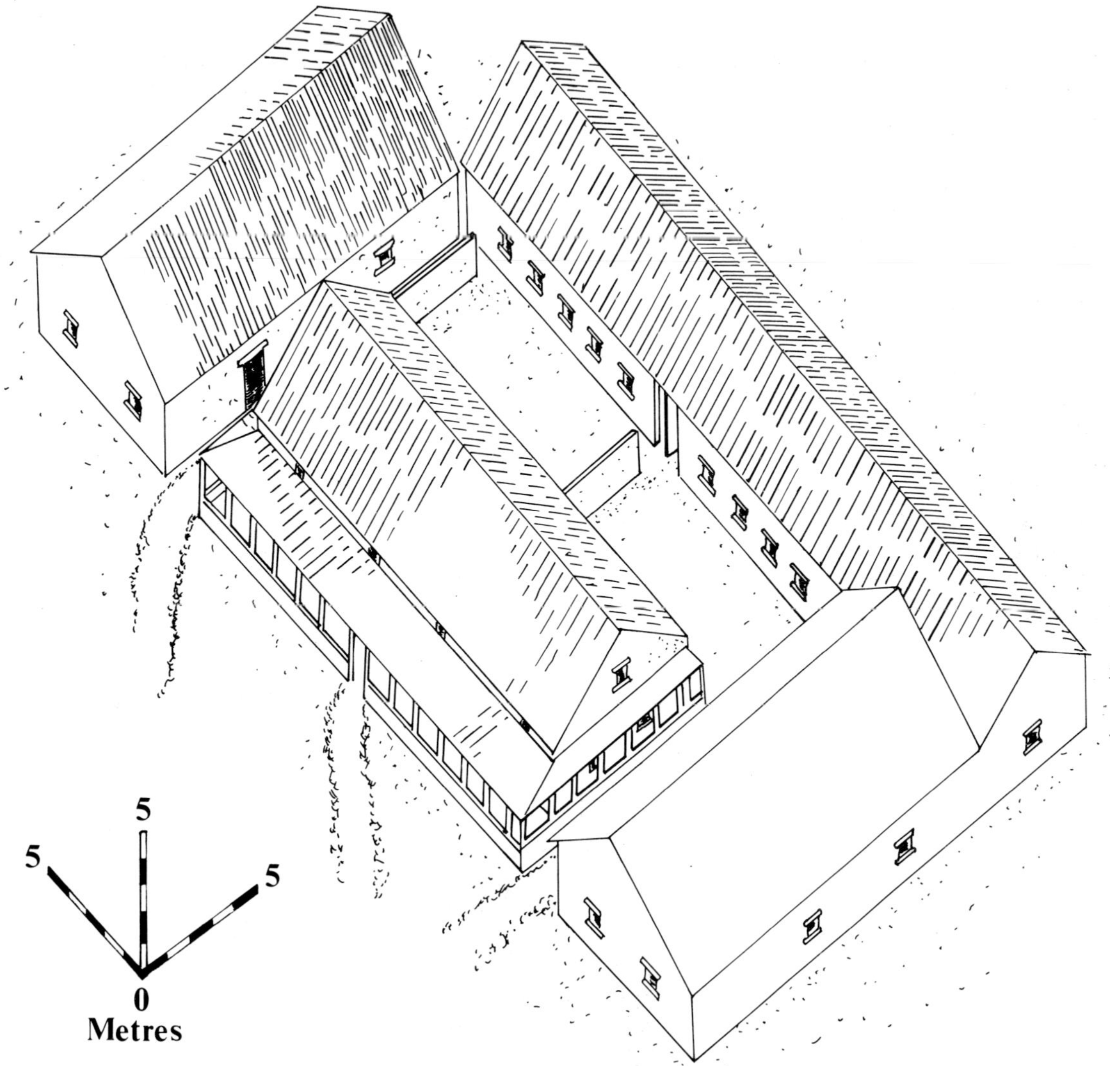

Fig.94 The conjectural reconstruction of phase I of the Roman villa dating to the early 1st century at Pentre Farm, Flint, excavated in the late 1970's and early 1980's.

Settlement Sites

Two sites are known in a lowland setting which fall into this category (excluding the industrial sites noted above), one at Rhuddlan the other at Ffrith. To this may be added the Dinorben hillfort (where romano-british occupation is attested) and possibly some of the hillforts along the Clwydian range where chance finds have been made.

At Rhuddlan the romano-british settlement has been traced in a number of excavations by Henrietta Quinnell in 1969-73 north of Twt Hill, and more recently by John Manley at Lon Hylas

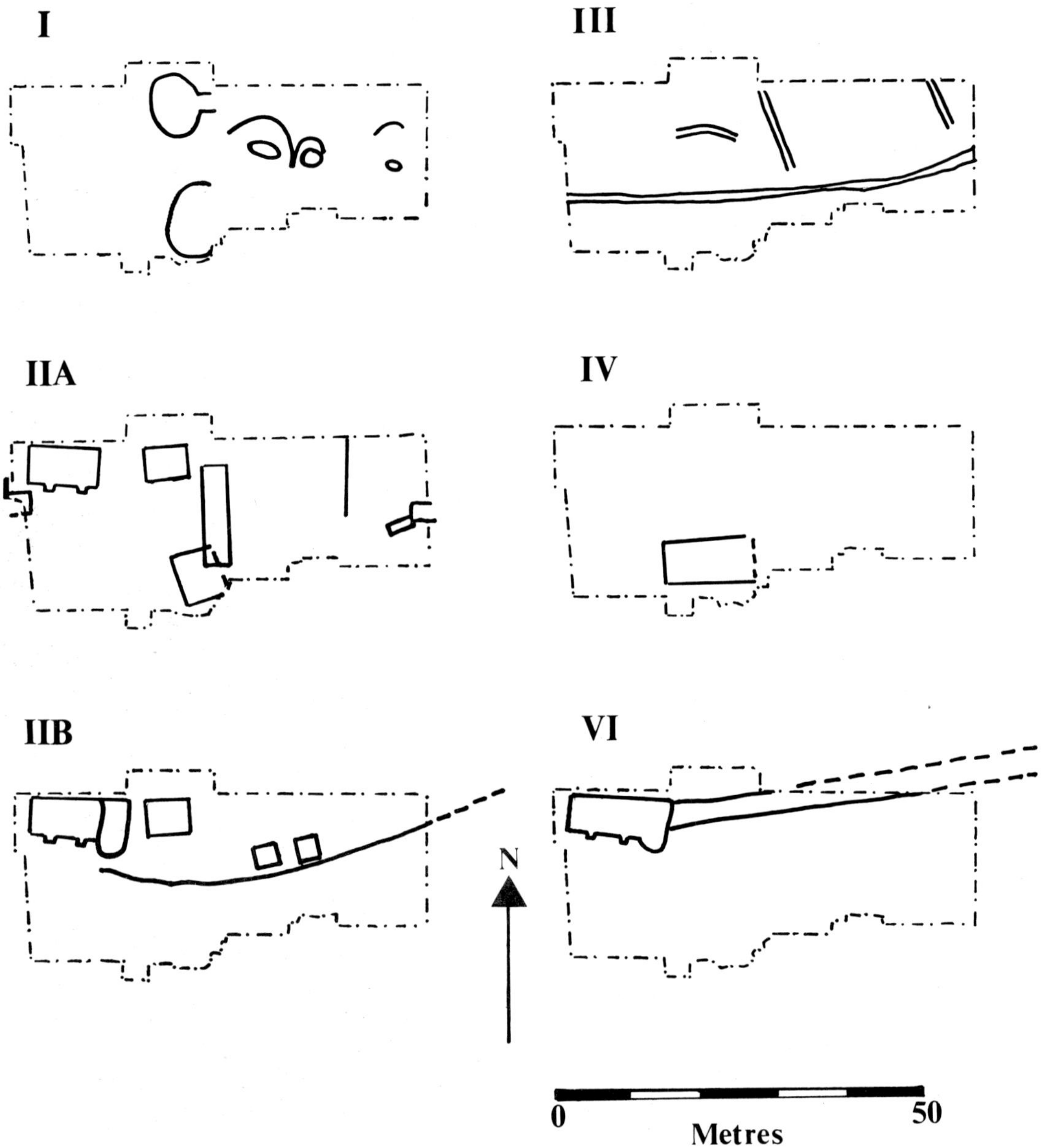

Fig.95 Plans of the Prestatyn Bath-house site showing its development from the late iron age through to the final phases of the bath-house in the mid-second century AD.

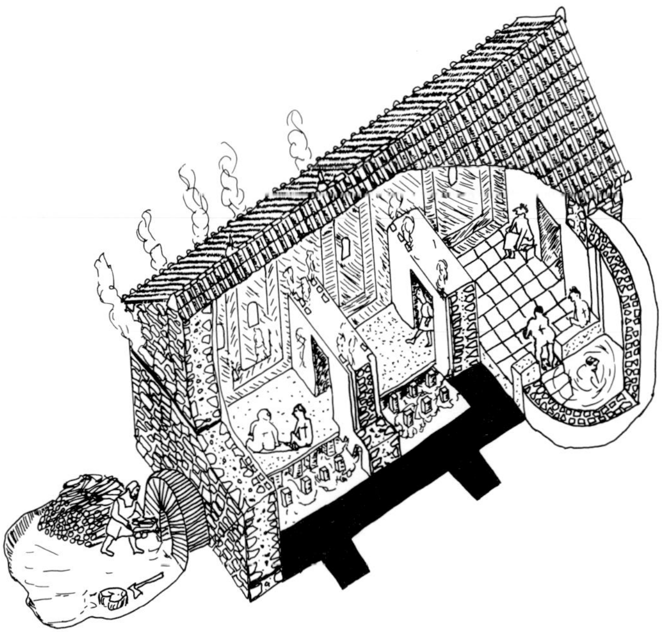

Fig.96 A reconstruction showing the Prestatyn bath-house in use at sometime during the second century AD.

and 'Town Ditch'. The 1969-73 excavations revealed drainage gullies of a circular timber building (much rebuilt) and a possible rectangular timber building. Pottery from the sites indicates an initial period of occupation of late first/early second century date, but with most of the activity dating to the late third and fourth centuries. More recent work by John Manley on Town Ditch, south of the site of the Dominican Friary, revealed a series of drainage gullies and an unstratified coin, AD 218-22. Rescue excavations at the junction of Lon Hylas and Castle Street uncovered a ditch 2m wide and 75cm deep containing sherds of pottery datable to the late first/early second centuries. Finally one sherd of samian ware was found at Hendre and is datable to AD 160-90. In conclusion, the features excavated north of Twt Hill and at Town Ditch indicate at least one native farmstead with associated field systems. The ditch at Lon Hylas would not be out of place on a native farmstead and no military presence is proven at Rhuddlan by the findings to date.

At least two masonry buildings are now known at Ffrith (Fig.93). Excavations by the late Mr. Bevan Evans revealed an extensive masonry bath-house. Stamped tiles of the Twentieth Legion were found and this may well have been the same structure noted in Camden's *Britannia*. Finds from the 16th, 19th and 20th centuries are detailed by Mr. Ellis Davies, and include bronze brooches, pins and a seal-box lid. Recent finds by the late Mr. Bevan Evans in the 1960s and 1970s comprised a silvered bronze spoon, seal

Fig.97 The bath-house at Prestatyn during excavation. The very young archaeologist is sitting on a drain adjoining the cold plunge bath.

Fig.98 A portable oven was found at Prestatyn. The oven would be used to cook small items such as bread, over a bed of hot charcoal. The only other British example of this type of oven comes from Holt, Clwyd.

box lid, silver signet ring, toilet implements, decorated bone pins and two military belt fittings of second century type. Pottery from the site was produced at Holt (Fig.98), North Wales and the Cheshire Plain, and also included imports of samian ware and amphorae. The seal-box lid is said to have been found with a coin of Commodius, AD 161-92. Military belt fittings, stamped tiles and cremations suggest a military presence, perhaps as a posting station. The finds are of good quality and indicate that the site attracted a wide range of goods. That the settlement was situated on the Roman road from Chester to Caer Gai indicates that it may have served as a market centre for the area. Coins of Theodosius (378-95) and Arcadius (383-408) suggest activity in the area in the late fourth/early fifth centuries. The Ffrith settlement contrasts well with the Rhuddlan site; the latter produced no fine wares from Holt and no small finds of any quality.

Other possible sites, of unknown status, where finds have been made are Dyserth Castle and Basingwerk Abbey. A number of cave sites in the Clwydians have also yielded romano-british finds, in particular Big Covert Cave, Orchid Cave and Lynx Cave. The latter produced six human burials. It must be noted however that these sites were not well excavated and the nature of the deposits and function of the sites remains unknown.

Religious Sites

A probable religious site is known near Ruthin, in the Vale of Clwyd, where a square enclosure has been found by aerial photography (Fig.99). It may well represent a temple precinct or sacred courtyard *(temenos)* enclosed by a broad ditch, the whole being surrounded by a double wall *(porticus)* with an internal colonnade. Inside the ditched *temenos* are the faint traces of a possible temple. (See also Manley's article, CAR 4205).

Other sites of a religious nature are known from the location of small finds. In 1979/80 a hoard of bronze objects was found at Llys Awel, Abergele, by a metal-detector user. 535 coins were recovered representing at least three hoards (one of Constantine, one of Magnentius and Constans and the third of Valentinian); a small number of earlier coins were also found. The hoard also produced a remarkable collection of votive objects including two crudely made figurines of seated dogs (Figs.100,101), a flat running dog of greyhound stature, two votive plaques (one a figurine standing, the other an engraved dog), and a figure of Mercury. The finds suggest a shrine or sanctuary nearby.

Four bronze *paterae* were found in 1879 near Coed Ial, Llantysilio and are likely to have come from a rich grave whilst the find of a

Fig.99 Aerial view of a possible Temple site near Ruthin. Few examples of this type of monument are known. Perhaps the best parallel for this site in Clwyd is that at Gosbecks Farm, near Colchester, Essex.

bronze figurine near Ruthin and a bronze horse at Gwaenysgor provide further evidence of a religious nature. A miniature amphora found at Coe Clogwyn, Hope, is likely to be modern and a probable tourist souvenir. A full size Dressel 2-4 Amphora was recognised at Rhos-on-Sea in 1985; it had been a garden ornament since 1977!

Cemeteries

The sites of three possible cremation cemeteries are known. At Ffrith in 1828, urns were found containing calcined bones associated with 26 coins, brooches, a mutilated altar and a lamp. Urns with cremations inside were also found near Bodfari in 1808 but these may be bronze age finds (since lost). More recently in 1981 at least two beakers were found near Ruthin Hospital which may have contained cremations (see above). Inhumation burials are known from Pentre Farm, Flint, one sealed with a lead cover probably reused from a water tank. Other inhumations were found in Ship Field, Flint, in 1923 and 1924.

Fig.100 and 101 Two seated dogs, probably votive objects, found as part of a hoard of metalwork at Llys Awel, Abergele.

Late Roman Occupation

The majority of romano-british sites excavated in Clwyd (Ffrith, Flint, Prestatyn, Rhuddlan and Dinorben) have yielded late Roman sherds of pottery. All but the Ffrith site have produced sherds of calcite-gritted jars dating to the late fourth century. At Ffrith the coin sequence ends with coins of Theodosius (378-95) and Arcadius (383-408). Coin hoards from various parts of Clwyd terminate in coins of Constantine, save Llys Awel which ends in a hoard of Valentinianic coins.

Other Finds

Many miscellaneous finds have been made throughout the county and are too numerous to note here. Full details may be obtained from the Sites and Monuments Record housed at Shire Hall, Mold and in reports on recent excavations.

Conclusions

In this brief study of the known romano-british sites in Clwyd one is struck by the absence of military sites, in particular auxiliary forts. Industrial sites of the 70s which produced the early lead pigs are also lacking. It is envisaged that the fort sites may be found near St.Asaph, Ruthin and Corwen, whilst the early industrial sites may lie on Halkyn Mountain and its coastal slopes. Such sites would benefit from more extensive aerial photographic surveys, in conjunction with field walking and watching briefs on development sites.

Numerous native farmsteads, similar to that at Rhuddlan must exist, probably in a lowland setting along the Vale of Clwyd and on the north coast.

Of the few known romano-british sites in Clwyd, two are currently under threat of destruction by ploughing. One is the possible temple site near Ruthin, which would repay total excavation, even though it may already have been extensively damaged by ploughing. Very few temple precincts of this type are known in Britain. The best parallel for the Clwyd precinct is that at Gosbecks Farm, near Colchester. Two further possible examples are known in Powys and one in Gloucestershire. The site is therefore an important one for Wales as a whole. The second site under threat is the legionary works depot at Holt. Here the sequence of production of tiles and pottery is not adequately known and extensive geophysical surveys and fieldwalking should be carried out before any further excavation is undertaken.

Sites with good stratification, such as Ffrith, Rhuddlan and Holt should be investigated at any opportunity, particularly in an attempt to fill the gap of third century occupation on many of the sites. Excavations must be on as large a scale as possible for us to understand the social and economic aspects of the sites. Small-scale work should be limited to the location of new sites, since they are often misleading and wasteful of manpower and money.

THE DARK AGES
by Nancy Edwards

The period c.400-1050 AD in Clwyd can be described with some justification as a 'Dark Age'. Our knowledge of the history and archaeology of Wales as a whole at this time is very limited and the evidence difficult to interpret, but the impression gained is that the north-east remains even more shadowy than many other parts, for example Gwynedd, Dyfed and Glamorgan.

The key to this may be that Clwyd was essentially a border area throughout the period. The powerful kingdom of Gwynedd to the west and increasing Anglo-Saxon penetration from the east may have meant there was little opportunity for the emergence of any strong regional identity. Indeed, at one time the land to the east of the river Conwy was termed *Y Berfeddwlad* (The Middle Country), perhaps meaning the land between Gwynedd and Powys. In the first half of the period there are indications of small kingdoms based on the later cantrefs of Rhos and Rhufoniog in the west and of the emergence of the Cadelling dynasty in the east who later supplied the kings of Powys. Parts of Clwyd were definitely in Powys as the 9th-century pillar of Elise, just outside Llangollen, testifies. Though the inscription is now illegible, in 1696 Edward Lhuyd recorded it as having been set up by Cyngen to commemorate his great-grandfather Elise who had annexed land for Powys at the expense of the English.

The rise of the Kingdom of Mercia in the 7th century posed a powerful threat in the east and the flatter, more fertile countryside of the Vale of Clwyd and the Vale of Llangollen were obvious targets for English attack. Offa's and Wat's Dykes, almost certainly constructed by Mercia towards the end of the 8th century in the face of Welsh raiding, are good evidence of both Mercia's power and border warfare. From the 9th century onwards English domination of large areas of north-east Wales may have been a reality, and the rise of Gwynedd at the expense of Powys left Clwyd the subject of almost constant hostilities. At the beginning of the 10th century the hiberno-norse settlement of the Wirral offers the possibility of Viking penetration as well. At the end of the period the fact that the whole of Flintshire and much of Denbighshire were included with entries for Cheshire in Domesday Book, together with the place-names and the method of recording, indicate the extent of English and then Norman control. Land east of Wat's Dyke is described in exactly the same way as the rest of Cheshire while information about what lay to the west is much more obscure. Along the borders the many vills recorded as waste in Domesday Book are an indication of continuing Welsh raids.

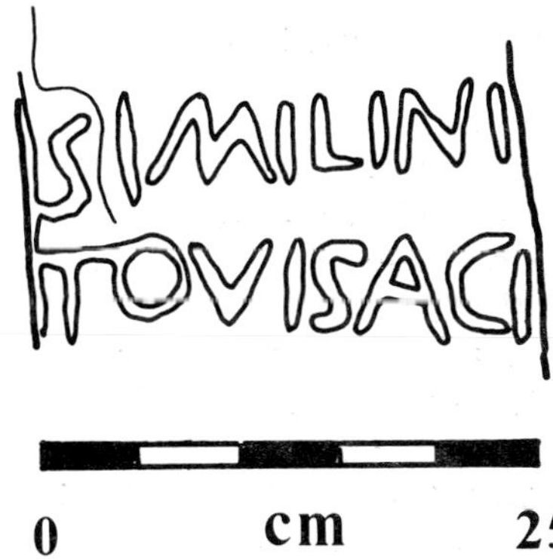

Fig.102 The inscribed stone from Clocaenog. The inscription in latin commemorates Similinus the Prince. The inscription is also recorded in ogham script suggesting some Irish influence in the region.

Set against this historical background the difficulties of the archaeology are more understandable. Areas such as the fertile Vale of Clwyd, where one would expect a comparatively large farming population are also those where the evidence is most likely to have been destroyed. The evidence for the early medieval church is inevitably more plentiful than other aspects because of the long continuity of some church sites which has led to the survival of a considerable corpus of stone sculpture. At the same time there has been almost no archaeological investigation of these sites simply because of their continued use. As elsewhere in Wales very little can be said of secular settlement sites throughout the period with the possible exception of some hillforts. These are obvious features in the landscape, which have been the subject of archaeological excavation, primarily because of their prehistoric use though some evidence of dark age occupation has also been recovered, largely as a by-product. Over the last fifteen years, with the extensive investigation of Offa's and Wat's Dykes and excavations at Rhuddlan, our knowledge of Anglo-Saxon activity has greatly increased but there are as yet few indications of Viking settlement. The aim of this paper is to provide a short review of the archaeological evidence and where possible to give some suggestions for future work.

The Early Church

We know remarkably little of Welsh ecclesiastical organisation or religious foundations before the 12th century. Some information can be gained from the historical sources but only thirty-five religious foundations may be identified throughout Wales before the Norman conquest from documentary references excluding charters, and of these only four in Clwyd: Llanelwy, which may have had some pre-conquest episcopal tradition (though the see of St.Asaph was probably not founded until 1141), Abergele, Llangollen and Bangor-Is-y-Coed. There is no early medieval archaeological evidence from any of these sites though a 12th-century stone shrine fragment from Llangollen does suggest its importance at that time. We are therefore very much dependent upon the archaeological evidence for the identification of early medieval ecclesiastical sites in Clwyd and the presence of early medieval stone sculpture in particular. However, in order to identify potential sites the archaeologist should also take into account later historical sources and the more recent descriptions of antiquarians who may have visited them when more survived than is now visible. Folk traditions may also have to be investigated but great care is needed. The possibility that sites with later medieval sculpture could indicate foundations which were also important at an earlier date should also be considered, though the lack of Romanesque architecture in Clwyd is a severe blow to

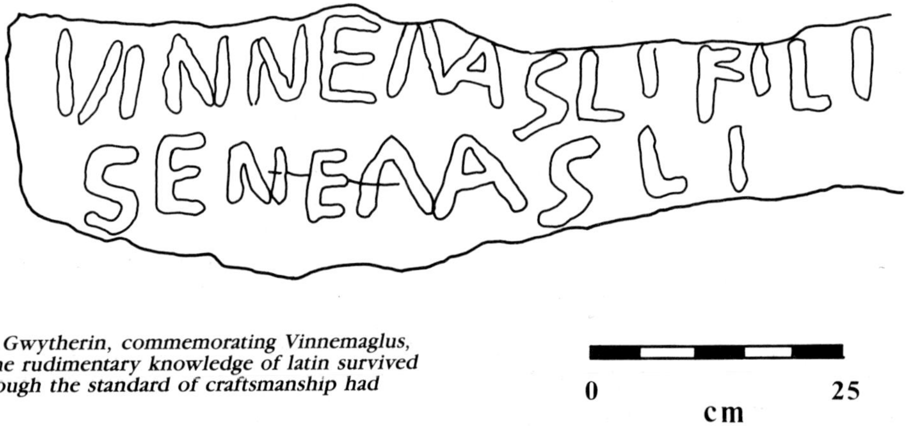

Fig.103 The stone from Gwytherin, commemorating Vinnemaglus, son of Senemaglus. Some rudimentary knowledge of latin survived into the dark ages, although the standard of craftsmanship had deteriorated.

Fig.104 This plan shows the excavated features from the multi-period cemetery at Tandderwen, near Denbigh. The dark age graves some with square enclosures and all aligned east-west, can clearly be seen.

gauging the importance of ecclesiastical sites in the 11th and 12th centuries. The topography of church sites can be important, the size and shape of the graveyard, the possible survival of early enclosure lines, perhaps only visible from the air, or early records of glebe land, can all provide valuable clues. *Llan* names, thirty-eight in Denbighshire but only four in Flintshire, and church dedications should also be taken into account but we should bear in mind that linguistic changes in place-names and changes of dedication may have distorted the evidence.

Probably the earliest evidence for Christianity in Clwyd are the latin inscribed stones of the 5th and 6th centuries AD. These were set up to commemorate the dead but there is at present little evidence to suggest that they are directly connected with the graves of those remembered. There are very few examples in Clwyd compared with Gwynedd, and stones from Pentrefoelas, Gwytherin (Figs.103,105), and the recent addition from Llangernyw, may be seen as an extension of the Gwynedd group while the stone from Clocaenog and that from Caerwys or Ysceifiog, now in Whitford church, are easterly outliers (Fig.106). Whether there were once many more inscribed stones and whether there were originally inscriptions on wood as well as stone is unknown but the distribution suggests influences coming from the west and along the Irish Sea routes rather than from the east.

This is certainly true of the Clocaenog stone (Fig.102) where the inscription is recorded not only in latin (SIMILINI TOVISACI) but also in the ogham script, (S[I]B[I]L[I]N[I] // [TO]VISACI) commemorating Similinus the Prince. Whether the personal name is British or Irish is unclear, but the use of ogham undoubtedly suggests Irish connections and raises the possibility of a ruling Irish element in the population some way to the east of where such settlement is historically attested. Irish influence is also suggested by the formula 'X son of Y' on the vertical inscription from Gwytherin (VINNEMAGLI FILI SENEMAGLI) commemorating Vinnemaglus, son of Senemaglus. Unusually, this stone seems to be still *in situ* and its location is interesting. It is the most westerly in a line of four small standing stones, the other three apparently uninscribed, located to the north of the 19th century church at Gwytherin. The ecclesiastical importance of this site and its connection with the cult of Gwenfrewi will be discussed later, but its antiquity is clear. However the significance of the stone line is obscure. The recent discovery of the incomplete inscribed stone (VERE[ ) from Bryn Gwylan, Llangernyw is not surprising considering the cross-inscribed stones in the churchyard not far away. The stone from Pentrefoelas was found in 1820 during the construction of Telford's road between Lima and Cernioge when forty long-cist graves were uncovered in a field called Dôl Trebeddau. The stone was found face-downwards on top of one of the graves, clearly reused. This is the only known long-cist cemetery from Clwyd and again would seem to be an extension of the group known from Gwynedd and from Anglesey in particular. The inscription from Pentrefoelas (BROHOMAGLI /IATTI (h)IC IACIT / ET VXOR EIVS CAVNE) commemorating Brohomaglus Iattus and his wife Caune uses the HIC IACIT formula ultimately demonstrating links with Christians in southern Gaul who used a similar formula. The same formula is also used on the Caerwys/Ysceifiog stone (HIC IACIT MVLI/ER BONA NOBILI(s)) and it is interesting to note that this again commemorates a woman, Bona the wife of Nobilis. The mention of women on these early Christian inscribed stones is relatively rare. These inscribed stones therefore suggest not only Christian and Irish elements in the population of 5th- and 6th-century Clwyd, but also the survival of some degree of latin learning which made their execution possible.

Apart from the long-cist cemetery at Pentrefoelas, there is little evidence of early Christian graves in Clwyd, though the existence of a burial in a stone cist under the mound on the site of the pillar of Elise may be significant. The recent excavation of east-west aligned graves without grave-goods, each enclosed by a rectangular ditch, at Tandderwen (Figs.104,110), Denbigh, is, however, an interesting discovery. They have radiocarbon dates centring on the 6th

Fig.105 The inscribed stone from Pentrefoelas commemorates Brohomaglus Iattus and his wife Caune. This inscription shows links with Christians in 'southern Gaul', through the use of the HIC IACIT formula.

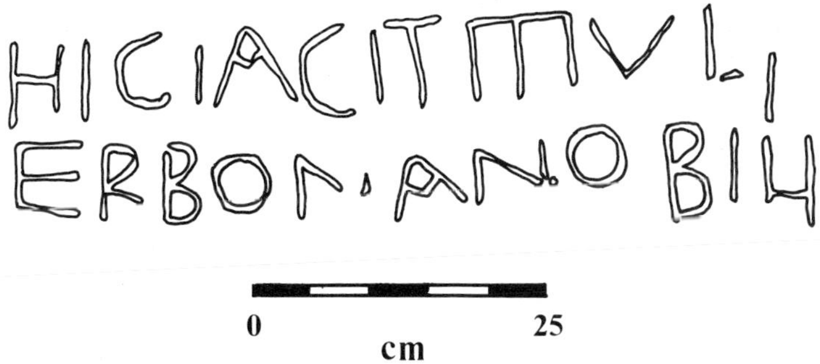

Fig.106 This stone from either Caerwys or Ysceifiog commemorates Bona, the wife of Nobilis. Some of these inscribed stones may have marked graves.

century and may be compared with similar examples in Gwynedd: a rectanglar ditched grave enclosure at Llandegai and the square structure enclosing two graves with a third set into the entrance at Capel Eithin on Anglesey.

The distribution map shows the location of both definite and possible early church sites in Clwyd and the nature of the evidence (Fig.108). Suffice it here to consider some of the more interesting examples in order to demonstrate the range of the material. The inscribed stone at Gwytherin has already been mentioned, but there is also a considerable body of other evidence suggesting the importance and antiquity of this remote site. *The Survey of the Honour of Denbigh* tells us that in 1334 there were still 'abbots' at Gwytherin who were supported by bond under-tenants suggesting that there had been a much earlier ecclesiastical community. A documentary reference in the 12th-century life of Wenefred (Gwenfrewi) by Robert, Prior of Shrewsbury suggests her close association with Gwytherin and that this is where she was buried. Indeed, at that time her body seems to have been transferred from Gwytherin to the Abbey of St Peter and St Paul in Shrewsbury. In addition, at the end of the 17th century, Lhuyd refers to the existence of a separate 'Kappel Gwenfrewi' in the southern part of the graveyard though this was destroyed around the beginning of the 18th century. Multiple churches are a feature of early Welsh religious foundations and it seems almost certain that this was a *Capel y Bedd* which may be compared with others still surviving at Clynnog, Caer Gybi and Llaneilian. Lhuyd has also left us a tantalising illustration of the shrine of Gwenfrewi (Fig.107). Although this is only a rough sketch and there is no indication of size, its shape strongly resembles the early 12th century shrine of St Manchan from Ireland: a

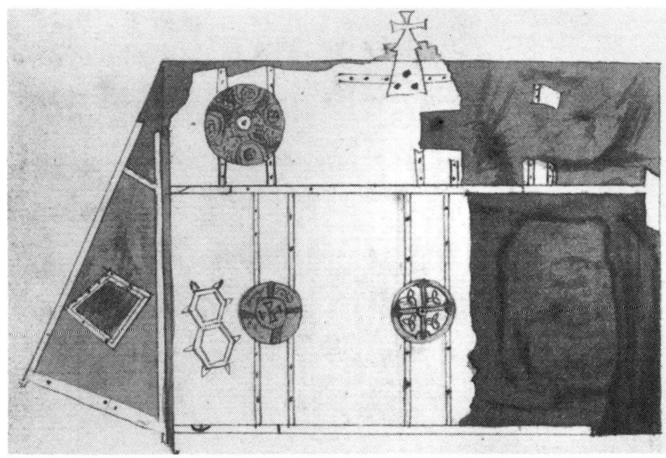

Fig.107 A rough sketch by Edward Lhuyd of the Shrine of St. Gwenfrewi which was still kept at Gwytherin in the seventeenth century. It was a wooden box covered with metal plates. The ornament suggests it was of dark age date.

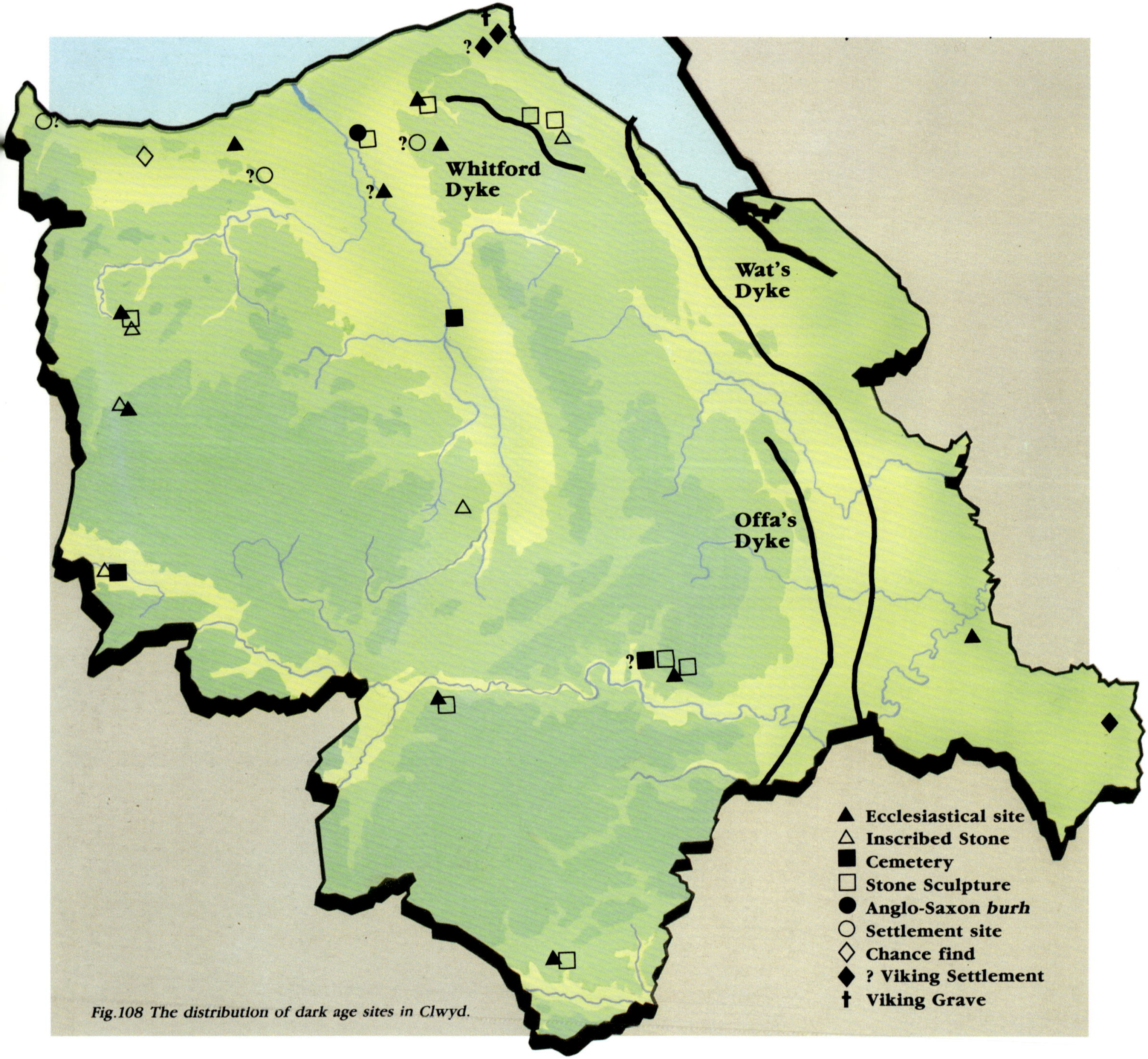

Fig.108 The distribution of dark age sites in Clwyd.

tent-shaped wooden box decorated with plates of metal. A glance at the decorated metal plaques in Lhuyd's drawing suggests that the shrine may have been composite, but the small cross-ornamented roundels are very similar to other cross motifs known from early medieval hiberno-saxon metalwork. Since no major pieces of early medieval Welsh metalwork survive apart from bells this sketch provides a very important glimpse of the ecclesiastical metalwork which might once have existed. The topography of Gwytherin is also interesting, a small but pronounced promontory with steep drops to the south-east and north, where there is a little stream (Fig.109). A few miles northwards Llangernyw church, with its two cross marked stones, is situated in a similar position on a prominent knoll which falls steeply to the east. Such locations may be closely compared with many early church sites in Ireland.

The possession of the body of the founder saint was a valuable asset to any religious foundation and some examples of elaborately carved stone shrines which were built in the 12th century to house these remains have survived. The best example is just within Powys in the remote church at Pennant Melangell, but there are also small fragments not far away at Llanrhaeadr ym Mochnant and at Llangollen. Llanrhaeadr ym Mochnant seems to have been an important native church dedicated to St Doewen, the ecclesiastical centre of the

Fig.109 An aerial view of Gwytherin. Note that the churchyard is unusually large.

commote of Mochnant. Later medieval documentary references which mention a community of clergy there in the time of Edward I hint at the earlier importance of the site and this is confirmed by the sculptural evidence. In addition to the shrine fragment there are two earlier pieces, possibly of 9th or 10th century date. The first with its well-executed fret pattern might be architectural. The second, an upright slab with a ringed cross decorated with plaitwork, frets and simple spirals, bears the commemorative inscription + COCOM FILIU(S) EDELSTAN, the hybrid anglo-welsh name Gwgan son of Elstan which demonstrates English influence very clearly in this secluded area of the kingdom of Powys. It has been suggested that the Edelstan mentioned could be Elstan Glodrydd, a prince of Powys (*floruit* c. 1010-40) but the sculptural motifs suggest an earlier date for the monument. The topography of the site, which completely dominates the modern village, should also be noted. The church is situated in an extremely large churchyard which slopes gently down to the river Rhaeadr, a tributary of the Tanat. Churchyards far in excess of the needs of the parish for burial are a feature of other important early religious foundations, for example Meifod, and may represent the original extent of the monastic enclosure.

Corwen, the major church of the commote of Edeyrnion, and formerly known as Corfaen, also has a very large churchyard (Fig.111). A reference in the Shrewsbury Cartulary shows there were sixteen clerics at Corwen in the early 13th century and again the sculptural evidence demonstrates the earlier importance of the site. The major piece is a cross shaft with a scalloped top decorated with crude interlace. It has been compared with the 9th-century pillar of Elise which demonstrates Mercian influence, but it is quadrilateral rather than cylindrical and Nash-Williams' suggestion of a later date, perhaps as late as the 12th century, seems more likely. In addition some rather crudely incised and unfortunately illegible runes of late 11th century or 12th century date have been identified on the north face, probably a religious graffito. Other early medieval sculpture from the site consists of a cross-inscribed stone reused as a lintel in the south door and two fragments decorated with interlace found in the 19th century but now lost.

In the Vale of Clwyd early medieval sculpture suggests sites at Whitford, Rhuddlan and Dyserth. The place-name Dyserth is derived from the latin *desertum* meaning desert, recalling the location of hermitages in the early centuries of Christianity, and was used at other early medieval monastic sites such as Dysert O Dea in Ireland. Situated not far from the famous waterfall, the only remains are a cross and a cross base, though the possible existence of a second cross is also recorded. The carving on both surviving pieces is rather crude but the cross may undoubtedly be grouped with other North Welsh crosses, 'Maen Achwyfan' near Whitford, and Penmon and is therefore likely to be 10th-century rather than later. Outside the churchyard Lhuyd mentions the holy well of St Cwyfan, the saint originally connected with the site; the church is now dedicated to St Ffraid.

A word should be said about holy wells in general. Seventy-six wells are known from Denbighshire which could still be located thirty years ago and fifty-one from Flintshire. Many of these are dedicated to saints and some, like Dyserth, are closely associated with church sites of possibly early origin. The most famous is that of St Wenefride (Gwenfrewi) at Holywell. It is first mentioned in 1093 when it was granted to St Werburgh's, Chester and the first evidence of visiting pilgrims is in 1119. No archaeological evidence survives, and the present well house

Fig.110 This reconstruction drawing shows families tending the dark age graves found at Tandderwen, in the Vale of Clwyd near Denbigh.

was built at the beginning of the 16th century, but the story of St Wenefride and the restoration of her severed head to her body by St Beuno and how a spring gushed from the ground her blood had stained is perhaps an echo of a much more ancient, even pagan, well cult.

It should be noted that local memory of many holy-well sites is fading and that the above ground remains of many need recording before their location is forgotten. For example, the well of St Mael and St Sulien situated in the vicarage wall at Cwm is fast disappearing under a swathe of ivy and the vicar did not know where it was, even though I was told it had been visited by an old man for water until only eight years ago. There are indications of a possible ancient ecclesiastical site at Cwm since Lhuyd mentions the story that three bells had been found on the hill near the church, the yellow bell of Cwm, the white bell of Abergele and the blue bell of Llanddulas. The shape of the bells *(cornelog)* and their association with colours suggests they were of Celtic type. A small hand-bell is also mentioned in 1769 but it is now lost.

Therefore, although our knowledge of the archaeology of the early church in Clwyd is fragmentary and difficult to quantify, there is some potential for future work on sites of

Fig.111 Birds-eye view of Corwen, its church and large churchyard.

known or suspected early medieval activity. It is difficult to excavate on active church sites, but it is essential to keep an eye on the tidying of graveyards, their extension or the alteration of enclosure lines. Similarly, it is possible to investigate church interiors during repairs or alterations and opportunities may arise to look under floors. An eye should be kept on redundant churches where more extensive work might be carried out. A thorough study of maps and documents should be undertaken to record the size, shape and topography of churchyards and glebe land holdings, and, as at Llanynys, this can be backed up by air photography.

Secular Settlement

It is more difficult to know how we may increase our knowledge of dark age settlement in Clwyd, since, apart from hillforts, we do not yet understand what the characteristic settlement types of this period may have been. We are therefore faced with a virtual stalemate and until some breakthrough is made it is likely that more sites will only be identified in the course of more general archaeological investigations.

There is only one hillfort with some archaeological evidence of dark age activity: Dinorben, which has been the subject of extensive excavation during destruction by quarrying. However, the earlier reports now need a detailed reassessment and Guilbert's excavations of 1977-9 await final publication. While there is substantial evidence of Roman occupation c.260-360 AD indicated by artefacts including coins, Savory's claim that he had excavated a large late Roman round-house superseded by a possibly sub-Roman aisled structure now seem very doubtful. However Guilbert's excavations did produce radiocarbon dates from Ditch 3 suggesting the possibility of an extra-mural settlement during the 5th century. In addition, there is an Anglo-Saxon gilt-bronze buckle fragment of late 6th or early 7th-century date, but unfortunately, unstratified, and possibly a dark age bead, an iron slotted pointed object and a Viking silver ingot. Glanville Jones' work, though controversial, suggesting the continuing importance of Dinorben, may also be significant. It is notable that a hearth at Dinorben is mentioned in the 10th century 'Stanzas of the Graves' *(Englynion y Beddau)*, that the *llys* for the commote of Rhos Is Dulas was located at a farm near Dinorben in the 14th century and that the bond settlements around Dinorben were responsible for the construction of the court buildings. Though it is impossible to prove, this could suggest that Dinorben remained an important site from the late bronze age right through to the later medieval period.

A second hillfort, Bryn Euryn, is also worthy of note. It has been claimed that this is the 'ear's stronghold', the fortress of Cuneglasus, one of the tyrants castigated by the 6th-century monk Gildas. But at present there is no archaeological evidence to support this.

Anglo-Saxon Penetration

Offa's and Wat's Dykes (see following article) are dramatic testimony of a Mercian presence in Clwyd at the end of the 8th century. However, excavations on the east bank of the river Clwyd at Rhuddlan demonstrate that by the early 10th century the Anglo-Saxons must have had at least temporary control of an area considerably to the west of Basingwerk, the northern terminus of Wat's Dyke. The *Anglo-Saxon Chronicle* tells us that in 921 Edward the Elder founded a *burh* or fortified town at *Cledemutha*. There has been considerable discussion concerning the identification of *Cledemutha* but Wainwright's suggestion that it should be translated as 'Clwyd mouth' makes Rhuddlan the most likely candidate, and this has now been supported by archaeological evidence. *Cledemutha* was the last in a series of *burhs* constructed during the early 10th century to consolidate the West Saxon advance northwards through western Mercia at the expense of the Vikings. It was built, almost certainly with the acquiesence of Gwynedd, specifically to curb Viking raids on North Wales and to stop further hiberno-norse infiltration into north-west England.

The precise area enclosed by the Anglo-Saxon *burh* defences at Rhuddlan has been tested by excavation. A section across the southern side of the town ditch led the excavator to suggest that this was the line of the *burh* defences because radiocarbon dates centring on the 9th century obtained from hearths under the bank provided a suitable *terminus post quem*. The area enclosed, seventy-four acres, is very large in comparison with the neighbouring *burhs* of Eddisbury, Runcorn and Manchester.

More evidence of Anglo-Saxon activity has been detected in the area between the Edwardian castle and Abbey Road within the Norman borough defences. Several trenches were dug between 1969 and 1971 but the Anglo-Saxon significance of what was found has only recently been recognised. Sections across the Norman borough defences indicated a complex sequence with at least three ditches having been constructed before c.1280. In one area two Anglo-Saxon *grubenhauser* or sunken-floored huts were excavated as well as other possible Anglo-Saxon features. Artefacts included sherds of late Anglo-Saxon pottery such as Chester ware and a bun-shaped loom weight. A further possible sunken-floored hut has been excavated together with evidence of antler working and a bone trial piece with a zoomorphic motif. These sunken-floored huts and associated artefacts are therefore very good evidence of Anglo-Saxon activity, presumably

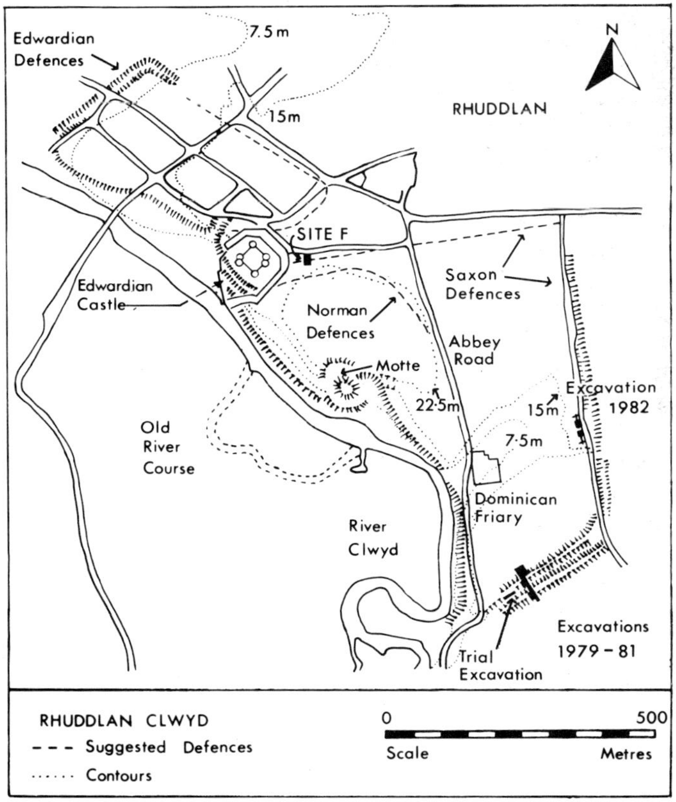

Fig.112 From this plan of Rhuddlan the extent of the Saxon burh of Cledemutha *can be seen. The large, enclosed area south-east of the later castle is much greater in extent than the English town of Edward I.*

Fig.113 The beautiful gold ring, found on Llysfaen Common in the late 18th century, might have belonged to the English Bishop Alhstan (AD 817-67).

connected with the *burh* of *Cledemutha*. The extent of the occupation and the success of this Anglo-Saxon plantation have yet to be determined and it is important to take advantage of any future opportunities which may arise for further excavation.

Other evidence of Anglo-Saxon activity consists of chance finds. Characteristically Anglo-Saxon bun-shaped loom weights have been found in a possible occupation layer at Bryn Llithrig near Rhuallt and could indicate a settlement site. Another interesting artefact is the gold ring found on Llysfaen Common during the 18th century (Fig.113). The inscription suggests that it could have belonged to Bishop Alhstan (817-67) of Sherborne and it may reflect the Anglo-Saxon custom of ring-giving by the powerful to their followers.

The Vikings

In 904, after an unsuccessful attempt to conquer Anglesey, Ingimund and his hiberno-norse followers, who had been expelled from Dublin, were given permission to settle on the Wirral. This is the only documentary account of a single episode in what must have been a fairly large-scale hiberno-norse immigration into north-west England at the beginning of the 10th century and such activity may have spilt over into north-east Wales. There is a small group of norse placenames in Flintshire: Axton, Kelston and Linacre, which are almost certainly indicative of Viking settlement, and the isolated placename of Croxton in Maelor Saesneg could indicate further infiltration along the river Dee.

Archaeological evidence is, however, largely absent. The only find which has been hailed as Viking is the grave at Talacre but, unfortunately, it was not scientifically excavated and the finds are now lost. It seems to have consisted of a stone cist buried in sand overlooking the sea. The skeleton had been placed on its back and a spearhead and knife were found amongst the bones. The cist, the artefacts and siting, which is similar to the only other possible Viking grave from Wales on Anglesey, would seem to tally with other Viking graves from the British Isles.

Less direct evidence of Viking contact may be detected in the form of artistic influence. This may be seen particularly well on the cross called 'Maen Achwyfan' near Whitford (Fig.114). The most diagnostic feature is the solid circle head with rolls set in the arm-pits of the cross. 'Maen Achwyfan' also has Viking ornamental motifs such as the 'T' fret and ring-knot as well as two unidentified figures, a man with a spear and a man with a staff, who could be warriors of the type found in anglo-scandinavian mythology. The distribution of these circle-headed crosses is predominantly coastal, four in North Wales, including a second example in Clwyd at Dyserth, over twenty from north-west England and two outliers from Cornwall. Such a distribution provides compelling evidence for sea traffic between these areas during the 10th and 11th centuries and the consequent spread of Viking artistic influences. As one might expect 'Maen Achwyfan' shows particular links with the Cheshire group.

Thus, though the documentary sources and placename evidence make the existence of Viking settlement very likely, at least in Flintshire, there is at present little archaeological evidence to support it. However this is not completely unexpected. It has proved almost impossible to find archaeological evidence of Viking rural settlements in the British Isles, outside northern Scotland.

Conclusion

The archaeological evidence for Clwyd c.400-1050 AD is therefore extremely fragmentary. This is the period of the formation of Wales and yet the north-east remains a shadowy border region where Anglo-Saxon influence is more distinctive in much of the archaeological evidence than the native Welsh. It is only in the ecclesiastical archaeology that we are able to detect the native population with any feeling of confidence; their inscribed stones, their graves, their monasteries, and some of their religious sculpture. The secular archaeology, apart from hillforts, is relatively obscure. In such a situation, when a single chance find or the discovery of one new site can radically increase our knowledge, it will take many years of intensive survey and archaeological excavation, together with parallel work on the documentary and placename evidence, to begin to build a more detailed picture.

Fig.114 The cross of Maen Achwyfan, dating to about AD 1000, stands in a field on the outskirts of Whitford. It is an impressive 3.4m high and has a small disc head. It is mounted on a sunken base and is probably in its original position. The carving shows Viking influence.

OFFA'S AND WAT'S DYKES
by David Hill

The largest archaeological monument in Britain is the earthwork complex known as the Offa's and Wat's Dykes. It must follow therefore that the dykes are also the largest archaeological monuments in Clwyd, *but* are they the most, or even among the most, *important* archaeological monuments in Clwyd? These earthworks with a ditch on their west (Welsh) side enter the county in the south; the Offa's Dyke crossing the Ceiriog at Chirk Castle (SJ 264 376) and the Wat's Dyke (near SJ 300 410) crossing the Dee at Ruabon (Wynnstay Park). They both mark off the high ground, Offa's Dyke running along the eastern limit of the plateau and the Wat's Dyke along the western edge of the plain, but the Offa's Dyke turns swiftly into a side valley and peters out near Llanfynydd (SJ 274 573) having completed only 13 miles (20 kilometres) of the way to the coast. The altogether more impressive and well engineered Wat's Dyke passes through Wrexham and then follows the north and east side of the Alyn valley, skirts Mold and runs parallel to the Dee estuary marking off the better agricultural land before reaching the sea at Basingwerk (SJ 198 775), a distance of 28 miles (45 kilometres). In addition there is a piece of earthwork of indeterminate length traditionally called the Offa's Dyke (and which we now generally refer to as the "Whitford Dyke") which is to be found inland from the sea at Trelawnyd (SJ 104 793) and at Whitford (SJ 130 771). I will return to this earthwork later.

The Offa's Dyke would appear to be an 8th century work associated with Offa, King of Mercia and overlord of southern Britain (759-98) and the Wat's Dyke is therefore dated by analogy to roughly the same period, Stenton suggesting the reign of Aethelbald (716-757). In reality, however, there is no secure dating for the Wat's Dyke.

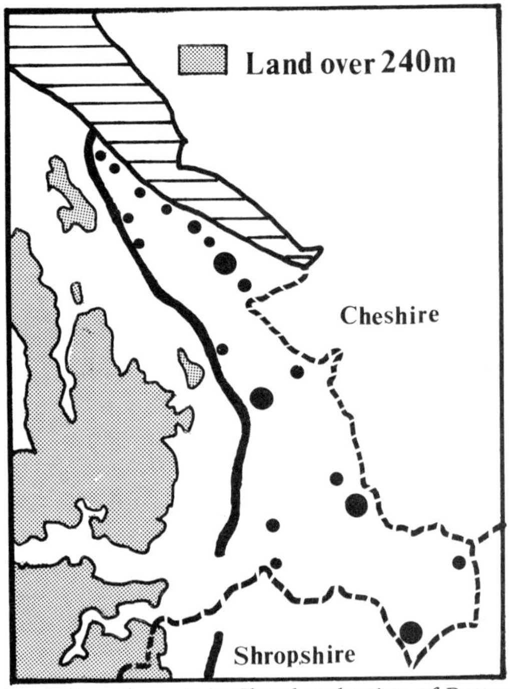

Fig.115 'English' settlements in Clwyd at the time of Domesday in 1086. Note that all the settlements are east of Wat's Dyke and Offa's Dyke.

So much for the introduction, we now know where the Dykes are — or do we? Again the question of the exact line must wait a paragraph or two, but before we go further perhaps we should attempt to assess if the journey is worthwhile — are the Dykes important? They are certainly large and they deserve respect for their age. Ancient Monuments should be protected. But what else? Firstly we should consider the map of Clwyd (Fig.116) and note that the Dykes split off a third of the county on the east and two-thirds on the west and they thus indicate the dual heritage of this border shire with its long English history in the east and the Celtic heritage to the west. The Dykes are two fixed points in a very long (and ill recorded) period when Celt and Saxon confronted each other but where the east of the present county was permanently Anglian

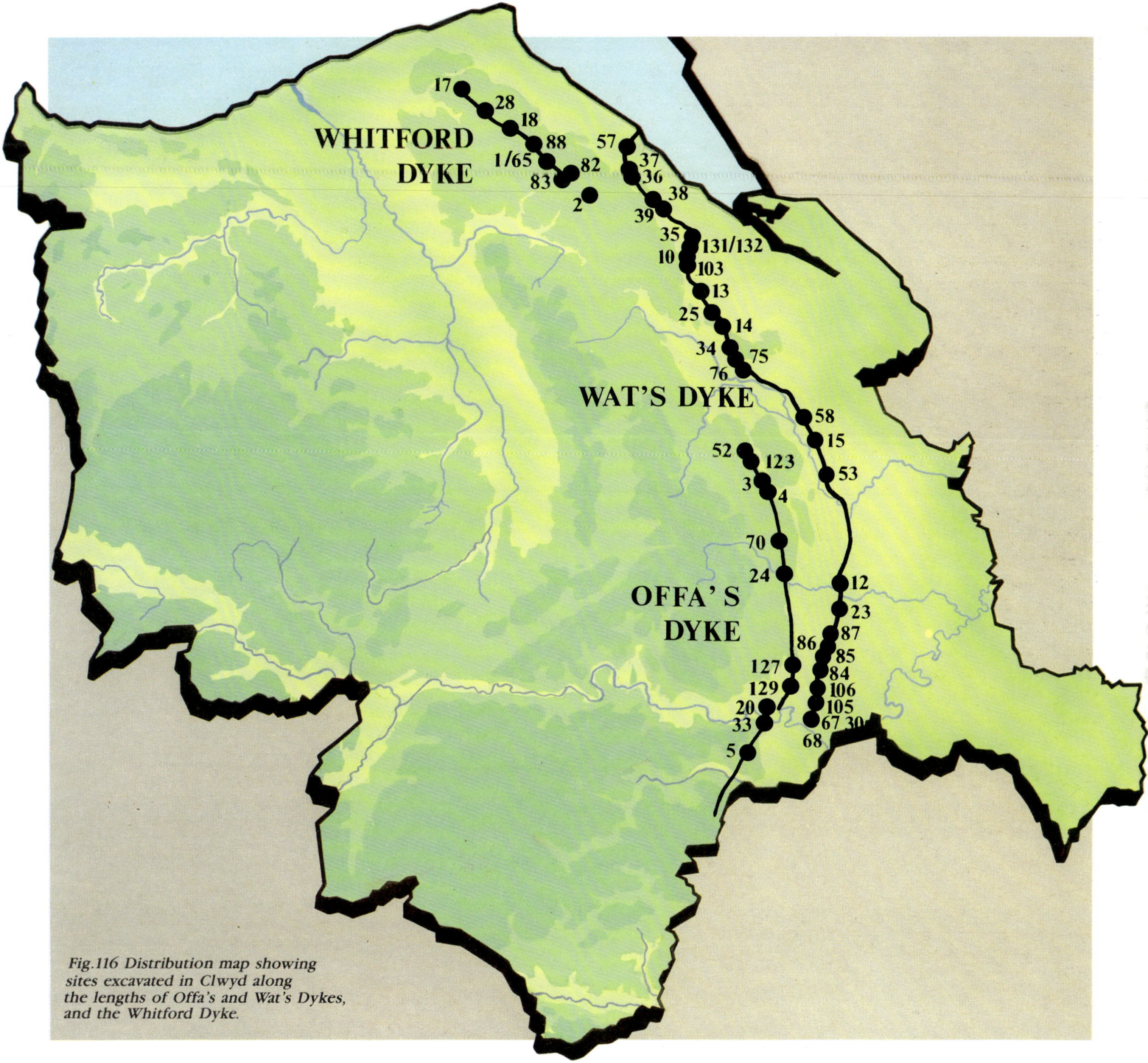

Fig.116 Distribution map showing sites excavated in Clwyd along the lengths of Offa's and Wat's Dykes, and the Whitford Dyke.

Fig.117 An aerial view of Offa's Dyke west of Rhostyllen near Wrexham. The Dyke is often preserved under later field boundaries and in the photograph runs from bottom-left to top-right.

or Saxon. The Domesday distributions confirm this (Fig. 115). But we should recognise that *Cledemutha* was built as an English town and it may be that from 826 until the battle of the Conwy in 881, for at least two generations, all of Clwyd was under Anglo-Saxon rule.

Secondly the Dykes should tell us of the nature of English settlement, and its organisation, by the predominant Saxon kingdom of the period 750-850, into a defensive net against Welsh raids.

Thirdly the Dykes mark off Welsh, tribal, Wales and they ought to give some insight into those problems that Nancy Edwards deals with elsewhere in this volume, the nature of the Welsh kingdoms and their economy. For across this barrier of the Dykes we should expect movements; not simply the attempt at criminal or military movements, raids and warfare; but we must ask ourselves how the large economy of the Anglo-Saxon kingdoms affected the smaller Welsh kingdoms? Should we not expect traders as well as raiders? And should this not be reflected archaeologically in passageways through the Dykes? Should we not expect toll-stations, custom posts or other control points? Did salt, pottery or silver pass the frontier and if so in what form; there seems to be no known trade demonstrated by artefacts or finds from the collapse of Roman rule until the 10th century coin of Hywel Dda.

The business of the archaeologist is to recreate the past, to allow us to visualise the past in the context of the physical remains and it must be admitted that in relation to the Dykes this is not easy, they are a "dead monument in an empty landscape" (Fig.117). It is possible to suggest the sequence of events leading to its construction, more difficult to suggest how, or if, the Dykes "worked". We might proceed more efficiently if we asked ourselves the questions of "what", "where", "when", and "why".

"I keep six honest serving men
(they taught me all I knew)
their names are "what" and "why" and "when"
and "how" and "where" and "who".

(C.Kipling)

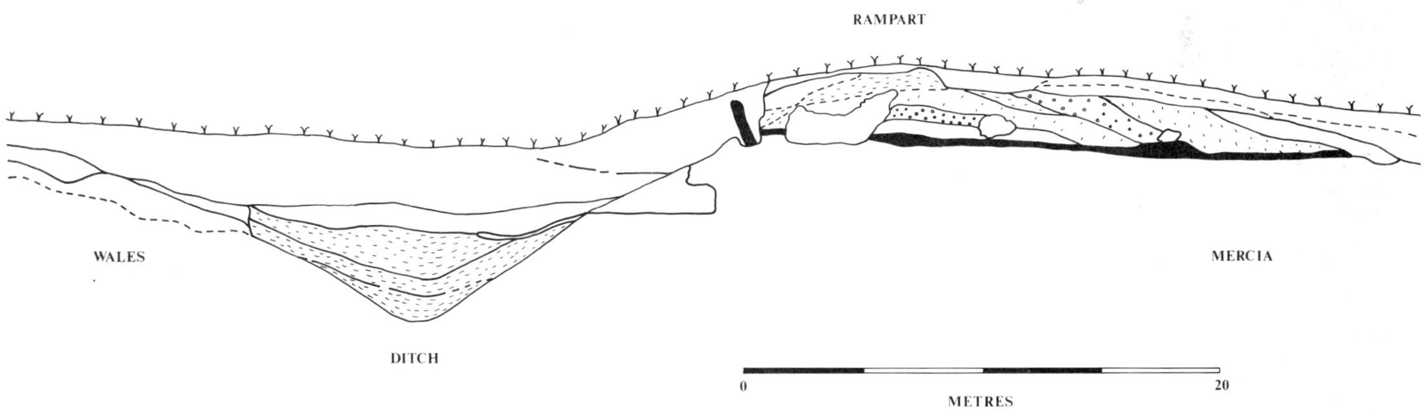

Fig.118 A section excavated across Wat's Dyke at Sychdyn near Mold, which clearly revealed the former extent of the wide ditch.

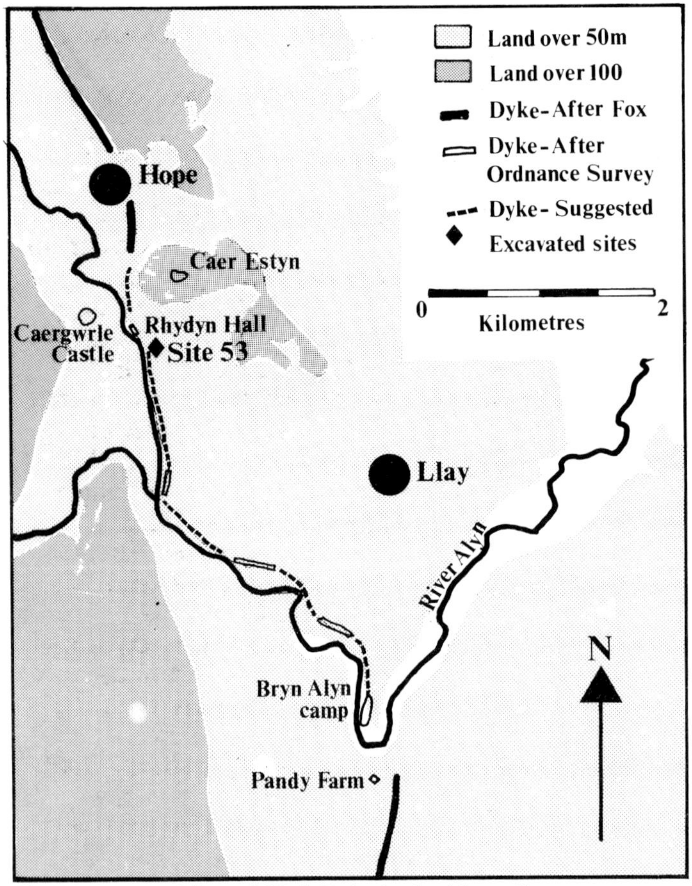

Fig.119 Suggested line of Wat's Dyke in the Alyn valley near Wrexham. According to Sir Cyril Fox the Dyke did not exist in this area but more recent work has discovered new lengths of Dyke.

The Dykes are best described in terms of "what" by considering Site 25, Sychdyn (Fig.118). The Wat's Dyke here near Mold, consists of a low earthern bank crowned with hedges or trees about 1 - 1.5m high with a shallow, sometimes waterlogged ditch in front of it. The whole construction is some 2.4m across. When excavated however the shallow ditch turns out to be 6m wide and some 2.4m deep with a cleaning slot at the bottom. Behind this considerable obstacle the bank appears to consist of a turf front to an earth bank itself stabilised with layers of turf. From a reconstruction of the shape of the bank it probably stood originally some 2m high. If one postulates a palisade then the whole obstruction from the bottom of the ditch to the top of the palisade would have been 6m high. In Clwyd the question of a palisade or wall may have been answered by Site 52, Llanfynydd Schoolfield, SJ 279 567. This site was excavated to confirm that the Offa's Dyke had reached to this point, it was being assumed that the road marked the line of the bank of the Dyke. In the Schoolfield at the base of the bank upon which the road was constructed the ditch was located (Fig.127). In the primary silt of the ditch were blocks of stone; the interpretation was therefore that the bank had been crowned by an unmortared stone wall. With or without a wall or palisade on the top or an *abattis* of thorn in the ditch, the Dyke would have been a very considerable barrier.

"Where" is a problem of great complexity which the Offa's Dyke project has concerned itself with for many years and with considerable success. It is a controversial matter and will have to be discussed here. The simplest Dyke is the Wat's Dyke so let us start with that. The line runs clearly northwards from the Wynnstay Park in Ruabon (SJ 303 423) over Pentre Clawdd hill (SJ 313 443) to Erddig (SJ 326 485) and through Wrexham, all this is as described by Sir Cyril Fox. However at the river Alyn (SJ 333 534) Fox lost the line of the earthworks and disbelieved the Ordnance Survey (Fig.119). The surveyors of the Ordnance Survey had felt that they could recognise the Wat's Dyke for two thirds of the distance of 5.4km whereas Fox declared "the Alyn ravine itself represented the line of the frontier". Now these are loaded expressions for to call the Alyn a "ravine" conjures up to the armchair or library-fast archaeologist a picture which is not the situation on the ground. At most seasons of the year the Alyn can be forded at any point and the sides of the ravine can easily be climbed . The "ravine" is a clear landscape feature and a considerable natural obstacle but "ravine" implies impassibility for a stretch of 5.6km and this description is not appropriate. In fact at Site 53, Hope, Rhydyn Hall, (SJ 312 569) Eric Foster excavated the ditch of the Dyke. (Fig.121). The "known" line of the Dyke can therefore be extended over much of the distance. Fox's line continues from Hope past Mold to the Afon Conwy west of Northop; here Fox thought the Dyke had never been completed although he recognised short sections at Holywell and at the Nant-y-Flint.

> "it can hardly be doubted that these were constructed to bar access to the coastal flat between Basingwerk and Flint at the only points where natural obstacles were non-existent. In the case of the latter construction was started on either flank of the vulnerable portion but was not carried to the centre . . .when it is remembered that incompleteness, equally inexplicable on topographical grounds, marks Offa's Dyke in this region, it is legitimate to suggest that — to the Mercians — it was a remote, difficult, and dangerous countryside, and that in the case of both Dykes the constructional and perhaps the military effort involved was too great to be sustained to the end. The attempted construction of Wat's Dyke hereabouts shows how essential to the Mercians the control of the south shore of the Dee estuary must have been, presumably as helping to secure the safety of Chester."

Fig.120 Aerial view of Offa's Dyke in the south of the county near Chirk.

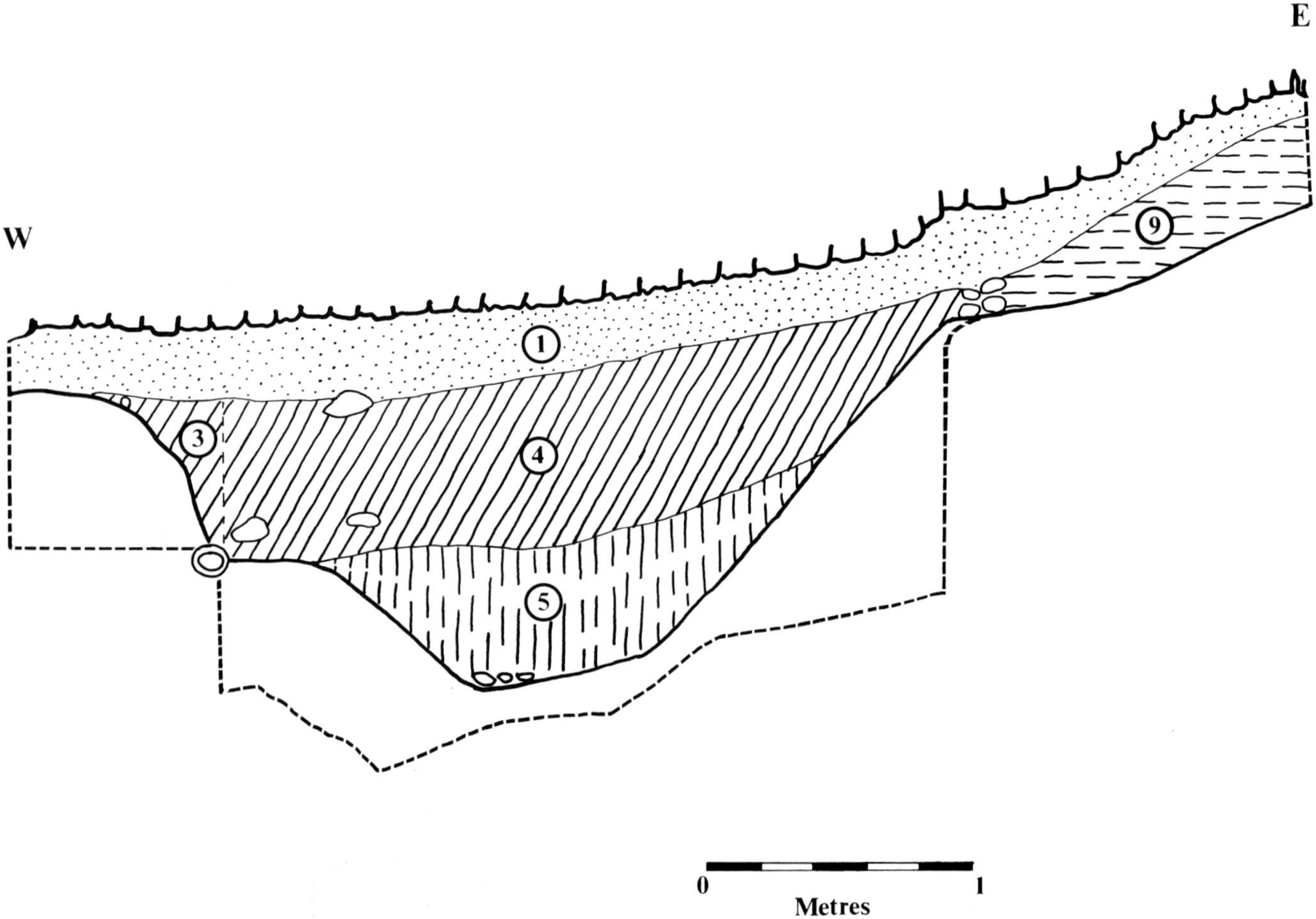

Fig.121 Excavated section across Wat's Dyke at Rhydyn Hall. Again the original size and extent of the ditch can clearly be seen.

Now this section of the Dykes and its interpretations shows Fox to be deeply confused about the area, having to square its "incompleteness" with its strategic importance by a tale of bungling. It is even more difficult to understand the paucity of the fieldwork. Fig.122 shows a completely different picture to that claimed by Fox, in fact only in two areas on this stretch from where Fox thought it terminated near Northop to its actual termination on the coast are there still sections of the Dyke yet unrecognised. A number of excavations have taken place.

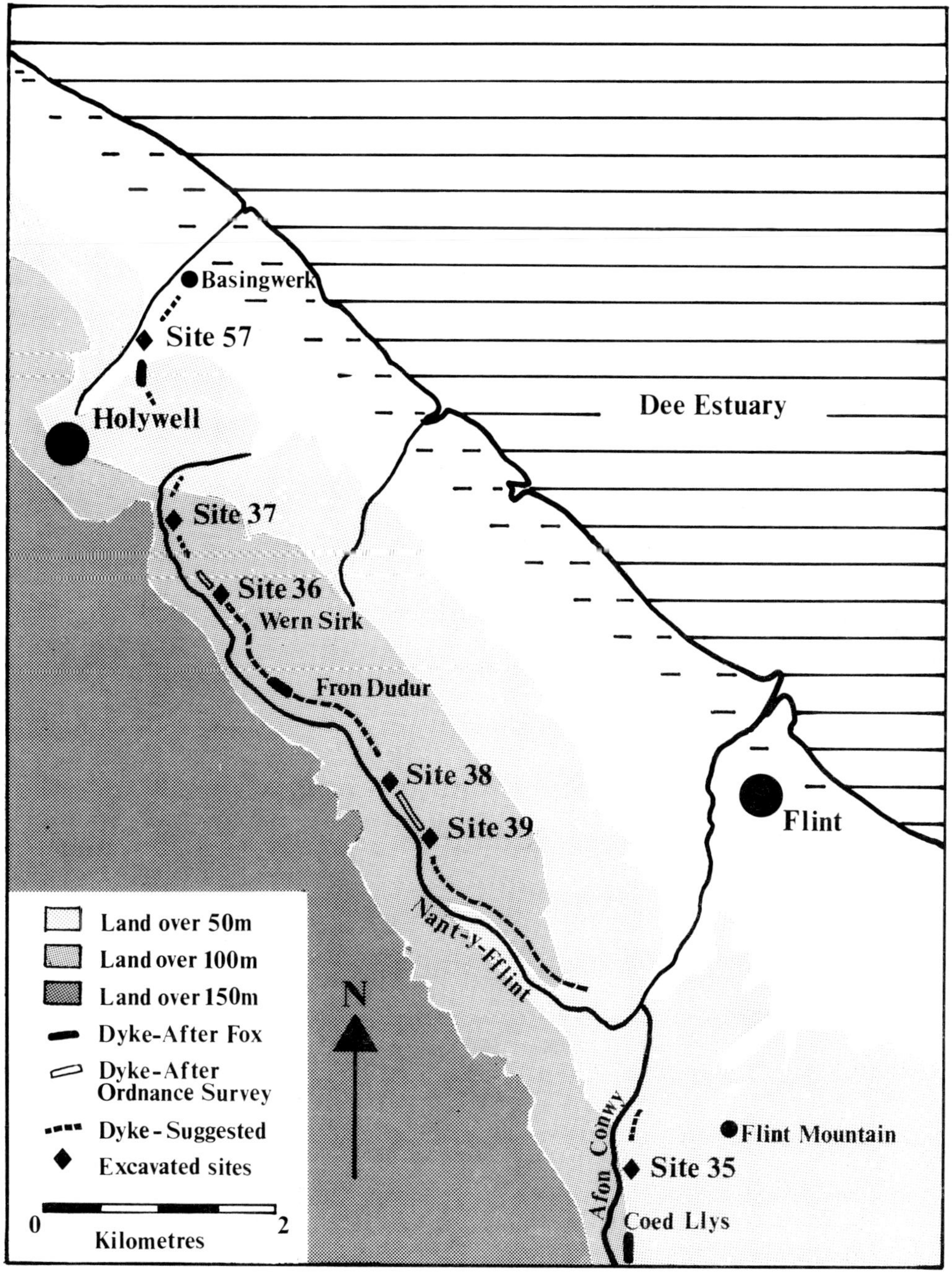

Fig.122 The northern end of Wat's Dyke between Flint and Holywell. Sir Cyril Fox thought that the Dyke had never been completed in this area, despite its strategic importance. Once again recent work has shown that the Dyke was originally continuous.

Site 36	Holywell, Coetia Clwyd	SJ 198 745
Site 37	Holywell, Coed Llwybr-y-bi	SJ 196 747
Site 38	Flint, Bethel Chapel	SJ 213 731
Site 39	Flint, Fernside Cottage	SJ 216 727
Site 57	Holywell, Coed Strand	SJ 917 767
Site 138	Flint, Northop Bypass	SJ 232 698

There really can be no doubt that the Dyke has been conclusively proved as passing through these areas. The discovery of these two important stretches within Clwyd, at the Alyn valley and in the north, is a major achievement of the Offa's Dyke Project.

If one looks at the line of the Wat's Dyke in simplified plans it is noticeable that such maps as appear in *Domesday Geography* or the *Ordnance Survey Map of Dark Age Britain* show smaller gaps in the line in Clwyd. We have dealt with the major gaps in the areas of the Alyn and the northern termination. It is to two small gaps that we should now turn. These were considered to be caused, according to Sir Cyril Fox, by forest so dense that a man could not pass. I have dealt with these gaps elsewhere and we have proved, archaeologically, that these gaps are caused by agriculture and the Dyke had been continuous. The proof is still lacking at Bryn-y-Baal where we have suggested a line across the fields (Fig.126).

The Offa's Dyke is, however, more fractious (Figs.120,123). It runs continuously along the plateau edge through Coedpoeth (SJ 293 540) and into the Cegidog Valley (SJ 284 554) (Figs.124,125). From there the Dyke is lost at Llanfynydd; it *may* run up the hill towards Treuddyn for some way as the Ordnance Survey shows it, for it is certain that it is at Site 52 (SJ 279 567) in Llanfynydd. What happens is uncertain and the very attractive idea (to me at least) that the Offa's Dyke then linked to the north with the Wat's Dyke, argued in two previous notes, cannot now be sustained, at least in its original form. The 1974 theory suggested that the original line of the Offa's Dyke came from the south to Llanfynydd in the way described above and then crossed over to the Wat's Dyke "corner" (perhaps at SJ 268 627) and followed the Wat's Dyke to the sea. This would have made the whole of the Wat's Dyke south of the "corner" phase II or the replacement of Offa's Dyke. The excavations at:—

Site 15	Hope, Pigeon House Farm	SJ 306 593
Site 75	Mold Rural, Watergate Estate	SJ 263 637
Site 76	Mold Rural, Bod Offa Farm	SJ 264 636

reveal the fact that the structure of the Wat's Dyke at these two widely separated points on the north and on the south of the "corner" are such that it is almost certain that they are of the

Fig.123 View of the very well-preserved stretch of Offa's Dyke at Tatham Road near Ruabon.

Fig.124 A scheduled stretch of Offa's Dyke at Brymbo, near Wrexham as it appeared before any management work was undertaken by the Clwyd Archaeology Service.

Fig.125 The same stretch of Dyke at Brymbo, near Wrexham, after management work had been carried out by Clwyd's Sites Management Officer with the complete co-operation of Brymbo Steelworks (the owners of the site) and Manweb (who own land adjacent to this stretch of Dyke).

same "build" and constructed by the same people and at the same time. At the time when I wrote the two notes mentioned above I considered that the placenames on the Dyke were significant. However there now appear to be "Wat's Dyke" names on the Offa's Dyke; "Offa" names on the Wat's Dyke; the possibility that the Offa's Dyke was called in one section (not in Clwyd) *Rough Ditch* similar to the present derivation of the Herefordshire *Rowe Ditch*; and finally the Wrexham stretch of the Wat's Dyke was probably called *Devil's Ditch* (on the original drawings for the first edition of the Ordnance Survey now in the Map Room of the British Museum). In view of all this I feel that the placename evidence should be left to someone more qualified to discuss it.

What is clear is that the structure known generally as Offa's Dyke at Ysceifiog, Whitford and Trelawnyd is not similar to any other section of the Offa's or Wat's Dykes. The gap of 30.6km from the last known point at Llanfynydd (Site 52) should warn us of problems and the prevalence of short dykes in the central Marches offer a parallel to this exposed fragment. It is

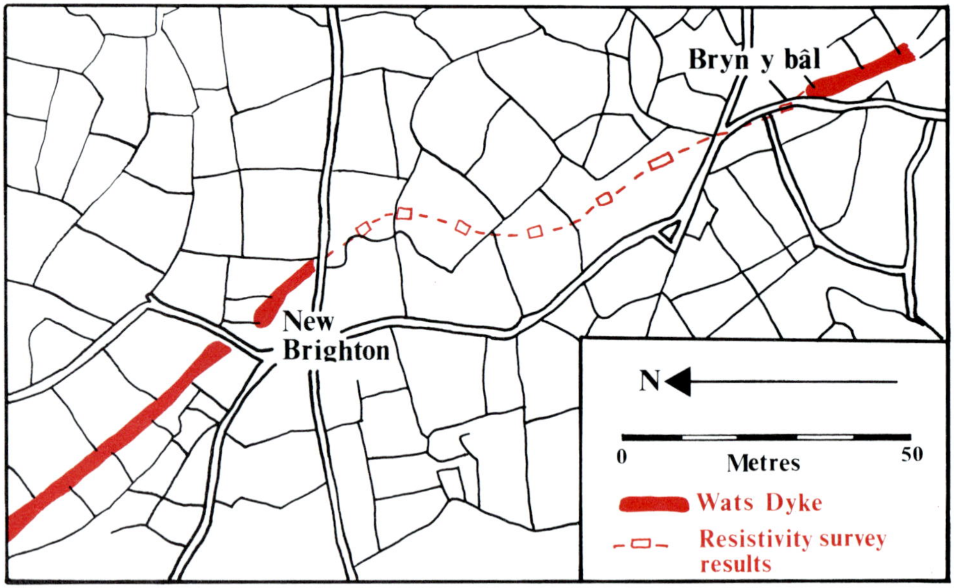

Fig.126 Results of a resistivity survey across fields at Bryn y bâl, near Mold, indicate the line of Wat's Dyke, although its existence here has not yet been proven conclusively by excavation.

the nature of the excavated and observed dyke, consisting as it does of a low earthwork between two quarry ditches at

Site 65 Whitford, Brynbella SJ 129 771
Site 82 Whitford, Rhydwen Farm SJ 133 766

which is clear proof that this earthwork is not part of the Offa's Dyke system although we still await confirmation of its date. This earthwork does not exist at Ysceifiog (Site 2) and we have demonstrated the termination of this Dyke in Pen-y-Gelli wood (Site 83, SJ 135 764). There was no sign of any earthworks in the considerable cut made between Ysceifiog and Pen-y-Gelli wood by the road improvements to the A55 at Site 121 at SJ 136 759.

There are still major problems associated with the line of both the Wat's Dyke(Fig.128) (with detailed work still being needed on the crossing of the Afon Conwy and within the confines of Holywell) with the Whitford Dyke where we do not know its western end and with the northern end of the Offa's Dyke to the north of site 52 at Llanfynydd.

"When" were the Dykes built? It would obviously be perverse to argue against the entry in Asser's *Life of King Alfred* written by a Welshman at the West Saxon court in 893 associating the Dyke with Offa in the late 8th

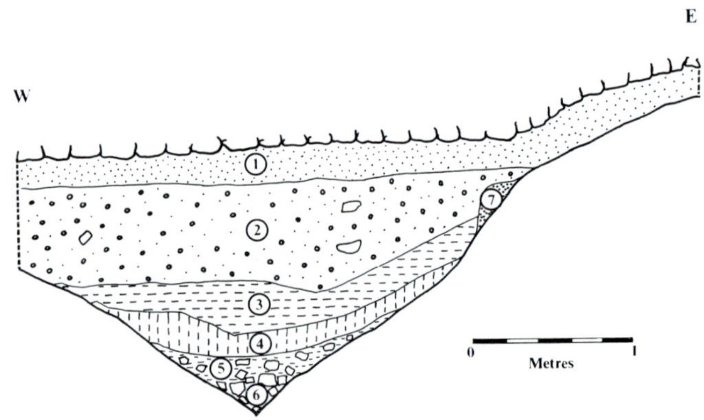

Fig.127 A section across Offa's Dyke at Llanfynydd. Offa's Dyke has not yet been shown to run further north than Llanfynydd.

Fig.128 Wat's Dyke as it appears today running through Rookery Wood at Erddig near Wrexham.

century. And this traditional view of the dating is borne out by the placename of the Dyke and the traditions attached to it. It is certain that the Dyke has always been known; knowledge of it has not been lost and the knowledge attaching it to the great Mercian king survived through the Middle Ages to appear on the first of the maps and to be recorded by the first of the antiquaries. However it should be noted that the statement by Asser and its context is important. Asser spends a considerable amount of time recounting the infamy of a certain wife of a West Saxon king, a tale quite suitable for the collections of the brothers Grimm. This lady was accused of all kinds of misdemeanours not least in accidentally poisoning King Beorhtric, her husband, in 802 whilst successfully poisoning a "certain young man very dear to the king" apparently a pastime in which she often indulged. In the midst of this fable, told to explain why the West Saxons did not afford the title of "Queen" to the wife of the king, Asser offers the information:—

> "There was in Mercia in fairly recent times a certain vigorous king called Offa, who terrified all the neighbouring kings and provinces around him, and who had a great dyke built between Wales and Mercia from sea to sea."
> *Rex nomine Offa, qui vallum magnum inter Britannium atque Merciam de mari usque ad mare fieri imperavit.*

The only other evidence we have for the date of the Dykes is the fact that the Offa's Dyke had been shown archaeologically to overlie, and therefore be later than, Roman remains at Ffrith (SJ 284 553).

So to "why" and "how" and "who". The reason lying behind the construction of such an enormous work has led to people making

Fig.129 An extremely well preserved stretch of Offa's Dyke in the area close to Chirk Castle.

guesses about its use for centuries. Until this century those guesses were seen almost entirely in terms of warfare and defence although there were some guesses which saw it as a legal barrier. However Fox suggested that the whole thing was "an agreed frontier" and quoted in evidence two places where he thought that the line of the earthworks demonstrated this.

It should be noted, however, that the line of the Dyke does NOT prove that Offa's Dyke is an agreed frontier. A possible scenario for the construction of Offa's Dyke (Fig.129) is as follows:

1. There were a series of devastating raids into England that Offa and the Mercians could not answer. Attempts to reply by counter-raids did not succeed and the farmers in the border area abandoned their fields and withdrew.
2. The king decided to apply a typical dark age solution and faced the most hostile Welsh kingdoms with a bank and ditch (these are known both on the continent, in East Anglia and with the Wansdyke in Wiltshire).
3. The king and his advisors, possibly an ealdorman, (the highest rank of Saxon official) talked it over with the council or *witan* and decided on a line for the works to follow. What is difficult to conceive for those days before maps is the intense understanding of the shape of the kingdom and the depth of local knowledge that allowed them to plan the line.
4. Rough sightings were probably made and checked with beacon fires etc. for line.
5. The crisis in the area could not have been very great for there was time to survey and layout the line making the very best use of the landscape, the hillsides and rivers. Long lines were laid out so that they took into account the number of river crossings (always a weak point) and the control of fords. A line was worked out which always attempted to be in a strong position with good visual command to the west.
6. Enormous fires were lit to clear the ground and the sight lines. A plough marked out the line in the open fields and pastures. Marker posts were erected on some stretches and in particularly difficult or complex parts there were built small banks and ditches as marking out features.
7. During the winter the king, meeting with his *witan*, ordered men from every village and settlement under his control (and we have a tribute list of the time, the *Tribal Hidage*) to report to the frontier, probably under their own reeves and ealdormen where they were assigned their areas to work. Those who did not go on this construction expedition would have contributed to those that did (one could expect about 5 men to a village) by loaning tools, ponies, giving food etc. It probably would be constructed in the late spring or early summer, at the Rogation days, the traditional time for such work in medieval Europe, just before Whitsuntide.
8. On arrival at the marking out bank or plough mark each group would find the length they had been assigned and they would set about digging and building this section.
9. The turf would be stripped off and in most cases used to stabilise the bank, it would also be used to build the front. Using whatever local materials were to hand, stone if they could find it in easy blocks, or timber, they would construct a palisade or wall. In a very short time the ditch and bank would also grow its obstruction of blackthorn and bramble.
10. The work was then ready. How precisely it worked I am unsure and so it is clear that much more work is left to do.
11. However it was not a success and the better engineered, thought out and constructed Wat's Dyke replaced it (Fig.130). The line also includes a series of hillforts and strong points; were these in use?

12. Even this did not succeed and in 822 the Mercians invaded North Wales and ruled for two generations, thus doing away with the frontier raids that had led to the construction of the Dykes in the first place.

Modern parallels such as the relations between Lebanon and the Israelis may help us to understand these works, designed as barriers to raids rather than walls against major armies, and as such are to be seen throughout history.

1.	Whitford, BRYNBELLA	1926 SJ 129 771	WHIT
2.	Ysceifiog, CIRCLE	1926 SJ 152 753	WHIT
3.	Frith, VILLAGE	1927 SJ 284 553	OFFA
4.	Frith, HALL	1927 SJ 288 548	OFFA
5.	Chirk, CAEAU-GWYNION	1928 SJ 273 395	OFFA
10.	Northop, MIDDLE MILL	1955 SJ 233 691	WATS
12.	Acton, WAT'S DYKE SCHOOL	1975 SJ 334 523	WATS
13.	Sychdyn, CLAWDD OFFA	1975 SJ 243 678	WATS
14.	Mold, BYPASS	1976 SJ 257 653	WATS
15.	Hope, PIGEON HOUSE FARM	1974 SJ 306 593	WATS
17.	Trelawnyd, VILLAGE	1973 SJ 089 798	WHIT
18.	Whitford, TRE-ABBOT-BACH	1973 SJ 112 784	WHIT
20.	Cefn, WATERLOO TOWER	1976 SJ 285 422	OFFA
23.	Wrexham, EXCHANGE STATION	1972 SJ 329 509	WATS
24.	COEDPOETH	1973 SJ 293 512	OFFA
25.	Sychdyn, PIPELINE	1974 SJ 252 659	WATS
28.	Trelawnyd, PENTRE FFYDDION	1976 SJ 104 790	WHIT
30.	Ruabon, WYNNSTAY PARK	1976 SJ 308 425	WATS
34.	Mold Rural, MYNYDD ISA	1957 SJ 262 639	WATS
35.	Flint Mountain, BRYN-Y-GARREG	1977 SJ 232 698	WATS
36.	Holywell, COETIA CLWYD	1976 SJ 198 745	WATS
37.	Flint, COED LLWYR-Y-BI	1977 SJ 196 747	WATS
38.	Flint, BETHEL CHAPEL	1977 SJ 213 731	WATS
39.	Flint, FERNSIDE COTTAGE	1977 SJ 216 726	WATS
52.	Llanfynydd, SCHOOLFIELD	1978 SJ 279 567	OFFA
53.	Hope, RHYDDYN HALL	1978 SJ 312 569	WATS
57.	Holywell, Coed Strand, CUPID'S GROVE	1978 SJ 191 767	WATS
58.	Hope, CLAWDD OFFA	1978 SJ 299 607	WATS
65.	Whitford, BRYNBELLA	1979 SJ 129 771	WHIT
67.	Ruabon, BOAT HOUSE	1980 SJ 308 432	WATS
68.	Ruabon, NANT-Y-CAE-COCH	1980 SJ 307 423	WATS
70.	BRYMBO, Area of	1892 SJ 29 52	OFFA
75.	Mold Rural, WATERGATE ESTATE	1981 SJ 263 637	WATS
76.	Mold Rural, BOD OFFA FARM	1981 SJ 264 636	WATS
82.	Whitford, RHYDWEN FARM	1981 SJ 133 766	WHIT
83.	Whitford, PEN-Y-GELLI	1981 SJ 135 764	WHIT
84.	Erddig, THE ROOKERY	1982 SJ 324 478	WATS
85.	Erddig, CISTERN	1982 SJ 325 480	WATS
86.	Erddig, BIG WOOD	1982 SJ 325 485	WATS
87.	Wrexham Regis, COURT WOOD	1982 SJ 328 489	WATS
88.	Whitford, CORNEL CAE	1982 SJ 125 775	WHIT
103.	Northop, MIDDLE MILL	1984 SJ 233 691	WATS
105.	Ruabon, PENTRE CLAWDD	1984 SJ 313 443	WATS
106.	Ruabon, BLACK BROOK KNOLL	1984 SJ 321 456	WATS
121.	Whitford, A55 IMPROVEMENT	1986 SJ 136 759	WHIT
123.	Llanfynydd, COED ISA	1986 SJ 282 562	OFFA
127.	Johnstown, HARRINGTON'S	1986 SJ 300 457	OFFA
129.	Ruabon, TATHAM ROAD	1987 SJ 302 448	OFFA
131.	Flint Mountain, COED LLYS	1987 SJ 232 698	WATS
132.	Northop, COED LLYS	1987 SJ 232 698	WATS

Fig.130 View of the excavated section across Wat's Dyke at Sychdyn near Mold.

MOTTES AND MOATED SITES
by Jack Spurgeon

A. The Mottes

The castles of the Norman conquest were mostly of earth and timber. Stone castles were rare. Timber castles were usually founded on mottes, though an embanked ringwork was substituted at about a quarter of them. In Wales we may ascribe to the period 1066-1200 some 242 mottes, 77 castle-ringworks and 27 far less surely-established stone castles. The totals for Clwyd are striking: 26 mottes; no ringworks; no certain early stone castles. To the 26 mottes we may also expect to add some of the eight motte-like mounds requiring archaeological investigation, and probably the vanished Overton Castle. These figures are largely based on David King's comprehensive gazetteer and bibliography of the castles of England and Wales. His chapters on Denbigh, Flint and Merioneth correct and extend the list that might be compiled from the relevant inventories of the Royal Commission and supersede his earlier lists in *Archaeologia Cambrensis*. Information has also been gleaned from the Clwyd Archaeological Record and the unpublished records of the Ordnance Survey.

Clwyd is the only county in Wales with no ringworks. Two explanations have been advanced. Noting that Cheshire also lacks ringworks, David King suggests that the accident of personal preference was at work: the Earls of Chester simply favoured mottes and this naturally influenced castle-building in adjacent North Wales, their zone of activity. Alternatively, it may be suspected that geological considerations are involved. Recent work in Glamorgan show that its 16 mottes lie within the limits of the glacial drift, while all but a few of its 23 ringworks occupy shallow soil over rock. In Clwyd most if not all the mottes are composed of glacial drift and many were formed by re-shaping prominent glacial landforms. These landforms are common in the county, and though unaware of the absence of ringworks, the geologist, Dr. Neaverson, suggested in 1947 that *Drift deposits . . . in North Wales . . . obviously determine the distribution of the artificial mounds on which early Norman castles were built . . . The construction of these strongholds required the presence of a suitable substratum which could be rapidly formed into conical mounds*".

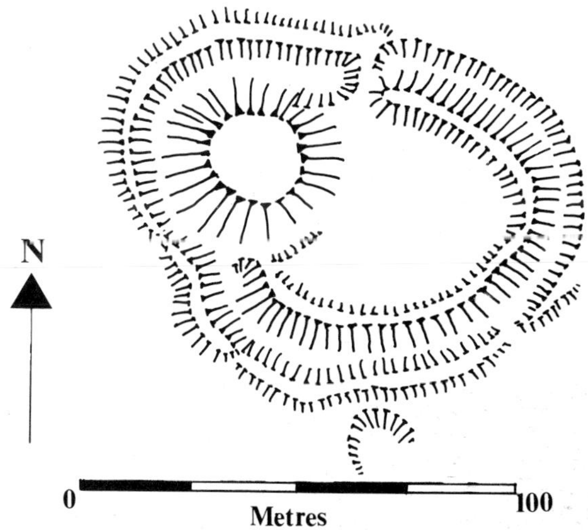

Fig.131 A plan of the impressive Welsh motte and bailey of Tomen y Rhodwydd, Llandegla, between Ruthin and Llangollen.

The distribution of our mottes is unremarkable (Fig.132), though its interpretation is bedevilled by the complex of medieval political entities comprised by the present county. About a half are closely concentrated between the Clwyd and the Dee in the greater portion of Flintshire which was effectively the border area of Cheshire. The remainder are more widely dispersed. Most lie on low hills or promontories, though a few are on scarp-edges and Prestatyn occupies flat marshy ground. In size they vary greatly, from the huge motte at Hawarden, rising 15m. from its ditch, to the little mound a metre high at Prestatyn (Fig.133).

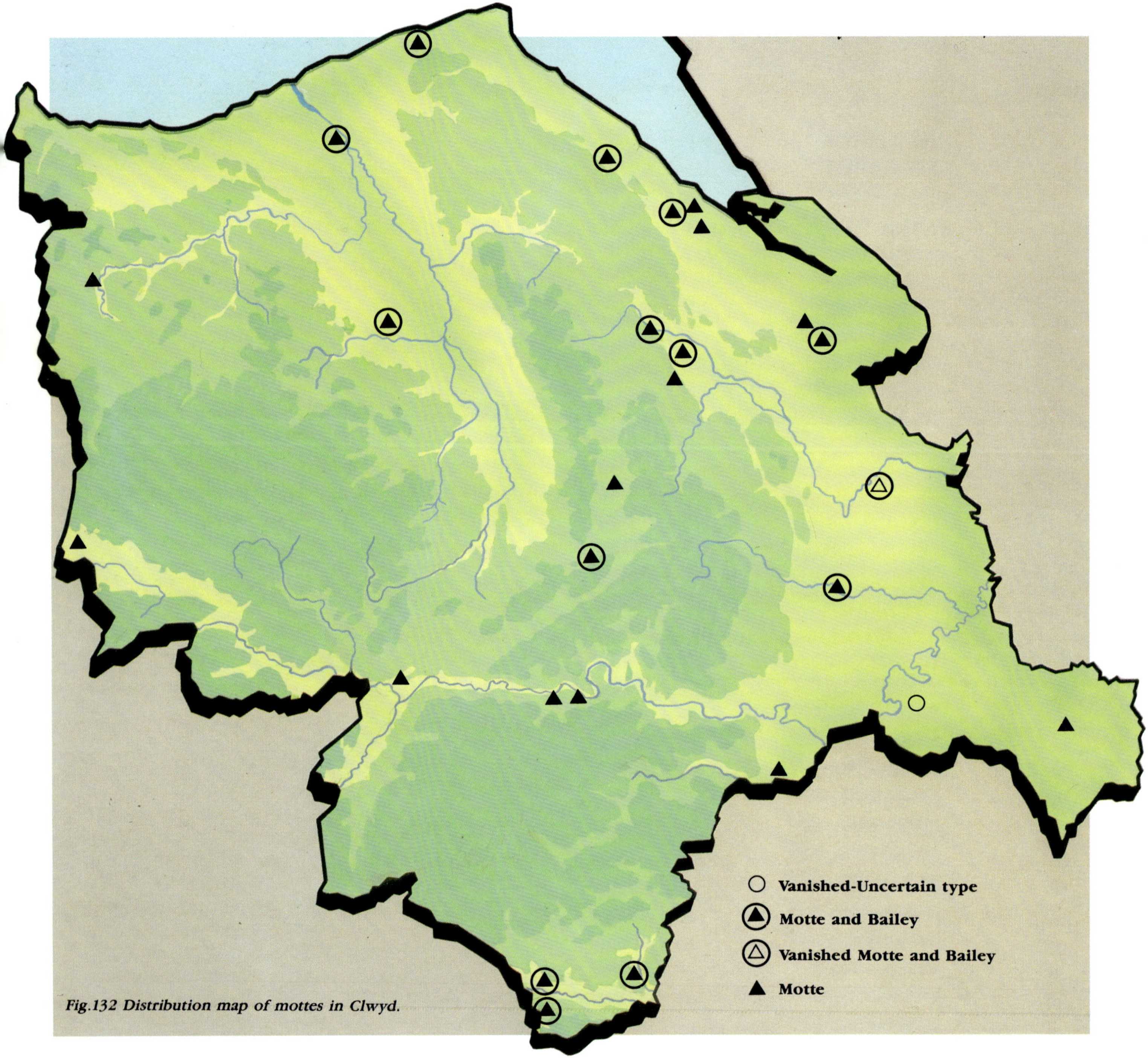

Fig.132 Distribution map of mottes in Clwyd.

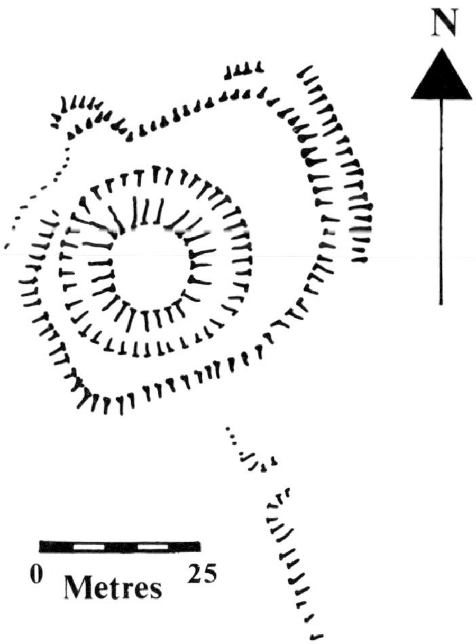

Fig.133 A plan of the low motte at Prestatyn where traces of masonry were noted during excavations carried out in 1913. Prestatyn is mentioned in the Domesday Book of 1086.

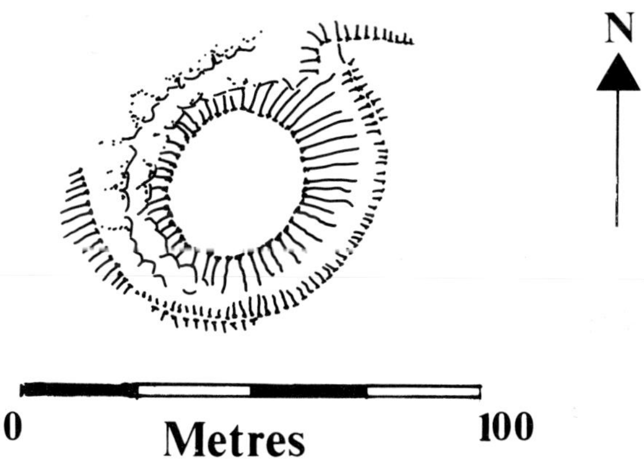

Fig.134 Tomen y Faerdre, Llanarmon yn Iâl, is one of the finest mottes in Clwyd and was possibly the caput *of Earl Hugh in the 12th century.*

Baileys adjoin 14 sites, though the evidence is sometimes slight. Bailey Hill at Mold has two baileys. Undue emphasis should not be placed on the absence of baileys at 12 sites, particularly in the light of the flimsy palisade discerned at Hen Blas. The finest mottes in the county are Mold, Erddig (Fig.137), Hawarden, Rhuddlan, Sycharth, Tomen y Rhodwydd (Figs.131,138) and Tomen y Faerdre (Fig.134). Hawarden is particularly strong, double-ditched all round and with an earthwork barbican.

Documentation is exceptionally good for the first Norman advances into North Wales in the late 11th century. Though the motte at Rhuddlan is the only castle recorded in Clwyd before 1100, it is possible to identify others which were probably as early. In 1070 William the Conqueror came to Chester and granted that county to Hugh of Avranches, commanding that a castle was built at Rhuddlan and given to Hugh's cousin Robert, so that he might contain the Welsh. Robert of Rhuddlan exceeded the king's order. Crossing the Clwyd he soon established another castle, possibly of stone, at Degannwy. Though now within the modern county of Gwynedd, Degannwy was anciently a part of the cantref of Rhos and, like Rhuddlan, a Welsh commotal llys. With his capture of Gruffydd ap Cynan in 1081 Robert assumed control of Gwynedd. In 1086 the Cheshire Domesday records a small borough at Rhuddlan, with its mint, church, iron-mines and fisheries. From the north shore of Tegeingl to Maelor a belt of thriving vills occupied lands that were waste in 1066. Rhos and Rhufoniog are recognisable as *Ros* and *Reweniou*, territories held of the king by Robert. His castle at Degannwy, in Rhos, has already been noted. If we seek his *caput* in Rhufoniog, we might begin with the large mound of Y Foelas, or the possible motte claimed to be masked behind the Crown Hotel at Denbigh. Beyond the Conwy Robert held *Nortwales*, or Gwynedd, from the king, rendering £40 annually. Hawarden was held by Earl Hugh and its motte may well be his; the largest are generally the earliest, and its double-ditching recalls Roger de Montgomery's Hen Domen, which certainly figures in

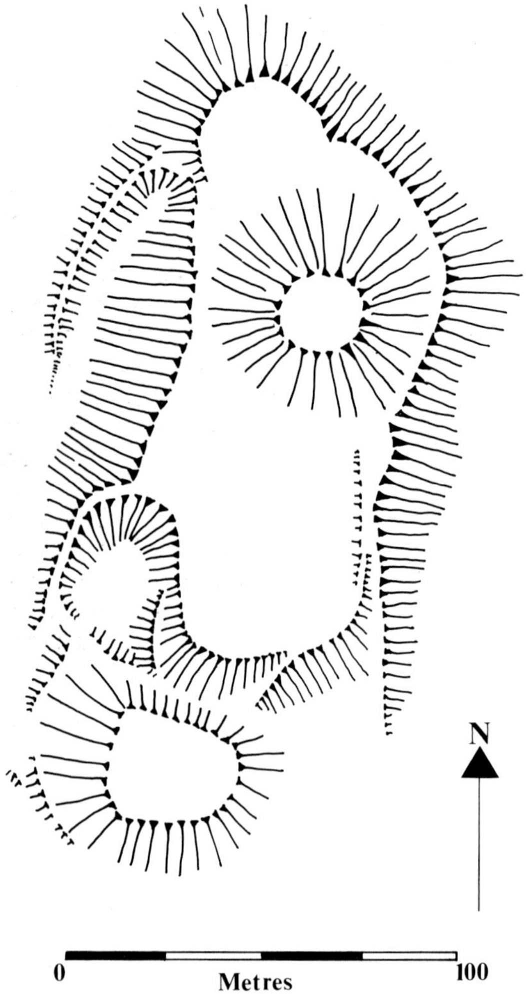

Fig.135 A Plan of the motte at Bailey Hill, Mold. This motte is unique in the county in having two baileys.

Domesday. To the south the commotes of Iâl, Cynllaith and Edeyrnion figure as *Gal*, *Chenlei* and *Derniou* in the Shropshire Domesday, for they pertained to Powys. Iâl was held by Earl Hugh, of Roger de Montgomery, and Tomen y Faerdre may well have been his *caput*. Cynllaith and Edeyrnion had fallen to Roger's sheriff, Rainald, and the mottes of Sycharth and Rûg are his likely administrative centres. Sycharth was another Welsh llys, while Rûg is the presumed location of *Ruc*, where Gruffydd ap Cynan had been captured in 1081.

It may now be accepted that Robert of Rhuddlan was slain by Welsh raiders below the Great Orme in 1093, rather than in 1088 as previously claimed. It follows that he was surely involved in the raising of castles in Gwynedd at Aber, Aberlleiniog, Caernarfon, and perhaps at Tomen-y-mur. His death perhaps inspired the Welsh revival of 1094. Gruffydd ap Cynan, now at liberty, soon drove the Normans back to the Conwy and seized their castles in Gwynedd.

Despite two expeditions by William Rufus, Gwynedd was not recovered and the Norman hold on Clwyd was soon challenged. By 1118 Rhos and Rhufoniog had fallen to Gruffydd and his sons, and in the third quarter of the 12th century his heir would even enjoy a period when his rule extended to the Dee. The four cantrefs of Perfeddwlad witnessed almost perpetual warfare throughout this century, while to the south, Powys became a client-kingdom of the crown under Henry I and recovered its northern commotes, including the two Maelors. In these circumstances it is not surprising that Clwyd lacks early stone castles, demonstrating David King's paradox of castle-building: danger inspired castles, but they could only be built strongly in conditions of peace. Throughout the 12th century and well into the 13th century, therefore, our mottes were of necessity in the forefront of the long struggle for the mastery of this most disputed area. About 15 of them are recorded, usually when destroyed by the Welsh, sometimes when restored by the Normans. Owain Gwynedd was especially active, capturing Mold (Fig.135) in 1146, building Tomen y Rhodwydd in Iâl in 1149, and capturing 'Basingwerk' in 1166 and Prestatyn and Rhuddlan in 1167. Tomen y Rhodwydd is the finest motte in the Principality which may be attributed to the Welsh. Though we may suspect

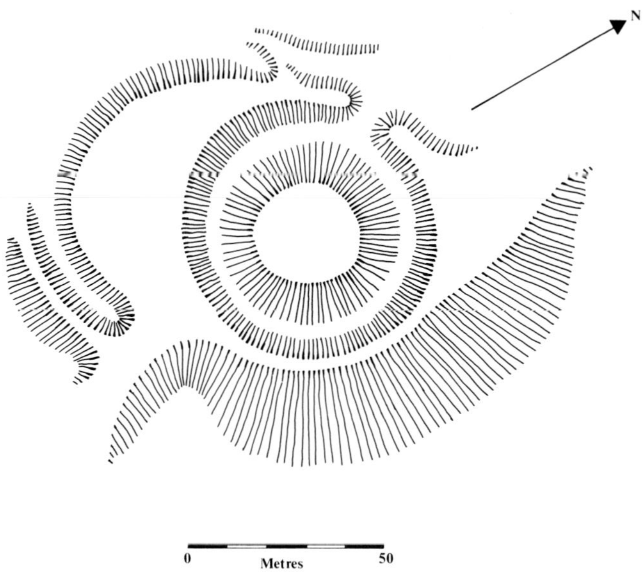

Fig.136 Sycharth motte, Llansilin, was partially excavated in the 1960's. It was in use until the early 15th century and contained the timber hall of Owain Glyndŵr.

that a few others in Clwyd may have been built by them, the majority are probably Norman works.

Mottes continued in use well into the 13th century. Timber defences were repaired at Rhuddlan in 1241, and renewed at 'Coleshill Castle' in 1244, this last no doubt one of three mottes near Flint. We may doubt that Owain Glyndŵr's timber hall on the motte at Sycharth was fortified, but it is of interest that its occupation was ended in the flames of war as late as 1403.

The archaeological potential of Clwyd's mottes will be evident from their rich historical context. To date only a few have been excavated. No data are available for 19th century work at Trueman's Hill and Hawarden (Fig.139), while the short note on masonry uncovered at Prestatyn is quite inadequate. Excavations at Rûg, near Corwen, were undertaken in the late 19th century and again in 1921. It is fortunate that the records made by Charles Wynn and Willoughby Gardner were adequate for the posthumous publication of a useful illustrated report in 1961. This shows that the motte was raised over a bronze age barrow containing a cist burial. A similar sequence is known at Treoda, (Nr. Cardiff), and at York, while effort was similarly minimised at Tomen-y-mur (Gwynedd) and Colwyn (Powys) by siting mottes over the remains of Roman fort gates. The historic motte at Sycharth was excavated in 1962-63 (Figs.136,141). No evidence was found to support the enduring suspicion that this motte was raised in the late 11th century. It should be added, however, that only two very small trenches were opened in the bailey, and that the quarter of the summit explored was greatly disturbed by the vestiges of Glyndŵr's hall and other structures destroyed by Prince Henry in 1403. A central core of stones was revealed within the motte but it proved too dangerous to establish its nature; it is uncertain

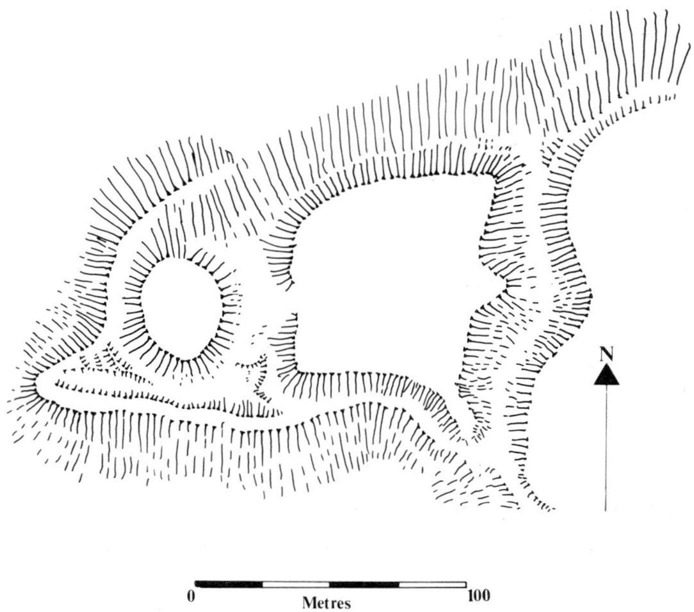

Fig.137 Plan of the large motte and bailey at Erddig, in the grounds of Erddig Hall, near Wrexham.

Fig.138 Aerial view of Tomen y Rhodwydd at Llandegla. The motte is the mound at centre-left and the circular defensive bank of the bailey can be clearly seen.

whether this represents another cairn, or the initial make-up of the motte. Rubble cores have also been noticed, but not investigated, in Montgomeryshire and Breconshire. No excavations have explored the motte at Rhuddlan (Fig.142), but the general disposition of the defences of its Norman borough has been established by trial trenching, as well as the location of its church.

One final excavation dissipates the needless pessimism that might be engendered by the disappointment of the far more limited exploration of Sycharth. At Hen Blas Mr. G.B. Leach tackled a reputed castle site with no signs of a motte (Fig.140). His outstanding work demonstrated the former existence of a small 12th century motte dominating an inner bailey formed by isolating a spur. Early in the 13th century most of this motte was levelled to fill the ditch separating it from the bailey, providing space for new buildings. Post-holes for a light palisade around the bailey were recorded, and within the outer bailey a chapel and lime kiln were excavated. The site was rich in finds, and Leach's admirable reports are well illustrated and supported by illuminating appendices.

With their rich historical context and the surprising wealth of archaeological evidence surviving at Hen Blas, it is not necessary to emphasise the need for the strictest protection of Clwyd's surviving mottes. The Roft motte at Marford and that suspected at Overton have already vanished. Of the remaining 25 listed, it is reassuring that all but two appear to be scheduled. This protection, however, requires constant local vigilance, and it should also be

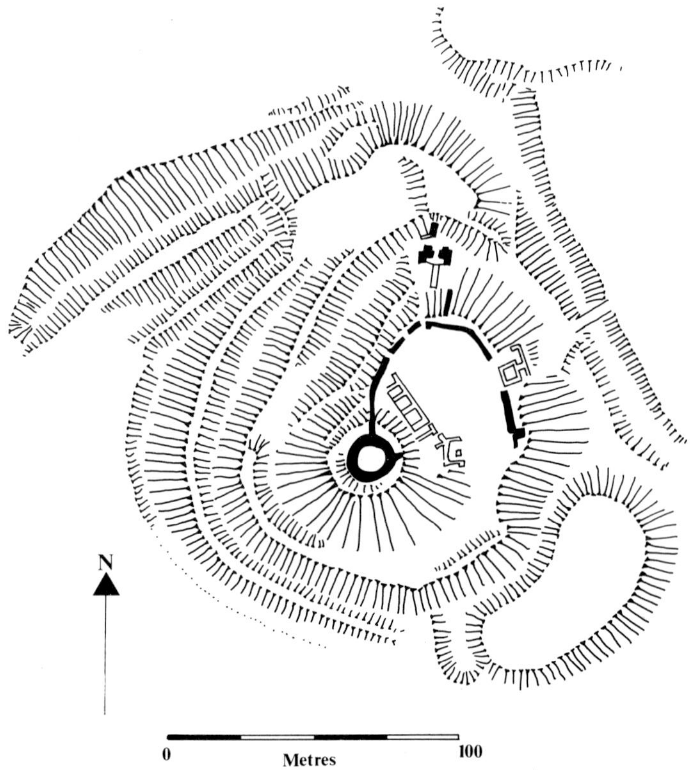

Fig.139 Plan of the strong, double-ditched motte at Hawarden. A later, stone castle was constructed on top of the earthen fortification.

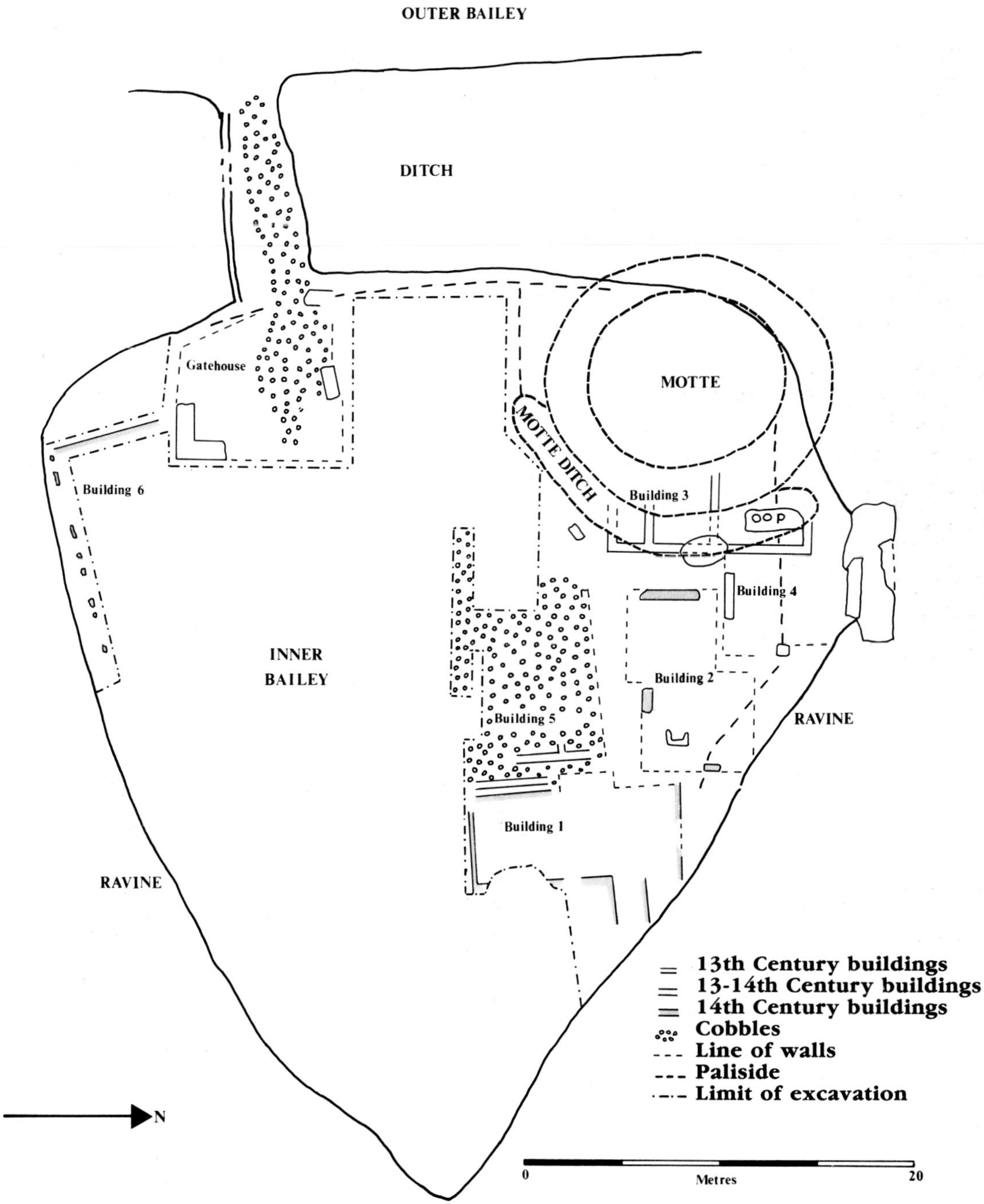

Fig.140 Plan of the excavated features at Hen Blas, near Flint. Long suspected as the site of a motte, its existence was not confirmed until the careful excavations of G.B. Leach were completed in the 1950's.

Fig.141 Aerial view of the motte and bailey at Sycharth, Llansilin.

noted that scheduled areas may well exclude adjacent ground where vanished baileys may be strongly suspected. Ploughing in such areas would soon destroy such evidence as that revealed in the two baileys at Hen Blas.

The excavation of mottes is a time-consuming and complex task. After 26 years excavating Hen Domen, Montgomery, Philip Barker has only recently exhausted the potential evidence that awaited his careful trowel in just half of the bailey. Until such protracted meticulous and desirable attention can be given to one of the Clwyd mottes, the priority is to protect them all for that happy day. Meanwhile, the following modest objectives might be urged:
1) The eight possible mottes should be investigated carefully, if necessary employing trial trenching. Confirmed mottes should be recommended for scheduling.
2) At mottes with no surviving traces of baileys, trial trenching should explore any adjacent area where ambiguous surface features or topographical limitations would suggest their probable locations.
3) Accurate and detailed large-scale plans and profiles of most sites are an urgent priority.

It goes without saying that before any motte is unavoidably mutilated or destroyed, it should be excavated as fully as possible. It is also self-evident that much is still to be gained from intensive study of the records, particularly in regard to early families and the descent of manors. Such study may often shed new light on early castles, even where they are not actually mentioned. This approach has greatly assisted current work on the early castles of Glamorgan.

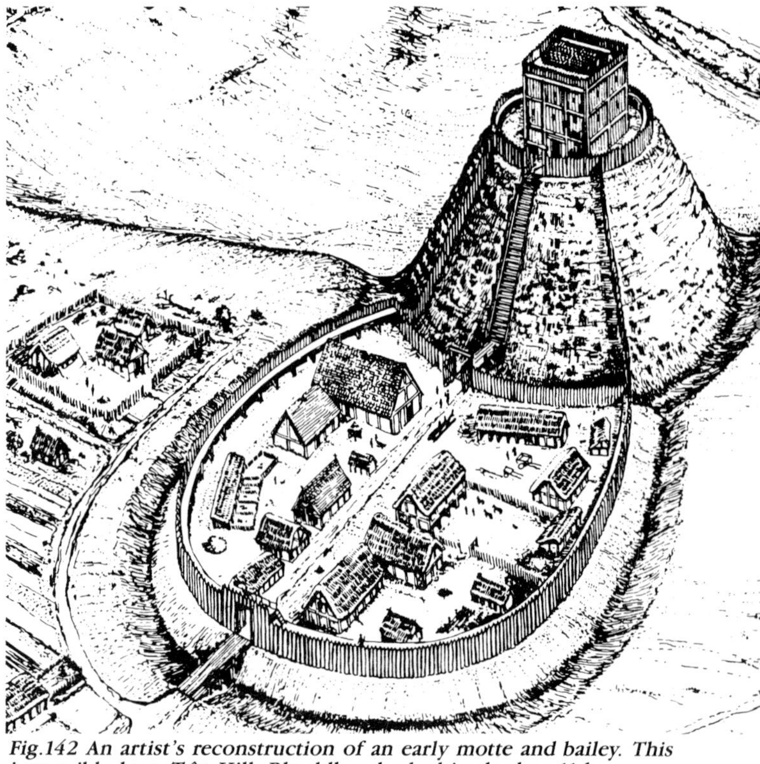

Fig.142 An artist's reconstruction of an early motte and bailey. This is possibly how Tŵt Hill, Rhuddlan, looked in the late 11th century.

B. The Moated Sites

'Moated sites', the current term for the 'homestead moats' first recognised in 1901 as a class of medieval monument, are usually square or rectangular, occasionally round or irregular. They vary greatly in size. In Wales the average area is one fifth of a hectare enclosed. With few exceptions, they are sited to ensure wet moats. Water-retaining banks, leats or dams occasionally survive, though such works were usually avoided by tapping immediately adjacent streams or springs, or by the reliance on seepage and runoff on impervious ground. Most were of manorial status, the homes of lords or their stewards. A few pertained to ecclesiastical institutions, but only the records will differentiate moated granges, parsonages or episcopal seats from those of lay lords. Occasional ancillary moated enclosures protecting orchards, gardens, animals or produce are hardly known in Wales, though in Clwyd we should note the moated haystacks recently noticed in the 14th century accounts of a manor in adjacent Cheshire. Dating evidence for moated sites indicates their introduction in the 12th century and a proliferation between 1200 and 1325. Thereafter, they continued in use, though were less frequently founded, until the 16th century.

The defensive capabilities of moated sites were negligible. Only three in Wales are known to have had stone walls and towers, but these sites, Llys Edwin (Clwyd), Roche Castle (Dyfed) and Pencoed Castle (Gwent), were hardly castles. Minimal protection against wild animals and marauders was only one function of the moat. It also proclaimed status, a contemporary motive best displayed in Clwyd by the absurdity of the stone defences of the entrance front at Llys Edwin, where timber served for the other walls and angle towers. More prosaically, the moat provided fish and fowl and a convenient watering-place for stock, not forgetting the insurance of a convenient source of water to fight fires. More detailed discussion of the form and function of moats is in print and need not be elaborated here.

There are about 100 more mottes in Wales than the 140 or so known or suspected moats. This difference is surely exaggerated or illusory. Many more moats await discovery, but it is not likely that our roll of mottes will be greatly increased. In England moats vastly outnumber mottes. Medieval archaeology has enjoyed much attention since the war, and following the formation of the Moated Sites Research Group in 1972, moats have been particularly closely studied. In 1972 it was possible to list rather more than 3,000 moats in England and Wales, a figure which has been almost doubled. Typical of this surge of discovery, known moats in Cheshire trebled from 55 to 180 between 1974 and 1982. In 1963 the episcopal moated site of Hen Gwrt (Gwent) was taken into state care, partly due to a presumed rarity of moats in Wales. Even then, some 41 moats had been mentioned in the first nine Inventories of the Royal Commission. By 1969 Emery could estimate a total of about 50 or 60 Welsh moats, and this had risen to 130 by 1979. The current total for Wales is now close to 150, and two general discussions of Welsh sites have appeared.

English moats form particularly impressive concentrations in East Anglia and the Midlands. Most Welsh sites may be seen as an extension of the Midlands sites into the richest and most manorialised areas of Wales. Clwyd exemplifies this English context, particularly with its impressively clustered sites in the eastern finger of Maelor Saesneg.

At present we may identify 43 certain or possible moats in Clwyd, though 12 of these are vanished, and others mutilated. A further 18 are dubious, and are listed, but not plotted on our map (Fig.143). Scant published information is available. The relevant Inventories mention only 21 moats in Clwyd, three now consigned to our

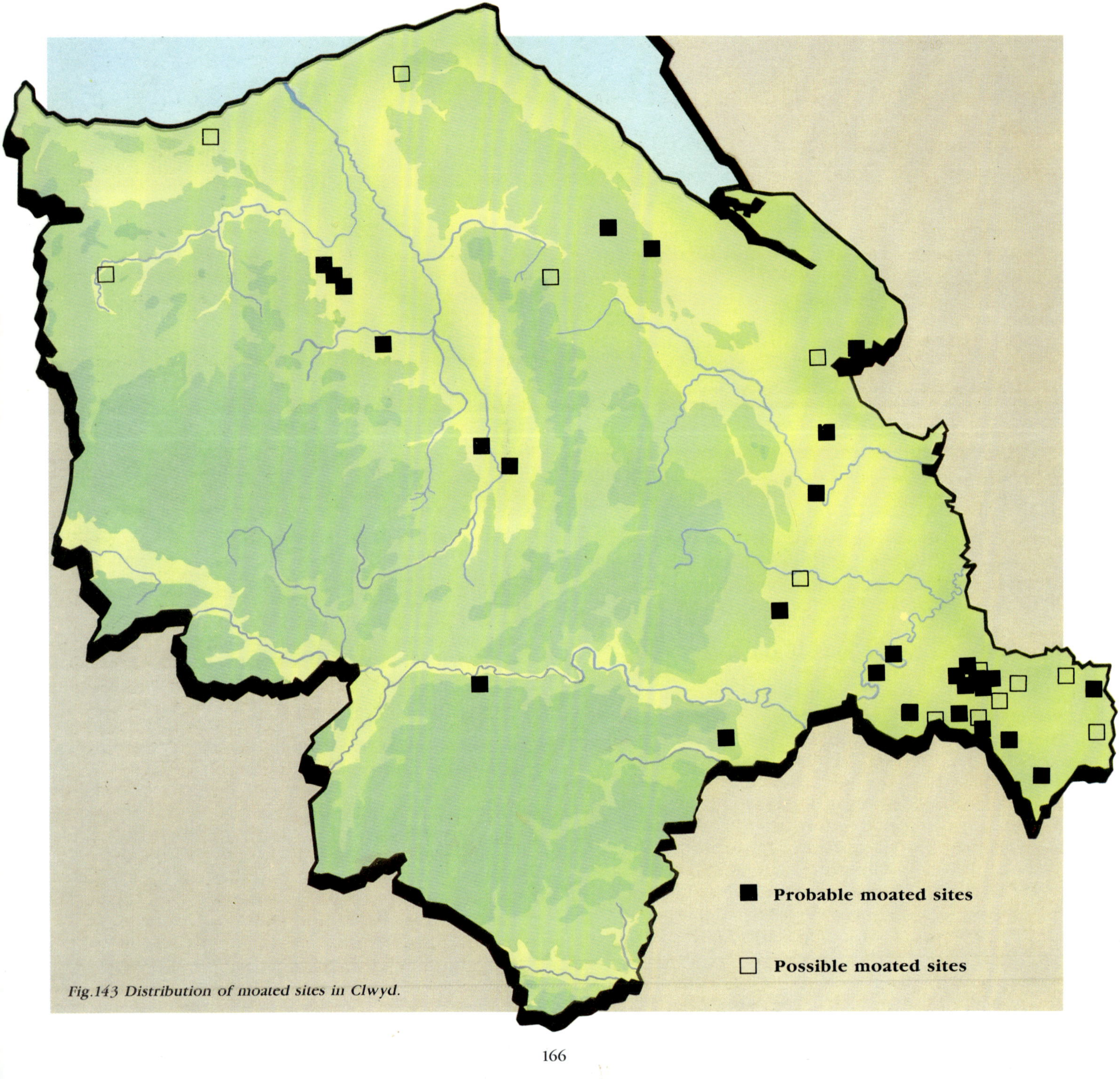

Fig.143 Distribution of moated sites in Clwyd.

Fig.144 Aerial view of Chapel Garth Moat, Peartree Lane, Halghton in the Maelor. Note the field-system at top-left of the photograph.

'dubious' list. A fascinating account of excavations at Llys Edwin was obscurely published in 1934, but left many questions unanswered. Rigg discussed and illustrated a new site at Green Lane, Hawarden, in 1961. In 1964 there followed a pioneering and perceptive study by Derrick Pratt of the moats in Maelor. This well-illustrated survey set high standards, particularly in its informed integration of historical information. Comparable studies have since appeared in England, but excepting the Commission's recent account of the moats of Glamorgan, it is sad that Pratt's example is yet to be followed in other areas of Wales. Finally, in 1981, maps and some plans of sites in the three 'old counties' appeared, together with lists and brief general notes.

The Clwyd moats cluster thickly in Maelor Saesneg, with lesser groups in Dyffryn Clwyd and Maelor Gymraeg. Pratt convincingly argued that those in Maelor Saesneg may well represent 14th century colonisation of dense woodland. This probability is strengthened by the presence of only one motte and no stone castles in the area. It is also tempting to see our other groups as assarting and manorial expansion following the pacification of the region in 1282. We have noted the continued use of mottes in the 13th century, and it is difficult to envisage the construction of many moated mansions in Clwyd before Edward's conquest. Thereafter, they could well represent the settlement of lesser lords, rewarded for their services with marginal lands in the hinterland of new baronial castles at Caergwrle, Chirk, Denbigh, Holt and Ruthin.

Moats in Clwyd were clearly sited to ensure wet moats: where information is available, no less than 22 sites lie on impervious boulder clay typified at Lightwood Green, Overton (Fig.145). This contrasts with our mottes, which mainly occupy glacial landforms of sand and gravel. Leats were hardly necessary, and stone-revetted moats are only recorded at Coed Henblas and Llys Edwin, while Penley Hall alone retains traces of a stone bridge.

In form Clwyd moats are square or rectangular (Fig.144), with the single exception of the oval Vicarage Meadow. The acreage of 22 sites is known. Of these, the average for 15 in Flintshire is one third of a hectare, an average unsurpassed in Wales, and surprisingly much greater than that of a little over one tenth of a hectare for seven sites in Denbighshire.

Fig.145 Aerial view of Lightwood Farm, Overton. Ridge-and-furrow fields can be clearly seen surrounding the moated site.

The manorial status of Clwyd moats is clear. Llay Hall is one of four late medieval aisle-trussed halls which were moated. The others were Horseman's Green, Lower Berse and Althrey Hall. Llay Hall was also a manor of the Hanmers, who also held Haulton Ring. Other moats pertained to the Ravenscrofts (Bretton Hall), the Pulestons (Emral Hall), the Dymocks (Penley Hall) and the Lloyds (Willington Old Hall), while that thoroughly anglicised Welshman, Owain Glyndŵr, held Glyndyfrdwy. The names of our moats also indicate seigneurial status: 13 incorporate 'Hall', 4 'Plas', and 4 'Llys'.

The rarer moats pertaining to ecclesiastical institutions are only represented by the vanished Llys Farm, at Prestatyn, a former seat of the Bishops of St.Asaph, though we should note Vicarage Meadow, Hanmer, our only circular site. This lies near the church, and may be the former parsonage, like others at Llandrinio and Meifod in Montgomery, though it has been claimed that it was a possession of Haulmond Abbey until the Dissolution. There is also the site called Peartree Lane, which lies in Chapel Garth, a name by which we prefer to know it.

Fig.146 Aerial view of Halghton Lodge moat, Halghton. Note how the ridge-and-furrow patterns cross the site and are therefore, in this instance, of later date.

The only excavated moat in Clwyd is Llys Edwin. In 1931 Glenn demonstrated that the motte of the Inventory was in fact a mound masking a substantial stone building in the north quarter of a large moated enclosure. The moat was 10m wide and revetted in stone. Charred oak stakes from a palisade along a water-retaining counterscarp bank were found in the moat. On the main north-west front two square projecting towers flanked a gate which faced an opposed stone bridge abutment. A portcullis protected the passage which led to a small cobbled yard. To the left the hall, kitchen and pantry were identified, together with an incorporated square tower which stood at the north angle of the moat. This impressive northern block was dated to the first half of the 13th century. It had replaced a former half-timbered building, and this had been preceded by another timber building indicated by post-holes. Quite clearly, if Glenn was correct, the site had been founded in the 12th century. By tradition it is associated with Edwin of Tegeingl, who figures in Domesday. A stone wall extended from the north block to a stone tower at the north-west angle, completing a stone façade along the entrance front. On other sides a timber palisade sufficed, and timber towers stood at the rear angles. Lesser buildings of timber lining the main inner court included a forge and stables. Unfortunately the finds and stratigraphy were inadequately described and not illustrated.

Moated sites are very vulnerable. Twelve Clwyd sites have vanished, a recent tragic case being Talant Cottage, Burton. Discovered in 1961 and still well-preserved in 1963, this fine site had been completely destroyed and put to agricultural uses by 1975. Sites still occupied are particularly vulnerable and usually mutilated. Such sites include Halghton Hall (Fig.146), Hollybush Farm and Wolvesacre Hall. In 1979 a discussion document assessed priorities for the preservation and excavation of Welsh moats,

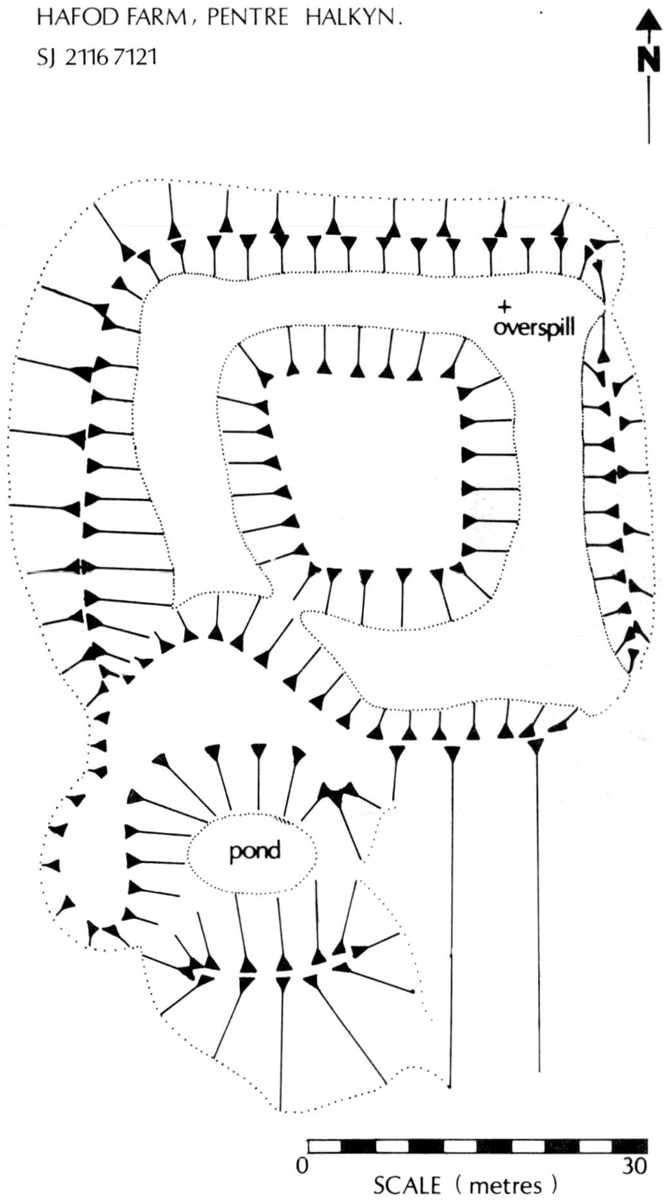

Fig.147 A plan of Hafod Farm moat, Pentre Farm, Halkyn, discovered during management of woodland by André Berry, now the Archaeological Sites Management Officer for the Clwyd Archaeology Service.

Fig.148 An artist's impression of the Hafod Farm moat in the late medieval period.

and the M.S.R.G. issued its policy statement in 1985. The first priority is the preservation of undisturbed sites unencumbered by post-medieval buildings and offering the maximum potential for eventual excavations. Such sites exist in Clwyd. The eight already scheduled do not include Chapel Garth and Halghton Lodge. At the very least, the limited protection of scheduling is urged for such sites, though preservation is most assured through state care or guardianship. Local authorities might be encouraged in this regard. Moated sites must be clearly explained to the public, and particularly those concerned with farming and land management. Where unavoidably threatened, all moats should be fully excavated; even when in-filled, the moat will conserve valuable archaeological information.

Regarding future work, recent aerial reconaissance by Chris Musson has located two 'new' moats as crop-marks: one at Bronington, the other at Hen Efail, Llanrhaiadr yn Cinmerch. Others no doubt await discovery, both from the air, and on the ground where small isolated illogical thickets are always worth exploring (Figs.147,148). As Llys Edwin is one of only three Welsh moats to have been extensively excavated, research excavation is badly needed, but priority must be given to the full excavation of threatened sites. Finally, it is essential that the comparatively untapped wealth of documentary evidence is searched. Unsuspected contemporary information relating to moats no doubt exists. Its transcription and dissemination will enhance the archaeological potential of sites and greatly assist us in the essential task of winning public support for their preservation.

A List of Mottes in Clwyd, including possible sites and those rejected

A. Mottes with Baileys **Pre-1974 county**

1.	Bailey Hill, Mold Urban.	(F1)	SJ 2353-6431
2.	Erddig.	(De)	SJ 3272-4869
3.	Hawarden.	(F1)	SJ 3197-6537
4.	Hen Blas, Coleshill Fawr.	(F1)	SJ 2214-7344
5.	Holywell, Bryn y Castell, Holywell Urban	(F1)	SJ 1857-7617
6.	Llys Gwenllian, Llanrhaiadr yn Cinmerch	(De)	SJ 0564-6440
7.	Marford — The Roft, Marford and Hoseley.	(F1)	SJ 3572-5623 (vanished)
8.	Prestatyn.	(F1)	SJ 0723-8331
9.	Rhuddlan — Tŵt Hill.	(F1)	SJ 0264-7766
10.	Sycharth, Llansilin.	(De)	SJ 2053-2587
11.	Tomen Cefn Glaniwrch, Llanrhaiadr ym Mochnant.	(De)	SJ 1487-2537
12.	Tomen y Maerdy, Llanrhaiadr ym Mochnant.	(De)	SJ 1488-2396
13.	Tomen y Rhodwydd, Llanarmon yn Iâl — Llandegla.	(De)	SJ 1770-5160
14.	Tyddyn Mount, Mold Rural.	(F1)	SJ 2527-6328

B. Mottes with no trace of Baileys

15.	Bryn Castell, Flint.	(F1)	SJ 2242-7353
16.	Bryn y Cwn, Flint.	(F1)	SJ 2383-7145
17.	Chirk-Castell y Waun.	(De)	SJ 2912-3756
18.	Hendom, Corwen.	(Me)	SJ 1357-4298
19.	Leeswood Mound, Mold Rural.	(F1)	SJ 2527-6150
20.	Llangernyw.	(De)	SJ 8742-6883
21.	Owain Glyndŵr's Mound, Corwen.	(Me)	SJ 1253-4313
22.	Pentrefoelas — Y Foelas.	(De)	SJ 8700-5225
23.	Rug, Corwen.	(Me)	SJ 0560-4387
24.	Tomen y Faerdre, Llanarmon yn Iâl.	(De)	SJ 1932-5615
25.	Trueman's Hill, Hawarden.	(F1)	SJ 3126-6597
26.	Tybroughton — Mount Cop.	(F1)	SJ 4703-4096

C. Vanished Site, probably a Motte

27.	Overton Castle.	(F1)	SJ 3569-4345 (Near)

D. Possible Sites (Not plotted on map)

1.	Bryn-ffanigl-uchaf, Abergele.	(De)	SJ 9215-7436
2.	Bryn y Castell, Mold Rural.	(F1)	SJ 2717-6210
3.	Coed Allt-y-tywod, Whitford.	(F1)	SJ 1444-7696
4.	Denbigh I — Crown Hotel Mount.	(De)	SJ 0510-6610
5.	Llangwm — Maesmor Hall.	(De)	SJ 0128-4458
6.	Maesgwyn, Pentrefoelas.	(De)	SJ 8633-5241
7.	Maes William, Mold Rural.	(F1)	SJ 2458-6121
8.	Scrape Cottage Mound, Hanmer.	(F1)	SJ 4407-3888

E. Rejected Sites **(IA = iron age; BA = bronze age)**

1.	Abergele, The Mount/Peel. (More probably a moated site)	(De)	SJ 9477-7764
2.	Bryn Euryn, Llandrillo-yn-Rhos. (not a medieval site. Internal 'citadel' probably I.A.)	(De)	SJ 8320-7983
3.	Gwernhaylod Banks, Overton. (I.A. rather than outwork of Overton Castle)	(F1)	SJ 3688-4336
4.	Hafod y Bwch, Esclusham Below. (Natural or B.A. barrow)	(De)	SJ 3090-4770
5.	Maesmynan, Aberwhiler. (Natural with B.A. burial)	(De)	SJ 1128-7212
6.	Plas Cadwgan, Esclusham Below. (Natural mound or B.A. barrow)	(De)	SJ 2985-4876
7.	Tomen y Castell, Gwyddelwern. (Natural mound)	(Me)	SJ 0723-4573
8.	Ucheldre House Mound, Corwen. (a natural hillock)	(Me)	SJ 0485-4525

A List of Moated Sites grouped as probable (A), Possible (B) and Uncertain/Rejected Sites (C)

The letters 'S' and 'V' following the grid references of some sites identifies those which are *scheduled* and those which are *vanished*, including a few known only as crop marks.

A. Probable Moated Sites

1.	Bretton Hall, Hawarden.	(F1)	SJ 3658-6375	— —
2.	Bryn Moat 'B', Hanmer.	(F1)	SJ 4272-4098	— —

3.	Chapel Garth — Peartree Lane Moat, Halghton.	(F1) SJ 4369-4166	—	—
4.	Coed Clattwn Moat, Henllan Urban.	(De) SJ 0451-6879	—	—
5.	Coed Henblas, Llanfair Dyffryn Clwyd Rural.	(De) SJ 1471-5518	—	—
6.	Emral Hall, Worthenbury.	(F1) SJ 4190-4417	—	V
7.	Eyton Old Hall, Erbistock.	(De) SJ 3486-4369	—	—
8.	Ffynogion, Ruthin.	(De) SJ 1282-5624	S	—
9.	Glyndyfrdwy — Owain Glyndŵr's Moat, Corwen.	(Me) SJ 1276-4311	S	—
10.	Halghton Hall, Halghton.	(F1) SJ 4158-4240	—	—
11.	Halghton Lodge Moat, Halghton.	(F1) SJ 4181-4324	—	—
12.	Haulton Ring, Hanmer.	(F1) SJ 4689-3727	S	—
13.	Hen Efail, Llanrhaiadr ym Cinmerch Urban.	(De) SJ 0630-6400	—	V
14.	Henllan — Pysgodlan, Henllan Urban.	(De) SJ 0398-6930	—	—
15.	Hollybush Farm Moat, Worthenbury.	(F1) SJ 4091-4390	—	—
16.	Lightwood Farm Moat, Overton.	(F1) SJ 3889-4099	S	—
17.	Llay Hall Moat, Llay.	(De) SJ 3262-5568	—	—
18.	Llyntro Moat, Esclusham Below.	(De) SJ 3042-4819	S	—
19.	Llys Edwin, Northop.	(F1) SJ 2369-6933	S	—
20.	New Hall Moat, Chirk.	(De) SJ 2745-3895	—	—
21.	Penley Hall Moat, Penley.	(F1) SJ 4168-4045	S	—
22.	Plas Heaton Moat, Henllan Urban.	(De) SJ 0415-6905	—	—
23.	Plassey Moat, Erbistock.	(De) SJ 3500-4517	—	V
24.	Talant Cottage, Town Ditch Moat, Burton.	(De) SJ 3297-5903	—	V
25.	Tallarn Green Moat, Willington.	(F1) SJ 4469-4390	—	—
26.	Wolvesacre Hall Moat, Iscoyd.	(F1) SJ 5065-4241	—	—
27.	Hafod Farm Moat, Pentre Halkyn	(F1) SJ 2116-7121	S	—

B. Possible Moated Sites

1.	Abergele — The Mount, Peel.	(De) SJ 9477-7764	—	—
2.	Althrey Hall Moat, Bangor.	(F1) SJ 3791-4408	—	—
3.	Bronington Cropmark, Hanmer.	(F1) SJ 4470-3930	—	V
4.	Fenns Old Hall, Bronington.	(F1) SJ 5055-3960	—	—
5.	Green Lane Moat, Hawarden.	(F1) SJ 3340-6379	—	—
6.	Henllys, Llanfair Talhaearn.	(De) SJ 9085-6959	—	V
7.	Hill Farm, Penley.	(F1) SJ 4001-4000	—	—
8.	Horseman's Green, Willington.	(F1) SJ 4473-4145	—	V
9.	Llys Farm, Prestatyn.	(F1) SJ 0618-8144	—	V
10.	Lower Berse, Bersham.	(De) SJ 3122-5008	—	V
11.	Maes y Groes, Iscoyd.	(F1) SJ 4985-4306	—	V
12.	Mulsford Hall, Worthenbury.	(F1) SJ 4306-4384	—	—
13.	Peartree House, Halghton.	(F1) SJ 4325-4180	—	V
14.	Plas Yw, Cilcain.	(F1) SJ 1584-6708	—	—
15.	Vicarage Meadow, Hanmer.	(F1) SJ 4580-3980	—	—
16.	Willington Old Hall — Yew Tree Farm Moat, Willington.	(F1) SJ 4557-4240	—	V

C. Uncertain and Rejected Sites

Note: The 18 sites here have all been advanced as possible moated sites. Some are vanished sites supported only by tradition or early accounts. A few may prove to have been moated sites, but all are listed here to assist future field workers.

1. Abergele Enclosure. (De) SJ 9082-7445
   (Rectangular enclosure on air photo - ?roman)
2. Bowen's Hall, Willington. (F1) SJ 4420-4200
   (Vanished. Local tradition only)
3. Bryn alleged moat, Halghton. (F1) SJ 4295-4107
   (Tithe Sched. — 'Moat meadow'. Tradition, but only modern drainage ditches survive)
4. Cae Haidd, Llanrwst Rural. (De) SJ 8510-5457
   (Uncertain rectangular earthwork. Too small for a moated site?)
5. Cae Moat, Penley. (F1) SJ 3935-3900
   (Field name only)
6. Fox Hall Enclosure, Henllan Urban.
   (Uncertain circular enclosure) (De) SJ 0345-6740
7. Ffridd Ddu, Llanfihangel Glyn Myfyr.
   (Uncertain circular enclosure) (De) SJ 9798-5016
8. Hen Ddinbych, Llanrhaiadr-yng-Nghinmerch. (De) SJ 9905-5636
   (Too large — ? A grange enclosure)
9. Hully, Tybroughton. (F1) SJ 4789-4193
   (Tradition only)
10. Kiln Farm, Marchwiel. (De) SJ 3373-4649
    (Reputed moat in 'Moat Field', ? clay pits)
11. Llanerch Park, Trefnant. (De) SJ 0590-7200
    (Moats reported. No information)
12. Llyn-tro Moat, Burton. (De) SJ 3460-5772
    (Reputed moat, filled in)
13. Marchwiel Old Hall. (De) SJ 3507-4722
    (Reputed moat — ? drainage ditch)
14. Motlands, Halghton. (F1) SJ 4350-4150
    (Uncertain earthwork)
15. Old Sontley, Ruabon. (De) SJ 3290-4580
    (Uncertain circular earthwork)
16. Redbrook Moat, Upper House, Malpas.
    (Reputed moat. No signs) (F1) SJ 50 * * 41**
17. Red Hall Moat, Ellesmere. (F1) SJ 3955-3965
    (Very dubious air-photo feature)
18. Rodens Hall, Sutton. (De) SJ 4070-4890
    (Alleged moat - dubious)

* *Unknown figures*

THE STONE CASTLES
by David Cathcart King

While it is difficult to find a good word to speak for the 1974 counties, or rather *départements*, it must be admitted that Clwyd is not by any means the most disastrous of these: it is not falsely named after an ancient kingdom, but occupying a different area; and the two counties destroyed for it — Denbigh and Flint — only date from Henry VIII's reorganisation. They corresponded closely with the Perfeddwlad, the Four Cantrefs of the Middle Country that made up Gwynedd below the Conwy — commonly held, none too firmly, by the rulers of Snowdonia. Henry VIII's surveyors had added to Denbigh the princedom of Powys Fadog to which the authorities have recently added some of the valley of the upper Dee. Obviously our own bureaucrats, normally extremely tidy-minded, have left us with two enclaves: Maelor Saesneg in the south-east, and opposite in the north-west, the outlying fragment of Caernarfonshire around the Great Orme. The first of these is no concern of this paper, but the second is another affair: to attempt the history of the Middle Country without mentioning the great fortress of Degannwy would be foolish.

We have thus three areas to consider: Tegeingl — essentially the historical county of Flint — the narrow corridor along the shores of the Dee, widening to enclose the lower Clwyd, the whole having many castle sites, reflecting its long history of dispute between England and Gwynedd; the other cantrefs of the Middle Country — Rhos, Rhufoniog and Dyffryn Clwyd — where the castles are much less numerous; and finally Powys Fadog. This, the northern part of the great lordship of Powys, has comparatively few early castles; it occupies a part of the borderland where there was surprisingly little castle-building on either side. This was due to the pro-English policy of its rulers, and the resulting lack of English

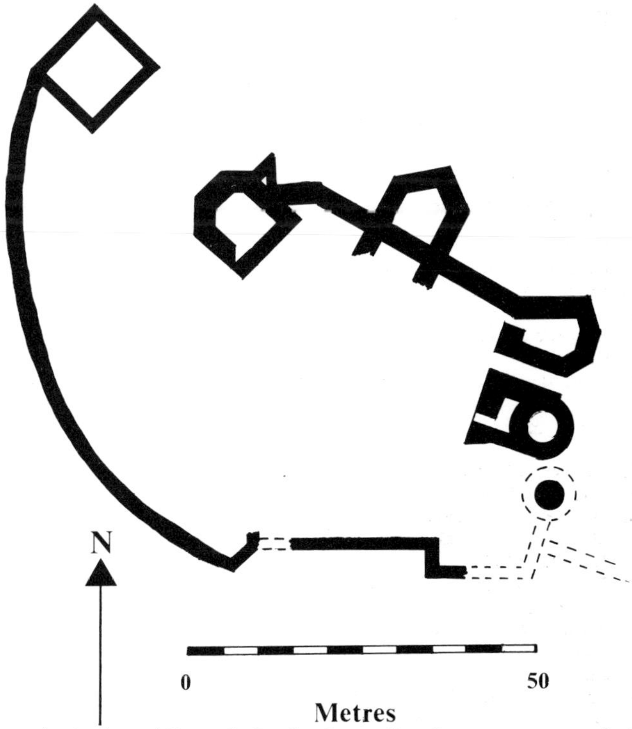

Fig.149 A plan of Dyserth Castle, the earliest known stone castle in Clwyd, constructed by Henry III in 1241.

aggression. We even find Welsh lords entrusted with the castles of Whittington and Ellesmere, while the rulers of Powys were allowed to enjoy the rule of a wide Welsh 'trespass' to the east of Offa's Dyke, and even the grotesque Maelor Saesneg, standing out like a sore thumb into England. (It is perhaps merely a freak of Henry VIII's border that has put the evidently Welsh Castell Brogyntyn into Shropshire). This wealthy little buffer-state took the side of Llywelyn ap Gruffydd in the Edwardian wars, and was extinguished at the conquest of Wales. (Southern Powys, siding with the king, survived this). Around Mold and Hawarden, where Powys Fadog marches with Tegeingl, there is a region of complicated history, reflected by a set of castles, built by a variety of lords.

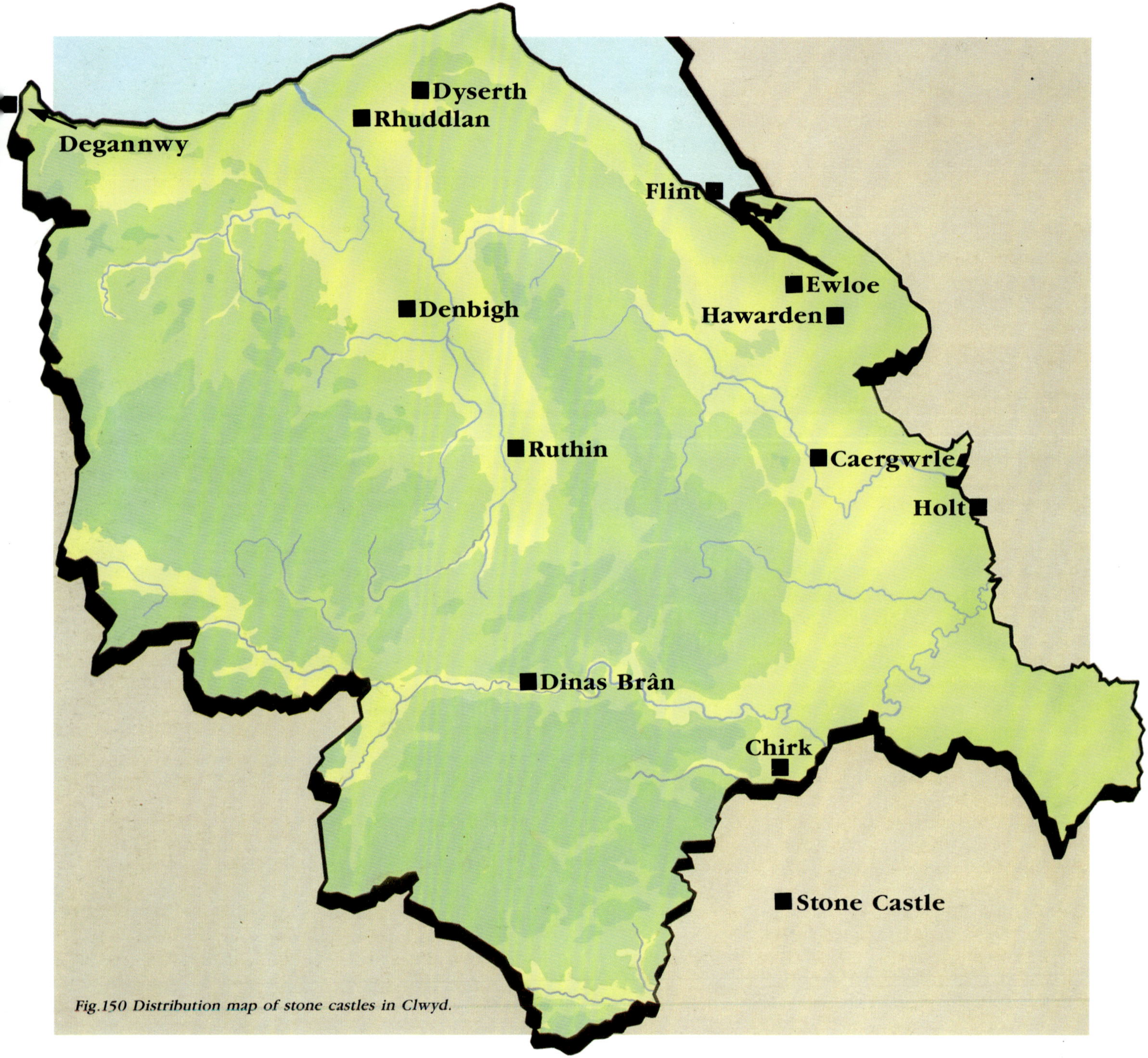

Fig.150 Distribution map of stone castles in Clwyd.

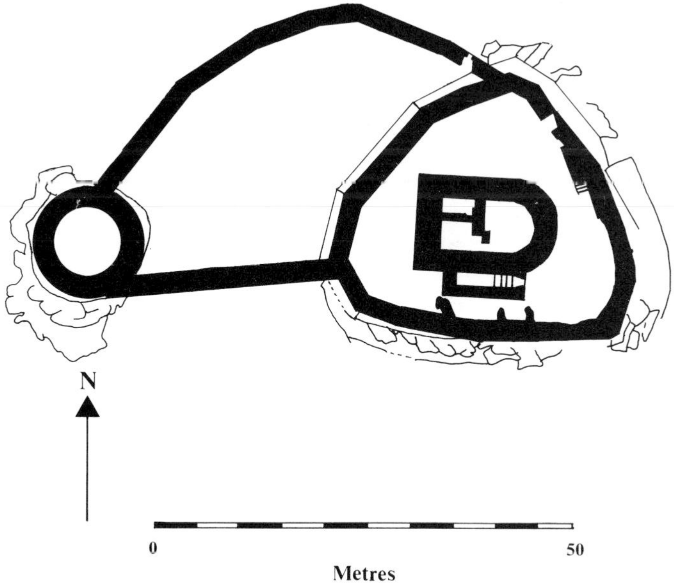

Fig.151 Plan of Ewloe Castle, built sometime in the 1250s by Llywelyn ap Gruffydd.

There are no stone castles of early date in the area of Clwyd (Fig.150). On the ancient site of Degannwy there are the remains of some early occupations of which nothing is to be made now and there is no sign of any masonry at any of the other castles mentioned in the 12th century. At Pentrefoelas the motte had a stone revetment, and Overton (swept away by the Dee) *may* have been a stone structure. Apart from these, the earliest stone castle in the district only appears in 1241, when Dafydd ap Llywelyn Fawr, the new ruler of North Wales, was forced to surrender Tegeingl to King Henry III, who built in it a castle, not at the ancient site of Rhuddlan, but a few miles away on the rocky escarpment, at Dyserth (Fig.149). The site was shifted in the course of construction, and very little of site or structure has survived the works of a massive quarry: it seems to have been a small strong masonry ward with a twin-towered gatehouse and at least two other towers, either round or polygonal; there were stone outworks.

At war with Dafydd in 1245, Henry advanced to Degannwy and got to work on a new castle, bringing up masons and labourers under cover of an army. The programme was successful; in face of the prince's furious opposition the castle was carried through to a defensible condition and when Sir John Edward Lloyd described the king's return as 'a confession of failure' he was being more patriotic than plausible. This style of advance had been used from the first years of Henry III's reign; it had been realised that the hastily-erected earth-and-timber castles of the 12th century were useless against the Welsh; something more powerful, in the form of up-to-date stone castellation, was needed to contain

Fig.152 An aerial view of Ewloe castle which occupies an unusual position, constructed in a valley and partially overlooked by higher ground.

Fig.153 Aerial views of both Denbigh (above) and Caergwrle castle (below). English workmen repaired Caergwrle Castle in the summer of 1282 and in the autumn of that year began working on the construction of Denbigh Castle.

their fury. But this kind of structure was demanding both in time and in resources, and could only be carried out under the protection of a concentration of troops. My own belief is that this method of proceeding was invented by the great William Marshal, Earl of Pembroke and Regent of England. He had suffered a good deal from the arms of Llywelyn the Great, while his own were devoted to the task of preserving the Plantagenet monarchy. Certainly as early as 1223, only four years after Marshal's death, we find his son using this method in the south-west of Wales, and his royal pupil doing the same at Montgomery. It was a means of making war that was suited to the talents of Henry III; he was much better at building than fighting.

The site of Degannwy is one of the oddest in Wales; England can offer only one similar, the Red Castle near Wem. Vaerdre Hill, the traditional site at Degannwy, has two summits; the larger is the site of the main ward, whose shape is determined by the cliffs. There was one large round tower, which seems not to have been a keep. Unfortunately, only 100 yards away there was a second summit, on which for security reasons was built some kind of apsidal structure, known as Mansell's Tower. The saddle between the two summits was enclosed to form a bailey, but only one side of this was ever built in stone. Here there was a powerful and very up-to-date double-tower gatehouse.

In 1256, when Llywelyn ap Gruffydd — Llywelyn the Last — entered the Perfeddwlad, he initiated a period of Welsh ascendancy. In particular, he isolated Henry III's new castles. Even with truces and English expeditions to spin out their survival for seven years, in 1263 the end came; Dyserth was taken by storm, apparently from a starving and exhausted garrison, and Degannwy opened its gates. Llywelyn dismantled it with extreme violence. At some time, approximately 1257, Llywelyn 'built a castle in the corner of the woods,' which was clearly Ewloe (Figs.151,152). This

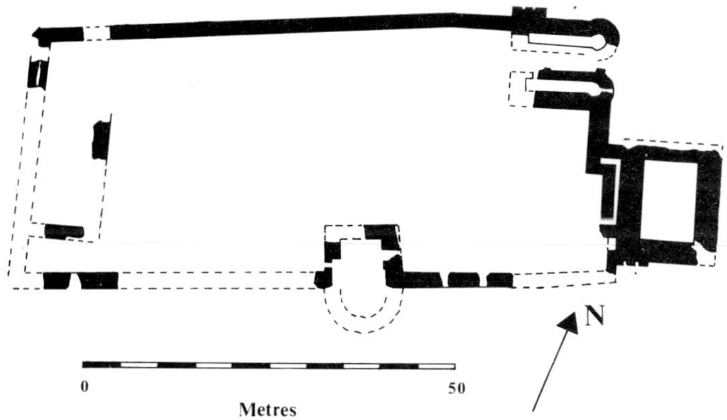

Fig.154 Plan of the castle of Dinas Brân, built around 1270, within an iron age hillfort. Dinas Brân is now owned by Clwyd County Council and visitors to the site are welcome.

was a very advanced example of the prince's power, menacing the English claims of Mold and Hawarden, and ousting those of Powys Fadog. The castle was built down a headlong valley-slope — a most extraordinary position, which would have been quite untenable if the castle had not been built from the first as a fairly high stone structure. The two wards have rather a random trace; the keep is one of those apsidal towers which had a certain vogue in North Wales. Welsh castles of the period were less ambitious than those of the English; towers generally seem to have had only two floors; flanking defence is generally lacking, and such novelties as portcullis-grooves and newel stairs are missing. Ewloe castle appears in recorded history only as a ruin; it was hardly worth defending against Edward I, and was overrun in 1277, probably without a fight.

Visitors to Llangollen are vividly aware of the ruins of a castle perched high overhead on a steep conical hill. This is Dinas Brân (Fig.154), a castle of the lords of Powys, built probably a little before 1270, inside the *dinas*, an iron age hillfort. The tourists who make the arduous climb are likely to be well-rewarded; there is more to see at the top than can be seen from the valley including some spectacular views of the Eglwyseg escarpment. Despite its ruinous condition there are noteworthy features of this long, rectangular castle. At its approachable end there is the stump of a big square keep — a rather primitive feature; alongside is a much more advanced and 'English' structure, a twin-tower gatehouse. There was a hall outside the keep — a feature rare in Wales — and an apsidal wall-tower *may* have stood three storeys high. But the most remarkable feature is the opulent detail of the work in the entry passage. Judging by the numerous freestone fragments lying about the castle, other parts may have been equally richly ornamented. Rich and splendid though this castle was, no attempt was made to defend it in 1277; instead, its lords burnt it. The ruin was garrisoned by the English, and then falls out of history.

When Edward I reached Coleshill in 1277, he sited the first of his castles on a rocky outcrop on the foreshore of the Dee — *Y Fflint* (Fig.155) in the mongrel dialect of those parts. There were two wards, the outer a simple walled enclosure, the inner a compact square ward with four powerful round angle-towers. The largest of these, overlooking the small gate,

Fig.155 Flint Castle, situated on the Dee Estuary, looks out across the marshy river to the Wirral.

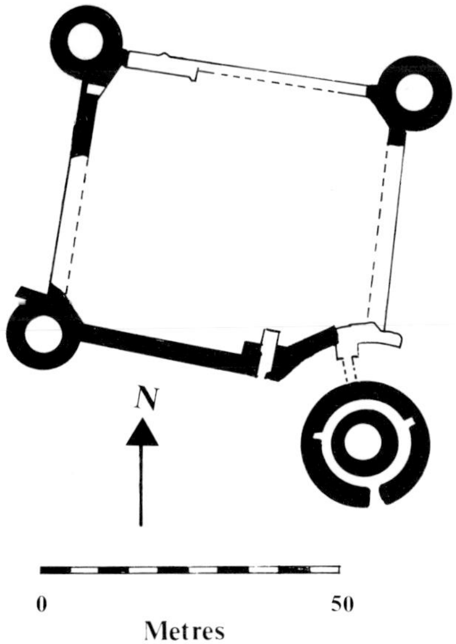

Fig.156 A plan of Flint Castle showing the mighty round keep which overlooks the entrance.

is a mighty round keep (Figs.156,160). There seem to have been little in the way of domestic buildings; in fact, the castle was evidently never finished. The great keep stands only two storeys high, instead of the four which we should expect, and the latrine-shafts cannot all be matched with their chambers. At a later date a timber storey was added on the top.

Proceeding to Rhuddlan, the king founded his second castle; it was an example of the concentric defence, with double lines of walls and towers (Fig.157). The lofty inner ward is square, with twin-tower gatehouses on opposite corners; the other angles are capped by single towers. It commands the narrow outer ward and afforded a second level of fire for its defence. At one point the outer ward is widened, to give access from the Clwyd. Edward arranged his castles to be supplied by sea; he had the Clwyd straightened and dredged for navigation. Finally,

Fig.157 An aerial view of Rhuddlan Castle on the banks of the river Clwyd. At the bottom right of the picture lies the motte of Tŵt Hill, which pre-dates the masonry castle.

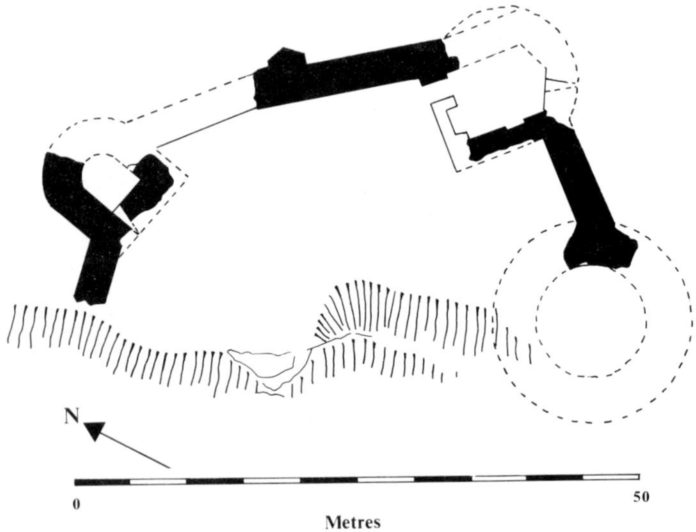

Fig.158 A plan of Caergwrle Castle. The castle's history is short, (it was occupied for perhaps only 4 or 5 years), but eventful. Dafydd probably launched his attack on Hawarden from Caergwrle and it was the first Welsh castle to be re-taken by Edward I in 1282.

Edward advanced to Degannwy, and encamped about the ruins of the castle. It has been noticed that he made no attempt to refortify either of his father's castles; Dyserth was simply in the wrong place, several miles from an open beach, and Degannwy had been starved out once and might be again. One comes across the statement that Edward chose to fortify Conwy instead; so he did, but only in 1283, when the whole of Gwynedd was in his power.

Llywelyn was obliged to surrender his conquests, and hand over the Perfeddwlad to the king. The principal beneficiary of Edward's largesse was no other than the prince's brother Dafydd, who had been in the English army during the war. He was rewarded with two of the Four Cantrefs — Rhufoniog and Dyffryn Clwyd, in which to begin a castle at Denbigh, and the territory of Hope, to begin one at Caergwrle (Figs.153,158). He had help and advice from the king and his staff; what he did at Denbigh is uncertain; but at Caergwrle he began a small, massive castle, whose features mirror his own character — part Welsh princeling, part English officer: two angle-towers of the current English plan, a short apsidal D; one of these with a habitable chamber at ground level — unusual in England, but thoroughly English in detail; traces of two newel-stairs; on the other hand, no proper flanking by the towers, a most extraordinary arrangement in the second tower, and the beginnings of a huge round keep some 50 feet in diameter. The castle stands on the summit of a hill, inside and backed against a formidable declivity. On this side there are no stone defences it is possible that there never were.

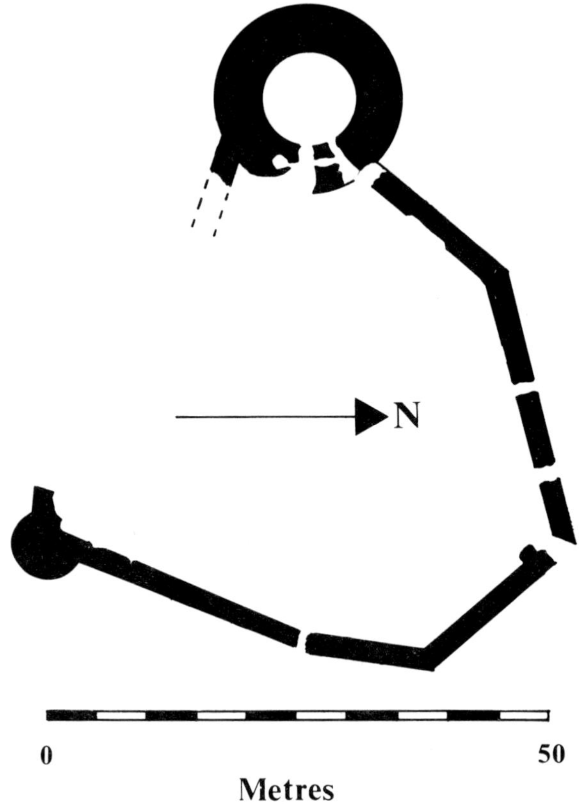

Fig.159 The strong, stone defences of Hawarden Castle were constructed in the late 13th century.

Fig.160 Aerial view of Flint Castle with its massive round keep.

Fig.161 An aerial view of the seemingly impregnable round keep at Hawarden castle. It fell to Dafydd, however, in 1282 when its English garrison was slaughtered.

When Dafydd broke out in a campaign in 1282, directed against both his princely brother and his royal protector, he is likely to have sprung his attack from Caergwrle on the English castle of Hawarden (Figs.159,161), which he took. Subsequent attacks on the new castles of Flint and Rhuddlan failed. Both were complete to the extent of being defensible, but now, as Edward's power extended over all Wales, they fell behind newer castles in the competition for scarce resources; against Conwy, Caernarfon, Harlech and Aberystwyth, they were no longer important and were left unfinished. As to Caergwrle itself, Dafydd did not defend it; the English advance guard found it dismantled and its well blocked with stones. Edward brought up a great body of carpenters and refitted the castle, using it as an important headquarters, including his central accounting and pay office. But like Flint and Rhuddlan it suffered a loss of importance after the conquest of Wales, and it never seems to have recovered from a destructive fire in late 1283.

Hawarden castle was a big powerful motte and bailey belonging to the de Mohaut family. It had been taken at the beginning of Dafydd's outbreak, and was captured by the Welsh rebels again in 1294. Its strong stone defences appear to have been built soon after; they are unsystematically arranged, with a number of signs of alteration; but in fact I believe the whole was erected in the course of a single prolonged campaign of construction, rather on the *solvitur ambulando* principle, working things out as they went. What there was finally was a fine and ornate round keep on the motte, with a rather unscientific set of walls about its small bailey. Inside this a hall was built, and outside there were added a single round solid angle-tower; a great square tower whose basement (all that survives) contains prisons and a cesspit; and a very formidable set of sallyports.

Edward's victory, and his disposal of Dafydd, gave him the opportunity of being generous to his subordinate commanders. In the Four Cantrefs he kept Tegeingl, with its strategic castles of Rhuddlan and Flint, to himself; Rhos and Rhufoniog were granted to the great Henry de Lacy, Earl of Lincoln, and Dyffryn Clwyd to de Grey. The Welsh lords of Powys Fadog were deprived, and Yale and Bromfield were bestowed on the Earl Warenne; in the extreme

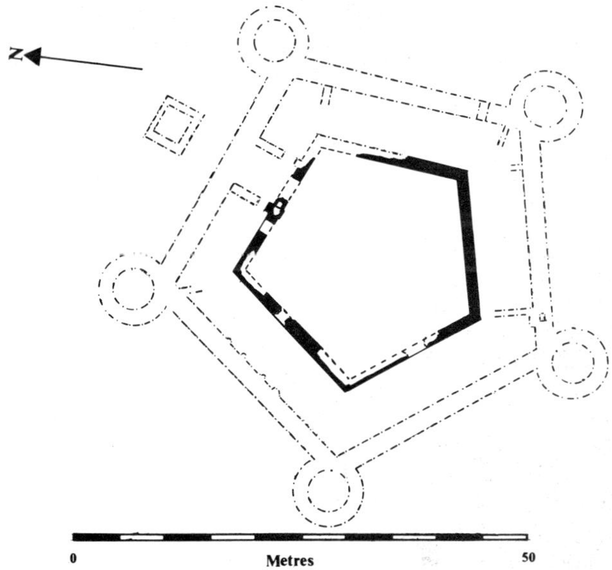

Fig.162 A plan of Holt Castle shows the scant remains of what was once a large and formidable castle.

Fig.163 An artist's reconstruction of Holt Castle. Perhaps this is how the castle appeared in the fourteenth century. Much of the masonry was removed in the late 17th century to help in the construction of Eaton Hall, Cheshire.

south, Mortimer was granted Nanheudwy and Cynllaith. All built their castles; Lincoln's was the important Denbigh (Figs.153,164), covering his substantial fief. The castle was aided by the king and his master-masons; at first it was built around the outer-fronts, joining up with the town-defences. This is the same arrangement as at Caernarfon, and had the same disastrous conclusion: the town being penetrated, the enemy could easily enter the castle. The later cross-defences were very much of the Caernarfon-style — massive polygonal towers, with an extraordinary three-tower gatehouse midway, a trap for assailants. Grey, in Dyffryn Clwyd, built the very substantial Ruthin castle, well supplied with round towers. At its top end there appears to be a fine twin-tower gatehouse, but also an uncapped angle. The building of the modern house has obliterated at least three of the big round towers; at the lower end there is a subordinate ward.

The Earl Warenne, master of Bromfield and Yale, possessed Dinas Brân castle, but for him it was a remote, inaccessible, and badly-damaged place. He moved his headquarters towards England. There is a note of rebellious tenants of Warenne, in about 1282, burning his castle of 'Glyn'. This is identified, rather uncertainly, as Erddig, generally treated as a big motte and bailey; it has certain unusual features, however. Finally, he settled, before 1311, at Holt, beside the Dee. This was a very unusual structure; a regular pentagon (an early surveyor charmingly calls it 'a five square') with large round corner towers. Its remains are slight, and singular: a pentagonal block of Old Red Sandstone with small traces of revetment. Originally this carried the enclosure; the defences, and the ring of buildings inside them, were built on the ground outside and below the central plan. There appear to have been four floors, two below the courtyard and two above; the uppermost was the *piano nobile*; what purpose the lowest level served I cannot say (Figs.162,163).

Fig.164 The three-towered gatehouse of Denbigh Castle. A statue, probably of Edward I, was mounted above the entrance.

In 1282 King Edward granted Chirk to Roger Mortimer 'the uncle'. There was an earlier motte-castle at Chirk town, now called Waun, but the great Edwardian castle seems to have been built soon after Roger's grant (Fig.165). I say, 'seems' for there is little evidence of any part of the castle's history. It is a remarkable structure, now inhabited as a Stately Home; the defences are enormously strong, with huge squat towers. Only one of them has an upper storey, and it seems likely that the whole castle was unfinished. Clearly, it was a very costly building; and this may explain the absence of any defences on the side of the declivity behind the castle; nevertheless in 1539 we find the redoubtable Bishop Rowland Lee reporting the fall of a piece of Chirk. This may explain the absence of defences at the rear of the castle.

Fig.165 Chirk Castle was built in the late 13th century with enormously strong defences. It has been occupied ever since and is now a stately home administered by the National Trust.

MEDIEVAL SETTLEMENT
by Glanville Jones

From written surveys of medieval date it is possible to determine the broad pattern of medieval settlement in the area that was to become the county of Clwyd (Fig.166). For parts of Clwyd, principally those in the east, there is the testimony of the survey whose results were summarized in Domesday Book in 1086. Nevertheless, for much of Clwyd the earliest testimony is that of surveys made after the Edwardian conquest of Gwynedd in 1282-3. Usually, however, only the broad distributional pattern of settlement can be ascertained from such surveys (Figs.167,169). Domesday Book provides a record of manors or estates and of the vill or vills which they comprised; and likewise the later surveys normally recorded only vills. Since a typical vill was a tract of land containing not only habitations but also arable land, pasture, and often woodland, it is difficult to determine from these surveys the precise form for any one vill, of the settlement, or the settlements, which lay within its boundaries.

There are few contemporary descriptions of settlement form but those which exist reveal that there were at least two distinct kinds of settlements. Gerald of Wales, writing at the close of the 12th century, observed that the Welsh 'neither inhabit towns, villages nor castles' of the kinds which, by implication, were inhabited by the English. Instead the Welsh led a 'solitary life in the woods', on the borders of which they contented themselves with 'wattled huts . . . constructed with little labour or expense, but strong enough to last a year or so'. That this was true of some medieval settlements in Clwyd is indicated by a record of 1284 which reveals that in seven vills, extending from the north-western limits of Little Leadbrook and Northop 'as far as Ewloe', the Welsh had 'small enclosures round their houses within the woods'. Yet, not all Welsh medieval settlements in Clwyd were of this kind for, as Gerald himself recorded, 'certain Welsh churches, with their villages and churchyards *(cum villis et coemeteriis)* had been burnt down by an English army', when, during the course of an expedition in 1165, it was moving westwards from Oswestry in order to cross the Berwyn mountains. These churches with their villages and churchyards were probably Llansilin and Llanrhaeadr-ym-Mochnant.

Similarly the Welsh medieval lawbooks reveal that there were two markedly different kinds of settlements. Some habitations were evidently scattered for, according to the lawbooks, every habitation ought to have two footpaths, one to its church and one to its watering place, as well as a bye-road to the common waste of the vill. On the other hand there were hamlets containing, notionally, nine houses so close together that fire was an ever present hazard. Again within every commote, which in theory contained 50 vills, there was one more important settlement in the *maerdref* (reeve's vill) which adjoined the king's court (*llys*). According to one 13th century lawbook which related to Gwynedd, the court contained a group of buildings, erected for the king by the bondmen or villeins of the commote. These buildings, within an enclosing wall or fence, comprised the hall, the food-house, the kitchen, the sleep-house, the stable, the porch and the privy. Outside the enclosure were the barn and the corn-drying kiln which were erected for the king, in the *maerdref,* by the bondmen of this reeve's vill. Near the court and the king's barn in the *maerdref* also stood a number of houses which could accommodate the officers and servants of the king when on circuit. Accordingly the settlement which contained the king's court, the *maerdref* hamlet, and other houses, was likely to have been at least a small nucleated village.

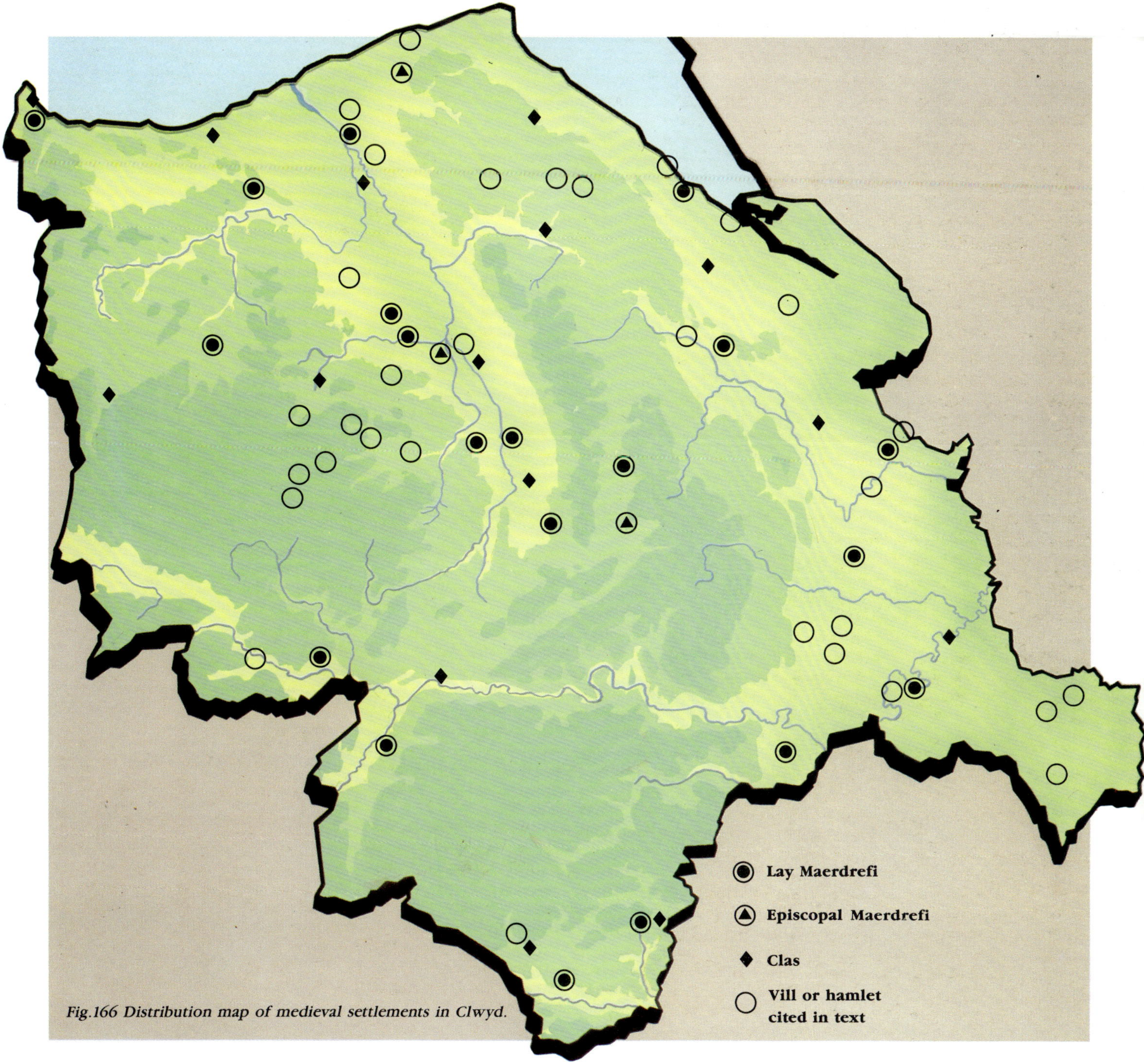

Fig.166 Distribution map of medieval settlements in Clwyd.

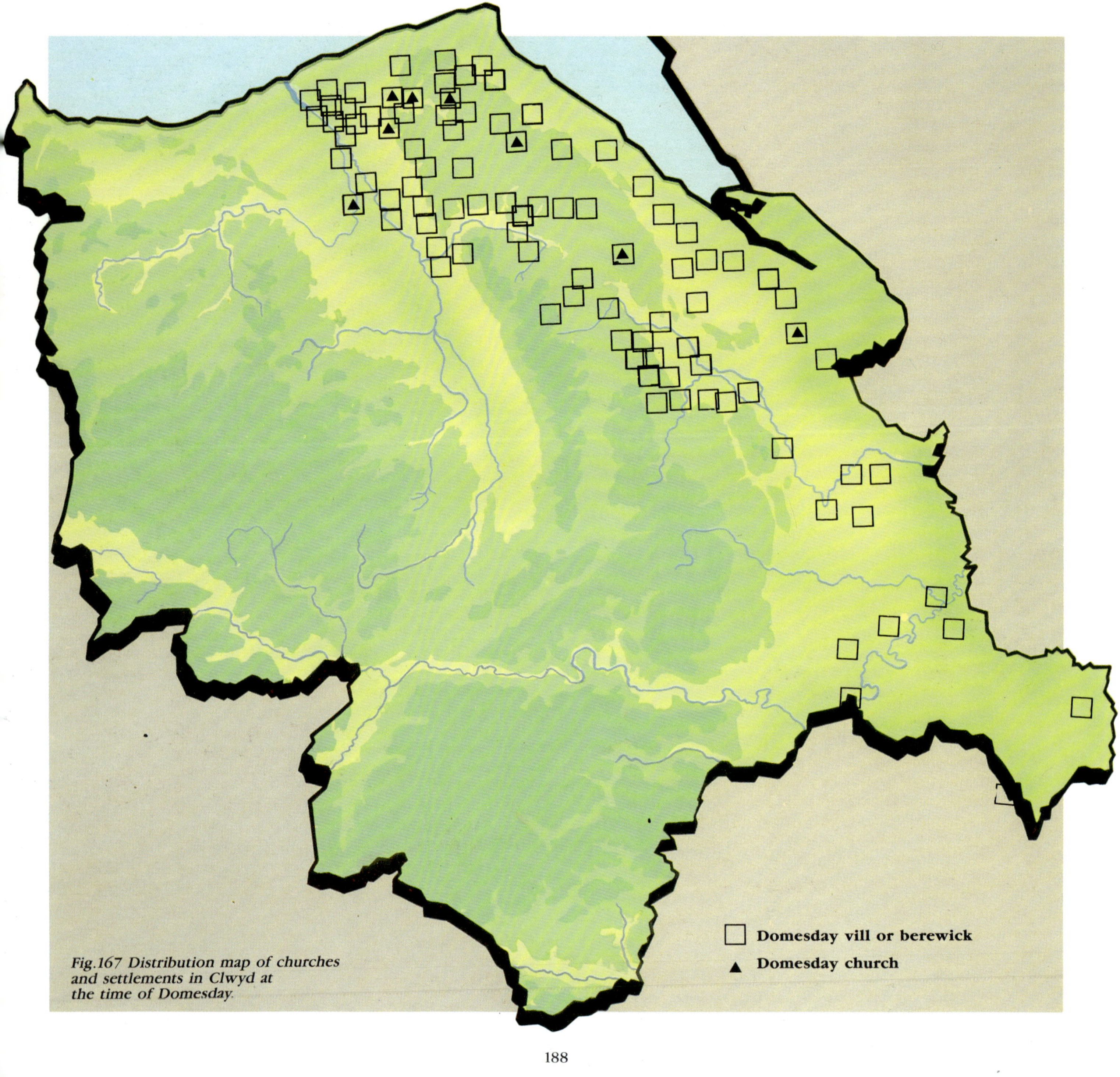

Fig.167 Distribution map of churches and settlements in Clwyd at the time of Domesday.

Fig.168 Aerial view of the motte, known as Tomen y Faerdre, Llanarmon yn Iâl. This was perhaps the site of the hall mentioned in a survey of 1315.

The vills of eastern Clwyd, although first recorded in Domesday Book, had been delimited long before 1086. Most of these vills bore English names and had been occupied by the Mercians from the early 8th century onwards. Subsequently English control had been effected as far west as Rhuddlan in Englefield where a Mercian *burh* was established *c* 921 called Cledemutha. Between 1055 and 1062 however there was a Welsh resurgence when Gruffudd ap Llywelyn of Gwynedd established his court at Rhuddlan. Gruffudd also acquired the English-named manor of Bistre in Moldsdale. There, in Bistre proper, and in two outliers or berewicks, he had '1 plough in demesne' that is he had in lordship arable land cultivated by one plough-team; and in 10 other berewicks his men had 6 ploughs. As Domesday Book records, when Gruffudd came to his court at Bistre his vassals rendered to him 'from every plough 200 *hesthas* (possibly loaves), a barrel full of beer, and a vessel of butter'. This was a substantial tribute so that even if the area tilled by each plough amounted to only 60 'acres', these were probably large units of 10,240 sq yds (8,560 sq m)

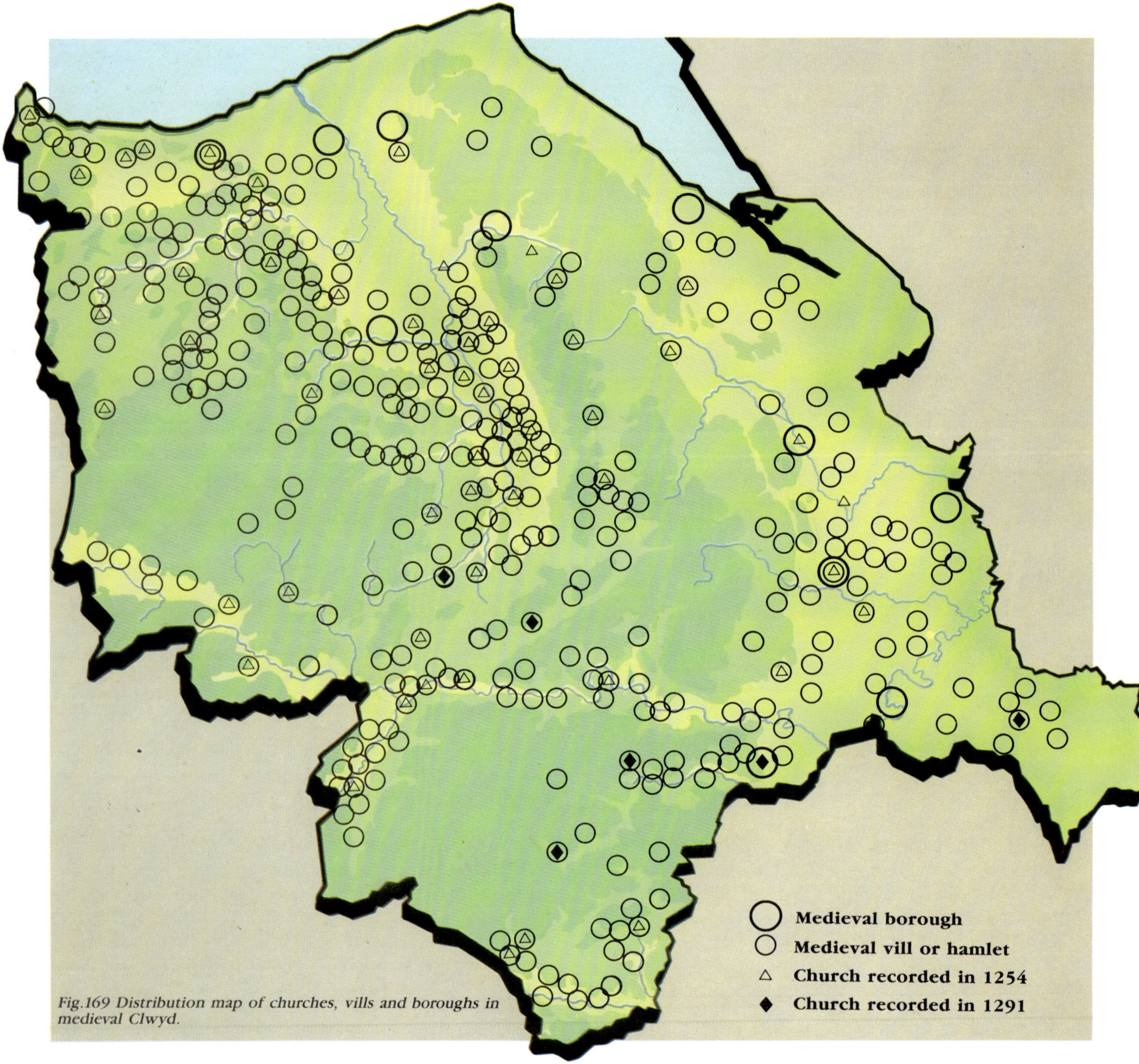

Fig.169 Distribution map of churches, vills and boroughs in medieval Clwyd.

Under Gruffudd's sway the whole territory as far eastwards as the Dee came under Welsh control, save for the lands along the estuary from Bagillt to Chester. Gruffudd, however, was expelled in 1063 and, as a result, Englefield and Bistre reverted to the control of Earl Edwin of Mercia. Nevertheless, according to Domesday Book, much of the area in 1066 lay waste, that is uncultivated and returning no income.

In, or about, 1070 the Merican thegns who held these lands were displaced by Norman grantees and by 1086 the ravages of war had been repaired. Thus at Rhuddlan, which was shared between Earl Hugh of Chester and Robert of Rhuddlan, there was a borough with 18 burgesses, a castle, a mint and a church; moreover, in the attached vill of Bryn with its outliers, there was land for 6 plough-teams which were there in lordship with 13 slaves. So too the numerous berewicks or vills of Rhuddlan in Englefield were now cultivated, mainly by villeins in the berewicks of Earl Hugh, but in those of Robert of Rhuddlan, who had enslaved many Welshmen, principally by smallholders and slaves.

Maelor Gymraeg, save for lands near the Dee, remained under Welsh control so that no vills were recorded here in 1086. Nevertheless, it would be wrong to assume that there were no vills here before 1086. The later surveys like the lay taxation returns of the late 13th century, reveal that there was a dense network of medieval vills throughout the greater part of Clwyd except for the uplands over 300m. So much is evident from Figs. 167,169 which indicate the probable main settlements within the recorded vills of Clwyd, and the churches, though not the chapels, recorded in the clerical taxation returns of 1254 and 1291.

In Maelor Gymraeg there were numerous vills bearing English names like Morton which must have been established before the middle of the 11th century, for in the 12th century they came to be occupied by Welsh kindreds claiming descent from the prominent Welsh notable, Rhys Sais, who in 1066 had held Erbistock as a free man. It was Tudor, his son, who in 1086 paid a tribute of £4 5s. for the commote of Nanheudwy to the Earl of Shrewsbury, and such payment implies settlement and the presence of vills in Nanheudwy. Similarly vills may be inferred for the commotes of Cynllaith and Edeirnion whence tribute was paid. In the commote of Iâl, likewise, no vills were recorded, but there were 11 plough-teams at work in 1086, and the recorded presence of two priests implies the existence of two churches, one probably at Llanarmon-yn-Iâl and the other probably at Llandegla. To the north-west in Rhos and Rhufoniog, the fee or holding which Robert of Rhuddlan held of King William, there were said to be extensive woods and moors. Nevertheless, it was valued at £12 and there was land here for 20 ploughs, although no churches were recorded. Presumably in Rhos and Rhufoniog, as was the case further west in North Wales which Robert of Rhufoniog likewise held of King William at a revenue of £40, 'the land of the Bishopric' was exempted.

The vills and berewicks actually recorded in 1086 ranged markedly in area. Most of those recorded for central Englefield covered only small areas. Thus, for example, the vill of Calcot contained only 212 hectares and the adjoining, hitherto unidentified, vill of Maen-caint only some 247 hectares. Such small vills imply a considerable density of settlement. Yet, to judge from the Domesday record, Calcot at most contained only land for a third of a plough, and Maen-caint only land for half a plough. Similarly in Caerwys, Llanelwy and Cyrchynan, which were recorded together, there was land only for 1 plough, which was there, worked by 6 smallholders and 1 slave. Even if, as is likely, the ploughlands were measured in large customary units the recorded arable area was so small that it was probably only a fractional share of the

Fig.170 The medieval enclosure site of Hen Dinbych, Bishopwall, sited at an altitude of 300m. It was probably built to manage the summer pasture which was linked with the maerdref *of the Bishops of Bangor at Llanrhaeadr.*

then existing arable land which came to be recorded in Domesday Book. Certainly in the case of these three berewicks the possessions of the Church are likely to have been excluded from the grant to Robert of Rhuddlan, and thus were not recorded in the Domesday survey. This would explain why, in spite of the name Llanelwy, no church was recorded for this berewick in 1086. Moreover, the fact that at a later date there was Church land in all three berewicks which belonged to Llanelwy (St.Asaph) supports this suggestion. In this event, despite the silence of Domesday Book about the church at Llanelwy, and the small size of the recorded population for the three berewicks, in 1086 there was probably a church hamlet around the ancient *llan*, or sacred enclosure, of Llanelwy.

In Maelor Saesneg the few manors recorded in Domesday Book appear to have covered large areas. Thus, for example, Bettisfield appears to have been co-extensive with the parish of Hanmer, which was later recorded as embracing six vills. Their combined area amounted to nearly 6,000 hectares, that is an average of some 1,000 hectares per vill. Altogether in the manor of Bettisfield there was said to be land for 8 ploughs in 1086, and this appears to have been disposed in a number of vills. At Bettisfield proper there was 1 plough in demesne with 2 slaves, and here in addition 3 villeins had a second plough. On the other hand, the plough held by the priest in the manor was undoubtedly at Hanmer for, although the church of St Chad was not named in Domesday Book, there were lands in Bettisfield manor which, it was claimed in the Domesday survey, had belonged in the time of King Canute, during the early 11th century, to the church of St Chad of Lichfield. Within the manor of Bettisfield there were probably also other distinct settlements, for in 1086 Domesday Book reports that 3 knights there had 3 ploughs in demesne, and no less than 9 villeins, 5 smallholders, 2 slaves and 3 other men had a further 3 ploughs between them. In view of the presence of 3 knights, one of these settlements was undoubtedly near the motte and bailey castle in the vill of Tybroughton.

Gresford in Maelor Gymraeg was an even larger manor in which there was land for no less than 12 ploughs in 1086. Gresford proper, with its church and priest, was a church hamlet, but the manor also embraced a number of outlying hamlets. Among these was Rossett some two miles north-east of Gresford, and, nearer Gresford, the hamlet of Marford which adjoined the Roft hillfort within which the Norman lord Osbern fitz Tesso had his hall.

Within the various manors and vills recorded in 1086 the hamlets, whose existence can be inferred from the testimony of Domesday

Fig.171 The romantic ruin of Valle Crucis Abbey, Llantysilio, near Llangollen. In the foreground the edge of the monks' fishpond can just be seen.

Book, appear to have resembled the hamlets portrayed in the Welsh law-books. This was undoubtedly true of Marford which emerged in the record of the early fourteenth century as the *maerdref* and the capital of the commote of Marford.

For some of the *maerdrefi* the testimony of the later medieval surveys gives an insight into the precise form of the settlement. Such is the case at Llanarmon-yn-Iâl, the capital of the commote of Yale. Here in 1315 the lord of the commote had a 'manor', a mill and an area of demesne land for the sustenance of the court. The hamlet, inhabited by bondmen, was nucleated around the ancient church in Tre'r Llan. A little way to the east on the west bank of the Afon Alyn was the lord's mill but the court, or 'manor' as it was called, was on the opposite bank of the river and thus some 300m distant from the church of Llanarmon. Erected and maintained by the labour of the freemen as well as the bondmen of the outlying vills in the commote, the 'manor' consisted of 'one hall, one chamber, one stable, one grange, and one cattle shed', roofed with laths rather than straw (Fig.168). Each 'house' was to be 19.5m in length and in breadth 'as is best fitting'. In 1315 the hall was perhaps located within the motte known as Tomen y Faerdre, but since this is only 24 m in diameter at the summit the remaining buildings of the manor, given their size, must have been sited within the bailey, probably on the north side of the motte near the significantly named Plas Isaf (Lower Mansion) where traces of earthworks have been discovered.

For Ystradowen, the capital of the commote of Ceinmeirch, a detailed survey of 1334 gives a very clear impression of the layout of the settlement (Fig.178). The court, known as Llys Gwenllian, comprised a motte on the western side of a roughly rectangular bailey enclosing about one third of a hectare. The 'capital messuage', as described in the survey, contained about three-quarters of a hectare within which were the court, a house for servants, two granges, a cattle-shed and two sheep-cotes. Thus, although the court was within the bailey, parts of the manorial complex, including no doubt the one house for servants and the 'houses' for livestock, must have lain outside its limits, probably to the south. The gateway of the manor opened eastwards on to the Greenway which led towards the church of Llanrhaeadr. Beyond the Greenway were the open arable demesne lands and meadows of the manor. To the south of the bailey was another roadway, and on the west the manor was adjoined by a clough containing over half a hectare of thick underwood. This clough, the ravine of an unnamed tributary flowing northwards to the Afon Ystrad, was included within the larger area of the capital messuage as a whole and, significantly, there are platforms on the steep side of the clough adjoining the bailey. According to the survey there was no dovecote nor garden at the 'manor of Ystradowen', but there were here in 1334 'two crofts enclosed around the manor (*due crofte incluse circa manerium*)' and said to contain an area of some 2.5 hectares. These must have been to the south of the bailey, but beyond the livestock houses of the court. In the vicinity of the house for servants there had been earlier cottages with crofts' which, according to the survey of 1334, were anciently in the tenure of certain bondmen who performed various services for the Welsh prince. After the conquest in 1282-3, however, these bondmen had been removed by the new lord, the Count of Lincoln, and settled elsewhere, including the upland hamlet of Pennant to which Madog Kinnock had been transferred. But clearly, before 1282-3, in the angle between the clough and the long clough of the Afon Ystrad, there had been a bond hamlet, or *maerdref,* adjoining the court of Ystradowen.

Within any commote the Welsh prince had, besides the lowland vill which contained his court and *maerdref* hamlet, a second vill which embraced his waste and summer pasture land *(hafod-tir)*. Such was the case in the commote of Ceinmeirch where the waste of Bishopswall, adjoining the boundary of Cernenyfed, contained an area of some 580 hectares at an altitude of well over 300m. In 1334 it was estimated that this pasture could sustain 8 bulls and 192 cows, in winter as well as in summer, and have sufficient hay for the sustenance of all these animals in winter. The presence of an embanked enclosure at Bishopswall proper suggests that this waste had been exploited long before 1282-3 for, as its name implies, it had earlier probably been a summer pasture linked with the *maerdref* of the Bishop of Bangor at Llanrhaeadr (Fig.170). Certainly the two upland hamlets of Aberberbo and Hafodlom, both attached to Bishopswall, had been established before the Edwardian conquest.

Similar pastures were also occupied by the tenants of lowland vills. Thus the tenants of the lowland bond vill of Prion had held before the conquest the 'hamlet' of Brynbach which embraced an area of some 220 hectares. The associated settlement was at Brynbach proper in a narrow upland valley at an altitude of over 300m. After the conquest this 'hamlet' had been leased to 8 English tenants in herbage but against

Fig.172 The remains of a long-house; part of an extensive medieval setlement on the edge of the moorland above Llandrillo.

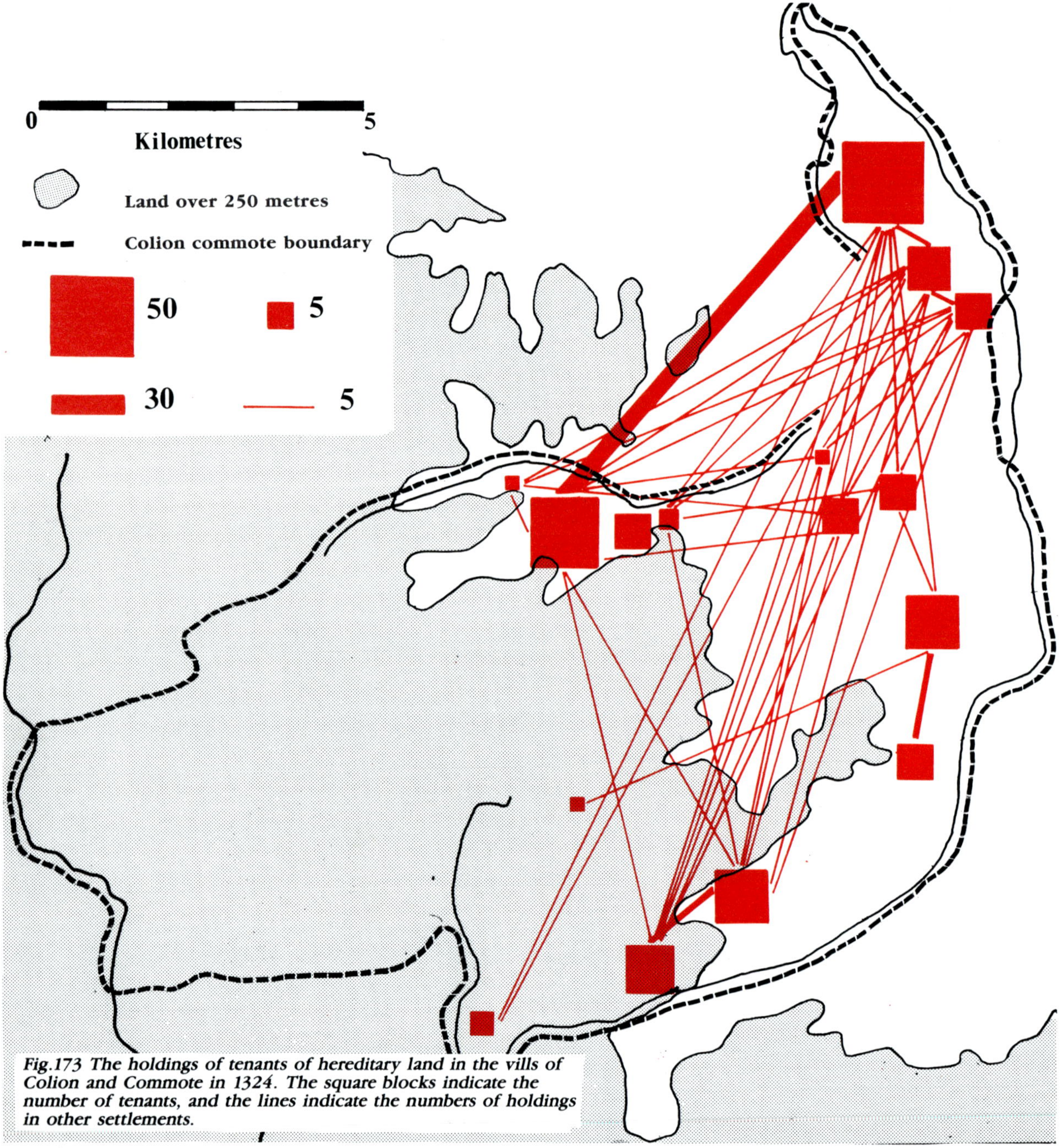

Fig.173 The holdings of tenants of hereditary land in the vills of Colion and Commote in 1324. The square blocks indicate the number of tenants, and the lines indicate the numbers of holdings in other settlements.

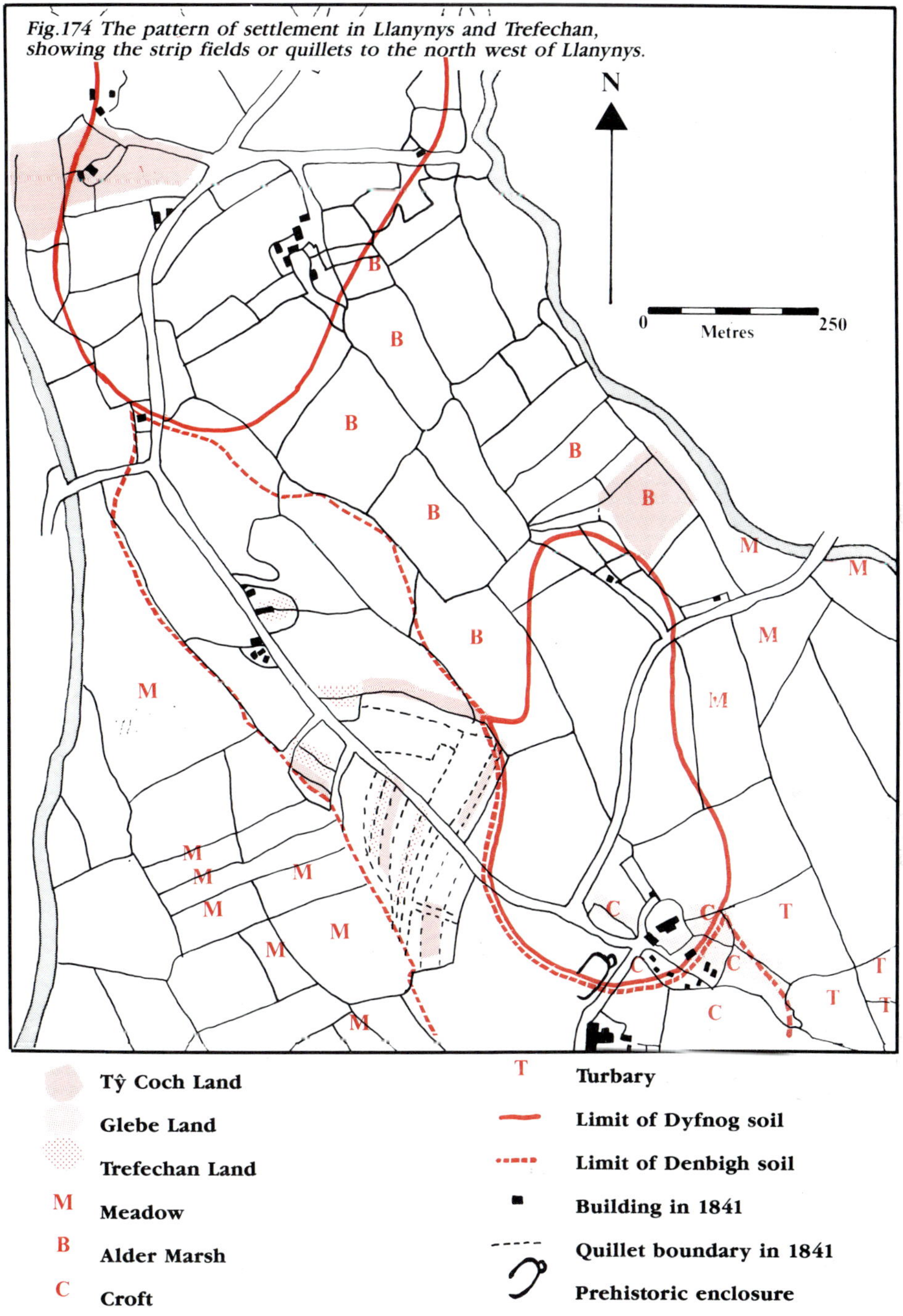

Fig.174 The pattern of settlement in Llanynys and Trefechan, showing the strip fields or quillets to the north west of Llanynys.

the terms of their lease these tenants, even at this altitude, had converted 82 hectares into arable land.

For the adjacent commote of Colion a register of tenants in 1324 provides an excellent insight into the detailed layout of settlement on hereditary land held by freemen (Fig. 173). Within the vill of Llanynys in 1324 there were no less than 48 tenants of free hereditary land but all save 9 of these also held land in one or more other vills. Thus, for example, Dafydd ap Gronw held one message or homestead in Llanynys with 0.6 hectares of land there and 1.5 hectares in Gyffylliog some 7km distant. Madog Fychan had a very much larger holding comprising one message and 6 bovates, that is probably 24 hectares of land in Llanynys, Maesmaencymro, Cefn-iwrch and Ysceifiog, plus 3.5 hectares 'with its particle of the mill of Bryncaredig', a mill which he shared with his kinsmen. The main linkages within holdings of free hereditary land were those between the lowland vill of Llanynys and the upland vill of Gyffylliog where 30 of the free tenants of Llanynys held hereditary land. To serve the needs of the free tenants of Llanynys permanent arable sharelands had been created in Gyffylliog. Thus David the dean *(decanus)* of Llanynys and Gronw his brother held two messuages, and half a carucate or ploughland, that is probably 12 hectares, in Llanynys and Gyffylliog. Together the two brothers also held one message and 6 hectares in Gyffylliog as well as further areas of 1.5 hectares and 3 hectares there. In addition, Gronw alone held one message with 0.1 hectare in Gyffylliog. Yet David the dean of Llanynys, Gronw ap Llywarch, Gruffydd Goch, Madog Fuchan, Ithel Foel and the 'community of the vill of Llanynys' (*communitas ville de Lannanys*) held by charter 12 hectares in the moor of Cefn at an altitude of over 300m in Gyffylliog, 3.5 hectares in the moor of Cefn-iwrch, 7.5 hectares in the moor of Trefechan, 19 hectares in the moor of Isllan (below the *llan*), and 22 hectares in the moor of Uwchllan (above the *llan*) with appurtenances in Llanynys. One of this group, Gruffudd Goch, held one messuage and two bovates, probably 8 hectares of land in Llanynys and Gyffylliog; but in addition at Llanynys he had 3 curtilages with 4.5 hectares and 0.6 hectare and '1 rod of land' which appear to have been smallholdings of hereditary land probably held by bond undertenants.

The church at Llanynys, on its island site between two rivers (Fig. 174), was recorded in verse of the 9th century as 'Lanfawr (Great Church) beyond Bannawg, where the Clwyd joins the Clywedog'. Alike in 1254 and in 1291 it was one of the richest churches in North Wales. Long before the 13th century it had become a *clas* or community of canons under an abbot, all sharing the revenues of the church. Of the 24 portionaries later recorded as 'the abbot and *clas* men' only one, whose portion was commonly called the portion of David the priest, had the cure of the souls of the parishioners. The *clas* had become a hereditary ecclesiastical corporation comprising members of progenies who succeeded their fathers as holders of all portions save that recorded in 1291 as the portion of David the chaplain. The portionaries evidently held free hereditary lands, among them the messuage 3.25 hectares held by Bleddyn Sant (Saint) in Llanynys and Gyffylliog. They also included the lands of free inheritance which David, the dean of Llanynys, shared with his brother Gronw.

Llanynys, placed perhaps significantly near a prehistoric enclosure, occupied an island-like spread of well-drained soils elevated above the floor of the vale. The church and church-yard lay within the northern part of what appears to have been a larger roughly-circular enclosure, perhaps the original *llan,* or sacred enclosure,

Fig.175 Aerial view of the setting of the quillets at Llanynys.

within which the dwellings of the canons were located. Outside this enclosure were the dwellings of undertenants; and beyond lay their small gardens or quillets disposed in radial fashion like the surviving croft of glebe land, one of a group of Gerddi duon (black gardens) in the field known as Cae'r llan (enclosed field of the *llan*). To the north in Bryn Castell there were other radial gardens, but beyond them, in turn, were some of the hereditary lands held by the portionaries of the *clas* (Fig.175). As in Maes isa (lower open field) and Maes ucha (upper open field), where quillets of former hereditary land survived until 1971, the arable lands of any heir consisted of long narrow strips lying intermingled in unenclosed sharelands (Fig.176). These rights of the portionaries in parcels of arable land were exercised over the well-drained soils. Attached to these arable parcels were appurtenant rights over meadow and common pasture; with the meadows, as indicated by their field names, on the fringes of the arable sharelands and the common pastures on ill-drained lands designated as alder marsh, bog or turbary. It was, however, proximity, usually to their largest shares of arable land, that determined the locations of the homesteads of the heirs of free hereditary land in Llanynys. These homesteads were initially probably at Llanynys proper but they came to be sited on the outer edges of the arable sharelands, as at the northern limits of Maes isa and Maes ucha or at Tŷ Coch and Pwll y Chwyaid Bach on the margins of the former sharelands at the northernmost Trefechan (Fig. 174).

In the medieval period there would have been larger numbers of such homesteads disposed around the outer edges of the sharelands, in girdle fashion. Given partible inheritance, and the ensuing fragmention of arable parcels, many holdings proved to be uneconomic and were acquired by estate-makers

Fig.176 Ploughing one of the last surviving quillets in Maes isa, Llanynys, in the mid-20th century.

who consolidated morcellated arable lands along with fringing meadows and unenclosed pastures into larger enclosed farms. Thus there came to be smaller numbers of homesteads than in the 14th century, although those that survived were rebuilt, as at Pwll y Chwyaid Bach. The process had been arrested in the vill of Llanynys, hence the fragmented make-up of farms like Tŷ Coch and Trefechan even in 1841; hence too the survival, in part at least, of girdles of outlying homesteads and, at Llanynys proper, of a few radial hamlet gardens (Fig.177).

Such dispositions whereby medieval holdings of hereditary land were made up in part of outlying homesteads with adjoining arable lands, and in part of the quillets of hamlets, whether occupied by undertenants or not, appear to have been characteristic of other *clas* settlements like Llanrhaeadr-ym-Mochnant with its outlier at Henfachau or Llanelwy. Similar dispositions obtained on holdings of hereditary land in some of the vills of the Bishop of St. Asaph, like Henllan.

Pickhill, on the other hand, despite its English name was a Welsh secular bond vill within which in 1315 there were 44 messuages and 15 cottages with, in all, 10 crofts and 9 curtlidges. Within Pickhill there were also 79 hectares of arable land of which 26 hectares were 'new land'. These were in the hands of 44 tenants of whom at least 27 occupying old land only, and 4 occupying both old and new land, were bondmen. In addition, there were probably 43 hectares of demense land. Thus, nearly a quarter of all the land in Pickhill was arable. In the earlier fourteenth century this arable land consisted of small Welsh quillets which lay in

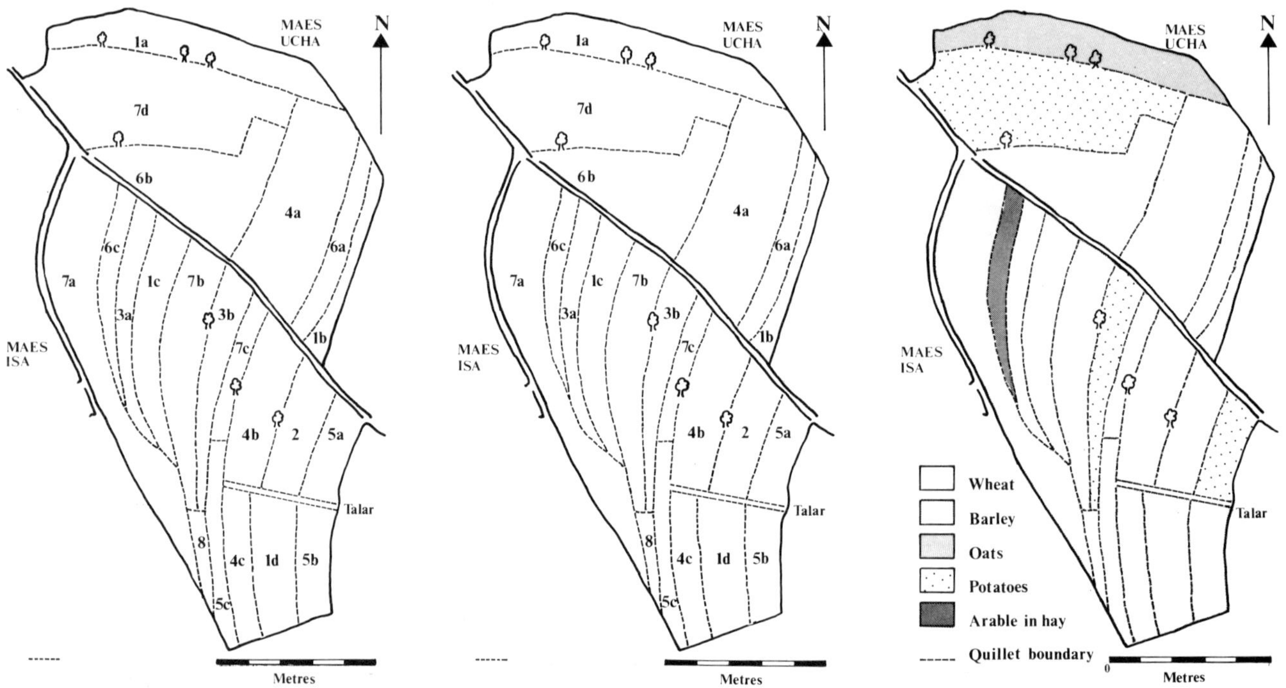

Fig.177 This information is drawn from the Tithe Apportionment and Map of Llanynys in 1841. The six quillets in Maes ucha and the fifteen quillets in Maes isa formed part of six distinct estates. Thcsc twenty one quillets formed part of eight separate farms. On five of the 'greensward' boundaries betweeen eight quillets there were seven trees. That between quillets 7c and 4b is the tree in Fig.176 (of a horse ploughing) and was a gnarled oak tree. The 'talar' shown was a headland on which ploughs were turned.

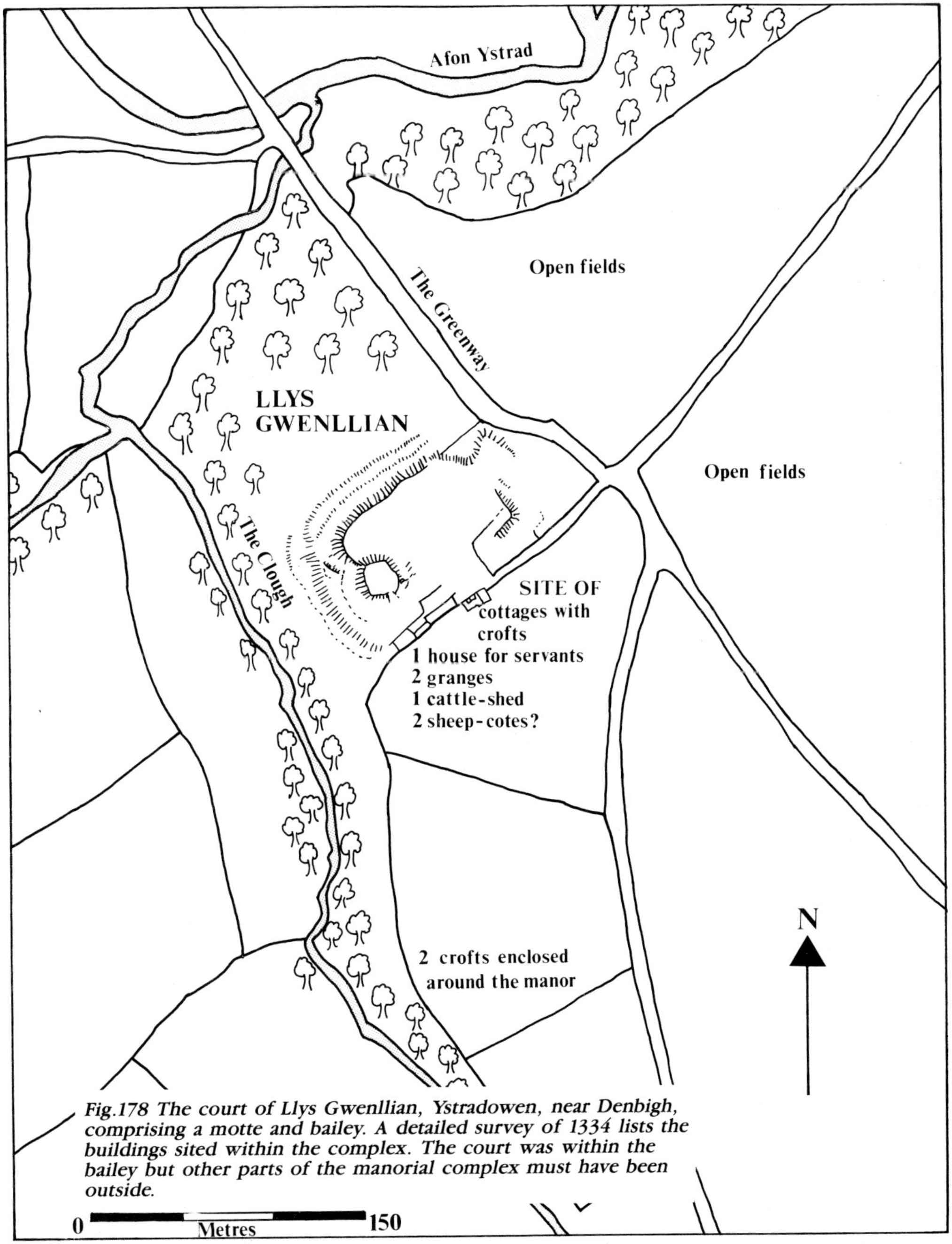

Fig.178 The court of Llys Gwenllian, Ystradowen, near Denbigh, comprising a motte and bailey. A detailed survey of 1334 lists the buildings sited within the complex. The court was within the bailey but other parts of the manorial complex must have been outside.

Fig.179 An impressive aerial view of surviving ridge-and-furrow fields at Pickhill Hall (near Wrexham).

open-field furlongs. Subsequently the vill lands were consolidated into a small number of estates but, although their arable land was enclosed and laid down to pasture, the form of the quillets was preserved. Thus, as a recent aerial photograph shows (Fig. 179), the layout of the medieval arable land has survived (at SJ 39 47), fossilised in ridge-and-furrow.

Survival of medieval ridge-and-furrow is fairly rare in Clwyd except towards its eastern boundary. Similarly, medieval settlement layouts can only be discerned infrequently save in ruins like those of former long-houses as on the moorland (at SJ 031 337) (Fig.172) near Llandrillo (Edeirnion); or in the ruins of monastic precincts such as Valle Crucis Abbey (at SJ 20 44) in Llantysilio (Iâl) (Fig. 171). At the main rural settlements within medieval vills most hereditary holdings have been consolidated into ring-fence farms. Most bond hamlets lacking a church have disappeared, and most *maerdref* hamlets have rarely survived unchanged. Sometimes the *maerdref,* as befits a commote capital, became the site of a borough as at Chirk, Wrexham, Rhuddlan, Denbigh, or Ruthin. Other *maerdrefi,* with their demense lands granted even before the Edwardian conquest to Welsh noblemen, as was the case at Dinerth and Llysaled, were consolidated, like hereditary lands, into ring-fence farms. Nevertheless, since *maerdrefi* were by far the most important of the medieval Welsh settlements their recorded sites should command investigation into the future.

VERNACULAR ARCHITECTURE
by A.J. Parkinson

Vernacular architecture is the traditional building style of the people, following ideas about design transmitted from master to apprentice over several generations, using local materials, and built by and for people who spent the majority of their working lives in a single area. Although many of the ideas can be traced back to prototypes outside the region (often to London or beyond), by the time they had reached as far as Wales, Cornwall or Yorkshire they had become modified so that truly regional styles can be identified. Until the appearance of published architectural pattern-books in the 18th century, mass-produced brick and slate in the 19th century, and cheap and rapid transport in the middle of the 19th century, every region had its own style of architecture. While the styles of adjacent areas may have graded into one another, each area had an architecture as distinctive as its dialect or accent.

The vernacular architecture of Clwyd reflects its variety of geology and geography. Broadly speaking, a series of blocks of highland are divided by more or less wide valleys - the Conwy valley, the Vale of Clwyd and the Dee valley. While the richest farmland is to be found in these lower areas, there are old farmsteads well up into the foothills of the mountains (Figs.182,188). This is a result of the historical development of settlement in the region. The Welsh system of *gavelkind* continued in some places until the middle of the 16th century: as the best land became fully occupied, new farmland was enclosed from the surrounding waste, so that the level of agriculture crept higher as new farms were created. The surviving old farmhouses indicate the wealth of the area: many of the houses built during the period 1450-1700 must have represented a very heavy capital outlay for families dependent entirely on agriculture.

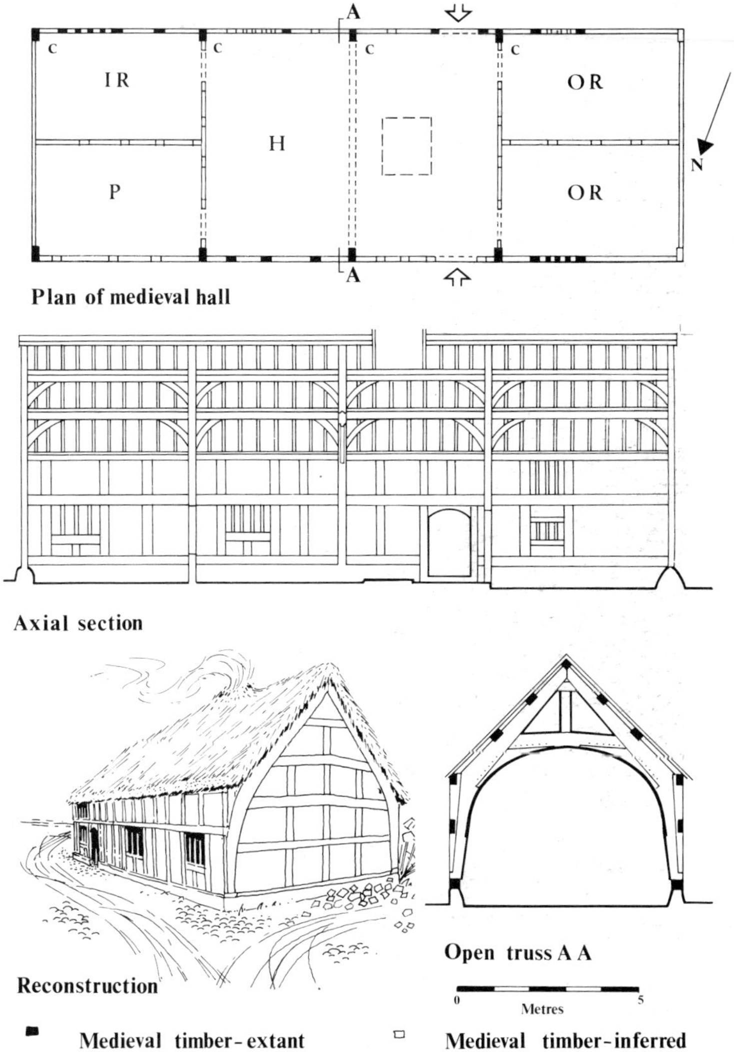

Fig.180 The Old Ship, Ruthin, a medieval cruck-framed hall-house with a two-bay hall, arch-braced central truss, and wind-braces. The rooms at either end of the hall were storeyed.

Building materials generally were those from the immediate locality. Hence there is considerable variety within Clwyd, since there are four different major materials available in various places: sandstone in the south, carboniferous limestone around the Vale of Clwyd and elsewhere, brick-clay in the Vale of

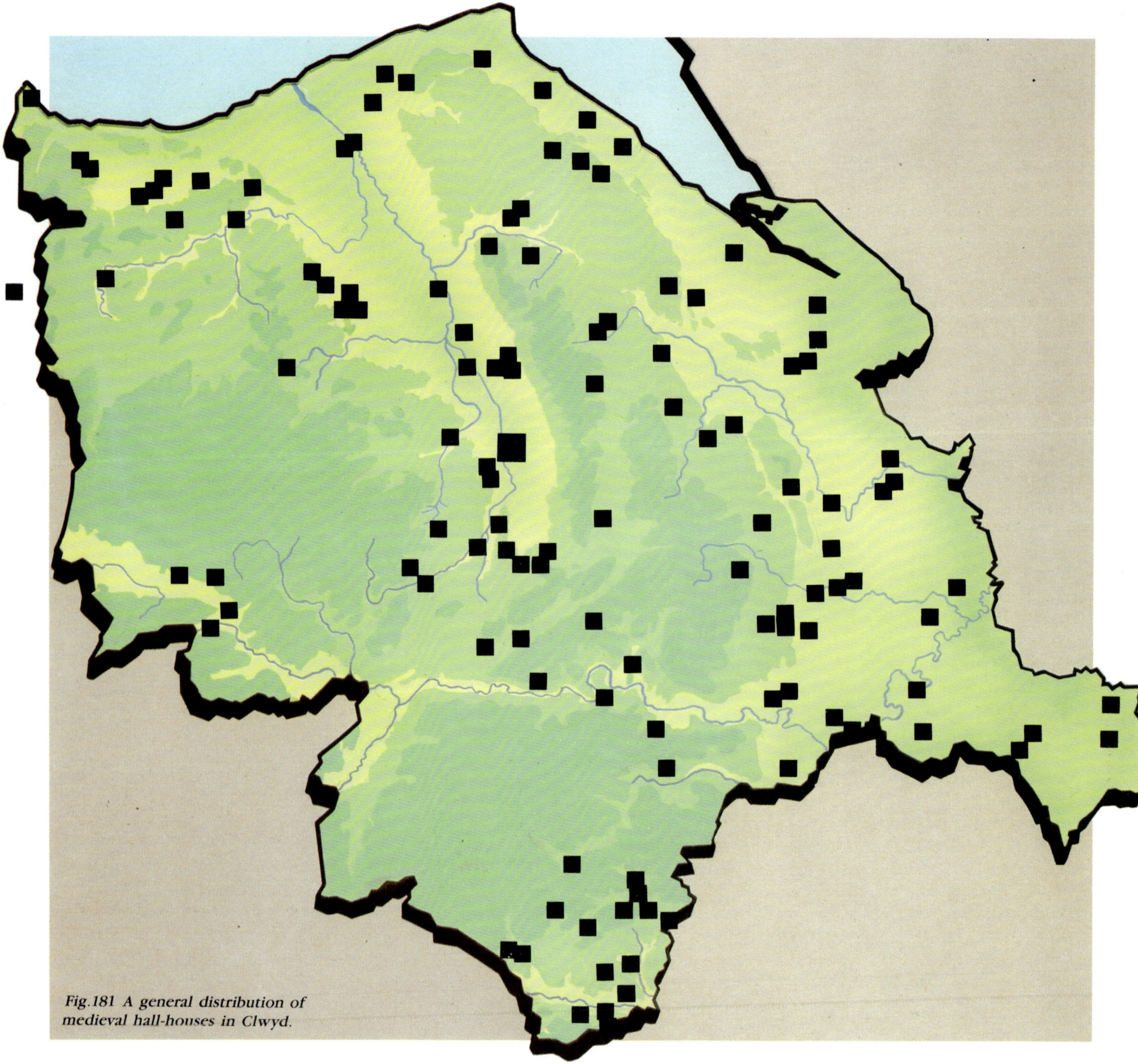

Fig.181 A general distribution of medieval hall-houses in Clwyd.

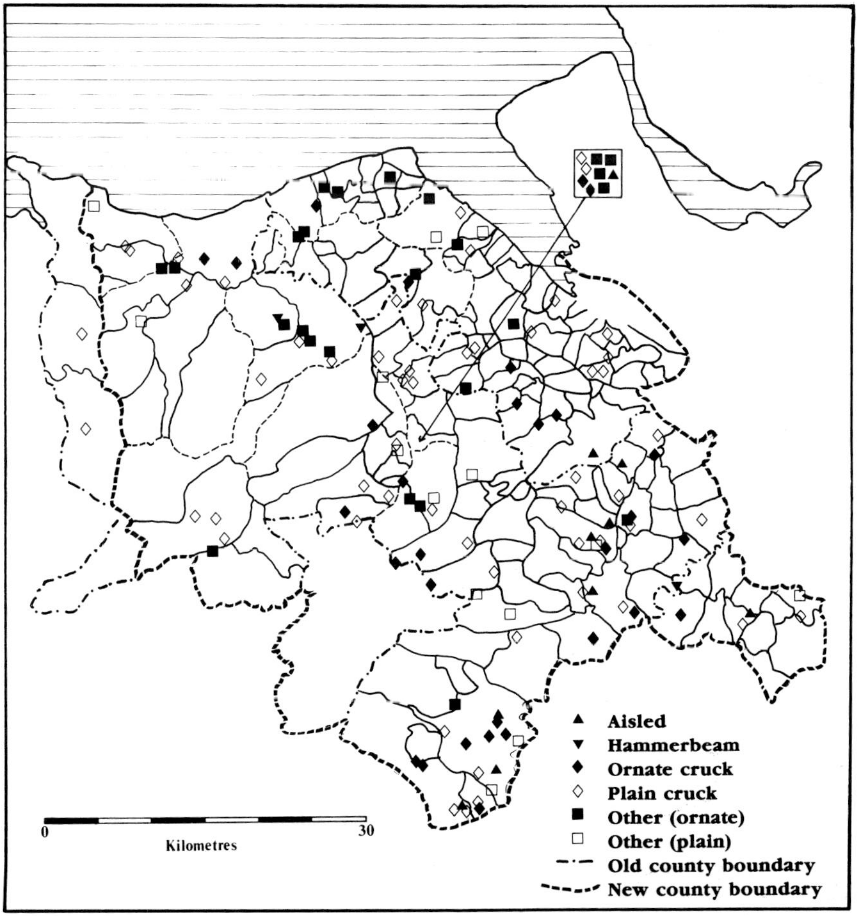

Fig.182 The distribution of hall-house roof types, in relation to township boundaries of Clwyd.

Clwyd and around Mold and Ruabon, and timber almost everywhere. The importance of timber was paramount, since it was used not only for the entire framework of buildings in the lowlands and the towns, but also for framing roofs and partitions in houses with mass walls.

Medieval Buildings

The majority of surviving medieval houses in Clwyd are timber-framed, either box-framed or more commonly cruck-framed (Fig.182). The difference is fundamental: a box-framed building consists of a framework of four walls which carry the whole weight of the roof, whereas the roof of a cruck-framed building is carried on cruck couples, paired beams running from the roof to the ground (Figs.180,183). Because of their self-supporting properties crucks were ideal for open halls (Fig.181), but since they could not be extended upwards (unlike box-framed houses) they fell out of favour when storeyed houses became popular.

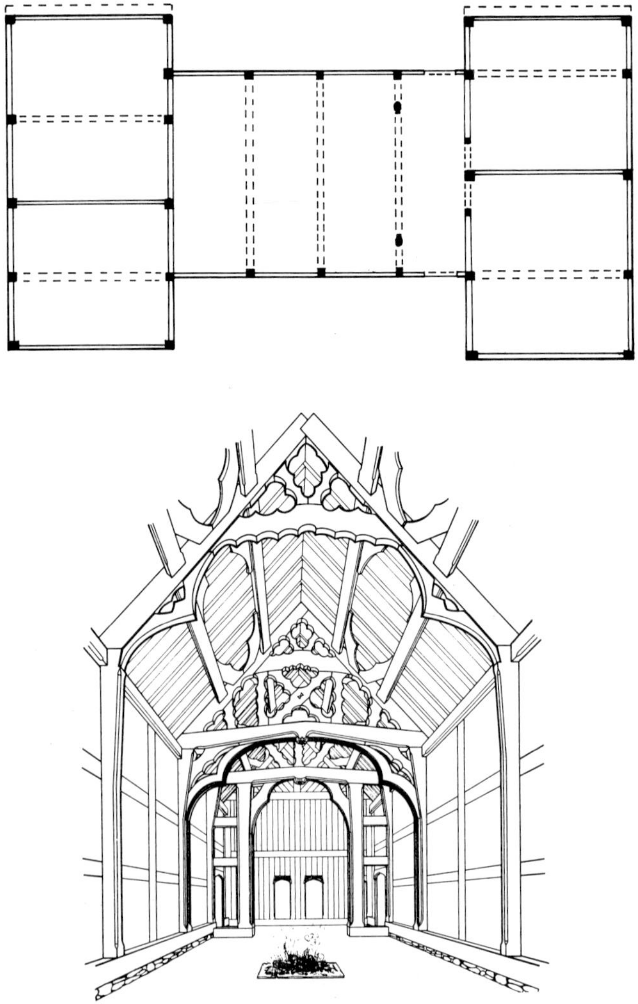

Fig.183 Plasnewydd, Ruabon: a box-framed H-plan hall-house with one aisled truss by the passage. The reconstructed drawing (below) may be modified by recent discoveries suggesting that the framing was more elaborate.

The earliest surviving houses in Clwyd date from the later middle ages, probably no earlier than the 14th century (eg Plas Cadwgan). Royal rule was becoming acceptable by then, so there was no need for defensible houses of the sort common in the Scottish Marches or in Ireland: almost the only tower house in north-eastern Wales is at Broncoed, near Mold. The majority of the farming population, whether gentry or tenants, built themselves more or less substantial houses on a pattern common to most of England and eastern Wales: this was the hall-house, in which the main living room was open from floor to roof, with the main fire on the floor. Hall-houses in eastern Wales are similar in style and numbers to those immediately over the border into England: a change takes place as one moves westwards into less hospitable country, where medieval houses become rarer and generally of a higher social status. Similarly there is a change from timber-framed buildings to stone-walled houses as one moves westwards.

Theoretically the simplest hall-house could consist of one large room like a barn. However, the simplest surviving examples consist of two units, a hall and a secondary room at one end (eg Hafod Adams), while the commonest type has the hall between secondary rooms at each end, sometimes with the end units subdivided into smaller rooms or ceiled over to give an upper floor (Figs.180,183). In rare cases (eg Ty-draw, Llanarmon Mynydd Mawr) there is evidence to suggest that the outer room may have been designed as a byre, with the cross-passage acting as a feed-walk. At a higher social level, the end-rooms might be enlarged into wings to give a T-plan (eg Plas-y-brain, Treuddyn (Fig.187)) or H-plan (eg Plasnewydd, Ruabon, (Fig.183)). Hall-houses were strongly symmetrical about their long axis. There were windows on each long wall and the entry was in the form of a passage between opposed doorways. The reason was purely practical: since glass was rarely used, only the leeside doorway and windows would be used and the rest kept closed and shuttered. Generally there would be wooden partitions at each end of the hall. At the passage end one or two doorways would lead into the service rooms, while at the other end there would be a raised dais for the high table. Occasionally there are traces of a fixed bench against the dais partition, which usually had two doorways leading into the small rooms beyond (eg Pentre, Ysceifiog, (Fig.186)): these were probably a small parlour and a bedroom. Above the dais there was sometimes a canopy, formed by cantilevering the joists of the parlour ceiling over the top of the partition to support the vertical partition above: this feature, probably in imitation of the 'tester' over royal thrones, is to be found in houses of widely differing social status (eg Pwll-y-chwiaid-bach (Fig. 185), and Gloddaeth, Llandudno). Since there was no chimney, the smoke found its way out through a vent in the roof, which may sometimes be identified by the small louvre-truss supporting the end of the ridge-beam (Fig.185).

Fig.184 Hafod Rhiwlas, near Llansilin, in the south of Clwyd.

Hall-houses varied greatly in size and sophistication. The smallest seem to have had three bays - inner room, hall and outer room - while most have a hall of two bays (Fig.180). In many of these the central truss is treated decoratively: for unlike later builders, medieval craftsmen tended to concentrate all their decorative skills on the inside of a house. External walls, even of timber-framed houses, tended to be quite plain (contrast Figs.180,197): but inside the visible structural timbers were enriched with arched braces, cusping, moulding

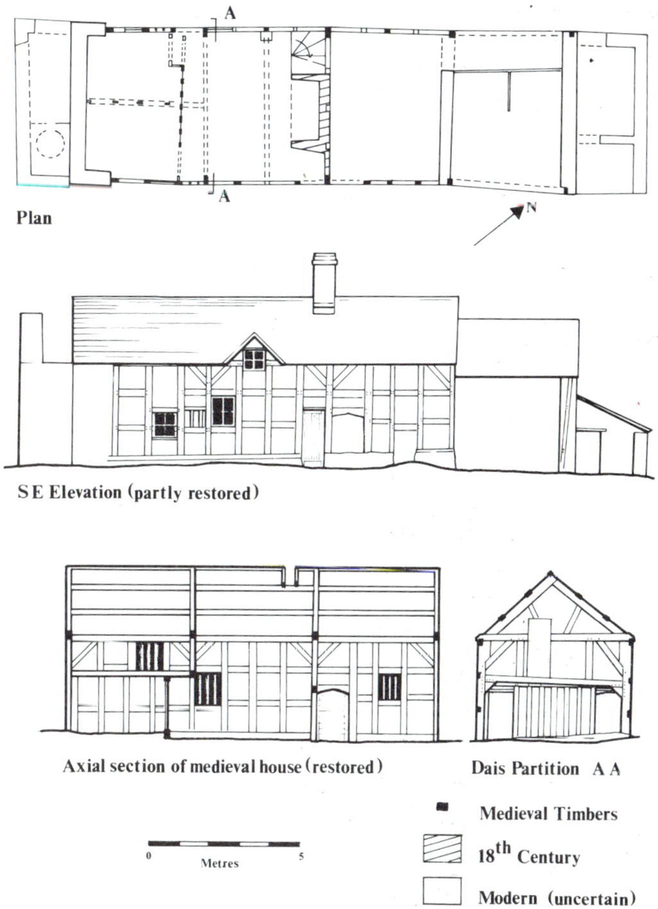

Fig.185 Pwll-y-chwyaid bach, Llanynys: a box-framed medieval hall-house converted to a storeyed lobby-entry house in the 18th century. The original cross-passage doorway, dais canopy and louvre-truss survive.

and bosses (Fig.183). Partitions were either framed and infilled with wattle-and-daub, or built of alternating thick posts and thin panels. The walls would have been plastered and probably decorated with painting or fabric hangings. Windows generally had closely-spaced wooden mullions to reduce draughts, and internal shutters. In the highest quality buildings the windows had stone mullions, not unlike those of contemporary churches: in fact the similarity between the open-roofed hall-house and the open-roofed church should not be overlooked.

At the top of the social scale houses were extremely elaborate, and for a short period at the end of the middle ages two forms of decorative roof-structure were occasionally used. One seems to be a revival of the archaic aisled building reduced to the minimum: the truss by the passage (and sometimes others) incorporated posts dividing the width of the building unequally into three parts (Fig.183). It is interesting to observe that several of these houses occupy moated sites, indicating perhaps 'manorial' status. In England aisle-truss roofs were generally superseded by the technically more complex hammerbeam roof by about 1400:

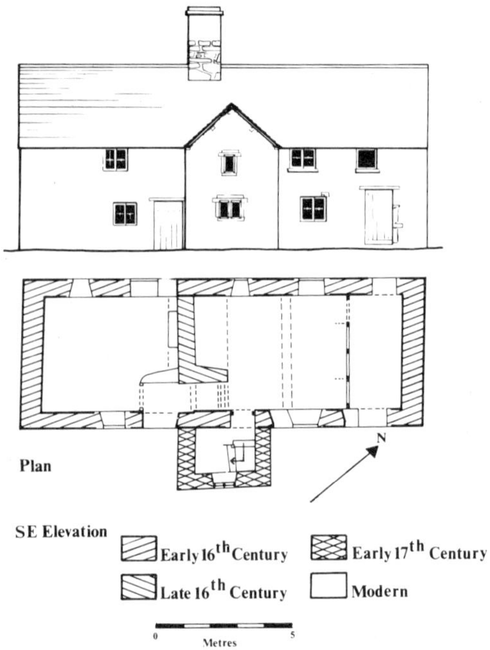

Fig.186 Pentre, Ysceifiog: a much-altered medieval hall-house, converted successively into an outside-cross-passage house and then a lobby-entry house. The staircase wing is 17th century. There is evidence that the lower end was at one time a byre. The dais partition has mortices for a fixed bench (plan after Delyn Borough Council).

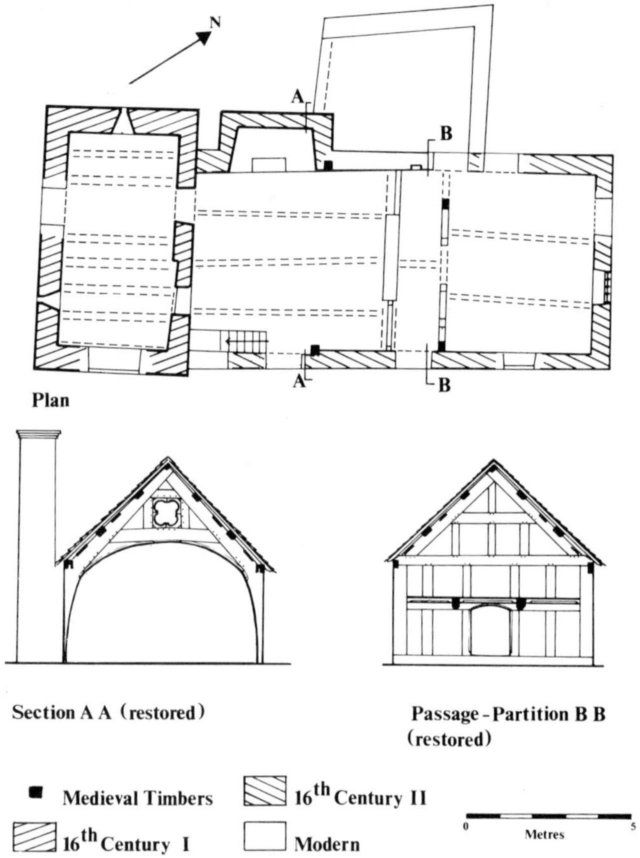

Fig.187 Plas-y-Brain, Treuddyn. A cruck-framed medieval hall-house, which was probably originally timber-framed. A stone chimney was added at an early date and is perhaps contemporary with the stone parlour block. The central arch-braced truss has cusping in the apex.

a simpler derivative of this, the 'false hammerbeam', became popular in the Vale of Clwyd for roofing churches and a few major houses at the very end of the 15th century. Such houses belonged to the greatest gentry families: one of the owners of Plas Cadwgan was Master of the Wardrobe to Elizabeth I. However, in terms of basic planning there was little difference between them and the smallest hall-houses.

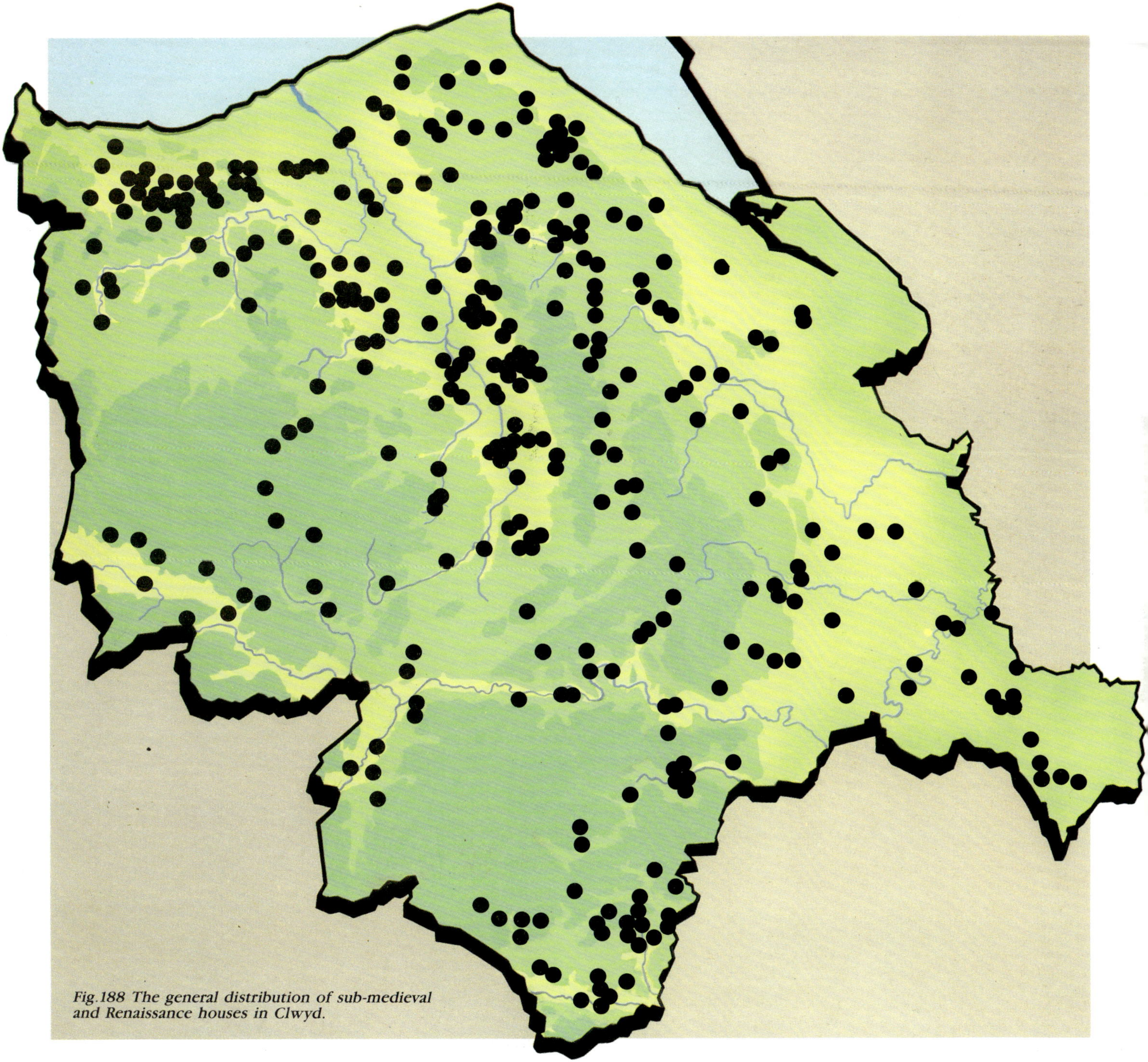

Fig.188 The general distribution of sub-medieval and Renaissance houses in Clwyd.

Sub-Medieval Houses (c.1550-1700)

One or two of the great hall-houses incorporated the innovation of a permanent fireplace and chimney. This was one of the two most

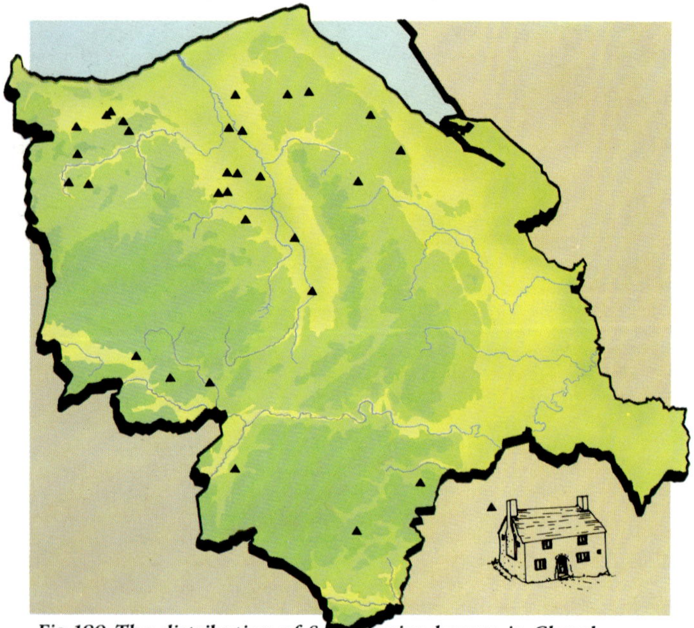

Fig.189 The distribution of Snowdonian houses in Clwyd.

Fig.190 Pen-y-bryn, Llansilin: the medieval house is now modernised. An open hall has been subdivided by the insertion of a floor and chimney. The degree of decoration on the original beams is typical of the region.

Fig.191 The distribution of lateral-chimney houses in Clwyd.

important improvements to the design of houses in the later 16th century, the second (related to it if not actually the result of it) being the provision of upper floors throughout the house. From about 1550 onwards all new houses seem to have been built with enclosed fireplaces, and very many older houses were converted by the insertion of chimneys and upper floors (Fig.185). The inspiration obviously came from the greater houses, and it is interesting to see how the basic idea was differently adopted in different regions.

In Wales during the period 1550-1650 there were four major house-types, which may be defined by the relationship between the main fireplace and the main entry. Although examples of each type may be found in any region, different types predominated in different regions. In Snowdonia and the Conwy valley the fireplace was on the gable wall and the main entry in the middle of the front wall, giving a room on either side of an entrance passage. In north-east and south-west Wales the chimney was frequently on the side wall with the entrance to one side of it. In south-east Wales the chimney was set inside the old hall, with the cross-passage immediately behind it: and in the Marches the chimney was set into the cross-passage so that there was a small lobby against the side of the chimney. The closest relation to the medieval hall-house was the type with the lateral chimney (Fig.192): the relationship between the rooms remained the same, and the chimney did not encroach on the living space. Although it was fairly common in Clwyd (Fig.191) it was by no means universal: the form with the lobby entry was almost as common in some areas (Fig.196). In some areas there were a

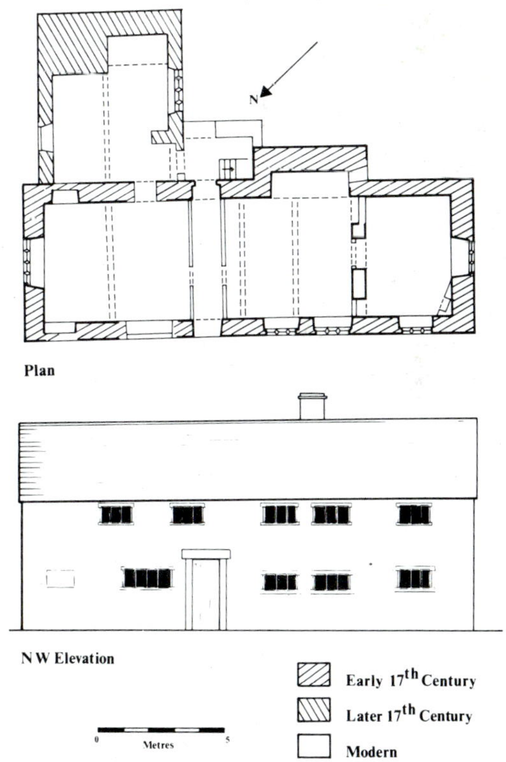

Fig.192 Pant-gwyn-mawr, Ysceifiog: a 17th century lateral-chimney house with a secondary (but still 17th century) rear wing. The spacing of the mullioned windows suggests Renaissance influence.

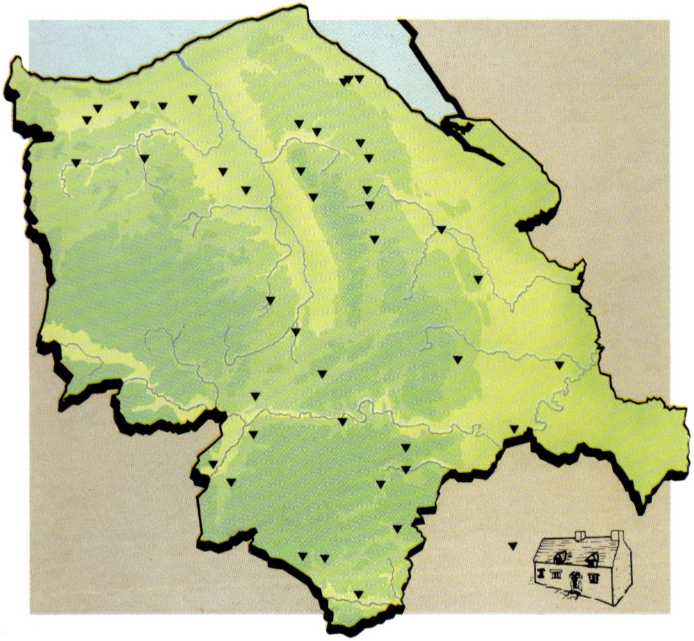

Fig.193 The distribution of outside cross-passage houses in Clwyd. Many of these are converted hall-houses.

few 'Snowdonian' houses, and there was a sprinkling of houses with the outside cross-passage (Figs.189,193) usually with a parlour at the lower end but occasionally with the lower room being a byre, giving the so-called 'long-house' type (Fig.186).

In many cases it is possible to see how a medieval hall-house was altered. A chimney may have been built against a decorated roof-truss, rendering it meaningless (eg the Blackamoor's Head, Rhuddlan), or a door may have been cut through a formerly solid partition to give access to the new first floor (Fig.185). However, the new storeyed houses were built to the same proportions as their predecessors, and in many cases the new grand chambers at the first floor were given decorated roofs exactly like those in the older open halls (eg Ty-isaf, Cilcain). Such decorated roofs remained popular in north-east Wales longer than anywhere else in the Principality.

Houses continued to be built using these plans until the mid-18th century. The relatively few dated examples suggest that in Clwyd the earliest may have been the type with the outside cross-passage, of which over half were converted hall-houses (Figs.186,194.); the latest may have been the type with the lobby entry, which became most popular after 1600 (Fig.195). The lateral-chimney house was the most common (nearly half of the surviving houses of the period 1550-1750 have this plan): it was already popular before 1600, but declined after 1700 (Fig.192).

By 1600 there were other changes as well. Cruck framing was no longer used in houses, since it provided insufficient headroom for an upper storey. However, it may have continued

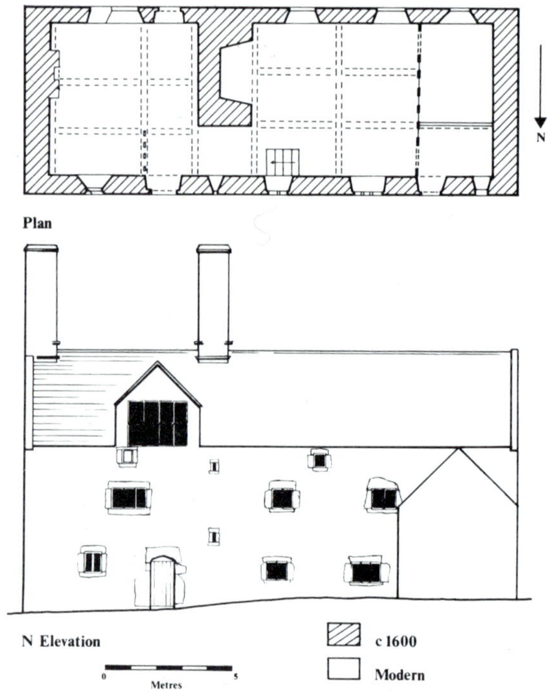

Fig.194 Faerdre, Abergele: an outside-cross-passage house, probably of c.1600. The megalithic door-head, mullioned windows and tall chimneys are typical of west Denbighshire. The large dormer window is a 17th century alteration, now removed.

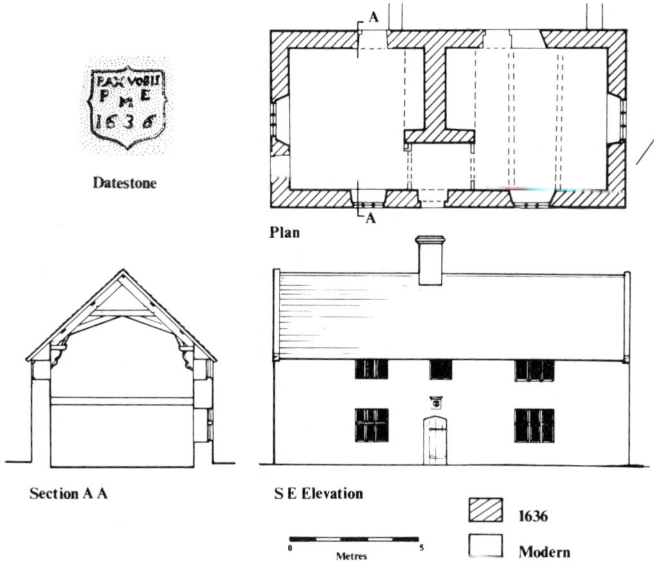

Fig.195 Coed-y-cra-uchaf, Northop: a lobby-entry house of 1636. The roof is probably the latest example of the Vale of Clwyd 'false hammer-beam' style. The formal elevation suggests Renaissance influence.

in use for barns, and an appreciable number of cruck barns prove to be disused medieval houses (eg Ty-draw, Llanarmon Mynydd Mawr), sometimes replaced by new storeyed houses in the same complex. Exterior timber framing became more elaborate, with close studding and various decorative designs being used (Fig.197). First floors were jettied, or cantilevered out - a technique only possible with box framing, and much used in town houses. Interior timberwork was decorated with mouldings and stops. Where good stone was available, it too was used for detailing: megalithic doorways were popular in some areas, as were tall chimney stacks (Fig.194).

Changes in location can also be seen. Whereas medieval houses were generally restricted to the lowlands and foothills (Fig.181), later houses were built on higher ground as well. It is interesting to note how many of the upland houses are of the lobby-entry plan, which may have become popular only during the 17th century (Figs.188,196).

Renaissance Houses (c.1580-1700)

At the end of the 16th century a totally new influence appeared, again initially at a high social level but slowly affecting almost the

Fig.196 The distribution of lobby-entry houses in Clwyd.

whole social spectrum. The Tudor court had attracted many ambitious Welshmen to London, and some of them brought back novel architectural ideas to their country estates. (Figs.200,202) The first appearance in north Wales of this new Renaissance style (which first appeared in England around 1510) was at Sir Richard Clough's prodigy house of Bachegraig, Tremeirchion, in 1567. This Flemish-style villa, based ultimately on Italian designs, had no lasting effects on its surroundings: nor did it derive anything from the traditional architecture of the area - even the materials are reputed to

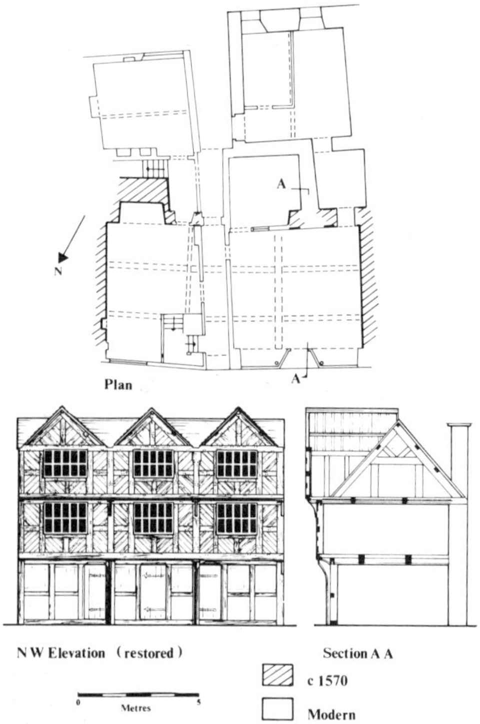

Fig.197 32-34 High Street, Denbigh: originally three shops, allegedly of 1570. The jettied front and elaborate framing is typical of town houses in eastern Wales and the Marches of c.1600, and of rural houses of quality.

Fig.198 Glan-tanat-isaf, Llanrhaeadr ym Mochnant in the Tanat valley, dating from the sub-medieval and Renaissance periods. The sub-medieval end-chimney plan is given external symmetry by more or less centralised windows.

have been imported. Perhaps more influential was Plas Mawr, Conwy, built by Robert Wynn between 1576 and 1595. While one wing still included a medieval-style ground-floor hall and cross-passage (as did many comparable houses in England), the rest made use of novel ideas then coming into fashion at the Elizabethan court such as exterior symmetry and thought-out circulation between rooms. This was a tremendous innovation, for until then houses had virtually no privacy: the nearest approach to an unused space between rooms was the lobby-entry of a Borderland house or the central passage of a Snowdonian house. For 'vernacular'

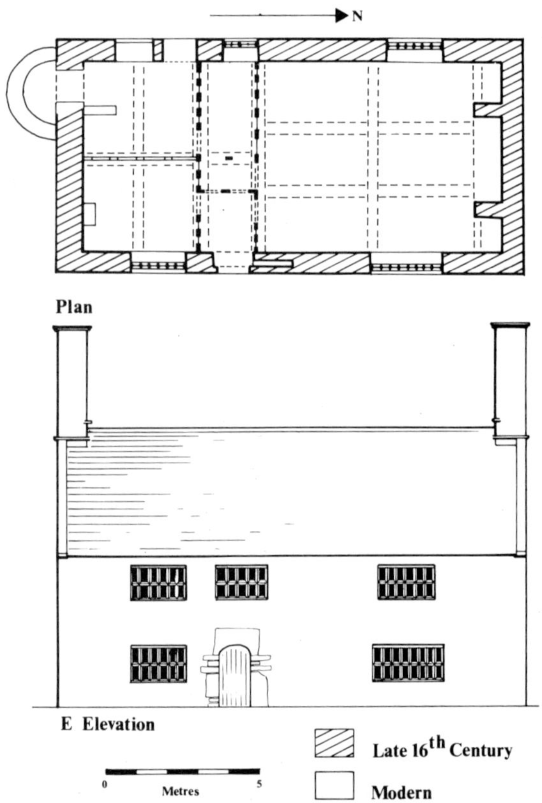

Fig.199 Dolbelydr, Cefn: a gable chimney house, the home of the grammarian Henry Salesbury in 1593. The circulation space inside the doorway, as well as the formality of the elevation, indicates Renaissance influence.

Fig.200 Faenol-fawr, Bodelwyddan: a formal Renaissance facade of 1597 with contemporary details (stepped gables and windows with stone mullions and transoms). The facade was altered by the insertion of eighteenth century sash windows.

buildings were not 'designed' in the modern sense, but built to traditional proportions without any consideration of basic design concepts: things had always been 'just so'.

But towards the end of the 16th century there appeared the figure of the designing architect (amateur or professional) whose training was more theoretical than practical. Men like Sir John Smythson or John Thorpe seem to have provided the court at London with innovatory house-plans (not always practical) based on abstract geometry and classical proportions, and incorporating some consideration of privacy. The idea of the circulation-space seems to have been taken into the vernacular tradition, often in conjunction with two other ideas, namely the grand stair and the imposing porch. Thus Dolbelydr, Cefn (Fig.199), home of the grammarian Henry Salesbury, was basically a sub-medieval house but with a true entrance-hall. Fferm, Hope, goes further: it has the sub-medieval plan of the lateral-chimney hall and subsidiary wing, but the entrance is through a porch into a passage, from which one may reach the rooms and the stair.

As the 17th century progressed, the great gentry houses were built to more formal Renaissance designs, with symmetrical facades and elegant detailing. At the same time the traditional plans continued in use, with perhaps a little more concern for external symmetry (Fig.192,195). Much of the change from sub-medieval to Renaissance architecture was more apparent than real, since the Renaissance elements were decorative rather than structural. The profoundest change was caused by the greater availability of glass, which led to a

Fig.201 Faenol-fawr, Bodelwyddan: interior detailing of 1597 (the panelling below the overmantel is later).

complete change in the style of the windows. It was no longer necessary to light every room from two sides: it was also possible to increase the size of the openings. So carved and moulded window-frames (in stone and timber) became common: some of the earliest had arched heads derived from medieval patterns, but soon rectangular windows with chamfered mullions and transoms became general (Fig.194,199). By the later 17th century there was also a change from the long low windows appropriate for the low-ceilinged sub-medieval rooms to taller windows more suitable for the taller rooms of the new houses.

There was also a new approach to decoration. Smaller and more elaborate motifs were introduced, often of foreign inspiration, and these were rapidly taken up by wood-carvers and plasterers. The exteriors of stone houses were decorated with pediments above the windows and carved panels and finials (eg Trevalun Hall), or the Flemish stepped gables probably introduced by Sir Richard Clough.

Fig.202 Golden Grove, Llanasa: a Renaissance facade betraying earlier origins. The status of the 'hall' is shown by its larger window (to the left of the porch). The stepped gables, mullioned and transomed windows and projecting porch are typical of the late sixteenth century in Clwyd.

Inside, the new chimney-pieces in particular were a focus for decoration, which often reflected one of the most extraordinary aspects of Clwyd during the Elizabethan and Jacobean periods (Fig.201). Coats of arms, initials and dates were proudly displayed on houses by their owners:

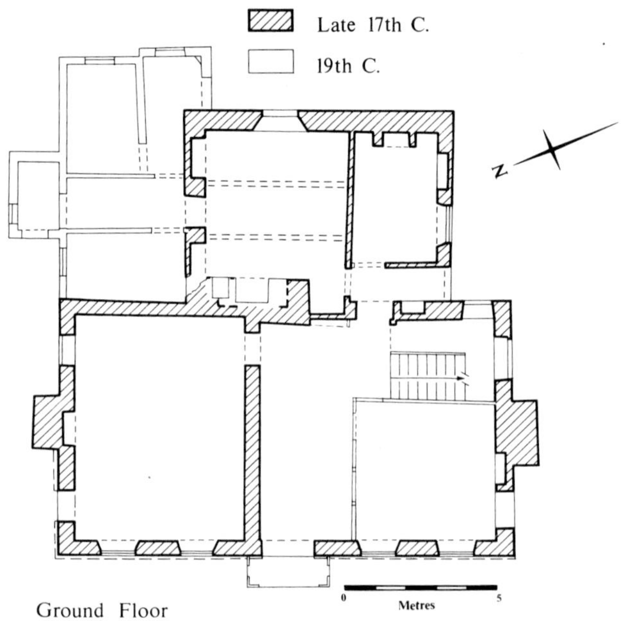

Fig.203 Plas-yn-dre, Holywell: possibly a house of the Pennant family. A late 17th century T plan house with very formal elevations.

there are more dated houses surviving in Clwyd from before 1600 than in the rest of Wales put together. The traditional Welsh pride in genealogy found a visible expression thanks to growing literacy fostered by the availability of books in English and Welsh as well as Latin, and these same books provided the models for up-to-date aesthetic taste. A series of carved screens and doorheads, which have the common features of classical guilloche moulding and decorative Renaissance lettering, include dates 'Anno Mundi' (from the creation of the world) which may have been taken from a now-lost almanac. Elsewhere, local carvers and plasterers took classical motifs into their repertoires: at Plas Tirion, Llanrwst, the amazing heraldic fireplace (with its possibly bogus coat of arms) has classical columns, up-to-date Jacobean strapwork and two figures probably derived from classical caryatids but in rather odd costume. Ceilings were decorated with carved and moulded beams or with moulded plasterwork similar to that in fashion elsewhere. There is increasing evidence that much more colour was in use than now survives: wooden and plaster overmantels were painted, so were walls and panelling.

After the Restoration there was a further change. The influences of London became stronger through the medium of the architectural pattern-book. Two new plan-types became popular, the T-plan house with service rooms at the rear (Fig.203) and the double-pile house two

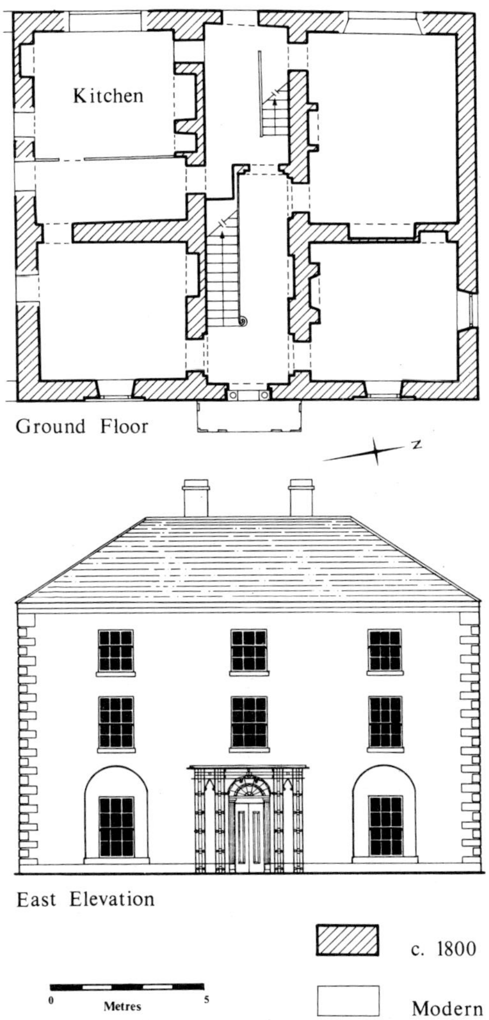

Fig.204 The Old Convent, Holywell: built c.1800 for Mrs. Smedley. A very stiff example of a pattern book, double-pile house. The arched recesses in the elevation are typical of the period.

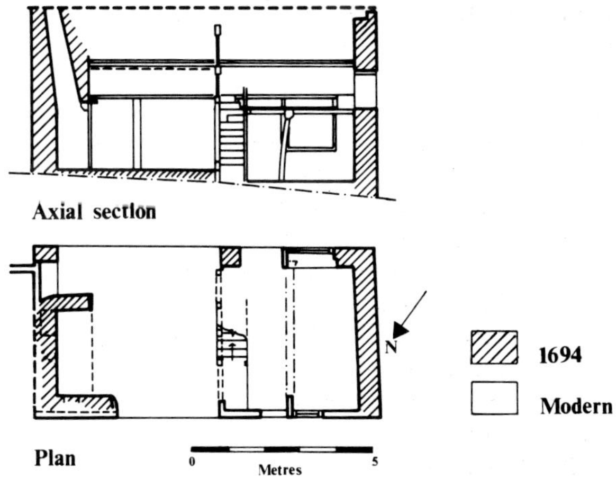

Fig.205 Cae-coch, Whitford: a lofted cottage dated 1694 on the fireplace lintel; essentially a hall-house in miniature. (Plan after Delyn Borough Council original).

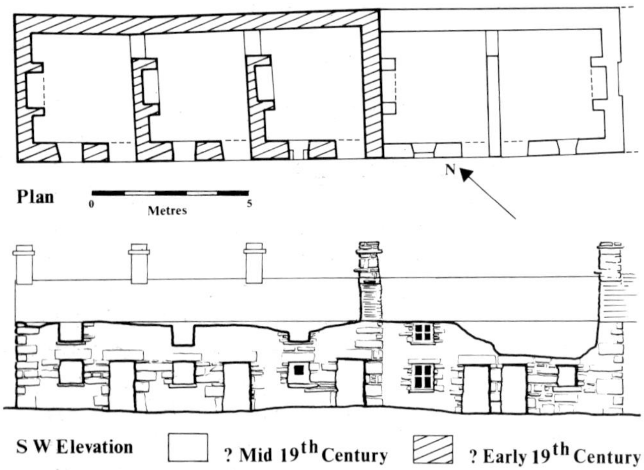

Fig.206 1-5 Acer Las, Cerrigydrudion: the earlier two phases of a row of ten cottages of c.1800-1870. The plans are 'industrial', but the construction is firmly traditional.

rooms deep around a central passage (Fig.204). These were favoured by the gentry, who by the 18th century were looking away from the locality for their architecture: under their influence brick and stucco replaced stone and timber framing, and sash windows became common.

However, at a lower social level vernacular traditions of planning and construction continued. Cottages were still built on a basically medieval pattern until the 19th century: there are large numbers where the living-room was open to the roof and a loft over the parlour (called the Croglofft) was reached by a ladder (Fig.205). Timber-framed walls and thatched roofs (often now covered with corrugated iron) survived longest in this type of building. Further west the use of rough rubble masonry continued, as at Acer-las, Cerrigydrudion (Fig.206). This row of cottages is unlikely to be earlier than 1800, and although the plans may be derived from the industrial Midlands the style of building is purely local and traditional.

Fig.207 Brithdir-mawr, Cilcain: a sub-medieval interior, with wooden mullioned windows, beamed ceiling and post-and-panel partition.

CLWYD IN THE INDUSTRIAL REVOLUTION
by Stephen Grenter and Ann Lloyd Williams

Introduction

The modern County of Clwyd consists largely of the former counties of Flintshire and Denbighshire. Although primarily a rural area, the east of the County was once intensively industrialised, with mainly heavy industries, such as coal and lead mining; iron, steel and copper manufacture; quarrying; pottery and brick production. Many of these industries played a significant role in the development of the Industrial Revolution in Britain, and although most have now disappeared from Clwyd, their remains are still a common feature of the landscape.

The Iron Industry

Throughout the 17th and 18th centuries, iron manufacture in Clwyd was concentrated in East Denbighshire, an area rich in ironstone, limestone and coal. By the middle of the 17th century, blast furnaces had been established at Bersham, Ruabon and Plas Madoc, producing pig iron for local forges, such as Pont y Blew, near Chirk.

During the 18th century, Bersham became a major concern, successfully smelting iron by burning coke in 1721, and thereafter developing a specialisation and expertise in the production of cast iron goods, which was eventually to rival any ironworks in Britain. After 1763, Bersham became the main works of the ironmaster John Wilkinson, manufacturing cannon (Fig.208) and cylinders for the Boulton and Watt engine, the quality of which was made possible by Wilkinson's invention of very accurate boring machines, the first of these patented in 1774. Wilkinson also founded an ironworks at Brymbo in 1793, which later became Brymbo Steelworks.

In the 19th century, with the notable exception of the Hawarden works which closed in 1844, iron manufacture continued to be concentrated within East Denbighshire, with new works being established at Coed Talon, Ffrwd and Acrefair between 1817 and 1825. The British Iron Company established at Acrefair was one of the most successful companies in North Wales, employing around 1,500 people at its peak. A drop in the price of pig iron after 1825, however, led to a depression in the industry, which the very large, modern integrated works of South Wales were better able to weather. Between 1830 and 1847 iron production in South Wales increased by 150%, whereas in North Wales virtually no increase took place. This decline was accelerated by the invention of the Bessemer steel making process in 1856, when only those works with sufficient capital to purchase this new equipment prospered.

Fig.208 The Octagonal Building at Bersham, near Wrexham. Built by John Wilkinson in the late 18th century, probably as a cannon foundry.

Fig.209 Distribution of industrial sites in Clwyd, mentioned in the text.

Fig.210 Brymbo ironworks in about 1860.

It was not until the opening of John Summers' great steel making plant at Shotton (Fig.209) on the Dee Estuary at the end of the 19th century, that Clwyd once again came to play an important role in the industry. Steel production ended at Shotton in 1980, with the loss of 8,000 jobs, although a modern cold rolling and strip coating mill still continues in production.

Surviving remains of the iron industry are rare. Only at Bersham and Brymbo (Fig.210) do substantial remains survive. At Bersham, notably at Mill Farm, two buildings still stand, both probably foundries. This site is currently under excavation by the Clwyd Archaeology Service and is revealing further substantial structures, including a blast furnace, air furnaces and coking ovens (Fig.213). At Brymbo, a late 18th century blast furnace survives, together with an associated casting house. Nearby is Pentre Saeson foundry, which was probably established

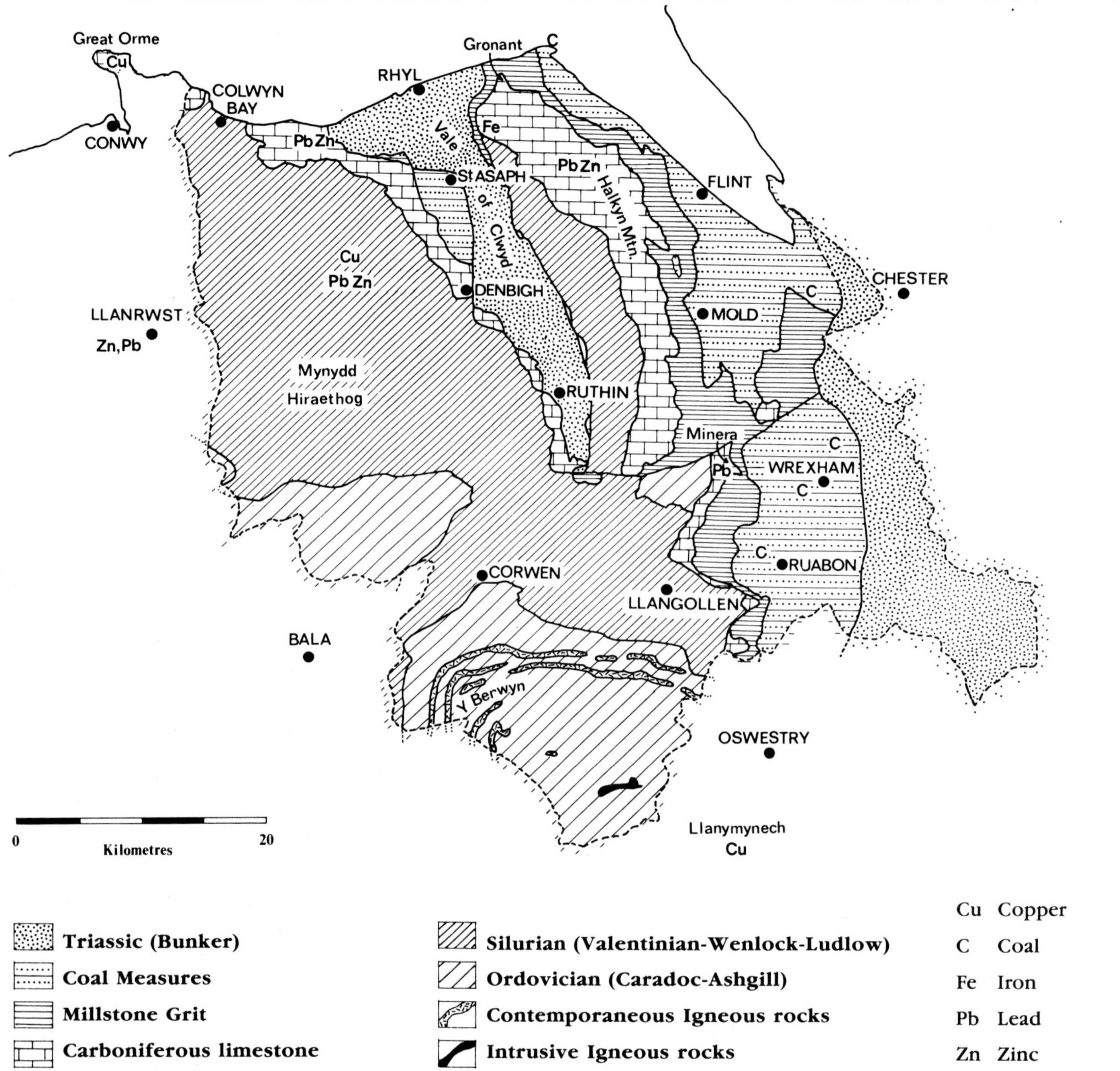

Fig.211 The geology of an area was closely related to where industries became established. The Coal Measures and limestone were particularly important for coal, clay, ironstone, limestone, lead and zinc.

by Wilkinson and worked until 1981. Buckley Foundry, established in 1792 and Rhuddlan Foundry are still working today.

The Coal Industry

The coalfield in Clwyd extends in a narrow strip northwards from near Oswestry to the coast at Point of Ayr (Fig.211). Split into two sections by the Bala fault, the Flintshire and Denbighshire coalfields developed in different ways. This was largely due to geographical factors, significantly the poor state of the road network, the effect of which was substantially mitigated by Flintshire's location on the coast. The Denbighshire coalfield, without easy access to the sea, could therefore only cater for a local market.

Fig.212 Bersham Colliery, the surviving No. 2 Headgear and Winding House can be seen on the right.

Fig.213 Excavations in progress at Bersham in 1990. The remains of the blast-furnace can be seen to the right of the mill building.

In Denbighshire, mining had been carried out on a small scale since the medieval period. From 1414, for example, the burgesses of Holt were given the right to dig for coal in Brymbo and Coedpoeth. From the 18th century, largely due to the demands of an expanding iron industry and an ever improving transport network, coal mining had become widely established. John Wilkinson, the ironmaster, had 41 pits in Brymbo alone.

A new era began in the Denbighshire coalfield at the beginning of the 20th century, with the sinking of deep pits. Llay Main No. 1 shaft eventually became the deepest in the country at 3000ft. At the time of nationalisation in 1947, five collieries remained in the coalfield: Bersham, Llay Main, Gresford, Hafod and Ifton (Shropshire). By the 1980s only Bersham colliery survived and following its closure in 1986, the major heavy industry of Denbighshire had disappeared.

Records of coal mining in Flintshire also first appear in the medieval period, but in this smaller coalfield, it was the demands of the lead, pottery and copper smelting industries, which provided a stimulus to its early growth. The mines also played a central role in the expansion of towns such as Mold and Holywell. By 1795 Pennant described the coal mines on the Dee Estuary as "the most flourishing I ever remember . . .", but by the mid-19th century, as in Denbighshire, the Flintshire coalfield had gone into decline. This was due to many factors, notably the concentration of industry in areas more suited to industrial growth. Copper smelting, for example, moved from Greenfield to Swansea which was better located to receive ore from Cornwall after the demise of the copper mines of Parys Mountain. At the time of nationalisation, only the Point of Ayr colliery, near Prestatyn remained and it is now the only surviving colliery in the County.

With the exception of Point of Ayr, surprisingly little of this once great industry survives today. The No.2 Winding Engine House and Headgear survives at Bersham (Fig.212), as do the engine houses at Wynnstay Colliery, Ruabon, built in about 1855, and at Bettisfield colliery, Bagillt. These examples are the exceptions, however. Usually the only clues to the existence of former coal mines are the ubiquitous coal tips. Even these are now rapidly vanishing through reclamation schemes.

The Lead Industry

The lead bearing region of Clwyd extends from Talargoch (Fig.214), near Prestatyn in the north-west to the Halkyn Mountain area in the east and to Minera (Fig.215) in the south. Lead mining began in Clwyd during the Roman period, when it was used for piping, cisterns, baths and coffins. Possible sites associated with the industry are known at Flint, Prestatyn and Ffrith, and lead ingots or pigs have been found at Carmel, near Holywell, and in Chester. Both mining and processing developed throughout the medieval period and are attested by the survival of place names such as Waun y Balls, near Flint and Pen y Ball, near Holywell. Ball is a likely derivation of bole, an early form of lead smelter. The increasing significance of the industry is reflected in the privileges granted to miners at both Minera and Holywell in the 14th century, which included freedom from some tolls and taxes and the right to hold their own courts.

Fig.214 The Clive engine house, Talargoch, near Prestatyn constructed in 1860 to house a massive 100 ins pumping engine.

Although the industry began to expand in the late 17th century, it was not until the 18th century and the Industrial Revolution, that large scale extraction took place with substantial

Fig.215 City Engine House, Minera built in 1847.

concerns at Minera, Halkyn and Talargoch. The extraction of the ore in Clwyd was generally hampered by flooding. A mining venture, therefore, usually required a great deal of initial capital outlay in installing expensive and ever more sophisticated drainage systems, allowing deeper extraction to continue. Very few mine owners had the foresight or the wealth to carry out this essential drainage. Notable exceptions were Paul Panton (Senior) at Talargoch and John Wilkinson at Minera. At Talargoch, Panton had to endure many years of loss before the mines showed a profit. In the last quarter of 1768, for instance, expenditure of £230 16s 7d was set against ore receipts of only £10. However, between 1794 and 1812 dividends totalling over £18,000 were paid to shareholders in spite of a serious accident in 1802 and a general depression in the local industry from 1802 - 1807.

At Minera, Wilkinson installed the latest Boulton and Watt engines to pump out the mines and over the six years following 1810, the mines raised over 50,000 tons of ore. Water continued to be a major problem, despite the attention of seven engines and the mines closed for almost 25 years from 1822. However, the digging of new drainage levels by John Taylor in

1845, led to the re-opening of the mines, and between 1849 and 1909 over £3,000,000 worth of ore was raised by the Minera Mining Company, which he established in 1849. Similarly, the Halkyn mines also suffered from flooding. In 1876, an Act of Parliament was passed to incorporate the Halkyn District Mines Drainage Company of which Taylor was the engineer. The later success of the Halkyn mines resulted from the excavation of the subsequent drainage level.

Between 1845 and 1938, Clwyd produced some 13% of the total British output of lead ore and 27% of zinc. However, by the turn of the century, cheap imports from abroad led to a drop in the price of British lead, which fell from an average of £21 per ton between 1853 and 1877 to £9 5s in 1894. This resulted in a collapse of the industry. The Talargoch mines ceased extraction in 1905. The Minera company closed in 1914. Halkyn, however, continued in production until 1947, and although no lead was raised after that date, the Company was not finally wound up until 1987.

The surviving remains of this industry litter the landscape in the lead producing areas. At Minera the remains of several engine houses survive to varying degrees, the City Engine House (Fig.215), erected in 1847, being the best preserved. A lead processing plant has also recently been revealed at the site. At Talargoch the former mine site is dominated by the Clive Engine House (Fig.214), erected in 1860 to house a massive 100 ins engine. The most common features surviving in the Halkyn area are bell pits. Engine houses survive at Pennant, near Rhuallt and at Hendre in the Wheeler Valley, while traces of the many mines in the Alyn Valley, such as the Glan Alyn mine at Loggerheads, can still be seen.

In Clwyd, the smelting of the mined ores was predominantly concentrated on the Dee Estuary, allowing easy transportation by sea. The use of coal, instead of wood, for smelting followed the successful development of a reverberatory furnace by the London Lead Company at Gadlys, near Bagillt in 1703. John Wilkinson established smelters at Brymbo for his Minera mines and at Buckley for his mine at Llyn y Pandy, near Rhydymwyn. The Brymbo Bottle chimney of his works still survives although the top was blown up in 1962 (Fig.216). On the Dee, near Mostyn, surviving buildings and part of a large chimney from the Llannerch y Mor smelting works are still standing.

Fig.216 The Brymbo Bottle Chimney. Part of a lead smelting plant built by John Wilkinson in the late 18th century. The top of the chimney was blown up in 1962.

The Clay Industry

It was the Romans who were the first to use clay on an industrial scale, as reflected in Clwyd by the legionary tilery at Holt. Although small scale pottery production took place in the County throughout the medieval period, it was not until the 18th and 19th centuries that Clwyd became famous for the manufacture of pottery, bricks, tiles and terracotta.

Fig.217 Buckley Potters at work. A watercolour, completed in 1823 by Lady Delamere.

The industry was concentrated in two main areas, Buckley and Ruabon, where suitable clay deposits were available. There were fourteen potteries in Buckley by the end of the 18th century, with Catheralls and Hancocks being the main manufacturers, producing mainly tiles, firebricks and a huge assortment of domestic wares (Fig.217). Vast amounts of Buckley ware were shipped from the Dee to Ireland and all around the Welsh coast.

In Ruabon, although bricks had been produced locally in the 18th century, it was in the 19th and 20th centuries that brick, tiles and terracotta manufacture became an important industry, especially when increased house construction in the Victorian period led to greater demand for red brick. At the same time detailed terracotta work became very fashionable. Two main companies operated in the Ruabon area. J.C. Edwards was established in about 1860, and later had works at Penybont, Trefynant and the Coppi, Rhos. In addition to numerous British contracts, products were exported to India, Canada, Egypt, Panama and Singapore. Henry Dennis established the other company in 1878, building a new works at Hafod brickworks in 1893 which manufactured ridge tiles, chimney pots, facing bricks and quarry tiles.

Throughout the clay manufacturing areas, the impact of the clay industry is still reflected in the large numbers of red brick buildings, many of which have attractive terracotta detailing. In Buckley, little survives of the potteries, although most of their locations are known. Pottery production has now ended, but brick and tile manufacture still continues at the Lane End brickworks, now owned by Butterley Brick Ltd. Dennis Ruabon is also still in operation and produces over half of Britain's quarry tiles, exporting over one third of these. An example of a beehive brick kiln, from Abenbury brickworks, Wrexham, can be seen in the Clywedog Valley at King's Mill.

Quarrying

Until the Industrial Revolution, quarrying in Clwyd was an essentially local industry meeting the demand for building stone. From the middle of the 18th century, in addition to stone and slate for building, there was an increasing requirement for stone for a variety of other purposes. Limestone was needed to produce lime, much sought after as a fertiliser, as a constituent of mortar, and as a fluxing agent in the smelting of iron. Hardcore was needed for building new roads and silica was also in demand for glass and refractory brick manufacture.

By far the most important stone extracted in Clwyd was limestone, which at one time was exported to Liverpool from Llanddulas, near Abergele and is still extensively worked in the County. Slate was also quarried in the Llangollen, Corwen and Glynceiriog areas, with the quarries of Glynceiriog and Llangollen employing over 600 men in the 1870s. Although locally important, slate quarrying in Clwyd was on a very small scale compared to the industry in Gwynedd.

Quarries, both in use and disused, are a common feature of the landscape, with many limestone, sand and gravel quarries still operating. The need to convert limestone into lime for mortar and fertiliser led to the construction of hundreds of small limekilns, structures which are still a common sight in the limestone areas. In addition, large industrial limekilns survive at Minera, near Wrexham, and at Padeswood and Gwernymynydd, near Mold. The Hoffman kiln (No.1) at Minera, built in 1868 and used until 1929, could hold 120 tons of limestone, had 24 chambers, and a chimney 275ft high (Fig.218). The kiln itself is still reasonably intact, although the chimney no longer stands.

Fig.218 The Minera Lime Company quarries, near Wrexham, in about 1910. In the background can be seen the chimneys of the Hoffman lime kilns, erected in 1868 and 1874.

The Copper Industry

Copper was not mined in Clwyd, although copper goods were produced in the Greenfield Valley, near Holywell, from the 1730s. It was at Greenfield from 1780 that Thomas Williams, the so called Copper King, set up his works to process copper mined from Anglesey by the Parys and Mona Mining Company. The works expanded in 1787, when Williams built a new rolling mill on the site to manufacture brass plate, utensils and wire. Greenfield also produced copper sheeting for ship-bottoms as well as trinkets for the African slave trade. By 1800 Williams controlled half of the British copper industry and his capital value was nearly £1,000,000. Using over 1000 tons of coal per day, the Greenfield works also had a significant impact on the expansion of the Flintshire coalfield.

After Williams's death in 1802 and the decline in the Anglesey mines, Greenfield's significance as a centre of the British copper industry waned, although production continued for some time. By the end of the century however, Clwyd's copper industry had disappeared.

Fig.219 Copperworks in the Greenfield Valley in 1796. Greenfield Mills, the copper battery works, can be seen in the foreground. The Valley contained a series of millponds providing water power for various manufacturing processes,

The remains of Williams' copper works can still be seen today at Greenfield Valley, where they form part of a Heritage Park. Archaeological excavations were carried out on the site between 1977 and 1981 and revealed buildings dating from 1766, including part of a copper and brass battery works (Fig.219).

Transport

The transportation of manufactured goods to the market place was a major factor in the siting of these industries. Many industries, therefore, were located on the banks of the Dee Estuary, with easy access to the sea. Cargo ships have transported goods along the Dee Estuary since the Roman period, and the industrialisation of Clwyd gave a great impetus to ship-building enterprises at ports such as Connah's Quay. Easy access to the sea, however, was not always possible, for example, the extractive industries had to be located where the minerals occurred. At the beginning of the Industrial Revolution, before an extensive road, canal or rail network had become established, the success or failure of many of these industries depended upon the development of often quite complex tramway systems.

From the middle of the 18th century, networks of horsedrawn tramways were developed to transport, for example, Buckley pottery to the sea; raw materials to the ironworks, as at Bersham from the 1750s; and slate from the quarries of Llantysilio Mountain, near Llangollen.

Canals in Clwyd also date from this period, with the first being built at Saltney Marsh in 1768, to take coals from Hawarden to the River Dee. The main canal project in Clwyd, however, was the construction of the Ellesmere canal from 1793. Major Denbighshire industrialists such as coalmine owner Richard Kyrke, and ironmaster John Wilkinson, were shareholders in this scheme, designed to link the rivers Severn, Dee and Mersey. Due mainly to problems with water supply, very little of this canal was actually built in Clwyd, apart from the Llangollen feeder branch, which considerably helped the transportation of slate from the quarries at Llangollen.

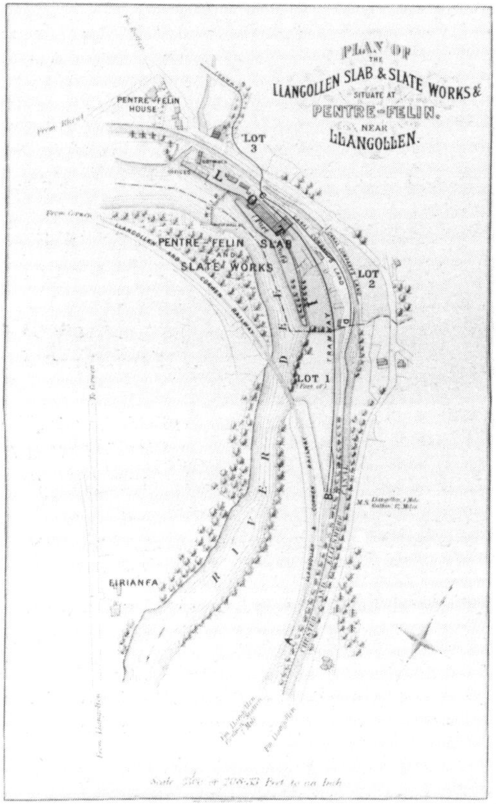

Fig.220 Plan of the Ellesmere Canal showing tramways and railways in the area around Llangollen in 1897.

The transportation problems of Clwyd's industry were substantially eased with the coming of the railways in the early 19th century. In Flintshire, work had begun on the Chester to Holyhead line in 1844 and although it was to be of little assistance to the main industries of the County, it did in fact promote a new industry, tourism.

To help the heavy industries of Denbighshire, and to open up, "the rich coalfields of Wrexham and Ruabon", the railway from Wrexham to Chester was begun in 1844, and a mineral branch from Wrexham to Brymbo was opened in 1847. In 1846, the line to Ruabon had been opened, and two years later, the Dee, which George Stephenson had considered impracticable to cross, was finally bridged by Henry Robertson and the link to Shrewsbury opened. Other lines such as the Wrexham-Mold-Connah's Quay line and the Mold-Denbigh railway, were laid after this date.

The remains of this transport network are a common feature of the modern landscape. The scars of former tramways are evident in many parts of the County, notably in the Buckley area and on Llantysylio Mountain, near Llangollen. The Ellesmere canal (Fig.220) with its impressive aqueduct at Pontcysyllte is still in use today, and part of the aborted section in Ffrwd is still visible. Unfortunately, many of the railways established in the early 19th century did not survive the Beeching cuts of the 1960s. However, the lines of some of them can still be seen.

Conclusion

This article has aimed to provide a general introduction to the history and archaeology of the Industrial Revolution in Clwyd. Although it has concentrated on Clwyd's major heavy industries, many more industries, such as textiles, brewing, paper making, leather and printing, have also been significant at times, especially to urban development.

Industrial archaeology is a relative newcomer to the field of archaeology. It is only very recently that it has gained the interest of a growing number of archaeologists. As a result, industrial remains are increasingly receiving the attention usually reserved for older and more traditional archaeological sites. Although many industrial sites have been lost since the 1960s their importance in Clwyd's industrial past is now being recognised and many are being preserved.

BIBLIOGRAPHY

The Environment

Ball, D.F., 1960 *The soils and land use of the district around Rhyl and Denbigh* Memoirs of the Soil Survey of Great Britain, Harpenden

Battiau-Queney, Y., 1984 "The pre-glacial evolution of Wales" *Earth Surface Processes and Landforms 9,* 229-252

Boswell, P.G.H., 1949 *The Middle Silurian Rocks of North Wales* Arnold, London

Brown, E.H., 1960 *The Relief and Drainage of Wales,* Cardiff

Brown, E.H. and Cooke, R.U., 1977 "Landforms and related glacial deposits in the Wheeler Valley area, Clwyd" *Cambria 4,* 32-45

Embleton, C., 1961 "The geomorphology of the Vale of Conway with special reference to its deglaciation" *Institute of British Geographers 29,* 49-70

Embleton, C., 1964 "Late glacial drainage in part of north east Wales" *Proceedings of the Geologists Association 67,* 393-404

Embleton, C., 1970 "North-Eastern Wales" pp.59-81 in *The Glaciations of Wales and Adjoining Areas,* (ed.) C.A. Lewis, Longman, London

Evans, J.G., 1975 *The Environment of Early Man in the British Isles* Elek Ltd., London

Green, S., 1984 *Pontnewydd cave — a Lower Palaeolithic hominid site in Wales. The First Report* National Museum of Wales, Cardiff 227pp.

Heyworth, A. & Kidson, C., 1982 "Sea-level changes in south-west England and Wales" *Proceedings of the Geological Association 93,* 91-111

Hibbert, A., (in preparation) Report on "Palaeobotany" in *Excavations in the Brenig Valley* (ed.) F. Lynch, Cambrian Archaeological Monograph

Ince, J., 1983 "Two Post-glacial pollen profiles from the uplands of Snowdonia, Gwynedd, N. Wales" *New Phytologist 95* 159-172

Lea, W. & Thompson, T.R.E., 1978 *Soils in Clwyd I Sheet SJ 35 (Wrexham North)* Record No.50, Soil Survey of England & Wales, Harpenden

Lowe, S., 1981 "Radiocarbon dating and stratigraphic resolution in Welsh Late-glacial chronology" *Nature* 293, *210-212*

MAFF, 1985 "Agricultural Land Classification of England & Wales" *Map and Technical Report No.11,* HMSO, London

Peake, D.S., 1981 "The Devensian glaciation of the north Welsh Border" pp.49-59 in *The Quaternary in Britain,* Eds J. Neale & J. Flenley, Pergamon, London

Preece, C.C., 1978 *The biostratigraphy of Flandrian tufas in southern Britain* Unpublished Ph.D. thesis, University of London

Rowlands, B.M., 1971 "Radiocarbon evidence of the age of an Irish Sea glaciation in the Vale of Clwyd" *Nature (Phys.Sci.)* London, 230, 9-11

Rudeforth, C.C., Hartnup, R., Lea, J.W., Thomson, T.R.E., & Wright, P.S., 1984 *Soils and their use in Wales* Bulletin No.11, Soil Survey of England & Wales, Harpenden

Seddon, B., 1962 "Late-glacial deposits at Llyn Dwythwch and Nant Ffrancon, Caernarvonshire" *Philosophical Transactions of the Royal Society,* London, B244, 459

Shackleton, N. & Opdyke, 1973 "Oxygen isotope and palaeomagnetic stratigraphy of Pacific core V28-238; oxygen isotope temperatures and ice volume on a 10^5 and 10^6 year scale." *Quaternary Research* 3, 39-55

Smith, B. & George, T.N., 1961 *British Regional Geology — North Wales* H.M.S.O., London

Smithson, F., 1963 "The micromineralogy of North Wales Soils" *Journal of Soil Science*

Thomas, G.S.P., 1984 "A late Devensian glaciolacustrine fan-delta at Rhosesmor, Clwyd, N. Wales" *Geological Journal* 19, 125-141

Thomas, G.S.P., 1985 "The late Devensian glaciation along the border of northeast Wales" *Geological Journal 20,* 319-340

Thomas, T.R.E., 1978 *Soils in Clwyd II Sheet SJ17 (Holywell)* Record No.50, Soil Survey of England & Wales, Harpenden

Warren, P.T., Price, D., Nott, M.J.C. & Smith, E.G., 1984 *Geology of the country around Rhyl and Denbigh* B.G.S. - N.E.R.C.; H.M.S.O. London

Worsley, P., Coope, G.R., Gord, T.R., Holyoak, D.T. & Robinson, J.E., 1983 "A Pleistocene succession from beneath Chelford sands at Oakwood Quarry, Chelford, Cheshire" *Geological Journal 18,* 307-325

The Palaeolithic

Arkell W.J., 1947 *The Geology of Oxford*

Blore, J.D., 1981 *Lynx Cave Excavations, Clwyd. 1962-1981. Second Report.*

Boswell, P.G.H., 1949 *The Mid Silurian Rocks of Wales*

Catt, J.A., 1981 'British pre-Devensian glaciations', in Neale, J. and Flenley, J., (eds.) *The Quaternary in Britain,* 9-19

Collcutt, S.N., 1984 'The Sediments', in Green, H.S., *Pontnewydd Cave. A Lower Palaeolithic Hominid Site in Wales: The First Report* (Cardiff), 31-76

Coope, G.R. and Brophy, J.A., 1972 'Late Glacial environmental changes indicated by a coleopteran succession from N.Wales', *Boreas* 1, 97-142.

Currant, A.P., 1986 'The Late Glacial mammal fauna of Gough's Cave, Cheddar, Somerset' *Proc. Univ. Bristol Spelaeol. Soc. 17* (3), 286-304

Dawkins, W.B., 1874 *Cave Hunting*

Dennell, R., 1986 'Needles and spear-throwers', *Natural History* (American Museum of Natural History, New York), *95*(10), 70-78

Embleton, C., 1960 'The Elwy river system, Denbighshire', *Geog.J.* 126, 318-334

Embleton, C., 1970 'North East Wales', in Lewis, C. (ed.) *The Glaciations of Wales and Adjoining Areas,* 59-82.

Embleton, C., 1984 'Location, setting and geomorphology' in Green, H.S., (1984), 23-29.

Foster, H.D., 1970 'Establishing the age and geomorphological significance of sorted stone stripes in the Rhinog Mountains, North Wales' *Geogr. Ann.* 52(A), 96-102

Green, H.S., 1981 'The First Welshman: excavations at Pontnewydd', *Antiquity* 55, 184-195

Green, H.S., 1984 *Pontnewydd Cave. A Lower Palaeolithic Hominid Site in Wales. The First Report* (National Museum of Wales)

Green, H.S., 1986 'The palaeolithic settlement of Wales research project: a review of progress 1978-1985' in Collcutt, S.N., (ed.) *The Palaeolithic of Britain and its Nearest Neighbours: Recent Trends* (University of Sheffield), 36-42.

Green, H.S., *et.al* 'Le site acheuléen de Grotte de Pontnewydd, Pays de Falles: géomorphologie, stratigraphie, chronologie, faune, hominidés fossiles, geologie et industrie lithique dans le contexte paléoélogiqueian' *L'Anthropologie* 93, i, 15-52

Hicks, H., 1886 Results of recent researches in some bone caves in North Wales' *Q.J. Geol. Soc.* 42, 3-19

Peake, D.S., 1981 'The Devensian Glaciation on the North Welsh border' in Neale, J., and Flenley, J., (eds.) *The Quaternary in Britain,* 49-59

Rowlands, B.M., 1971 Radiocarbon evidence of the age of an Irish Sea glaciation in the Vale of Clwyd', *Nature* 230, 9-11

Shotton, F.W. and Williams, R.E.G., 1971 'Birmingham University radiocarbon dates V' *Radiocarbon* 13 (2), 141-156
Shotton, F.W. and Williams, R.E.G., 1973 'Birmingham University radiocarbon dates VI' *Radiocarbon* 15 (1), 1-12
Shotton, F.W., 1977 'Chronology, climate and marine record. The Devensian Stage: its development, limits and substages. *Phil. Trans. R.Soc. Lond.B.* 280, 107-118
Stringer, C.B., 1984 'The hominid finds' in Green, H.S. 1984, 159-170
Smith, F.G., 1933 'Archaeology - a club evening'. *Proc. Dyserth and District Field Club'* pp.19-21.

Mesolithic

General:

Darvill, T.C., 1986 *Prehistoric Britain*
Jacobi, R.M., 1980 The Early Holocene Settlements of Wales in J.A. Taylor (ed) *Culture and Environment in Prehistoric Wales* British Archaeological Reports 76, 131-206

Rhuddlan

Manley, J. & Healey, E., 1982 Excavations at Hendre, Rhuddlan: the Mesolithic Finds *Archaeol Cambrensis* CXXXI, 18-48
Miles, H., 1971-72 Excavations at Rhuddlan 1969-71: Interim Report *Flints. Hist. Soc. Publs.* 25, 1-8
Miles, H., 1972 'Rhuddlan' *Curr. Archaeol.* 3, 245-8

Prestatyn

Clark, J.G.D., 1938 Microlithic Industries from Tufa Deposit at Prestatyn, Flints. and Blashenwell, Dorset *Procs. Prehist. Soc.* IV, 330-32
Clark, J.G.D., 1939 Further notes on the Tufa Deposit at Prestatyn, Flints. *Procs. Prehist. Soc.* V, 201-202
Neaverson, E., 1942 The Extent of the Tufa Deposit at Prestatyn *Procs. L'pool. Geol. Soc.* 18, 50-56
Smith, G.F., 1926-27 Prehistoric Remains at Bryn Newydd, Prestatyn *Trans. Llandudno, Colwyn Bay & District Field Club* 13, 62-72

Brenig

Lynch, F., 1975 Brenig Valley Excavations 1974 *Denbs. Hist. Soc. Trans* 24, 30

Neolithic

Atkinson, R.J.C., 1969 The Date of Silbury Hill, *Antiquity,* 43, 216
Atkinson, R.J.C., 1970 Silbury Hill, 1969-70, *Antiquity,* 44, 313-5
Brassil, K.S., Guilbert, G.C., Livens, R.G., Stead, W.H., and Bevan-Evans, M., 1981-82. Rescue Excavations at Moel Hiraddug between 1960 and 1980, *Flintshire Hist. Soc. Publ.*, 30, 13-88
Bowen, E.G., and Gresham, C.A., 1967 *History of Merioneth*. Vol. 1
Boyd Dawkins, W., 1874 *Cave Hunting*
Boyd Dawkins, W., 1901 The Cairn and Sepulchral Cave at Gop, Near Prestatyn, *Archaeol. Journ.*, 58, 322-41
Bradley, R., 1984 *The social foundations of prehistoric Britain.*
Britnell, W.J., 1982 The excavation of two round barrows at Trelystan, Powys *Proc. Prehist. Soc.*, 48, 133-201
Britnell, W.J., and Savory, H.N., 1984 *Gwernvale and Penywyrlod: Two Neolithic Tombs in the Black Mountains of Brecknock.* Cambrian Archaeological Monographs No.2
Burl, A., 1976 *The Stone Circles of the British Isles*
Clark, D.V., Cowie, T.G., and Foxton, A., 1985 *Symbols of Power at the time of Stonehenge.*
Clough, T.H.McK., and Cummins, W.A., (eds) 1979 *Stone Axe Studies.* C.B.A. Research Report No.23
Coles, J.M., and Simpson, D.D.A., (eds) 1968 *Studies in Ancient Europe*

Cummins, W.A., 1979 Neolithic stone axes: distribution and trade in England and Wales, in Clough and Cummins (eds), 5-12
Daniel, G.E., 1956 *The Prehistoric Chamber tombs of England and Wales*
Davies, E., 1929 *The Prehistoric and Roman Remains of Denbighshire*
Davies, E., 1949 *The Prehistoric and Roman Remains of Flintshire*
Day, W., and Savory, H.N., 1972 The excavation of a Bronze Age burial mound at Ysgwennant, Llansilin, Denbighshire, *Archaeol. Cambrensis* 121, 17-50
Eogan, G., 1983 A flint macehead at Knowth, Co.Meath, Ireland *Antiquity,* 57, 45-6
Garton, D., 1987 Buxton, *Current Archaeol.*, 103, 250-53
Glenn, T.A., 1914 Exploration of a Neolithic Station near Gwaenysgor, Flints *Archaeol. Cambrensis,* 14, 247-70
Glenn, T.A., 1935 The distribution of the Graig Lwyd axe and its associated cultures *Archaeol. Cambrensis,* 90, 189-214
Green, H.S., 1980 *Flint Arrowheads of the British Isles,* Brit. Archaeol. Rep (British Series No. 75)
Grimes, W.F., 1939 The excavation of Ty-isaf long cairn, Brecknockshire., *Proc. Prehist. Soc.,* 5, 119-42
Hemp, W.J., 1927 The Capel Garmon chambered long cairn, *Archaeol. Cambrensis,* 82, 1-43
Hart, C.R., 1981 *The North Derbyshire Archaeological Survey*
Jacobi, R.M., 1980 The Early Holocene Settlements of Wales in Taylor (ed.) 131-206
Joseph, J.K.St., 1980 Air Reconaissance: recent results, 49, *Antiquity,* 54, 47-51
Lynch, F., 1969 The Megalithic Tombs of North Wales in Powell *et al.* 1969, 107-148
Lynch, F., 1969 The Contents of Excavated Tombs in North Wales, in Powell *et al.* 1969, 149-74
Macinnes, I., 1968 Jet sliders in late neolithic Britain, in Coles and Simpson (eds.) 137-44
Megaw, J.V.S., and Simpson, D.D.A., 1979 *Introduction to British Prehistory*
Mercer, R.J., 1981 *Excavations at Carn Brea, Illogan, Cornwall, 1970-73,* reprinted from *Cornish Archaeology,* no.20
Musson, C.R., 1971 A study of possible building forms at Durrington, Walls, Woodhenge and the Sanctuary, in G.J. Wainwright, *Durrington Walls,* 363-77
Ó Nuallàin, S., 1972 A Neolithic House at Ballyglass, near Ballycastle, Co. Mayo *J.Roy. Soc.Antiq. Ir.,* 102, 49-57
Piggott, S., 1954 *The Neolithic Cultures of the British Isles*
Powell, T.G.E., 1954 Excavations at Gwaenysgor (Flints.) 1951 *Archaeol. Cambrensis,* 103, 109-11
Powell. T.G.E., Corcoran, J.X.W.P., Lynch F., and Scott, J.G., 1969 *Megalithic Enquiries in the West of Britain,* Liverpool
Powell T.G.E., and Daniel, G.E., 1956 *Barclodiad y Gawres*
RCAHM 1956 *An Inventory of the Ancient Monuments in Caernarvonshire, Vol. 1: East.* The Royal Commission on Ancient and Historical Monuments in Wales and Monmouthshire
Roe, F.E.S., 1968 Stone mace-heads and the latest neolithic cultures of the British Isles in Coles and Simpson (eds.) 1968, 145-72
Roe, F.E.S., 1979 Typology of stone implements with shaftholes, in Clough and Cummins (eds.) 1979, 23-48
Savory, H.N., 1980 The Neolithic in Wales, in Taylor J.A., (ed.) 207-32

Smith, I.F., 1979 The chronology of British stone implements in Clough and Cummins (eds.) 1979, 13-22
Taylor, J.A. (ed.) 1980. *Culture and Environment in Prehistoric Wales,* Brit. Archaeol. Rep. (British Series No. 76)
Wainwright, G.J., 1971 The excavation of a Late Neolithic enclosure at Marden, Wiltshire, *Antiq. J.,* 51, 177-239
Warrilow, W., Owen, G., and Britnell, W., 1986 'Eight ring-ditches at Four Crosses, Llandysilio, Powys, 1981-85', *Proc. Prehist. Soc.,* 52, 53-87
Whittle, A., 1977 *The Earlier Neolithic of southern England and its Continental Background,* Brit., Archaeol. Rep. (Supplementary Series No. 35)

Bronze Age

Barnwell, E.L., 1875 The Rhosnesney Bronze Implements *Archaeol. Cambrensis* 4, ser. VI, 1875, 70-3
Bevan-Evans, M., and Hayes, P., 1952-3; 1954-5. Report on the Cairn on Cefn Goleu near Moel Fammau *Flints, Hist. Soc. Publics.,* 13, 1952-3, 91-7 and 15; 1954-5, 112-37
Burgess, C.B., 1968 The Later Bronze Age in the British Isles and North West France *Archaeol. J.,* 125, 1968, 1-45
Burgess, C.B., 1974 The Bronze Age in A.C. Renfrew (ed.) *British Prehistory,* 1974
Burgess, C.B., 1980 The Bronze Age in J.A. Taylor (ed.) *Culture and Environment in Prehistoric Wales,* BAR 76, Oxford, 1980
Burgess, C.B., 1985 Population, Climate and Upland Settlement in Spratt and Burgess 1985, 195-230
CAR, Clwyd Archaeological Record
Clarke, D.V., Cowie, T.G., and Foxon, A., 1985, *Symbols of Power at the time of Stonehenge,* Edinburgh, 1985
Crew, P. *forthcoming* Excavations at Cracwellt; Interim reports in *Archaeology in Wales,* vol 23, 26 and 27
Day, W., 1972 The excavation of a Bronze Age burial mound at Ysgwennant, Llansilin, Denbs. (with report on the finds by H.N. Savory), *Archaeol. Cambrensis* CXXI, 1972, 17-50
Ellis Davies, 1929 *Prehistoric and Roman Remains of Denbighshire*, 1929
Ellis Davies, 1937 A small hoard of flanged bronze celts from Betws (or Bettws) yn Rhos, Denbighshire *Archaeol. Cambrensis* CXII, 1937, 335
Ellis Davies, 1949 *Prehistoric and Roman Remains of Flintshire,* 1949
Eogan, G.,1967 The Associated Finds of gold Bar Torcs *J. Roy. Soc. Antiq. Ireland* 97, 1967, 129-75
Forde-Johnson, J., 1964 A Hoard of Flat Axes from Moel Arthur *Flints. Hist. Soc. Publics.* 21, 1964, 99-100
Fox, C., 1926 The Ysceifiog Circle and Barrow, Flintshire *Archaeol. Cambrensis* 7 ser. VI, 1926, 48-85
Glenn, T.A., 1915 Prehistoric and Historic Remains at Dyserth Castle *Archaeol. Cambrensis* 6 ser.CV, 1915, 47-86
Green, H.S., 1985 Some recent finds of Bronze Age antiquities from Wales *BBCS,* 32, 1985, 275-82
Green, H.S., Smith, A.H.V., Young, B.R. and Harrison, R.K., 1980. The Caergwrle Bowl: its composition, geological source and archaeological significance *Rep. Inst. Geological Science,* 80/1, 1980, 26-30
Grenter, S., 1989, Gwernymynydd Axe Hoad *Archaeology in Wales,* 29, 1989, 46
Hayes, P., 1960 Archaeological Notes: Halkyn Copper Axe *Flints. Hist. Soc. Publics.* 18, 1960, 169-71

Hemp, W.J., 1921-3 A List of Mounds, Cairns and Circles on the North Flintshire Plateau *BBCS,* 1, 1921-3, 353-70
Hemp, W.J., 1950-2 Merionethshire cairns and barrows in Llandrillo and neighbouring parishes *BBCS,* 14, 1950-2, 155-65
Llwyd, A., 1847 Letter quoting MS of Rev. J. Llwyd. *Archaeol. Cambrensis,*II, 1847, 372-3
Lynch, F.M., 1971 Report on the re-excavation of two Bronze Age Cairns in Anglesey: Bedd Branwen and Treiorwerth *Archaeol. Cambrensis,* CXX, 1971, 11-83
Lynch, F.M., 1975 Brenig Valley Excavations 1974 *Trans. Denbs. Hist, Soc.,* 24, 1975, 13-37
Lynch, F.M., 1977 A Cinerary Urn from Llanrhaeadr near Denbigh, *Trans. Denbs. Hist, Soc,* 26, 1977, 155-7
Lynch, F.M., 1979 Ring Cairns in Britain and Ireland; their Design and Purposes *Ulster J. of Archaeol.,* 42, 1979. 1-19
Lynch, F.M. and Chambre, J., 1983-84. Report on the excavations of a Bronze Age Barrow at Llong near Mold. *Flints. Hist. Soc. Public.* 31, 1984-4, 13-28
Lynch, F.M., Grealey, S., Waddell, J. and Allen, D.W.H., 1974 Brenig Valley Excavations 1973 *Trans. Denbs. Hist. Soc.,*23, 1974, 9-64
Manley, J.F., 1984 Cerrig y Drudion Survey *Archaeol. in Clwyd, 6,*1984, 5-7
Manley, J.F., 1985 Fields, Cairns and Enclosures on Ffridd Bryn Helen, Clwyd in Spratt and Burgess 1985, 317-50
Miles, H. *forthcoming* Excavations at Rhuddlan.
Northover, P., 1980, The analysis of Welsh Bronze Age metalwork in H.N. Savory *Guide Catalogue of the Bronze Age Collections* National Museum of Wales, Cardiff, 1980
Powell, T.G.E., 1953 The Gold Ornament from Mold, Flintshire, North Wales *Proc, Prehist. Soc.,*XIX, 1953, 161-79
Savory, H.N., 1950-2 Excavations and Discoveries: Burial Cave at Llanferres (Denb) *BBCS,* XIV, 1950-2, 174-5
Savory, H.N., 1959 The Late Bronze Age in Wales: some new Discoveries and new Interpretations *Archaeol. Cambrensis,* CVII, 1959, 3-63
Savory, H.N., 1961 Bronze Age Burials near Bedd Emlyn, Clocaenog *Trans. Denbs. Hist. Soc.,*10, 1961, 7-22
Sheppard, T., 1941 The Parc y Meirch Hoard, St.George Parish, Denbighshire *Archaeol. Cambrensis,* XCVI, 1941, 1-10
Spratt, D.A., and Burgess, C.B., 1985 *Upland Settlement in Britain,* BAR 143, 1985
Stapleton, Rev. P., 1908 and 1909 The Bryngwyn Tumuli *Archaeol. Cambrensis* 6 ser, VIII, 1908, 359-76 and 6 ser, IX, 1909, 361-6
Williams, H., 1921 Excavation of a Bronze Age Tumulus near Gorsedd, Holywell, Flintshire *Archaeol. Cambrensis* 7 ser, I, 1921, 265-89
Wynne-Ffoulkes, W., 1851 Tumuli in Denbighshire: Plas Heaton Tumulus *Archaeol. Cambrensis,* 2 ser, II, 1851, 274-80

Iron Age

Davies, Canon Ellis, An early hanging bowl found at Cerrig-y-drudion *Archaeol. Cambrensis* vol 81, part II, 7th ser vol 6, 3, 35-339
Davies, Canon Ellis, *Prehistoric and Roman Remains of Denbighshire,* 1929
Davies, Canon Ellis, *Prehistoric and Roman Remains of Flintshire, 1949*
Gardner, W., Pen y Corddyn, near Abergele, *Archaeol. Cambrensis* 6th ser, vol 10, 1910, 79-156
Gardner, W., The native hillforts in North Wales and their defences. *Archaeol. Cambrensis,* vol 81, part II, 7th ser vol 6, 221-282

Gardner, W., and Savory, H.N., *Dinorben: A Hillfort Occupied in Early Iron Age and Roman times - Excavations, 1912-69.* Cardiff 1964 and 1971

Guilbert, G., Moel y Gaer: an area excavation on the defences. *Antiquity* LXI, 1975, 109-117

Guilbert, G., The guard-chamber gateways at Dinorben and Moel Hiraddug hillforts, and the problem of dating the type in North Wales. *BBCS XXVII,* 1980, 516-520

Harding, D., (ed.) *Hillforts, Later Prehistoric Earthworks in Britain and Ireland* London 1976

Hemp, W.J., A La Téne shield from Moel Hiraddug Flintshire *Archaeol. Cambrensis,* vol 83 Part II, 7th ser vol 8, 253-284

Houlder, C., Rescue excavations at Moel Hirraddug I, excavation 1954-55 *Flints. Hist. Soc. Public* 19, 1961, 1-20

Juvenal, *Book XIV.*

Morris, E., Prehistoric Salt distribution: Two case studies from Western Britain. *BBCS* XXXII, 1985, 336-379

Stead, I., The Cerrig-y-Drudion 'Hanging Bowl' *Archaeol. J.* 1982 LXII part II, 221-234

Small Settlements

Allen, D., and Vyner, B.E., 1977 Caldicot, *Archaeol. in Wales*, 17, 35-6

Bowen, E.G., and Gresham, C.A., 1967 *History of Merioneth*, 1.

Bradley, R., 1984 *The social foundations of prehistoric Britain*

Britnell, W., 1982 Collfryn hill-slope enclosure, *Archaeol in Wales*, 22, 17

Britnell, W., and Musson, C.R., 1984 Rescue excavation of a Romano-British Double-Ditched enclosure at Arddleen, Llandrinio, Northern Powys, *Archaeol. Cambrensis*, 133, 91-99

Chapman, J.C. and Mytum, H.C. (eds), 1983 *Settlement in North Britain 1000 BC — AD 1000*, BAR 118

Crew, P., 1980 Forden Gaer, Montgomery, *BBCS* 28, (4), 730-42

Cunliffe, B., 1984 *Danebury: an Iron Age hillfort in Hampshire,* 1 and 2. Council Brit Archaeol Res Rep 52

Davies, E., 1929 *The Prehistoric and Roman Remains of Denbighshire*

Davies, E., 1949 *The Prehistoric and Roman Remains of Flintshire*

Fried, M.H., 1967 *The evolution of political society*

Glenn, T.A., 1913a Earthworks on Bryn Goleu, *Northern Flintshire* 1, (1), 1-5

Glenn, T.A., 1913b Distribution of neolithic implements in northern Flintshire, *Archaeol Cambrensis*, 13, 6th Ser, 181-90

Greene, P., 1975 A cropmark site in Cilcain parish, west Flintshire, 1972, *J Chester Archaeol Soc*, 58, 97-8

Gresham, C., 1941 Ancient habitation sites in Caernarvonshire, *Trans Caernarvonshire Hist Soc*, 3, 1-8

Griffiths, W.E., 1951 Early settlements in Caernarvonshire, *Archaeol Cambrensis*, 101, 38-71

Guilbert, G., 1982a The Warren, *Archaeol in Wales*, 22, 43

Guilbert, G., 1982b Top Farm, *Archaeol in Wales*, 22, 44

Guilbert, G., 1983 Craig Fawr, *Archaeol in Wales*, 23, 12

Hemp, W.J. and Gresham, C.A., 1944 Hut circles in north-west Wales, *Antiquity*, 18, 183-96

Higham, N.J., 1982 The Roman impact upon rural settlement in Cumbria, in *Rural Settlement in the Roman North* (eds P. Clack and S. Haselgrove), 105-22

Houlder, C., 1974 *Wales: an archaeological guide*

James, H. and Williams, G., 1982 Rural settlement in Roman Dyfed, in *The Romano-British Countryside. Studies in rural settlement and economy* (ed D. Miles), BAR 103, (1 & 2), 289-312

Johnson, N., and Rose, P., 1982 Defended settlement in Cornwall, *The Romano-British Countryside. Studies in rural settlement and economy* (ed D. Miles), BAR 103, (1 & 2), 151-207

Jones, G.D.B., 1979 Aerial Photography in North Wales 1976-7, *Aerial Archaeol*, 4, 56-64

Jones, M.L., 1984 *Society and settlement in Wales and the Marches 500 BC to AD 1100*, BAR 121, (1 & 2)

Kelly, R., 1980 Moel Gerddi, *Archaeol in Wales*, 20, 30-2

Kelly, R., 1981 Erw Wen, Harlech, *Archaeol in Wales*, 21, 27-8

Kelly, R., 1982 The Ardudwy Survey: Fieldwork in Western Merionydd, 1979-81, *J. Merioneth Hist Rec Soc*, 9, (2), 121-62

Musson, C.R., 1981 Prehistoric and Romano-British settlements in northern Powys and western Shropshire: recent evidence from aerial photography and excavation, *Archaeol J*, 138, 5-7

Mytum, H., 1981 Drim Camp, Llawhaden, *Archaeol in Wales*, 21, 32-3

Mytum, H., 1983 Castell Henllys, Meline, *Archaeol in Wales*, 23, 24-5

Palmer, R., 1983 Analysis of settlement features in the landscape of prehistoric Wessex, *The impact of aerial reconnaissance on Archaeology* (ed) G.S. Maxwell, Counc Brit Archaeol Res Rep 49, 41-53

Palmer, R., 1984 *Danebury. An aerial photographic interpretation of its environs*, RCAHM (England), Supp Ser 6

Parkhouse, J., 1979 Biglis, Cadoxton, Nr. Barry, *Archaeol in Wales*, 19, 28-9

Perry, B.T., 1969 Iron Age enclosures and settlements on the Hampshire chalklands, *Archaeol J*, 126, 29-43

RCAHM (Wales), 1912 *An Inventory of Ancient Monuments in Flintshire*

RCAHM (Wales), 1914 *An Inventory of Ancient Monuments in Denbighshire*

RCAHM (Wales), 1921 *An Inventory of Ancient Monuments in Merionethshire*

RCAHM (Wales), 1937 *An Inventory of Ancient Monuments in Anglesey*

RCAHM (Wales), 1956 *An Inventory of Ancient Monuments in Caernarvonshire: Vol 1, East*

RCAHM (Wales), 1960 *An Inventory of Ancient Monuments in Caernarvonshire: Vol 2, Central*

RCAHM (Wales), 1964 *An Inventory of Ancient Monuments in Caernarvonshire: Vol 3, West*

RCAHM (Wales), 1976 *An Inventory of Ancient Monuments in Glamorgan 1 (2): the Iron Age and Roman Occupation*

Service, E.R., 1971 *Primitive Social Organisation*

Smith, C.A., 1977 Late prehistoric and Romano-British homesteads in north-west Wales, *Archaeol Cambrensis*, 126, 38-52

Smith, C.A., 1987 Excavations at the Ty Mawr Hut-circles, Holyhead, Anglesey, *Archaeol. Cambrensis, 127, 20-38*

Spurgeon, C.J., 1972 Enclosures of Iron Age type in the Upper Severn Basin, *Prehistoric Man in Wales and the West* (eds F. Lynch and C. Burgess), 321-44

St.Joseph, J.K.S., 1961 Aerial Reconnaissance in Wales, *Antiquity*, 35, 263-75

Stanford, S.C., 1972 The function and population of hill forts in the Central Marches, in *Prehistoric Man in Wales and the West* (eds F. Lynch and C. Burgess), 307-19

Vyner, B .E., 1982 Excavations at Woodbarn Rath, Wiston, 1969, *Archaeol Cambrensis*, 131, 49-57

Waddelove, E., 1983a The Roman road between Varis and Canovium, *Archaeol Cambrensis*, 132, 95-106

Waddelove, A.C.E. & E.P., 1983b A Roman military site in the Vale of Clwyd? *Trans Denbighshire Hist Soc*, 32, 129-30
White, R.B., 1977 Cefn Graeanog, *Archaeol in Wales*, 17, 30
White, R.B., 1978 Cefn Graeanog, *Britannia*, 9, 406-7
Williams, G., 1978 Aspects of later Prehistoric and Native Roman Carmarthenshire: Part I, *Carmarthenshire Antiq*, 14, 3-19
Williams, G., 1979 Aspects of later Prehistoric and Native Roman Carmarthenshire: Part II, *Carmarthenshire Antiq*, 15, 15-37
Williams, G., 1983 Woodside Camp; Dan-y-Coed Enclosure *Archaeol in Wales*, 23, 26-30

Roman

Arthur, P., 1978 The Lead Glazed Ware in Roman Britain Arthur, P., and Marsh, G., (eds.) *Early Fine Wares in Roman Britain* BAR 57, 293-356
Blockley, K., 1989 *Prestatyn: 1984-5 An Iron Age Farmstead and Romano-British Industrial Settlement in North Wales* BAR 210
Blockley, M. and Quinnell, H., forthcoming *Excavations at Rhuddlan 1969-73*
Camden. W., 1586 *Britannia*
Carrington, P., 1986 The Roman Advance into the North Western Midlands Before AD 71, J. *Chester Archaeol*. Soc. 68, 5-22
Davies, E., 1949 *The Prehistoric and Roman Remains of Flintshire*
Dudley, D.R., and Webster, G., 1965 *The Roman Conquest of Britain*
Gardner, W., and Savory, H.N., 1964 *Dinorben: A Hillfort Occupied in Early Iron Age and Roman times*
Goodburn, R., (ed.) 1979 Roman Britain in 1978 in *Britannia* X, 268-338
Green, M.J., 1978 *'Small cult-objects from the military areas of Roman Britain'* BAR 52
Greene, K., 1977 Legionary Pottery and the Significance of Holt, Dore, L. and Green, K., (eds.), *Roman Pottery in Britain and Beyond* BAR S30, 113-32
Grimes, W.F., 1930 Holt, Denbighshire: The Works Depot of the Twentieth Legion at Castle Lyons, *Y Cymrodor* XLI.
Hall, R.A., 1983 Miniature amphorae from Norton, North Yorkshire *Britannia* XIV, 262.
Hull, M.R. 1958 *Roman Colchester* Res. Rept. of the Soc, of Antiq. of London XX
Jones, G.D.B., 1980 Archaeology and Coastal Change in the North-West, Thompson, F.H., (ed.), *Archaeology and Coastal Change* Soc. of Antiq. of London, occ. paper, new series 1
Manley, J., 1986 'A Roman Amphora from Rhos-on-Sea, *Archaeology in Clwyd,* 8, 11-13
Mankey, J., (ed.), *Archaeology and Coastal Change* Soc. of Antiq. of London, occ. paper, new series 1.
Margary, I.D., 1973 *Roman Roads in Britain*
McWhirr, A., 1981 *Roman Gloucestershire.*
Nash-Williams, V.E., 1969 *The Roman Frontier in Wales*
Newstead, R., 1937 The Roman Station, Prestatyn: First Interim Report. *Archaeol. Cambrensis* XCII,ii, 203-32
Newstead, R., 1938 The Roman Station, Prestatyn: Second Interim Report *Archaeol. Cambrensis* XCIII, ii, 175-91
O'Leary, T.J., Blockley, K., and Musson C.R., 1989 *Excavations at Pentre Farm, Flint 1976-81* BAR 207
O'Leary, T.J. and Davey, P.J., 1975-6 *Flintshire Hist. Soc. Publ.* 27, 138-51
Rankov, N.B., (eds) 1982 Roman Britain in 1981, *Britannia* XIII, 328-95.
Smith, F.G., 1934 Visit to Roman Site Discovered by Mr.F. Gilbert Smith *Dyserth and District Field Club,* 60-3

Smith, F.G., 1935 Second Visit to Prestatyn Roman Site. *Dyserth and District Field Club*, 48-51

Stephens, G.R., 1984 Roman Holt: Personnel, Production and Water Supply, *Denbighshire Hist. Soc. Trans.* 33, 81-92

Waddelove, E., 1979 *A Roman Road in the Vale of Clwyd* (privately published).

Webster, G., 1952-3 The Lead-Mining Industry in North Wales in Roman Times *Flintshire Hist. Soc. Publ.,* 13, 5-33

Weetman, M.W.. Excavations at Croes Atti Lane, Flint, 1986 *Archaeology in Wales* 26

Whittick, G.C., 1982 Roman Lead-Mining on Mendip and in North Wales, *Britannia* XIII, 113-24

Dark Ages

Anon. 1819-20 Miscellaneous Intelligence, *The Cambro-Briton* 1, 359-60

Bailey, R.N., 1980 *Viking Age Sculpture in Northern England*

Camden, W., 1789 *Britannia*, Gough, R. (ed.), 3 vols

Campbell, J.(ed.), 1982 *The Anglo-Saxons*

Darby, H.C., and Maxwell, I.S., 1962 *The Domesday Geography of Northern England*

Davies, E., 1949 *The Prehistoric and Roman Remains of Flintshire*.

Davies, W.,1982 *Wales in the Early Middle Ages*

Edwards, N., 1985 A Possible Viking Grave from Benllech, Anglesey. *Trans. Anglesey Antiq. Soc.*

Edwards, N., 1986 Anglesey in the Early Middle Ages: The Archaeological Evidence. *Trans. Anglesey Antiq. Soc.* 19-42

Edwards N., and Lane, A. (eds.), 1988 *Early Medieval Settlements in Wales AD 400-1100*

Fisher, Canon, 1926 The Welsh Celtic Bells, *Archaeol. Cambrensis* 81, 324-34

Gardner, W., and Savory, H.N., 1964 *Dinorben*

Gresham, C., 1968 *Medieval Stone Carving in North Wales*

Guilbert, G., 1979 Dinorben *Archaeol. in Wales* 19, 14

Hamlin, A., 1976 The Archaeology of Early Christianity in the North of Ireland. Ph.D. Queens Univ. Belfast, unpublished

Hill, D., 1981 *An Atlas of Anglo-Saxon England*

Hubbard, E., 1986 *Clwyd*

Jackson, K., 1953 *Language and History of Early Britain*

Jackson, K., 1982 Gildas and the names of the British Princes, *Cambridge Medieval Celtic Stud.* 3, 30-40

Jones, F., 1954 *The Holy Wells of Wales*

Jones, G.R.J., 1960-3 The Tribal System in Wales: a reassessment in the light of settlement studies, *Welsh Hist. Rev.* 1, 111-32

Jones, G.R.J., 1961 Settlement Patterns in Anglo-Saxon England, *Antiquity* 35, 221-32

Jones, G.R.J., 1964 The Llanynys Quillets: A Measure of Landscape Formation in North Wales, *Denbighshire Hist. Soc. Trans.* 13, 133-58

Jones, G.R.J., 1972 Post Roman Wales, Finberg, H.P.R. (ed.), *The Agrarian History of England and Wales,* I, ii, 281-328

Jones, R.O., 1898 The Pool Park Inscribed Stone, *Archaeol Cambrensis* 373-77

Knight, J., 1981 In Tempore Iustini Consulis: Contacts between the British and Gaulish Churches before Augustine, in Detsicas, A. (ed.), *Collectanea Historica: Essays in Memory of Stuart Rigold,* 54-62

Lloyd, J.E., 1939 *A History of Wales from the Earliest Times to the Edwardian Conquest,* 2 vols. 3rd ed

Manley, J., 1984 The Late Saxon Settlement of *Cledemutha* (Rhuddlan), Clwyd, in Faull, M. (ed.), *Studies in Late Anglo-Saxon Settlement,* 55-64

Manley, J., 1987 Cledemutha: A Late Saxon Burh in North Wales, *Medieval Archaeol.*, 31, 13-46
Miles, H., 1971-2 Excavations at Rhuddlan, 1969-71; Interim Report *Flintshire Hist. Soc. Pub.* 25, 1-8
Moon, R., 1978 Viking Runic Inscriptions in Wales, *Archaeol. Cambrensis* 127, 124-6
Morris, C.D., 1982 The Vikings in the British Isles; Some Aspects of their Settlement and Economy, Farrell, F.T. (ed.), *The Vikings*,70-94
Morris, J. (ed.), 1978 *Domesday Book, Vol. 26, Cheshire*, Morgan, P. (ed.).
Morris, R.H. (ed.), 1909-11 Parochialia being a Summary of Answers to Parochial Queries issued by Edward Lhuyd, *Archaeol. Cambrensis* special supp. 3 vols
Musson, C., 1985 Clwyd-Powys Archaeological Trust, *Archaeol in Wales* 25, 4
Nash-Williams, V.E., 1938 Some Dated Monuments of the "Dark Ages" in Wales, *Archaeol. Cambrensis* 93, 149-88
Nash-Williams, V.E., 1950 *The Early Christian Monuments of Wales*
O'Kelly, M.J., 1964 The Belt-Shrine from Moylough, Sligo, *J. Roy. Antiq. Ir.* 95, 149-88
Oman. C.C., 1930 *Victoria and Albert Museum, Department of Metalwork, Catalogue of Rings*
Owen, E., 1886 *Old Stone Crosses of the Vale of Clwyd.*
Pierce, G.O., 1984 The Evidence of Place-Names, in Savory, H.N. (ed.), Glamorgan County History Vol. 2 Cardiff, 456-92
Radford, C.A.R., and Hemp, W.J., 1957 The Cross-Slab at Llanrhaeadr-ym-Mochnant, *Archaeol. Cambrensis* 106, 109-16
Radford, C.A.R. and Hemp, W.J., 1959 Pennant Melangell: The Church and the Shrine, *Archaeol. Cambrensis* 108, 81-113
Raftery, J. 1941 *Christian Art in Ancient Ireland*, vol.2
Rees, U., 1975 *The Cartulary of Shrewsbury Abbey* 2 vols
Rhys, J. (ed.), 1883 *Tours in Wales by Thomas Pennant, esq.*, 3 vols
Richards, M., 1960 The Irish Settlements in South-West Wales, *J. Roy, Soc. Antiq. Ir.* 110, 133-62
Richards, M., 1975 Norse Place-Names in Wales, Cuiv, B. (ed.), *The Impact of the Scandinavian Invasions on Celtic-Speaking Peoples c.800-1100 AD,* 51-60
Ross, A., 1974 *Pagan Celtic Britain,* 2nd ed.
Savory, H.N., 1971 *Excavations at Dinorben, 1965-9*
Smith, F.G., 1931-3 Talacre and the Viking Grave, *Proc. Llandudno, Colwyn Bay and District Field Club* 17, 42-50
Stalleybrass, B., 1914 Recent Discoveries at Clynnog Fawr, *Archaeol Cambrensis* 271-96
The Royal Commission 1912 *II County of Flint*
The Royal Commission 1921 *VI County of Merioneth*
Thomas, D.R., 1906-11, *History of the Diocese of St.Asaph,* 4 vols., 2nd ed.
Vinogradoff, P. and Morgan, F. (eds), 1914 *The Survey of the Honour of Denbigh 1334*
Wade-Evans, A.W., 1944 *Vitae Sanctorum Britanniae et Genealogiae*
Wainwright, F.T., 1945-46 The Scandinavians in Lancashire, *Trans. Lancs. Antiq. Soc.* 58, 71-116
Wainwright, F.T., 1948 Ingimund's Invasion, *Eng. Hist. Rev.* 63, 148-60
Wainwright, F.T., 1950 Cledemutha, *Eng. Hist. Rev.* 65, 203-13
Wainwright, F.T., 1959 Athelflaed, Lady of the Mercians, in Clemoes, P. (ed.), *The Anglo-Saxons* 53-69
Williams, I., 1945 *Enwae Lleoedd*
Williams, I. and Nash-Williams, V.E., 1937 Some Welsh Pre-Norman Stones, *Archaeol. Cambrensis* 92, 1-10

Offa's & Wat's Dykes

Keynes, S., and Lapidge, M., 1983 *Alfred the Great: Asser's "Life of King Arthur" and other contemporary sources*

Manley, J., 1987 *Cledemutha,* A Late Saxon Burh in North Wales *Medieval Archaeology* XXXI. 1987

Noble, Frank, 1978 *Offa's Dyke Reviewed, a critical re-assessment of published work and accepted opinions; with detailed re-consideration of the course of the Dyke through the Diocese of Hereford.* Open University M.Phil. Thesis

Ordnance Survey, 1986 *A Map of Britain in the Dark Ages*

Robinson, Peter, 1985 Land-systems mapping and the new Offa's Dyke Survey *Archaeology in Clwyd* 7

Stevenson, W.H., 1959 *Asser's Life of King Alfred* (New impression with an article by Dorothy Whitelock)

Weetman, Mike, 1986 Wat's Dyke, Coed-Llys, Northop (SJ 232 698) *Archaeology in Wales.* 26, 52-52

Worthington, M., Wat's Dyke: A comment on the work of Sir Cyril Fox in Clwyd *Archaeology in Clwyd 8*

Mottes & Moated Sites

Aberg, F.A., 1983 The Moated Sites Research Group, in Hinton, David A. (ed), *25 Years of Medieval Archaeology*, University of Sheffield, 1983, 97-101

Alcock, L., 1967 'Excavations at Degannwy Castle, Caernarvonshire,' 1961-66, *Arch.Journal*, CXXIV, 1967, 190-201

Darby H.C., 1962 (ed., with Haxwell, I.S.) *The Domesday Geography of Northern England* 1962, 383-91

Darby H.C., 1971 (ed., with Terret, I.B.) *The Domesday Geography of Midland England*, 1971, 158-62

Darby, H.C., 1977 *Domesday England*, 1977, 321-24 and 328-33

Edwards, J.G., 1956, 'The Normans and the Welsh March', *Proc. of the British Academy*, XLII, 1956, 155-77

Emery, F.V., 1969 *The World's Landscapes — 2 Wales*, 1969

Gardner Willoughby, 1961, 'The Mound at Rûg, Near Corwen', *Journ. Merionethshire Hist. Soc.*, IV, 1961-64, 3-6

Glenn T.A., 1934 *Excavation at Llys Edwin, Celyn Farm, Northop, Flintshire*, 1934 (reprinted from 'The Family of Griffith of Garn and Plasnewydd')

Green, J. Patrick, 1982, 'Moated Hay Stacks', *Landscape History*, IV, 1982, 69

Hague, Douglas B., and Warhurst, Cynthia, 1966, 'Excavations at Sycharth Castle, Denbighshire', 1962-63, *Archaeol Cambrensis*, 1966, 108-26

Hemp, W.J., 1926 'Denbigh Castle', *Y Cymmrodor*, XXXVI, 1926, 64-120.

Hogg, A.H.A., and King, D.J.C., 1963 Early Castles in Wales and the Marches', *Archaeol. Cambrensis*, 1963, 77-124

Hogg, A.H.A., and King D.J.C., 1970 Additions and Corrections to Hogg and King 1963, *Archaeol. Cambrensis*, 1970, 119-124.

King, D.J., and Alcock, L., 'Ringworks of England
and Wales', *Château Gaillard*, III, 1966 (1969), 90-127

King, D.J.C., 1961 'The Castles of Breconshire' *Brycheiniog*, VII, 1961, 71-94

King, D.J.C., 1983 *Castellarium Anglicanum; An Index and Bibliography of the Castles in England, Wales and the Islands*, 2 vols, Kraus, 1983(see also Hogg and King 1963 and 1970 and King and Alcock 1966)

Leach, G.B., 1957 'Excavations at Hen Blas, Coleshill Fawr, Near Flint — First Report', *J. Flints. Hist Soc.*, XVII, 1957, 1-15
Leach 1960 Second Report — *ibid.* XVIII, 1960, 13-60
Le Patourel, Jean, 1973 *The Moated Sites of Yorkshire,* Soc. for Medieval Archaeology, Monograph No. 5, 1973
Lloyd, John Edward, 1911 *A History of Wales from the Earliest Times to the Edwardian Conquest,* 2 vols, 1911 (later editions similarly paginated)
Miles, Henrietta, 1971, 'Excavations at Rhuddlan, 1969-71', Interim Report', *J. Flints. Hist. Soc.*, XXV, 1-8
M.S.R.G. *Annual reports of the Moated Sites Research Group.*
Neaverson, E., 1947 *Medieval Castles; A Study of Sites, Water Supply and Building Stones,* 1947
Ord. Vit. *The Ecclesiastical History of Orderic Vitalis,* Ed. Chibnall, Marjorie, For Clwyd see Vol. II, 1969 and Vol IV, 1973
Pratt, Derrick, 1964 Moated Settlements in Maelor, *J. Flints. Hist. Soc.,* XXI, 110-120 (and *J. Wrexham Local History Class, No.2,* May 1964, with additional map)
R.C.A.M. Inventories of the Royal Commission on Ancient Monuments (Wales):
R.C.A.M. 1912 *Flintshire.*
R.C.A.M. 1914 *Denbighshire.*
R.C.A.M. 1921 *Merionethshire.*
R.C.A.M. 1982 *Glamorgan*, Vol 3, Part 2 — General discussion of Welsh moated sites, 69-76.
Rigg, J., 1961 *J. Flints. Hist. Soc.*, XIX, 1961, 92-93
Smith, Peter, 1975 *Houses of the Welsh Country side; a study in Historical Geography*, H.M.S.O., 1975
Spurgeon, C.J., 1979, 'Medieval Moated Sites in Wales; Present Knowledge and Future Prospects'. A discussion paper prepared for the Ancient Monuments Board for Wales and published in *M.S.R.G.*, VI, 1979, 34-44 and *Archaeology in Wales*, XVIII, 1978, 18-29
Spurgeon, C.J., 1981 Moated Sites in Wales, in Aberg, F.A. and Brown, A.E. (eds), *Medieval Moated Sites in North-West Europe*, B.A.R. International Series 121, 1981
Spurgeon, C.J., 1986 The Castles of Glamorgan; Some sites and Theories of General Interest, *Château Gaillard*, XIII (1986), 1987
Tait, James, 1925 'Flintshire in Domesday Book', *Flints. Hist. Soc. Publications*, XI, 1925, 1-37
Taylor, A.J., 1955 *Rhuddlan Castle*, Official Guide Book, H.M.S.O., 2nd edition, 1955
Taylor, C.C., 1978 'Moated Sites; Their Definition, Form and Classification' in *Medieval Moated Sites*, Aberg, F.A. (ed), C.B.A. Research Report No. 17, 1978, 5-13
Wilson, David, 1982 'Moated Sites of Cheshire — A Brief Review', *M.S.R.G.*, IX, 1982, 9-13

The Stone Castles

Alcock, L., 1967, 'Excavations at Deganwy Castle, Caernarfonshire', *Archaeological Journal,* CXXIV 1967, 190-201
Butler, L.A.S., 1987, 'Holt Castle: John de Warenne and Chastellion', *Castles in Wales and the Marches, Essays in honour of D.J. Cathcart King,* ed Kenyon and Avent, 1987, 105-124
Clark, 1884, *Mediaeval Military Architecture* ii, 88-89
Glenn, T.A., 1915, 'Prehistoric and Historic Remains at Dyserth Castle', *Archaeologia Cambrensis,* 6th series, xv 1915, 47-86, 249-52
Hemp, W.J., 1926, 'Denbigh Castle', *Y Cymmrodor,* xxxvi 1926, 64-12
Hemp, W.J., 1929 *Flint Castle,* HMSO 1929

Hussey, 1951 Chirk Castle, Denbighshire, *Country Life* 1951, 896-9, 980-3, 1064-7, 1148-51
King, D.J.C., 1974, 'Two castles in Northern Powys: Dinas Brân and Caergwrle', *Archaeologia Cambrensis,* cxxiii 1974, 113-31
King, D.J.C., 1983, *Castellarium Anglicanum,* 1983
RCAHM. 1914, *Inventory of Royal Commission on Ancient Monuments in Wales and Monmouthshire,* Denbigh 1914

Medieval Settlements

Calendar of patent rolls, Edward I AD 1281-1292, 1893
Charles, B.G., 1938, *Non-Celtic place-names in Wales*
Chibnall, M., (ed) 1973, *The ecclesiastical history of Orderic Vitalis 4*
Dimock J.F., (ed) 1868 *Giraldi Cambrensis Opera VI,* Rolls ser 21
Davies, E., 1929, *The Prehistoric and Roman Remains of Denbighshire*
DB, Domesday Book, Cheshire (ed) P. Morgan, 1978
DB, Domesday Book, Shropshire (ed) F and C. Thorn 1986
Ellis, H., (ed) 1838, *The record of Caernarvon*
Ellis, T.P., (ed) 1924, *The first extent of Bromfield and Yale AD 1315*
Jack, R I., 1968, The lordship of Dyffryn Clwyd in 1324, *Denbigh Hist Soc, 17, 8-53*
Jenkins, D., (ed) 1963, *Llyfr Colan*
Jenkins, D., (ed) 1986, *The law of Hywel Dda,* The Welsh Classics
Jones, G.P., (ed) 1933, *The extent of Chirkland (1391-1393)*
Jones G.R.J., 1964, The Llanynys quillets: a measure of landscape transformation in North Wales, *Denbigh Hist Soc, 13,* 133-58
Jones G.R.J., 1983-4 The ornaments of a kindred in medieval Gwynedd, *Studia Celtica 18-9,* 135-46
Jones, G.R.J., 1986, Churches and secular settlement in ancient Gwynedd, in *Human Geography from Wales, Proceedings of the E.G. Bowen Memorial Conference* (ed W. K. D. Davies), 33-53
Lunt, W.E., (ed) 1926, *The valuation of Norwich.*
Owen, A., (ed) 1841, *Ancient Laws and Institutes of Wales, 2*
Palmer, A.N., 1886, The portionary churches of medieval North Wales, *Archaeologia Cambrensis,* 5 ser, *3,* 175-209
Palmer, A. N. and Owen, E., 1910, *A history of ancient tenures of land in North Wales and the Marches*
PRO Public Record Office E179/242/52
E179/242/53
E179/242/55
SC6/1143/22
SC6/1143/23
Wales 15/8
RCAHM. 1914, *An inventory of the ancient monuments of Wales and Monmouthsire IV, County of Denbigh,* 135-6. Royal Commission on Ancient and Historical Monuments
Taxatio ecclesiastica Angliae et Walliae auctorite P Nicholai IV circa AD 1241, Record Commission, 1862
Thorpe, L., (ed) 1978, *Gerald of Wales: The journey through Wales: The description of Wales,* Penguin Classics
Vinogradoff, P and Morgan, F (eds), 1914, *Survey of the Honour of Denbigh 1334*
Wiliam, A R (ed), 1960, *Llyfr Iorwerth.*
Williams, I (ed), 1953, *Canu Llywarch Hen*

Vernacular Architecture

Baggs, A.P., 1972, 'Pattern-books and vernacular architecture before 1790' *Vernacular Architecture* 3, 1972, 22-3
Hayes, P., 'Some Cottages in the Hawarden District' *Flints. Historical Soc. Publications,* 23, 1967-8, 54-73

Howell, P., Country Houses in the Vale of Clwyd I' *Country Life*, 22.12.77, pp.1906-7
Parkinson, A.J., 'A Master-Carpenter in North Wales' *Archaeol Cambrensis.* 124, 1975, 72-101
Smith, P., *Houses of the Welsh Countryside* 1st ed. 1975
Smith, P., 'Hall, Tower and Church', in R.R.Davies *et al*(eds.) *Welsh Society and Nationhood* 1984
Summerson, J., *Architecture in Britain 1530-1830* (London, 1963)
Wiliam, E., - 'A Cruck Barn at Hendre-wen, Llanrwst, Denbighshire' *Trans. Ancient Monuments Soc.*, 1976, 23-31
Wiliam, E., *Traditional Farm Buildings in North East Wales* 1982

Industrial Archaeology

Davies, K. & Williams, C.J., 1986, *The Greenfield Valley* (2nd Edition).
Dodd, A.H., 1951, *The Industrial Revolution in North Wales.*
Edwards, I., 1960, The Charcoal Iron Industry of East Denbighshire 1630-90, *Denbs. Hist. Soc. Trans.*, 9, 22-53.
Edwards, I., 1961, The Charcoal Iron Industry of Denbighshire 1690-1770, *Denbs, Hist. Soc. Trans.*, 10, 40-97.
Edwards, I., 1985, Slate Quarries in the Llangollen District, *Denbs. Hist. Soc. Trans.*, 34, 91-120.
Grenter, S. & Williams, A., 1990, *Bersham Ironworks.*
Lerry, G.G., 1946, *Collieries of Denbighshire.*
Lerry, G.G., 1949, *Henry Robertson, Pioneer of Railways.*
Lerry, G.G., 1957-61, The Industries of Denbighshire from Tudor Times to the Present Day, *Denbs. Hist.Soc. Trans.* 6-10.
Lewis, W.J., 1967, *Lead Mining in Wales.*
Messham, J.E., 1956, The Buckley Potteries, *J. Flints. Hist. Soc.*, 16, 31-87.
Palmer, A.N., 1897-1898, John Wilkinson and the Old Bersham Iron Works, *Cymmrodorion Soc.*
Rhodes, J.N., 1971-72, The Lead Mills at Mold, *J. Flints. Hist. Soc.*, 1971-72, 21-30.
Thorburn, J.A., 1986, Talargoch Mine, *British Mining* No.31.
Williams, C.J., 1980, *Metal Mines of North Wales.*
Williams, C.J., 1986, *Industry in Clwyd.*
Williams, C.J.,1987, *The Lead Mines of the Alyn Valley.*

The Editors of The Archaeology of Clwyd wish to acknowledge the following sources for the illustrations used.

Redrawn from Smith and George 1981: reproduced by permssion of the Director, British Geological Survey, Crown Copyright reserved. Fig 1.

Based on data from Embleton (1970), Peake (1981) and Thomas (1985): Fig 2

Clwyd County Council: Figs 3, 91, 114, 155, 164, 165, 171, 209.

National Museum of Wales: Figs 8, 9, 10, 13, 14, 15, 16, 17, 18, 20, 21, 22, 23, 25, 33, 44, 45, 46, 48, 49, 51, 73, 92.

Chris Musson: Figs 4, 7, 55, 63, 70, 85, 86, 87, 89, 109, 111, 117, 120, 129, 138, 141, 144, 145, 146, 52, 153, 157, 160, 161, 165, 168, 170, 179.

National Monuments Record: Figs 181, 182, 183, 185, 186, 187, 190, 192, 194, 195, 197, 198, 199, 200, 201, 202, 203, 204, 205, 206, 207.

Clwyd Record Office: Figs 210, 215, 217 218, 219, 220.

Clwyd-Powys Archaeological Trust: Figs 30, 71, 97 98.

Tim Morgan: Figs 88, 110, 148, 163

Frances Lynch: Figs 50, 54

Buxton Museum, Jackson Collection: Fig 19

Buxton Museum: Fig 23

After Jacobi: Fig 29

Henrietta Quinnell: Fig 31

After J.K.St.Joseph: Fig 42

British Museum: Fig 47

Peter Reynolds: Fig 72

National Museum of Scotland: Fig 74, 35

Cambridge University: Air Photographs Collection: Fig 99

Victoria and Albert Museum: Fig 113

David Hill: Fig 130

CADW: Fig 142

RAF Crown Copyright: Fig 175

Glanville Jones: Fig 176

Jon James: Fig 184

All the remaining illustrations have been produced by the Clwyd Archaeology Service.

The coloured base map of Clwyd, used throughout, was produced by Yan Den-Breejen.

PLACENAME INDEX

N.B.: - major references to placenames appear in bold type
- placenames occurring in captions appear in brackets

Abbey of St Peter & St Paul (Shrewsbury): 133
Abbey Rd (Rhuddlan): 139
Abenbury brickworks (Wrexham): 227
Aberberbo: 194
Abergele: 78,82,(85),(89),95,126,(127),130,137,(212),228
Aberystwyth: 182
Acrefair: 219
Acer-las (Cerrigydrudion): 218
Acton Park (Wrexham): (75)
Airdens (Sutherland): 59
Althrey Hall: 168
Alwen River: 117
Alyn ravine: 146
Alyn River: 74,146,150,193
Alyn Valley: 64,70,74,142,(146),150,226
Anglesey: 18,61,132,133,140,228
Arddleen: 109
Ardudwy (NW Wales): 59,67
Arenigs, the: 18,26
Axton (Flintshire): 140
Bachegraig (Tremeirchion): 213
Bagillt: 191,224,226
Bailey Hill (Mold): 159,(160)
Bala: 72
Ballyglas (Co. Mayo): 55
Baltic: 74
Bangor: (192)
Bangor-Is-y-Coed: (22),130
Bannawg: 198
Barcloddiad y Gawres (Anglesey): 61
Basingwerk: 139,142,160
Basingwerk Abbey: 126,147
Bellan nr Mold: 19
Bersham: 219,221,(223),224,229
Bersham,No.2 Headgear & Winding Hse: (223)
Bersham, Octagonal Building: (219)
Berwyn Range: 13,15,16,26,47,57,67,70,97,104,186
Bettisfield: 192,224 Betws yn Rhos: 76,(77)
Big Covert Cave (Clwydians): 126
Biglis (Glamorgan): 110
Bishopswall: 194
Bistre: 189,191
Blackamoor's Head (Rhuddlan): 212
Bodelwyddan: (215)
Bodfari: 127
Bovium: 119
Boyne Valley (Ireland): 59,61
Branas-uchaf (Llandrillo): 61
Breconshire: 161
Brenig: 23,25,49,51,54,70,74,(81)
Brenig '47'(marker cairn): 65
Brenig '51' (cairn): 67
Brenig Cemetery: 65,67,72,(79)
Brenig, Llyn (Denbigh moors): (71),(79)
Brenig Valley: 65,74
Bretton Hall: 168
Brithdir-mawr (Cilcain): (218)
Brittany: 76
Bromfield: 183,184
Broncoed (Mold): 206
Bronington: 170
Brymbo: (151),219,221,(221),223,226,230
Brymbo Bottle Chimney: (226)
Bryn: 191
'Bryn Carrog' coastline: 29
Bryn Castell (Llanynys): 199
Bryn Euryn: 138
Bryn Gwylan (Llangernyw): 132
Bryn Gwyn Hall (Delyn): 70
Bryn Helen: 67
Bryn Llithrig (Rhuallt): 140
Bryn Llwyn (Gwaenysgor): 55
Bryn Newydd (Prestatyn): 50,(53)
Bryn Polyn (St Asaph): 117
Bryn Sion (Ysceifiog): 78
Bryn Teg (Cerrigydrudion): (111),(112)
Bryn y bâl: (152)
Brynbach: 194
Bryncaredig: 198
Brynford (Delyn): (68),70,74
Brynhyfryd Park (Ruthin): 117
Bryn-y-Baal: 150
Buckley: 223,226,227,(227),229,230
Burton: 169
Butser Hill (Hamps.): (93)
Buxton (Derbyshire): 55
Cae Gwyn Cave: **39-44**,29,(41),(42),(43),45
Cae Trenches (Gwynedd): 114
Cae-coch (Whitford): (217)
Caer Ddunod: 107
Caer Drewyn (Corwen): (96)
Caer Gai (Gwynedd): 117,120,126
Caer Gybi (Gwynedd): 133
Cae'r llan (Llanynys): 199
Caergwrle: 78,(78),167,(176),180,(180),182
Caernarfon: 120,182,184
Caernarfonshire: 173
Caersws: 109
Caerwys: 23,99,131,132,191
Calcot: 191
Caldicot (Glamorgan): 110
Calderstones (Liverpool): 61
Canonium: 109
Capel Garmon: 59,60
Capel Eithin (Anglesey): 133
Cardiff: 161
Carmarthenshire: 111
Carmel (Holywell): 120,(120),224
Castell Brogyntyn (Shropshire): 173
Castell Henllys (Dyfed): 111

Castle Street (Rhuddlan): 125
Cefn: (214),215
Cefn Bannog: 67
Cefn Cave: **38-39**,29,(38),(39)
Cefn Goleu: 70,72
Cefn Graeanog (Gwynedd): 114
Cefn Rock: 26
Cefn Meiriadog: 26
Cefn-iwrch: 198
Cegidog Valley: 150
Ceinmeirch: 194
Ceiriog River: 142
Cernioge (Pentrefoelas): 132
Cerrig Gwynion: 107
Cerrigydrudion: 67,(80),90,95,(111),218,(218)
Chapel Garth: (167),168,170
Chelford: 23
Cheshire Basin: 13,23,93
Cheshire Plain: 15,18,61,74,97,126
Cheshire: 93,129,157,165,(183)
Chester: 117,119,120,126,136,147,159,191,224,230
Chirk: 142,(147),(154),167,184,(185),202
Chirk town (Waun): 184
Cilcain: 212,(218)
Cledemutha (Rhuddlan): 139,(139),140,145,189
Clocaenog: (68),70,71,,(129),131
Clocaenog forest: 67
Clwyd,Lake: 29,(30),51
Clwyd, mid: 117
Clwyd, north east: 74
Clwyd River: 29,47,49,59,65,117,139,157,159,173,179,(179),198
Clwyd, south: 72
Clwyd, uplands: 65,67
Clwyd, Vale of: (2),(20),13,15,18,19,24,26,(27),29,51,57,70,93,97,102,107,117,120,126,128,129,136,(137),203,208,(213)
Clwyd, east: 189
Clwyd, west: 97
Clwydian Range: 18,(20),26,(30),67,70,82,(82),84,85,97,123,126
Clynnog: 133
Clywedog River: 29,198
Clywedog Valley: 227
Coe Clogwyn (Hope): 127
Coed Hen Blas: 167
Coed Iâl (Llantysilio): 126
Coed Talon (Denbighshire): 219
Coedpoeth: 150,223
Coed-y-cra-uchaf (Northop): (213)
Colchester (Essex): (127),128
Coleshill: 178
'Coleshill Castle': 161
Colion: (196),198
Collfryn (Powys): 109
Colwyn: 13,(77)
Colwyn (Powys): 161
Colwyn Bay: 18,19,57
Commote: (196)
Connah's Quay: 229,230
Conwy: 180,182,214
Conwy Valley: 19,26,59,61,203,211
Conwy River: 16,47,117,129,147,152,159,173
Coppi (Rhos): 227
Corfaen (Edeyrnion): 136
Cornwall: 115,140,203,224
Corwen: (57),59,72,(96),117,119,120,128,136,(138),161,228
Craig Arthur (Newmarket): 55
Craig Fechan (Llanfihangel Glyn Myfyr): (114)
Crown Hotel (Denbigh): 159
Croxton (Maelor Saesneg): 140
Cumbria: 99
Cwm: 137
Cynllaith: 160,184,191
Cyrchynan: 191
Dan-y-Coed (Dyfed): 111
Dee River: 16,(22),47,70,(76),117,140,142,147,157,160,173,175,178,(178),184,191,221,224,226,227,229
Dee Valley: 19,57,61,(61),78,203
Degannwy: 159,173,175,177,180
Delyn: 55,57,59,72
Delyn Plateau: 67,70
Denbigh: 23,(30),49,51,(131),132,(137),157,159,167,(176),180,184,(184)(201),202,(214),230
Denbigh Moors: 26,(71),97
Denbighshire: 70,129,131,136,167,173,(212),219,223,224
Deva: 117
Devil's Ditch (Wrexham): 151
Derbyshire: 55,64
Ddol Rock: 26
Dinas Bran (Llangollen): (21),177,(177),184
Dinerth: 202
Dinorben: 82,85,(85),86,87,88,(88),89,(89),90,93,94,95,96,107,123,138
Dôl Trebeddau (Pentrefoelas): 132
Dolbelydr (Cefn): (214),215
Dominican Friary (Rhuddlan): 125
Drim (Dyfed): 111
Droitwich (Worcs.): 93
Dublin: 140
Duggleby: 61
Dyffryn Clwyd: 167,173,180,183,184
Dysert O Dea (Ireland): 136
Dyserth: 55,67,(89),(91),120,126,136,140,(173),175,177,180
Dyfed: 97,99,111,129,165
East Anglia: 155,165
Eaton Hall (Cheshire): (183)
Eddisbury: 139
Edeirnion/Edeyrnion: 136,160,191,202
Ellesmere Castle: 173
Ellesmere canal: 229,230,(230)
Eglwyseg, (Llangollen): 15,21
Eglwyseg escarpment: (21),178
Eglwyseg Mountain: 72
Elwy River: 26,29,117
Elwy Valley: 19,26,(27),(28),29,32,(33),(35),(36),38,(38),(39),59
Emral Hall: 168
England: 47,59,60,72,85,97,109,139,140,157,165,167,173,177,184,206,208,213

Englefield: 189,191
Erbistock: 191
Erddig: 146,(153),159,(161),184
Erw Wen (Gwynedd): 114
Essex: (127)
Ewloe: (175),177,186
Faenol-fawr (Bodelwyddan): (215)
Faerdre (Abergele): (212)
Fferm (Hope): 215
Ffordd Isa (Prestatyn): 122
Ffridd y Garreg Wen (Holywell): 70,71,74
Ffrith: 49,53,109,119,(122),123,125,126,127,128,154,224
Ffrwd (Denbighshire): 219,230
Ffynnon Beuno Cave: **39-44,**(40),29,(42),(43),45
Ffynogion (Ruthin): 95,(95)
Flint: 13,109,119,121,(123),127,128,147,(149),157,161, (163),(178),(179),(181),182,183,224
Flintshire: 129,131,136,140,141,157,167,173,219,223,224,228,230
Forden Gaer: 109
France: 90
Gaul: 87,132,(132)
Gerddi duon (Llanynys): 199
Germany: 76
Gladys (Bagillt): 226
Glamorgan: 109,129,157,167
Glan Alyn mine (Loggerheads): 226
Glanllynnau: 29
Glan-tanat-isaf (Llanrhaeadr ym Mochnant): (214)
Gledlom: 72
Glen Ballyre (Isle of Man): 41
Gloddaeth (Llandudno): 207
Glol: 107
Gloucestershire: 128
'Glyn' castle (Erddig?): 184
Glynceiriog: 228
Glyndyfrdwy: 168
Golden Grove (Llanasa): (216)
Gop Cave: 57,59,(62),64
Gop Cairn: 61,62,(62),(63),64
Gop Hill: (62)
Gosbecks Farm (Essex): (127),128
Graig Lwyd (Penmaenmawr): 16,59
Great Orme: 16,18,160,173
Green Lane (Hawarden): 167
Greenfield: 224,228,229,(229)
Greenfield Mills: (229)
Greenway: 194
Gresford: 192,224
Gryffiliog: 198
Gwaenysgor: 55,57,(62),(63),120,127
Gwent: 165
Gwernymynydd (Mold): 78,228
Gwynedd: 61,72,97,113,129,131,132,133,139,159,160, 161,173,180,186,228
Gwytherin: (130),131,132,133,(133),135,(135)
H.M. Stanley Hospital (St Asaph): 117
Hafod: 224,227
Hafod Adams: 206
Hafod Farm moat: (169),(170)
Hafodlom: 194
Halghton: (167),(168)
Halghton Hall: 169,170
Halghton Lodge: (168)
Halkyn: 76,(169),225,226
Halkyn Mountain: 16,18,97,102,120,128,224
Hampshire: (93)
Hanmer: 168,192
Hardings Down North (Glamorgan): 109
Harlech: 182
Haulton Ring: 168
Haulmond Abbey: 168
Hawarden: 157,159,161,(162),167,173,177,(180),182,(182),219,229
Hendre (Rhuddlan): 125
Hendre (Wheeler valley): 226
Hen Blas: 159,162,(163),164
Hen Denbych (Bishopwall): (192)
Hen Domen (Montgomery): 159,164
Hen Efail (Llanrhaiadr yn Cinmerch): 170
Hen Gwrt (Gwent): 165
Henfechau: 200
Henllan (Denbighshire): 70,71,200
Herefordshire: 99,151
Hesp Alyn: 15
High Street (Denbigh): (214)
Hiraethog: 16,24,26,70,72
Hiraithog, Capel: 72
Hiraethog moorland: 13,15,18,29,51,64
Hiraethog, Mynydd: 18,49,51-53,57
Hollybush Farm: 169
Holt: 109,117,**119**,(119),120,121,126,(126), 128,167,(183),184,223,227
Holyhead: 230
Holyhead Mountain: 113
Holywell: 23,71,120,(120),136,(149),152,(216),(217),224,228
Hope: 127,147,180,215
Horseman's Green: 168
Howe Hill (Duggleby): 61
Iâl: 160,191,202
Ifton (Shropshire): 224
Ireland: 23,55,59,61,115,133,135,136,206,227
Irish Sea: 18,23,47,76,131
Isllan: 198
'Kappel Gwenfrewi' (Gwytherin): 133
Kelston (Flintshire): 140
King's Mill (Clwyedog Valley): 227
Knowth (Boyne Valley, Ireland): 59
Lake District: 18,26
Land's End: 59
Lane End brickworks (Buckley): 227
Lichfield: 192
Lightwood Green (Overton): 167,(168)
Lima (Pentrefoelas): 132
Linacre (Flintshire): 140
Linden Walk (Prestatyn): 29
Little Leadbrook: 186
Little Orme: 29

Liverpool: 61,228
Liverpool Bay: 23
Llanarmon: 49,64,193
Llanarmon Mynydd Mawr: 206,213
Llanarmon yn Iâl: (45),70,(159),(189),191,193
Llanasa: (216)
Llanbedr: 84,(84),(85),96
Llanddulas: 137,228
Llandegai: 133
Llandegla: 64,90,(157),(162),191
Llandrillo: (8),61,(61),67,99,(195)
Llandrillo (Edeirnion): 202
Llandrinio (Montgomery): 168
Llandudno: 207
Llandyrnog: 70
Llaneilian: 133
Llanelidan: 19
Llanelwy: 130,191,192,200
Llanfair Dyffryn Clwyd: 70
Llanferres: 67
Llanfynydd: 142,150,151,152,(152)
Llanfynydd Schoolfield: 146
Llangernyw: 67,131,132
Llangernyw church: 135
Llangollen: 15,70,72,78,129,130,(157),177,(193),228,229,230,(230)
Llangollen, vale of: 107,129,135
Llangwm: (57),74
Llannerch y Mor (Mostyn): 226
Llanrhaeadr: 70,(192),194
Llanrhaeadr-ym-Mochnant (Tanat Valley): 64,(64),135,186,200,(214)
Llanrhaiadr yn Cinmerch: 170
Llanrwst: 217
Llansilin: 62,(69),(161),(164),186,(207),(210)
Llantysilio (Ial): 126,202
Llantysilio (Llangollen): (193)
Llantysilio mountain (Llangollen): 229,230
Llanymynech: 16
Llanynys: (2),138,(197),198,199,(199),200,(200),(207)
Llay Hall: 168
Llay Main: 223,224
Llifad (Gwynedd): 114
Llong: 71,74
Llyn Aled Isaf: **24-25**,(24),25,49,51,54
Llyn y Pandy (Rhydymwyn): 226
Llys Awel (Abergele): 126,(127),128
Llys Edwin: 165,167,168,170
Llys Farm (Prestatyn): 168
Llys Gwenllian: 194,(201)
LLysaled: 202
Llysfaen Common: 140,(140)
Llwynheiernin (Glamorgan): 109
Loggerheads: 226
Lon Hylas (Rhuddlan): 123,125
London: 203,215
Lower Berse: 168
Lynx Cave: **44**,(45),29,49,53,126
Maelor: (22),97,159,160,167,(167)
Maelor Gwmraeg: 167,191
Maelor Saesneg: 140,165,173,192
'Maen Achwyfan' (Whitford): 136,140,(141)
Maen-caint: 191
Maes isa (Llanynys): 199,(199),(200)
Maes ucha (Llanynys): 199,(200)
Maesmaencymro: 198
Maesmor (Corwen): (57),59
Maesol (Llangernyw): 67
Man, Isle of: 26,41
Manchester: 139
Mansell's Tower (Degannwy): 177
Marches, the: 151,211,(214)
Marches (Scottish): 206
Marden (Wilts.): 64
Marford: 162,192,193
Marion Bach (Delyn): (68),70
Meadows Estate (Prestatyn): 122
Meifod: 136
Meifod (Montgomery): 168
Meliden (Dyserth): 120
Mercia: 129,139,154
Merioneth: 157
Mersey river: 229
Mia Hall (Trelawnyd): 49
Middlewich (Cheshire): 93
Midlands: 59,165
Mill Farm (Bersham): 221
Minera: 15,16,224,225,226,228,(228)
Minera, City Engine Hse: (225)
Mochnant: 136
Moel Arthur: 76,82
Moel Famau: 19,(25)
Moel Fenlli: 82,85
Moel Hiraddug: 55,82,85,87,88,89,(89),90,(91),93,94,(94),96
Moel Sych (the Berwyns): 104
Moel Tryfan: 29
Moel Wnion: 29
Moel y Crio: 29
Moel y Gaer (Llanbedr): 84,(84),(85),96
Moel y Gaer (Rhosesmor): 55,(58),82,84,85,86,(86),87,(87),(88),89,93,95,107
Moel y Gerddi (Gwynedd): 114
Moelfre Uchaf (Betws yn Rhos): 76,(77)
Mold: 59,(73),74,78,(145),146,147,(152),(156),159,160,(160),173,177,205,206,224,228,230
Montgomery: 164,168,177
Montgomeryshire: 162
Morton (Maelor Gymraeg): 191
Mostyn: 226
Mynedd Poeth: 67
Mynedd Rhiw: 16
Nanheudwy: 184,191
Nannerch: 19,72
Nant Mawr River: 29
Nant y Fuach (Dyserth): 67
Nant y Glyn: 65

Nantwich (Cheshire): 93
Nant-y-Flint: 147
Netherlands: 76
Newmarket: 55
Northop: 147,148,186,(213)
Oakenholt (Flint): 121
Offa's Dyke: 129,130,139,**142-156**,(142),(143),(144),(147),(150),(151),(152),(154),173
Ogof Llyn Parc (Minera): 15
Old Convent (Holywell): (217)
Old Canonry (St Asaph): 117
Old Ship (Ruthin): (203)
Orchid Cave (Clwydians): 126
Oswestry: 13,15,186,223
Overton: 162,(168)
Overton Castle: 157,175
Oxfordshire: 29
Padeswood (Mold): 228
Pant y Dulaith (Delyn): 70,72
Pant-gwyn-mawr (Ysceifiog): (211)
Pant-y-Saer (Gwynedd): 113
Parc y Meirch: 78
Parys Mountain: 224
Peartree Lane (Chapel Garth): (167),168
Pen y Ball (Holywell): 224
Pen y Bryn (Llansilin): (210)
Pen y Corddyn (Abergele): 82,85,86,88,(89)
Penbedw Park (Nannerch): 72
Pencoed Castle (Gwent): 165
Penley Hall: 168
Penmaen: 29
Penmaenmawr: 59
Penmon: 136
Pennant: 194
Pennant Melangell (Powys): 135
Pennant (Rhuallt): 226
Pennines 61,74
Penrhos (Corwen): 117
Pentre (Flint): 121
Pentre (Ysceifiog): 207,(208)
Pentre Clawdd: 146
Pentre Farm (Flint): 121,(123),127
Pentre Farm (Halkyn): (169)
Pentre Halkyn: 78
Pentre Llyn Cymmer: 67,(80)
Pentre Saeson (Brymbo): 221
Pentrefoelas Castle: 175
Pentrefoelas (Gwytherin): 131,132,(132)
Penybont (Trefynant): 227
Penycloddiau: 82,(82)
Pen-y-Gelli wood: 152
Penywyrlod (Talgarth, Powys): 60
Perthi Chwarae (Llanarmon): 64
Pickhill: 200
Pickhill Hall (Wrexham): (202)
Plas Cadwgan: 206,208
Plas Isaf: 194
Plas Madoc: 219
Plas Mawr (Conwy): 214
Plas Tirion (Llanrwst): 217
Plas Uchaf (Llangedwyn): (112)
Plasnewydd (Ruabon): 206,(206)
Plas-y-brain: 206,(208)
Plas-yn-dre (Holywell): (216)
Point of Ayr (Prestatyn): 15,223,224
Pont y Blew: 219
Pontcysyllte: 230
Pontnewydd Cave: **32-38**,(28),(33),(34),(35),(36),(37),18,26,29,38,39,45
Powys: 60,109,128,129,135,136,160,173
Powys Fadog: 173,177,183
Prestatyn: 13,15,32,49,**50**,(53),55,61,92,(92),95,97,109,119,121,122,(124),(125),(126),128,157,(159),160,161,168,224,(224)
Prion: 194
Pwll y Chwyaid Bach: 199,200,207,(207)
Red Castle (Wem): 177
Reweniou (Rhufoniog): 159
Rhaeadr river: 136
Roche Castle (Dyfed): 165
Roft: 192
Rhos: 129,159,160,173,183,191,227
Rhos Is Dulas (Dinorben): 138
Rhosddigre (Llandegla): 64
Rhosesmor: 19,55,82,84,(86),87,(87),(88)
Rhos-on-Sea: 127
Rhostyllen (Wrexham): (144)
Rhuallt: 140,226
Rhuddlan: **49-50**,(49),(52),53,55,57,59,70,81,123,125,126,128,130,136,139,(139),159,160,161,162,(164),175,179,(179),182,183,189,191,202,212,223
Rhufoniog: 129,159,160,173,180,183,191
Rhyl: 23,53,57
Rhydmwyn: 226
Rhydyn Hall (Hope): 147,(148)
Rookery Wood (Erddig): (153)
Rome: 85
Ros (Rhos): 159
Rossett: 192
Rough Ditch: 151
Rowe Ditch: 151
Ruabon: 15,70,142,146,(150),205,206,(206),219,224,227,230
Rug (Corwen): 160,161
Runcorn: 139
Ruthin: 13,95,(95),117,(119),126,127,(127),128,(157),167,184,202,(203)
Quarnford (Staffordshire): 59
St Asaph: (60),117,120,128,130,192
St Chad (Lichfield): 192
St Cwyfan (Dyserth): 136
St Ffraid (Dyserth): 136
St Teila (Llandegla): 90
St Manchan (Ireland): 133
St Mael & St Sulien (Cwm): 137
St Werburgh's (Chester): 136
Salattyn: 74

Saltney Marsh: 229
Sanctuary, the (Wilts.): 64
Scotland: 18,26,47,141
Severn River: 17,229
Severn Valley: 62,97,99,109,116
Shotton: (76),221
Shrewsbury: 133,230
Shropshire: 173,224
Silbury Hill (Wiltshire): 61,62,(62)
Snowdonia: 13,16,18,19,23,26,65,93,173,211
Splash Point (Rhyl): **53-54**,49,(54)
Staffordshire: 59
Sutherland: 59
Swansea: 224
Sycharth: 159,160,161,(161),(164)
Sychdyn: (145),146,(156)
Talacre: 140
Talant Cottage (Burton): 169
Talar Goch (Dyserth): 120
Talargoch (Prestatyn): 224,225,226
Talargoch, Clive Engine Hse: 224
Talgarth (Powys): 60
Tan y Llwyn (Llangollen): 78
Tanat river: 136
Tanat Valley: 64,(64),70,102,107,(214)
Tandderwen (Denbigh): **51-53**,(51),49,53,70,(131),132,(137)
Tan-y-coed (Dee valley): 59
Tatham Road (Ruabon): (150)
Tegeingl: 159,173,175,183
Thames River: 17
Tomen y Faerdre (Llanarmon yn Iâl): 159,(159),160,(189),193
Tomen y Mur (Gwynedd): 161
Tomen y Rhodwydd (Llandegla): (157),159,160,(162)
'Town Ditch' (Rhuddlan): 125
Trefechan: (197),198,200
Trefnant: 18,19
Trefynant: 227
Trelawnyd: 49,151
Tremeirchion: (40),(41),(42),(43),213
Treoda (Cardiff): 161
Tre'r Llan: 193
Treuddyn: 150,(208)
Trevalun Hall: 216
Trueman's Hill: 161
Twt Hill (Rhuddlan): 123,125,(164),(179)
Tŷ Coch (Llanynys): 199,200
Ty Mawr (Gwynedd): 113
Ty Isaf (Powys): 60
Ty-draw (Llanarmon Mynydd Mawr): 213
Ty-isaf (Cilcain): 212
Tybroughton: 192
Tyddyn Bleiddyn (Elwy valley): 59,(60)
Ty-draw: 206
Urquart (Moray): 59
Uwchallan: 198
Vaerdre Hill (Degannwy): 177
Valle Crucis Abbey: (193),202
Varis: 109,117
Vicarage Meadow (Hanmer): 167,168
Wales, east: 206,(214)
Wales, mid: 61
Wales, north east: 76,97,99,109,116,129,140,206,211,212
Wales, north west: 59,113
Wales, south: 59,219
Wales, south east: 60,211
Wales, south west: 110,113,177,211
Wales, west: 97
Wansdyke (Wiltshire): 155
Watling Street: 120
Wat's Dyke: 129,130,139,**142-156**,(142),(143),(145),(146),(148),(149),(152),(153),(156)
Waun: 184
Waun y Balls (Flint): 224
Wem (England): 177
Wessex: 59,74,99,114,116
Whitton Lodge (Glamorgan): 110
Wheeler River: 29
Wheeler Valley: 19,67,226
Whitford: 102,140,(141),151,(217)
Whitford (Rhuddlan): 136,142
Whitford Church: 131
Whitford Dyke: 142,(143),152
Whittington Castle: 173
Willington Old Hall: 168
Wiltshire: 61,(62),64,155
Wirral: 129,140,(178)
Wolvesacre Hall: 169
Woodside Camp (Dyfed): 111
Woodbarn Rath (SW Wales): 113
Wrexham: 19,23,70,74,(75),76,142,(144),146,(146),151,(151),(153),(161),202,(202),(219),227,(228),230
Wynnstay Park (Ruabon): 142,146
Wynnstay colliery: 224
Y Berwyn: 18
Y Berfeddwlad [Perfeddwlad] (Rhos, Rhufoniog): 129,160,173,177,180
Y Foelas (Rhufoniog): 159
Yale: 183,184,193
York: 161
Yorkshire: 61,74,203
Yr Orsedd Wen (Salattyn): 74
Ysceifiog (Delyn): 70,78,131,132,151,152,198,207,(208),(211)
Ysgol y Castell: 49
Ysgol y Llys (Prestatyn): 122
Ysgwennant (Llansilin): 62,(69),70,71,74
Ystrad River: 29,194
Ystradowen: 194,(201)